Images of
American Society

A History of the United States

Images of American Society

A History of the United States

VOLUME I

G. D. LILLIBRIDGE
California State University, Chico

HOUGHTON MIFFLIN COMPANY/BOSTON

Atlanta   Dallas   Geneva, Ill.   Hopewell, N.J.   Palo Alto   London

Acknowledgment is made for permission to reprint the following materials, alphabetically listed by authors:

From Carl Becker, on p. 109, "Benjamin Franklin," from the *Dictionary of American Biography.* Reprinted by permission of Charles Scribner's Sons.

From R. R. Palmer, on pp. 145–146, *The Age of Democratic Revolution: A Political History of Europe and America, 1760–1800.* Volume I, *The Challenge.* Copyright © 1959 by Princeton University Press; Princeton Paperback, 1969. Reprinted by permission of Princeton University Press.

Cover photo courtesy of Nebraska State Historical Society, Solomon D. Butcher Collection

Printed in the U.S.A.

Library of Congress Catalog Card Number: 75-31017

ISBN: 0-395-21873-X

For Flo

Contents

Maps

Preface

Professor William McNeill remarked not long ago that an introductory course in history should be designed for citizens not professional historians. That seemed to me an eminently practical approach for an introductory American history. What I have attempted in this book, therefore, is to examine those major experiences, forces, and institutions that have occupied the time, energy, and lives of the American people and that *seem to me* to have most influenced us as a society, to have made us the kind of people we are today. I have sought to suggest a sense of humanity, a recognition that from the beginning this country has been made up of human beings who in terms of their own times and circumstances have suffered, agonized, exalted, loved, erred, lived, and died as human beings do in every age and time.

My concern has been with such powerful experiences as democracy, the frontier, war, and the city; with such forces as science, technology, and industry; with such institutions as the family and the church; with such interests as the arts, entertainment, and recreation; with such diverse fates as those of the immigrants, the blacks, and the Indians. I have tried to note the impact of all these upon the lives of Americans, and how their lives have been changed as a consequence. It has been my experience that this approach not only greatly appeals to students but also offers them a broad perspective enabling them to understand better the society in which they live.

As I have painfully discovered, it is not easy to organize such material so that one gets a sense of progression and time. The book is divided into four broad time periods that roughly cover (1) the seventeenth and eighteenth centuries, (2) the early life of the new Republic up to the Civil War, (3) developments from the Civil War to World War I, and (4) the period from 1920 to the present. Each chapter is preceded by a Spirit of the Times and followed by a Profile. I have used the Spirit of the Times to illuminate the chapter by focusing on a particular aspect of life during the period. I have deliberately avoided any set pattern to these, and they vary widely in approach. In each Profile I have chosen an individual, most of them well known but some unknown to the reader, and have provided a brief biographical sketch. The purpose of the Profile has been to use the life of one person to suggest the topic of the chapter and at the same time to remind the reader of the fact that American history is in the last analysis the story of individual human beings—the great and the obscure alike.

This is a personal book in some respects. It reflects, for example, my general optimism about the course of American affairs—no mean feat in these times. I become gloomy on many occasions as I look at the record of the past and the chronicle of the present, but in the long haul I see much to be hopeful about in the history of this country and the character of its people, and I have what may be an old-fashioned if wavering confidence that things will get better. At the same time, however, I have every conviction that we will always be plagued by problems and cursed with troubles that arise from the frailty of human beings. There may be those who believe that by genetic or legislative engineering, or by revolutionary revisions, we will eventually remove all the ills that flesh is heir to, but I am not one of those people. Being any kind of optimist at all about the human prospect, to say nothing of the American one, thus leads one to emphasize the good that lies in human achievement. Because as Americans we have certain black marks on our record—and I try to point these out—is no reason for failing to take pride in our achievements.

While it is impossible for us to avoid passing judgments on the Americans of the past, we should recognize that these judgments are not based on any superior moral wisdom, but rather upon the accumulation of experience and knowledge that we have access to but that of course was not available to those in the past. What I am suggesting is that we can at least try to understand the men and women of the past in terms of the circumstances in which they found themselves—circumstances which did not include the gift of viewing themselves from the vantage point of the twentieth century. I am not, for example, inclined to regard myself as morally superior to Thomas Jefferson because he thought blacks unequal to whites and I do not. I am more inclined to praise people for their accomplishments than to condemn them for their failures, though the latter should not be ignored. Hence my general optimism.

This book is a personal one also because it reflects my long interest in the image other peoples have held of America and the impact this country has had on other societies throughout the world. I think our understanding of ourselves is greatly enhanced by knowing what others think of us, even though their views may not coincide with the facts as we see them. Throughout this book, therefore, I have tried to use this theme to advantage.

Then, too, this book is a personal one in that here and there I have relied on experiences and associations special to me. Thus in the Spirit of the Times for the chapter on immigration, the words of Stephen Yakich on why he came to America were drawn from a taped interview I made with him, a man who had wandered and worked his way across America, married relatively late in life, and had a son who eventually married one of my daughters. The Profile of Phillip Mizel in the same chapter is also on a man I knew most of my life—the father of my oldest and closest friend. The Profile of Fred Burton in the chapter on World War II deals with a close friend of my youth whose diary and letters to me and to his family I have used.

This raises a point about the Profiles. Most of these discuss well-known people whose influence in American life was considerable. But a number are of Americans not generally known, yet whose lives exemplify certain experiences. Not many of us are familiar with Eliza Pinckney or Nannie Alderson, for example, and only friends and relatives know of Phillip Mizel or Fred Burton, but all in their own way were important Americans. And recognition of their importance enhances our realization of the importance of all Americans in the history of this country.

* * *

A number of colleagues in other institutions read all or part of the manuscript. I am very grateful to them for their criticisms, some of which were sharp and relentless, all of which were justified and productive. I have tried to respond to these to the best of my ability, and the book is, in my view, enormously improved as a consequence. My gratitude is therefore extended to: Gerald Danzer, the University of Illinois; Emile B. Jones, American River College; Robert McColley, the University of Illinois; Allan R. Millett, Ohio State University; J. Carroll Moody, Northern Illinois University; Stephen B. Oates, the University of Massachusetts; and J. V. Reese, Texas Tech University. I owe a special debt of gratitude to a number of my colleagues at California State University, Chico. During a period when I fell behind in my work because of the terminal illness of my mother, my dear friend Carl Hein did the basic draft for the chapters on Reconstruction and the black American. Lois Christensen did the Instructor's Manual, tested material on her students, and gave me frequent advice. Some of my colleagues read extensive parts of the manuscript and offered fruitful suggestions for improvement. Carl Hein read much of the manuscript and I benefited by his broader world view of America. William Hutchinson and Clarence McIntosh read the chapter on the last frontiers and made numerous suggestions of value to which I tried to respond. I am also especially grateful to two old and dear friends who read large portions of the manuscript on their own time, and encouraged me to persist in spite of their criticisms: Merle Curti, Frederick Jackson Turner Professor of History Emeritus at the University of Wisconsin; and the late Bert James Loewenberg, Professor of History Emeritus at Sarah Lawrence College.

In all instances, however, I bear sole responsibility for errors of fact, incautious judgments, slippery interpretations, and dangling participles.

Finally, I must note that any claims to originality must rest on the general approach I have taken (following Professor McNeill's suggestion) and on my utilization of such devices as The Spirit of the Times and the Profile. For, like most who attempt to cover so much ground, I have had to rely on the work of others. The Selected Reading at the end of the book includes most of the major sources from which I culled material in the development of my interpretation.

G. D. LILLIBRIDGE
California State University, Chico

Images of
American Society

A History of the United States

Part One

FOUNDATIONS OF AMERICAN CIVILIZATION

1492–1789

Chapter 1
"AN OTHER WORLD"

The Spirit of the Times
SEEKING OUT THE NEW

Wonders are many, but none, none is more wondrous than man.
Man moves over the grey sea, using the wind and the storm,
    daring the depths and surges.
Even the eldest of all the gods—Earth, inexhaustible Earth—man masters her. . . .
Language and thought, light and rapid as wind,
    man has taught himself these, and has learnt the ways of living in town and city. . . .
Cunning, cunning is man.
Wise though his plans are, artful beyond all dreaming,
    they carry him both to evil and to good.

So Sophocles described humanity to the Greeks. And so man and woman displayed their nature as Europe revitalized herself from the tenth century on—building inward, thrusting outward, daring the depths and the surges, mastering the earth, seeking new thought, advancing to both evil and good.

Daring Norsemen plowing the North Atlantic to the edge of the Western Hemisphere, their deeds disappearing in the wake of their ships . . . Crusaders carrying sword and banner to the Near East . . . Marco Polo tracing his route across Asia to the court of the Khan and recounting the fabulous wealth of the Orient to listeners at home . . . new towns and merchants prospering . . . trade and commerce . . . spices, silk, precious stones, dyes, oranges, cotton flowing by caravan from the East to Europe . . . the curious and eager seeking new trade routes to the Orient to bypass the avaricious merchants of Venice . . . Prince Henry the Navigator sending his ships around Africa . . . Columbus breaking through to the West . . . America . . . and the conquest with the blood flowing first and after that the wealth . . . and then the people from the city and the plow, from farm and shop.

Why did they do it?

Said Bernal Díaz, the explorer who followed Cortés in Mexico: "to serve God and his Majesty, to give light to those who were in darkness, and to grow rich as all men desire to do."

The fleet of Sir Francis Drake as it sailed into St. Augustine—one of the magnificent expeditions to the New World. Detail from Expeditio Francisci Drake equitis angli in Indias Occidentalis. *1588.*

Wrote Christopher Marlowe who stayed at home and thought about it:

Our souls whose faculties can comprehend
The wondrous architecture of the world
And measure every wandering planet's course,
Still climbing after knowledge infinite,
And always moving as the restless spheres
Will us to wear ourselves and never rest.

And an English ballad celebrating one of the voyages to Virginia sang:

We hope to plant a nation
Where none before hath stood.

To traverse unknown continents and ocean seas, to explore and exploit, to search out the new because the mind is restless and the body aches, to serve God and King, to get rich, to give birth to new nations, to construct a holy society as a model for all humanity! Wonders are many, but none more wondrous than man.

And so a new age began in 1492.

The New World and the Old

At the beginning there they stretched, the lands of the Western Hemisphere, "from the regions of eternal frost to the isthmus of Darien and thence to the plains of Patagonia," as orators were fond of saying a century ago. North America, South America, and cupped between them in the great sweep of the Caribbean the islands of the West Indies, Columbus's window onto the western seas.

These lands were vast and diverse: they held great mountain chains, extended plains, fertile valleys, barren deserts, mighty river systems, sparse plateaus, dense rain forests. Their plants, birds, and beasts were equally varied, and many of them were unknown to the rest of the world. Both continents were occupied by peoples of unfamiliar and divergent cultures, perhaps a million Indians in the North and several millions more in the South, peoples whose contacts with the rest of mankind had been lost in the unrecorded history of their migration from Asia some 25,000 to 40,000 years

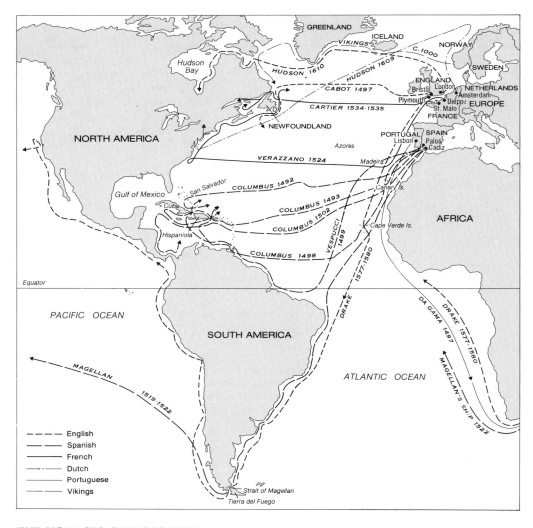

THE VOYAGES OF DISCOVERY

before—or were buried in forgotten meetings with ancient wanderers across the sea who left no record of their passing except perhaps in legend.

The exploration and exploitation of these new lands were to have a profound effect upon Europe. What was the European world like and what happened to it when the New World became a part of European life?

The European World   Take a look, for instance, at the Europe from which Columbus sailed, a continent whose future was to be deeply affected by the discovery, exploration, and settlement of the lands of the New World.

Fifteenth-century Europe was a world which, within its own framework, seemed as disturbing as our own time does to us: a world marked more by insecurity than security, more by disorder than order, more by despair than confidence. The loose confederation of European states known as the Holy Roman Empire had no real authority, and throughout the life of this political fiction inherited from the ancient world, anarchy was widespread. The Turks had taken Byzantium in mid-century and for decades afterwards moved threatening westward even to the gates of Vienna. Between 1337 and 1453 the Hundred Years' War had brought misery to England and France, and England had then moved from external conflict to internal strife in the Wars of the Roses which followed. Italy was plagued by conflict between her city-states and was ruled by assassination, and life was made insecure by bands of professional soldiers who roamed the land. The Universal Church, some of whose Popes were more agile on the battlefield or in the boudoir than before the altar, was rent by dissent and protest that culminated in Luther's Ninety-five Theses. One of the most popular themes in literature and painting was the Dance of Death. The historian Johan Huizinga has thus described the times:

> At the close of the Middle Ages, a sombre melancholy weighs on people's souls. Whether we read a chronicle, a poem, a sermon, a legal document even, the same impression of immense sadness is produced by them all. It would sometimes seem as if this period had been particularly unhappy, as if it had left behind only the memory of violence, of covetousness and mortal hatred, as if it had known no other enjoyment but that of intemperance, of pride and cruelty.

No wonder that attention had long been directed to the attractions of the past, the glories of the ancient world, as compensation for the miseries of the present and the uncertainties of the future.

At the same time, in spite of the sense of pervading gloom, there were strong signs of a new order. A more stable political environment was on the way in the rise of national states that were breaking down localism and giving rise to a new form of unity and cooperation. The stagnation of the medieval economy was being replaced by a new order resting on trade and commerce and dominated by a dynamic and confident new class. Shaken by protest that was to culminate in the Protestant Reformation, the Church was tightening discipline and raising its moral tone. This was the dawn of the Renaissance—the rebirth that was to see a great flowering of the arts, the revival of ancient learning, and the development of new ideas. Europe was thrusting outward rather than turning in upon itself, as the exploratory voyages by the Portuguese attest. With all this came a new sense of confidence. The future began to offer hope and opportunity rather than despair.

What happened at the end of the fifteenth century, with the four great voyages of Columbus and the rapid opening up of the New World to further exploration and exploitation by a Europe in transition, was that this great experience and activity served as a catalytic agent of change. What Europe needed at this moment was some great endeavor and commitment that

The Spanish conquest of Mexico. One scene from the Codex Florentino, part of the Indian Codices. The Spanish search for gold ultimately resulted in the destruction of the Aztec empire, concluded with the fall of the capital Tenochtitlan. The sophisticated weapons and sea support of Cortés' forces were finally able to defeat the Aztec warriors.

might absorb as well as nourish her restless and confined energies. The uncovering of the New World provided this new purpose and set in motion the modernization of Europe, the victory of the new order over the old. The effects were startling in economic life, in language and literature, upon social classes, upon political and religious thought, and in the expansion of scientific knowledge.

The Impact of America on Europe The New World proved to be a great treasurehouse of natural wealth out of which poured a profusion of plant, animal, and mineral resources profoundly affecting the economic, social, and intellectual life of Europe.

First, there was the impact made by the great influx of precious metals into the European economy. For three centuries after Columbus a steady stream of gold and silver found its way, through Spanish plunder and spending and English privateering, throughout Europe—an incredible expansion in specie that was out of all proportion to the rise in population, thereby extending greatly the basis for a money economy and stimulating the rise of modern capitalism. The consequences of this enormous increase in the supply of money were far-reaching. Large amounts of capital became available for enterprise and investment. Since all this was accompanied by a major price revolution in which prices rose while wages remained relatively low, the great profits stemming from this disparity meant even more money available for business expansion.

Great as was the wealth represented by precious metals, it was as nothing compared to the wealth generated by the agricultural and forest resources of the New World. In the long run these resources were to give a breadth and zest to the economic life of Europeans theretofore inconceivable. Many of these resources were those that replenished a diminishing European supply, such as the products of the forests: tar, pitch, ship timbers and masts, wood for fuel and handicraft, endless supplies of skins and furs for European comfort. Of even greater significance was the introduction of products previously unknown to Europeans: the potato, maize, kidney and lima beans, and the peanut, tomato, squash, avocado, maple sugar, watermelon, cucumber, and the Indian's secret weapon, tobacco. It is often forgotten that over half of the world's present agricultural produce consists of plants originating in the New World. Finally there were the herbs and drugs, rare and common, which brought from the New World "wonderful cures of sundry great diseases that otherwise than by these remedies they were incurable," as John Frampton joyfully and somewhat prematurely reported in 1577.

For almost three centuries after Columbus this wealth poured into Europe, stimulating commerce, trade, business enterprise, and economic life in general. Although the profits from this revitalization of economic life, especially in western Europe, naturally fell into the pockets and vaults of the organized entrepreneurs of the day, the products themselves—the foodstuffs, the produce of forest and wildlife—found their way into the broader economic and social arena and helped alter the habits and manner of living of even the masses of the population.

Tobacco is a good example. At first only a fad among the wealthy, extensive production soon after the plant had been refined by John Rolfe placed it within easy reach of all classes. Thus smoking became one of the few pleasures of life shared by poor and rich alike. Popes issued orders against it; King James I of England would not suffer what he called "the noxious weed" in his presence; and the Grand Turk Murad IV executed people who tried it (though ironically three centuries later a cigarette was named after him). But the simple pleasure and the relaxation it seemed to provide overrode all these threats.

More importantly, the potato very early became a cheap and abundant food, an important element in the sustenance of the masses. By 1630 it had become the staple of Ireland, and by the eighteenth century it was joined by another prolific American import, Indian corn or maize. These two nutritious plants became staples in the diet of the poor in most of Europe, and in large measure stimulated and supported the great population boom of the eighteenth and nineteenth centuries.

The infusion into Europe of this wealth from the New World, and the economic activity it stimulated, also had its impact upon the social class

The tobacco plant. It was to become a vital element in the economy of the New World, not only as the colonies' most important export, but actually as currency in Virginia, Maryland, and North Carolina.

structure. Quite naturally the commercial and business class—the merchants, bankers, shipowners, and other entrepreneurs—greatly increased in number and wealth, and consequently became a growing power in European social and political life. Their voice and influence had more and more to be taken into account by kings, nobles, and churchmen in whom power and influence had theretofore been centered.

Moreover, the new and expanding economic life called into being an urban working class, differing in function, organization, and numbers from the older restricted craftsmen of the medieval guilds. These were the sailors, clerks, bookkeepers, carpenters, dock workers, and others whose growing presence meant that another new and considerable element in European society had to be reckoned with by the traditional wielders of power.

At the same time that the economic and social boundaries of the Old World were being penetrated by the products of the New, its intellectual borders were being breached as well. For the Old World not only ate, inhaled, carved, wove, and shipped out on the products of the New, but the minds and imaginations of its people were nourished, enriched, and stimulated by the life and phenomena that lay across the Atlantic.

The New World, by the very fact of its discovery, gave man an expanded view of the physical earth. In the century and a half after Columbus dozens of accounts of voyages, travels, and exotic lands were published, forcing revision of older concepts of the earth. Europe shrank while the world grew. Beyond the bounds of Europe new life unfolded, richly varied and vast in its extent. Hundreds upon hundreds of unknown plant and animal forms were

The title page from a pamphlet describing the location and delights of New Brittaine. Such descriptions, seeking to encourage settlers to venture to the colonies, were one of the sources of Europe's first conceptions of the New World.

THE
DISCOVERY
OF
Nevv Brittaine.

Began *August* 27. *Anno Dom.* 1650.

By { *Edward Bland*, Merchant. *Abraham woode*, Captaine. *Sackford Brewster*, *Elias Pennant*, } Gentlemen.

From Fort *Henry*, at the head of *Appamattuck* River in *Virginia*, to the Fals of *Blandina*, first River in *New Brittaine*, which runneth West; being 120. Mile South-west, between 35. & 37. degrees, (a pleasant Country,) of temperate Ayre, and fertile Soyle.

LONDON,
Printed by *Thomas Harper* for *John Stephenson*, at the Sun below Ludgate. *M. DC. LI.*

discovered in America, thus broadening the knowledge of the world, stimulating the establishment and activity of scientific societies, promoting new and more accurate scientific classification of flora and fauna, and challenging long-held and cherished beliefs. For example, the New World was filled with such a variety of life unknown elsewhere that the Biblical theory that all the earth had been planted from one garden came under serious question. And in the minds of those unable to fit the New World Indian into any Biblical scheme of humanity, doubts were raised about the descent of the human race from Adam and Eve. Moreover, imagination and thought were greatly stirred by the opening up of the New World. One early traveler to the Americas prophetically noted that they offered "a fertile field for creative fanciful genius to explore, and may give rise to the most novel, elegant, and beautiful flights of imagination; and the brightest, most ingenious, and splendid embellishments of fiction."

How right he turned out to be. The common tongues of Europe were given new vitality by the popular accounts of voyagers and adventurers to the New World who wrote in a racy and vivid vernacular. Poets and playwrights found new themes and images to work with, and often simply turned the traveler's prose into verse, as Michael Drayton did in his *Ode to the Virginian Voyage,* in which he appropriated for his own purposes the very words of one of Raleigh's captains who explored Virginia in 1584. Shakespeare set his play *The Tempest* on a fanciful West Indies island and John Donne found a new way to exalt a woman's charms when he referred to his *Mistress on Going to Bed* as "O my America, my new-found land." Writers were intrigued with the image of the New World as the land of abundance and fertility. For the Elizabethan playwrights Beaumont and Fletcher, it was a place

> Where every wind that rises blows perfume
> And every breath of air is like an incense:
> The treasure of the Sun dwells here . . .
> Nothing bears a life, but brings a treasure.

Utopian literature, arguing the possibility of a future better life for humanity, found new sources of strength in the idea of the New World. Thomas More's *Utopia* was but one of such works stimulated by the discoveries of Columbus. Many writers were especially smitten by the romantic image of the Indian. The North American Indian in time became Rousseau's Noble Savage: the individual of nature whose life, stripped of the sin and superficiality of sophisticated cities, was a challenge to the restricted and often frustrating society of old Europe, and thus forced Europe to look critically at its own social arrangements and behavior.

In sum, the New World introduced so many new elements into European life and thought that it not only stimulated change but forced Europeans to re-examine themselves and their society. Its lands and wealth helped transform the economy and social structure of Europe; the vast profusion of its life poured forth rich and piquant food for an expanding knowledge to feed upon; its fresh and unspoiled scenery stretching endlessly into the unknown provided the stage upon which new bravery in thought and imagination might strut and find its way. And so Europe was drawn out from within itself, enticed to turn its eyes upon the world both near and far, brought down from the contemplation of the heavenly to find pleasure, profit, and excitement in the investigation of the earthly, and opened up to influences that helped free the European mind from provincialism.

Comparison: The New World of Space In seeking the significance of an event distant in the past, it is sometimes helpful if we have something closer at hand with which to compare it. In this sense, perhaps the exploratory adventures in space in the latter half of the twentieth century can help us to understand how it was that the ending of one era and the beginning of another is marked by a single voyage in 1492. Thus when Frank Borman, commander of Apollo 8 and a new kind of admiral of a new kind of ocean sea, slipped the bounds of earth for the first time in history and took his craft in orbit around the moon on December 24, 1968, it may well be that another new era in the history of the human race began.

Although these two extraordinary voyages of exploration almost five centuries apart were both made by men whose conviction, confidence, and intelligence give direction and purpose to their crafts, the voyages in themselves were not of course comparable. The times in which they took place were too different for that: the world of sailing ships, sealing wax, and kings was not the world of microcircuits, spacecraft, and piston rings. Yet in the

*The New World as envisioned by the Europeans. It was an image of
strangeness and abundance—of beasts and vegetation and gods unknown
on European soil and of welcoming Indians who shared their plentiful
harvest.*

broader sense of their place in history, their roles may well turn out to be
much alike.

On the day before his death in 1963 President John F. Kennedy recalled
the Irish writer Frank O'Connor who had told how as boys when he and his
friends out hiking came across an orchard wall that seemed too high to climb
they would throw their hats over the wall and thus have no choice but to
follow. The United States, said Kennedy in reference to the space program, is
tossing its hat over the wall. "We will climb this wall," he said. "And we
shall then explore the wonders of the other side."

With the Spanish commitment to the *Nina, Pinta,* and *Santa Maria* in 1492
Europe, as it were, threw its hat over the wall, and in climbing the wall after it
indeed found wonders to explore on the other side. Is it possible for us to say
that the flight of Apollo 8, in its own way, may someday be seen as the same
kind of opening wedge into the future, that like Columbus's journey it may
serve as a marking point for a new release of human energy, for the absorp-
tion of people in great new enterprises changing the face of the earth and the
life of each individual?

One must not, in the excitement of speculation, be moved to greater
confidence about the course of the future on the basis of the past than the
evidence warrants, particularly since history never repeats itself. But it is

Columbus planting the cross and distributing trinkets. This moment was the culmination of his vision.

difficult to deny that the movement into space in all its related aspects represents new ventures and activities which are catalytic in their impact, even though the hat has only just been thrown over the wall.

But the consequences and effects of this commitment have already been widespread and significant, opening as they have the door to a new treasurehouse of knowledge and achievement reaching out far beyond the space program itself. These developments have touched every field of endeavor and knowledge—industry, business, medicine, travel, communication—and we cannot even begin to assess the extent to which in the future they will alter the nature and character of human life and relationships, except to know that a new Other World is in the making and the real wonders still lie on the other side of the wall.

Moreover, all this has affected people's views and attitudes toward themselves and one another and the purpose of their lives, just as the discovery of the New World five centuries earlier challenged older ideas and assumptions. This has been true even in a negative sense in the arguments raised against space exploration. To ask why money and effort should be poured into space when such resources are needed to combat poverty, disease, ignorance, and misery here on earth has forced far sharper definitions and examinations of, and even commitments to, what is needed here on earth than we have ever had before. The simple irony of being able to place men on the moon and yet not know where to put our garbage here on earth has led many people to think more critically about our relationship to our earthly environment, to perceive not only the earth's minuscule place in the universe but its rare values as a life-supporting spacecraft in the sky. The very use of the word *spacecraft* to describe our present view of the earth as a planet of limited resources suggests the extent to which our thinking about the earth has been affected by the voyages of discovery into space.

For the view of earth from 250,000 miles out in space has raised with greater relevance than ever before the question of people living in harmony on this planet, "the good earth" as Frank Borman called it. In much the same manner that poets of five centuries ago appropriated the words of the voyagers to the New World, the poet Archibald MacLeish, relying on the words of the Apollo 8 astronauts, has written:

> To see the earth as it truly is, small and blue and beautiful in that eternal silence where it floats, is to see ourselves as riders on the earth together, brothers on that bright loveliness in the eternal cold—brothers who now know they are truly brothers.

Because we have the advantage of almost five hundred years of hindsight, we know for certain what started with Columbus. It may be five centuries more before we are sure of what started with Apollo 8. But just because we do know a great deal about the first, we can intelligently speculate on the meaning of the second.

What does seem clear is that both these great voyages of exploration serve as marking points for those rare moments in historical development when momentous shifts in the course of human affairs take place. Both occurred in periods of turbulent change, both seem to have prompted new examinations of the worlds people were already familiar with, and both directed new attention toward the future.

Profile: CHRISTOPHER COLUMBUS

Who was this curious, restless, greedy, God-fearing, stubborn, determined, proud, disappointed man who called himself Admiral of the Ocean Sea and discovered a world he refused to admit was new?

Born in 1451, the son of a weaver of Genoa, he was at sea on the Mediterranean by the age of twenty. Later shipwrecked off Portugal, he settled there for a time and on the island of Madeira, and made various voyages into the Atlantic including at least one to Guinea and the Gold Coast in Africa. These experiences proved fruitful. He learned that south of the Canary Islands the winds blew westward. Knowing that to the north the prevailing winds blew east, he reasoned that one could sail south to catch the westward winds to the Indies and then return by the northern route on the winds blowing east to Europe. Moreover, during his stay on Madeira he took notice of the strange driftwood and other objects cast ashore during storms, and he correctly deduced that this debris came from lands to the west.

By the early 1480s these experiences strengthened his conviction—mathematically unsound but historically fortunate—that the size of the world made it but an easy sail westward to reach the island of Japan and thus open up a short sea-route to the riches of the East. Ancient and medieval geographers knew the world was round and that it was therefore theoretically possible to reach the East by sailing west. Columbus agreed but differed with those learned men who had more accurate notions of the size of the globe than he had. People with a vision have a tendency to pick and choose the evidence which supports their dream, and Columbus was no exception. He relied upon the ancient Greek mathematician Ptolemy, the geography of Pierre d'Ailly's Imago Mundi, published in 1410, and the calcualations of Florentine geographer Paolo Toscanelli with whom he corresponded—all of whom so misjudged the size of the earth that the distance from Portugal to Japan was determined to be only 3000 miles, over 9000 miles short of the actual distance! So a voyage westward to the treasures of the East "is not only possible to make, but sure and certain," as Toscanelli put it.

Columbus's vision was also nourished by the legend of the West. For centuries, ever since the Greek poet Homer first sang of the Elysian Plain, that western abode of heroes after death, Europe had associated the West with some form of earthly paradise where life was idyllic—where all women were beautiful, men strong-limbed, and children sturdy; where innocence not guile prevailed, harmony not disorder; where the climate was perpetual springtime and the air perfumed by flowers. Among the many legends of this land blest by the gods was the voyage in the sixth century of the Irish monk St. Brendan, who supposedly found this paradise in the Fortunate Isles. So powerful was the legend of such a paradise that its location even appeared on maps under various names. Columbus himself believed that it was possible to locate, though not actually explore, the original paradise, the Garden of Eden. And on one of his later voyages to the New World he became convinced that he had determined its location, an accomplishment sure to bring him everlasting fame.

And so Columbus conceived his scheme to reach the East by sailing west. Utterly confident that he was right, as individuals of destiny invariably are, and stirred by visions of the titles and wealth which would come to him as a consequence of his success, he hawked his proposal—the Enterprise of the Indies as he called it—before various monarchs. Rebuffed by Portugal's King John II, he was also twice turned down by the monarchs of Spain. Then in one of those sudden turns of mind that sometimes initiate great events, Isabella agreed to support his expedition. Presumably she was much impressed by Columbus and thought there was little to lose and much to gain. He might be right after all. The expedition cost about $14,000. Her gamble paid off.

There had been remarkable voyages before and there were to be other remarkable voyages after, but none was of greater import than that which began when the Nina, Pinta, and Santa Maria slipped anchor out of Palos on August 3, 1492, and which climaxed on October 11 off San Salvador, the first land sighted in the Western Hemisphere.

It was the lushness of the new lands he uncovered on his four voyages between 1492 and 1504, the hint of paradise about them, the unmistakable suggestion of great wealth that so impressed the Admiral of the Ocean Sea as he cruised among the islands of the Caribbean on his first voyage:

> This island and all the others are very fertile to a limitless degree, and this island is
> extremely so. In it there are many harbors on the coast of the sea, beyond comparison
> with others that I know in Christendom, and many rivers, good and large, which is

marvelous. Its lands are high; there are in it many sierras and very lofty mountains, beyond comparison with Tenerife. All are most beautiful, of a thousand shapes; all are accessible and are filled with trees of a thousand kinds and tall, so that they seem to touch the sky. . . . The nightingale was singing and other birds of a thousand kinds, in the month of November, there where I went. There are six or eight kinds of palm, which are a wonder to behold on account of their beautiful variety, but so are the other trees and fruits and plants. In it are marvelous pine groves; there are very wide and fertile plains, and there is honey; and there are birds of many kinds and fruits in great diversity. In the interior, there are mines of metals and the population is without number.

And of another island he wrote:

Espanola is a marvel. The sierras and the mountains, the plains and the champaigns are so lovely and so rich for planting and sowing, for breeding cattle of every kind, for building towns and villages. The harbors of the sea here are such as cannot be believed to exist unless they have been seen, and so with rivers, many and great, and of good water, the majority of which contains gold. In the trees, fruits, and plants, there is a great difference from those of Juana. In this island, there are many spices and great mines of gold and of other metals.

All this was, in the appropriate phrase, a New World—"an Other World," as Columbus described it to Ferdinand and Isabella—its existence predicted by the ancients, its image preserved in European myth, and its presence finally uncovered on the most important of all voyages of exploration. With justifiable pride Columbus called attention to his accomplishment: "Over there I have placed under their Highnesses' sovereignty more land than there is in Africa and Europe." But he never received the grants and rewards he kept demanding for this achievement, and he died, worn out and bitter, in 1506.

Sir Walter Raleigh was later to say of his own voyages that he promoted them "To seek New Worlds for gold, for praise, for glory." The Admiral of the Ocean Sea got none of these in his own time, but praise and glory as the greatest discoverer and navigator in history will be his as long as people admire the restless, probing, and determined spirit.

Chapter 2
TOWARD A NEW SOCIETY: THE PEOPLE AND THE LAND

The Spirit of the Times
FIRST SETTLEMENTS

The roots of what became the thirteen English colonies were all planted in the seventeenth century, with the exception of Georgia where the first colonists did not arrive until 1733. By that date, colonial settlements stretched along 1200 miles of coast from Maine to the edge of Spanish Florida. After the desperate struggles of the first settlements, the task of colonization remained difficult but not uncertain. But in the earliest years it was touch-and-go. The sheer will to survive, a lot of luck, and the generosity of nearby Indians—these were the key ingredients that carried the colonists through the early years. Learning from the experiences of the early settlers and drawing upon the resources of established communities, later colonists had the odds in their favor.

But in the beginning, colonization was a grim experience, as the Jamestown and Plymouth ventures abundantly demonstrated. Virginia, the first colony, was founded when the London Company landed about a hundred men in May of 1607. The fate of their tiny settlement at Jamestown was precarious for over a decade. Wasting their efforts and energies in pointless searches for gold and passageways to the Far East, inexperienced in the ways of wilderness or farming, and ill-equipped for the perils of a new world, the settlers wallowed in their own ignorance and ineptitude. Sixty men perished of disease and famine the first year. One settler sadly observed with irony and a touch of wit remarkable under the circumstances: "The many birds and beasts were wild and we unskilled and they suffered not much from us." The settlement was reinforced, but disease, famine, and Indians in the winter of 1609–1610 wiped out most of the remaining original

An early settlement in Salem, Massachusetts.

settlers and their new companions. Finally beginning to understand the demands of a new environment, the London Company began sending out skilled workers, experienced farmers, and women as well in 1619, thus giving the settlement the assurance of permanence through families. The discovery that tobacco was more valuable than nonexistent gold gave the settlers a solid economic resource on which to build. But in the years from 1607 to 1622, only some two thousand of six thousand settlers survived, and they principally because of aid from the Powhatan Indians.

North in New England, the settlement of the Pilgrims at Plymouth in 1620 was equally grim. Sailing late in September, driven off course by storms, and forced to land in winter, the Pilgrims saw their numbers cut in half by spring. Governor William Bradford recorded of those difficult months:

> But that which was most sad and lamentable was that in 2 or 3 months time half of their company died, especially in January and February, being the depth of winter; and wanting houses and other comforts; being infected with the scurvey and other diseases which this long voyage and their inaccommodate condition had brought upon them; so as there died sometimes 2 or 3 of a day in the foresaid time; that of 100 and odd persons scarce 50 remained: and of these in the time of most distress there was but 6 or 7 sound persons; who, to their great commendations, be it spoken, spared no pains, night nor day, but with abundance of toil and hazard of their own health fetched them wood, made them fires, dressed them meat, made their beds, washed their lothsome clothes, clothed and unclothed them. In a word did all the homely and necessary offices for them, which dainty and queasy stomachs cannot endure to hear named.

But they made it. Aid from Squanto, the Indian friend who showed them how to plant corn and how to fish and hunt under wilderness conditions, proved to be a key factor in the settlement's survival. Since the Pilgrims were not drawn to the

New World by lures of gold, they were spared the fruitless activities that so drained and distracted the first settlers at Jamestown. And after their first harsh winter, they settled down to hard work and made a secure if not particularly prosperous place for themselves.

Later settlements all profited from the experiences of these earliest settlers—their failures as well as their successes. When the first heavy Puritan migration under John Winthrop sailed for America in 1630, for example, nothing was left to chance. The expedition of over a thousand persons was in essence a society in miniature, possessing adequate supplies, all essential equipment, and skills of every necessary kind. Moreover, subsequent settlements benefited from adjacent established settlements. The first small group of some two hundred farmers settled in Maryland by Lord Baltimore in 1634 was greatly aided by the flourishing Virginia settlements and consequently had few problems getting under way. And by the time William Penn established his colony in 1681, his lands lay between prosperous and developed areas to the north and south, a happy circumstance which greatly diminished the problems and fears of the first Quaker settlers.

Furthermore, a number of the colonies had their first communities either established or quickly reinforced by settlers on the move from other areas who were already experienced in the matter of colonization. The first communities of Rhode Island and Connecticut, for instance, were founded in the mid-1630s by Puritans leaving Massachusetts as a result of religious dissatisfaction with the Massachusetts authorities—Roger Williams and Anne Hutchinson and their followers into Rhode Island, Thomas Hooker and his friends into Connecticut. The first settlers in the Carolinas in the 1670s were either small farmers from the West Indies or farmers from Virginia, both groups with long experience behind them. Similarly, Puritans from long-established communities in New England moved into and helped to settle New Jersey after that area had been given as a grant by the Duke of York to two of his friends.

And so the process of colonization advanced. Group after group arrived, put down roots, grew, and expanded. By the time Georgia was on a firm base in 1750, the colonial population had grown from 100 to over a million. And an established society spreading along the eastern seaboard for hundreds of miles had been carved out of wilderness.

In the long millennia of human existence, individuals had struck out into new lands untold times: struggling for survival, creating a physical place for themselves, establishing families, developing societies in hostile environments. By the time of the discovery of the New World this process of creating civilizations and cultures in new and virgin lands on the globe was an experience located in the remote past beyond the memory of the living. In the seventeenth century that experience reoccurred in new form and for new purposes, but it tested the ingenuity, courage, and will of the people just as surely as had those earlier ventures of wandering men and families thousands of years before.

The People and Why They Came

For over a century after Columbus the great explorers sailed, the conquering captains from Castile moved like scythes through the ancient civilizations of the Aztec and the Inca, and the bureaucrats followed in their train to govern what had been discovered and possessed. By 1607, when the first English

THE DEVELOPMENT OF COLONIAL
SETTLEMENTS, 1630–1760

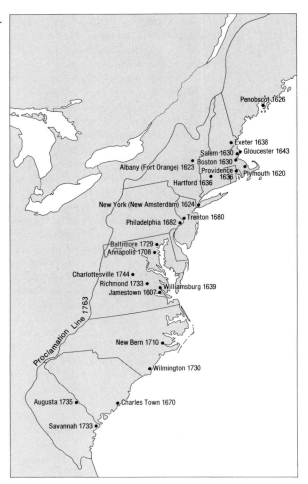

Penobscot 1626
Exeter 1638
Salem 1630 Gloucester 1643
Boston 1630
Albany (Fort Orange) 1623
Providence 1636 Plymouth 1620
Hartford 1636
New York (New Amsterdam) 1624
Trenton 1680
Philadelphia 1682
Baltimore 1729
Annapolis 1708
Charlottesville 1744
Richmond 1733 Williamsburg 1639
Jamestown 1607
Proclamation Line 1763
New Bern 1710
Wilmington 1730
Augusta 1735 Charles Town 1670
Savannah 1733

settlers landed at Jamestown, the Spaniards had created an empire which
stretched from Mexico and the Isthmus through South America, except for
Brazil and the plains of the far south.

Except for Mexico, fruitless searches for legendary cities of gold and
fountains of youth, and a few minor Spanish outposts in Florida and the
Southwest, the North American continent lay untouched and unexplored,
there for the taking. The interested takers were the English, French, and
Dutch. The English had early joined the exploration game, sending Cabot in
1497–1498 on a major expedition that was to form the basis for subsequent
English claims to New World territories. But the English were not prepared
to exploit these claims until decades later, and even then their initial efforts
were hardly encouraging.

Nevertheless, the unsuccessful English attempts to plant colonies on the
North American coast in the latter part of the sixteenth century—notably

The Arrival of the Englishemen in Virginia, from Thomas Hariot, A
briefe description of Virginia. *Hariot was a member of the first group
of English settlers who attempted to establish a post on Roanoke Island.
Unable to find the gold or the route to the Pacific they had come for, the
entire settlement returned to England with Sir Francis Drake.*

Raleigh's famous failure on Roanoke Island—did not dampen English interest, nor did the painful struggles of the Jamestown colonists to survive in
1607 or the agony of the Plymouth settlers over a decade later. Within a few
years there began that flow of peoples from the Old World to the New that in
less than two centuries was to result in the firm establishment of those
English-dominated colonies posed on the razor's edge of the North American continent, colonies that were ultimately to strike out on their own as the
independent United States. And it was this flow of human beings over the
generations that was to constitute Europe's great gift to the New World in
return for the treasure it took from forest, field, and mine.

Who these people were, why they came, what they brought with them;
what happened to them, their ideas, and their institutions after they arrived;
what kind of life they created in the wilderness—these are the primary
matters that concern us in the colonial era of American development. For it
was during this period of 156 years—from 1607 to 1763, when the revolutionary era began—that the roots of American civilization and culture were
put down. Here is our infancy and our childhood. Here were the formative

years of American values, ideas, institutions, and experiences that have shaped us as a people and drawn the fundamental lines of our character, interests, and attitudes. For although the colonists of the seventeenth and eighteenth centuries would scarcely recognize themselves in us, we can recognize ourselves in them, even though we have outgrown the world in which they lived.

As small children of ten, had we the gift to see ourselves at forty, we would be strangers to ourselves. But at forty it is possible to rediscover the sense of being ten, to see ourselves in that recollection, and thereby to understand ourselves better as we are now. Much the same holds true for a people or a community. It is no accident that the drive of contemporary black Americans for a new and more satisfying place in America involves not only a powerful and widespread search into the past for the roots of their identity, but also a deep conviction that the past will substantiate their claim on the present. Herein lies the significance and the excitement of our recollection of colonial society and life, for we are looking back upon ourselves, and the memories, whether pleasing or painful, illuminate our lives today.

Who were we then, whence did we come, and why?

Although by the end of the colonial period you could find in the thirteen colonies individuals from every part of the European and Mediterranean world, the major sources of immigration were few and the main one was England. The heaviest and most important period of English migration to America was the seventeenth century. The other significant groups came largely in the eighteenth.

The decision to pick up stakes, to abandon the familiar, to commit yourself to wave and tempest over three thousand miles of perilous seas, and finally to gamble on being able to create a new and better life in a strange environment—this was a decision not to be made lightly. The people who made it were not necessarily stronger, wiser, or more farseeing than those who did not, but they were different. They had crossed the psychological barrier that prompts individuals to bear those ills they have rather than flee to others they do not know. The pressures that helped thrust people through that barrier were, on the one hand, strong dissatisfaction with things where they were, and on the other, the conviction that westward across the Atlantic lay opportunity for a fresh start, a chance to change one's life for the better.

Religious Discontent in England In England in the seventeenth century circumstances conspired to foster a widespread discontent: many people were unhappy, especially among the middle and lower classes. Although the role of religion as a cause for emigration has been overestimated by those who point to the wisdom of the Almighty in founding the United States, it would be wrong to neglect the influence of religious dissatisfaction in persuading people that the time had come to move. It was important in the establishment of the tiny Plymouth colony in 1620, and in the initial Puritan migration to America from 1629 to 1640. The Stuart kings, who reigned from

1603 to 1642 and again from 1660 to 1688, wished to increase the power of the crown they wore. Since the monarch was also head of the established church, the enforcement of religious conformity became an important instrument in enhancing the authority of the king.

Thus royal policy fed the resentment of the Separatists of Plymouth who sought complete independence from the Church of England, of the Puritans who wanted to modify church government from within, and of the Catholics who still dreamed of reunification with Rome. It is worth special note that between 1629 and 1640, when Charles I ruled without Parliament and backed Archbishop William Laud's strict enforcement of the religious code, the Puritan migration was at its heaviest, and over twenty thousand English went to the New England colonies. But between 1641 and 1660, when the Puritans waged their civil war with Charles and governed England through the Commonwealth of Oliver Cromwell, Puritan migration fell off sharply.

To a lesser degree, religious pressure affected the sentiments of Catholics under the Commonwealth and the convictions of Quakers later in the century, and thus sent numbers of these people to what they hoped would prove havens for their own beliefs in the New World—the Catholics in Virginia and Maryland, the Quakers in Pennsylvania.

Economic Pressures Yet, powerful though this motive was—disagreeable and threatening as religious controversy could be to people for whom God and Heaven contained the final message of existence—other motives also thrust Englishmen into the New World. Among these were economic conditions. By the opening of the seventeenth century the transition from an economy of medieval self-sufficiency to one of modern commercialism had brought distress and concern to many of the middle and lower classes whose role in the new order had not yet been defined. Small landholders had been dispossessed of their holdings, artisan craftsmen found their old security threatened, small businessmen and merchants often lacked the financial resources to weather the ups and downs of the emerging economic order. Not until the end of the century, when England's trade and industry began its period of expansion (due in no small part to her American holdings), could an economic place be made for many of these people, and it is worth noting that when this happened English migration slackened.

Economic distress was understandably widespread in the seventeenth century. Even in the minds of those whose decision to move may have been largely shaped by religious motives, economic concern was a lurking presence. That Puritan stalwart, John Winthrop, who strongly felt the impact of his religious concerns, also had financial worries in the depression year of 1629. And even the saints of the *Mayflower* filled out their company with sinners who hoped to solve their economic woes.

In trying to understand why people came to the New World, it is not enough to reckon the power of their discontent. No one was likely to pack a bag for this alone. There had also to be a lively expectation of doing better somewhere else. Thus it was not just that people were *thrust out of* England (or anywhere else for that matter) by revulsion at what they had to put up with at home, but that they were also *attracted by* America, lured by the promise of the New World.

That promise was mainly economic, though as time went on there were growing social and political attractions as well: the opportunity for advancement, for material gain and benefit, for the improvement of one's lot in the world. No one can dispute the fact, of course, that from the beginning a kind of horror story about the New World circulated throughout Europe, a story that grew with every voyage and registered new tones of frightfulness with every telling. There were tales about the cruelty of the Indians—their skill and delight in torture, their taste for human flesh, their treachery, their practice of human sacrifice. And there were tales of terror about the furies of nature—the rage of rivers and seas, the horrifying beasts, the unimaginable extremes of climate, the crushing cold of the north and the violent heat of the south, the earthquakes and winds. But there is no better example of the power of the wish to better oneself than the fact that these tales of terror came in a poor second to the tales of glittering promise. From the days of discovery, as we well know, stories about the wealth of the New World, presumably there for the taking, had circulated widely. Only two years after the first landing at Jamestown, and despite the grimness of the struggle for survival there (which news of course did not circulate so widely), the Reverend Daniel Price in England was telling his congregation that the New World was a country

> not unlike to equalize . . . Tyrus for colours, Balsan for woods, Persia for oils, Arabia for spices, Spain for silks, Narcis for shipping, Netherlands for fish, Pomona for fruit and by tillage, Babylon for corn, besides the abundance of mulberries, minerals, rubies, pearls, gems, grapes, deer, fowles, drugs for physic, herbs for food, roots for colours, ashes for soap, timber for building, pastures for feeding, rivers for fishing and whatsoever commodity England wanteth. . . .

—a recital that must have whetted many an appetite, pious or no.

Francis Higginson, a member of the early group of Puritans migrating to Massachusetts Bay, was more restrained in his description of plentitude, but his more realistic account may for that very reason have been even more seductive:

> Great pity it is to see so much good ground for corn and for grass as any is under the heavens, to be altogether unoccupied when so many honest men and their families in old England . . . do make shift to live one by the other.

The desire to share in all this, to own one's own land, must have been quickened by the writing of one Plymouth colonist that "We are all freeholders, the rent day does not trouble us." Moreover, all this was free from Old World encumbrances upon the common people. No lordly huntsmen followed their hounds over the poor's cultivated fields; there were no feudal tithes, taxes, and rates. This economic lure of the colonies continued unabated throughout the seventeenth and eighteenth centuries. In the latter

Indian massacre at Jamestown, 1622.

part of the seventeenth century William Penn produced for prospective immigrants a description of Pennsylvania that would do credit to the Hawaiian Chamber of Commerce.

Finally, it should be recognized that there were those who came unwillingly. The reasons for this stemmed from a combination of economic and social circumstances at work not only in England but also in the colonies. In the seventeenth century England had what was regarded by the authorities as an excess of undesirable elements: beggars, wandering poor, criminals, all set loose upon the land by the disorder of a society in transition. Very early, transportation to the colonies came to be looked upon as a means of getting rid of such people and thus presumably improving the social atmosphere at home. Children of the poor, a financial burden to the parish, were often sent to America. Footloose women of fancy, from the streets and byways, found themselves shipped out to make their contribution to motherhood in America. In later years, lenient judges offered criminals transportation as an alternative to execution or long imprisonment. This desire to rid England of undesirable individuals coincided with the need of the colonies for labor, and such persons often found themselves bound in long service to colonial masters eager for workers.

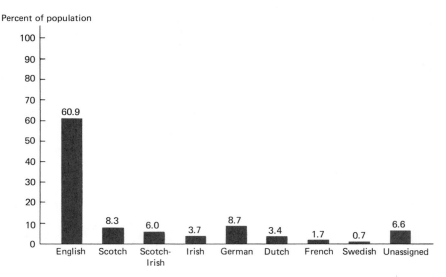

Percent of population

NATIONAL ORIGIN OF THE WHITE POPULATION, 1790

It was this need in the colonies that also made kidnapping if not widespread at least not uncommon. Ship captains made money selling such people into service in the New World, and the unscrupulous were not averse to trying any method to fill the holds before setting sail. Strongarm squads known as press gangs roamed the streets of port towns at night before the tide turned, picking up drunks and the young, and rapping any resisters over the head if necessary. Naive souls were sometimes enticed aboard by devious methods and then clapped under the hatches. There is also some evidence that persons with obnoxious relatives found ship sailings a handy solution to their problem.

Non-English Immigration   What held true for English migration in both the seventeenth and eighteenth centuries also held true in general for the handful of non-English folk in the colonies by the end of the seventeenth century as well as for the heavy non-English migration of the eighteenth century. Dissatisfaction and distress at home were abetted by the attraction and enticement of America.

Conversely, the relative absence of dissatisfaction at home prevented the Dutch from creating a genuine settlement in the New Netherlands where, with only a few farmers, a handful of patroons and their tenants, some commercial men, and a series of bungling administrators, they were outnumbered in their own colony and fell easily to English rule.

Special conditions of religious distress in France—prompted by the removal of protection for French Protestants when the Edict of Nantes was revoked in 1685—sent French Huguenots fleeing the country. And fruitful

Persecuted Lutherans leaving Salzburg for Georgia. James Oglethorpe, the founder of the colony, envisioned it as a place where the victims of injustice could start anew, and he sought settlers for his project throughout Europe, asking only that they be of good character.

economic and social opportunities in the New World attracted many of these industrious people, primarily to South Carolina, Virginia, New York, and Pennsylvania.

In the eighteenth century, social and economic conditions such as religious persecution, famine, and economic dislocation produced considerable distress in Germany, particularly in the Rhineland, and made Germans ripe for migration. Combined with the alluring propaganda put out by William Penn, this distress made German migration one of the heaviest of the century. The same held true for the famed Scotch-Irish, the largest migrating group of the eighteenth century—those Lowland Scots originally transported by England to Northern Ireland in the seventeenth century as a presumed counterweight to Irish rebellion. But suffering under harsh English economic and religious restrictions imposed on all of Ireland, the Scotch-Irish were drawn to the colonies in great numbers, especially by the opportunity to take up land along the frontier line of settlement. The Highland Scots, who also came in the eighteenth century though in far smaller numbers, had a special motivation. Most of these tough-minded people chose exile in America for political reasons after the crushing of the Stuart rebellions against the English in 1715 and 1745.

There were, of course, as always in the immigrant experience, those who came to the New World and for one reason or another found the experience so discouraging that they returned home. Such a one was Thomas Lechford who wrote of Massachusetts men in 1640: "I am not of them in Church or Commonweal . . . and loth am I here to stay, but am plucking up stakes with as much speed as I may." And he did.

The Ocean Voyage   No matter who, the people who came to America had to undergo the rigors of the voyage from Old World to New. The journey across the Atlantic in those days bore no resemblance to the pleasure jaunt it has since become on the great ocean liners and jet aircraft. The time of passage varied greatly—from a speedy three weeks to an agonizing three months—and depended on the weather, the condition of the ship, and the capacity of the captain for drink. Few immigrants had ever sailed before, and the perils of the North Atlantic could be terrifying and sometimes fatal. Few experiences are more frightening than a storm at sea, even in the finest vessels of today, and the small, cramped, "tempest-tossed" ships of an earlier time tested the faith of even the most devout that an omnipotent God would preserve them for a better destiny.

In his journal recording the crossing of one of the first Puritan groups in 1629, the Reverend Francis Higginson has left us a description of this experience:

> Wed. the 27th the wind still N. and calm in the morning, but about noon there arose a So. wind, which increased more and more, so that it proved to us that are landsmen a sore and terrible storm; for the wind blew mightily, the rain fell vehemently, the sea roared and the waves tossed us horribly; besides it was fearful dark and the mariner's mate was afraid; and noise on the other side with their running here and there, loud crying to one another to pull at this and that rope.

Disease also took its toll. A governor's wife in 1639 noted that "While crossing the Atlantic we have been pestered with people so full of infection that after a while we saw little but throwing dead bodies overboard."

Passengers had to bring their own supplies and if they ran out were compelled to purchase from the captains at high prices or do without. Food was often spoiled and water scarce or undrinkable by voyage end. A Dutch passenger in 1679 described an appetizing mealtime:

> There was not a bit of butter or vinegar on the food during the whole voyage except what we had purchased at Falmouth. I do not know how long it was we had nothing to eat except the heads of salt fish, and those spoiled for the most part. We had to eat them until they were thrown overboard. Most of the time we had white peas which our cook was too lazy to clean, or were boiled in stinking water, and when they were brought on the table we had to throw them away. The meat was old and tainted. The pork was passable but enormously thick, as much as six inches; and the bread was mouldy or wormy.

No company ever sailed with only the pious on board: all had their share of cheats, liars, gamblers, seducers, and hellers that the godly souls had to endure with much trial. The Reverend Higginson wrote of one such fellow,

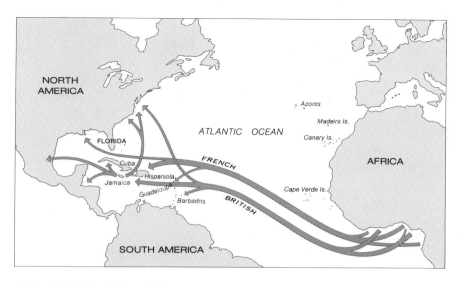

THE SOURCES AND DESTINATIONS OF THE SLAVE TRADE IN
THE EIGHTEENTH CENTURY

concluding with a flat statement that had behind it the certain conviction that
God is not to be trifled with:

> This day a notorious wicked fellow that was given to swearing and boasting of
> his former wickedness . . . mocked at our days of fast, railing and jesting
> against puritans, this fellow fell sick of the pox and died.

Yet all was not terror and wickedness. Life went on in its accustomed
ways. Meals were cooked, clothes washed, love made, babies born, trades
plied, books read, the good weather enjoyed, religious services held. Even so
the best of every voyage was its end, and few who made the trip wished to do
so again. It is probable that to many the perils facing them on land seemed
mild by comparison with the terrors they had faced at sea.

The Slave Trade   Second only in numbers to the English immigrants in
the colonial period were the blacks from Africa, transported against their
will. Few blacks had ever heard of the New World; indeed, few had even
seen or heard of the ocean that was to bear so many of them in misery and
terror to America. Many who ended up aboard slave ships were criminals
sold for punishment. Others were sold by their families in time of famine.
Some had been kidnapped by Europeans, though more by native gangs. Still
others were prisoners of war or slaves from birth.

Economic circumstances, not surprisingly, generated the slave trade.
Greed for profit drove the European traders and sea captains, as well as

The slave ship. The conditions in the slave quarters on the Abanoze *were depicted by Meynell, a young British naval officer on board.*

African chieftains and slavers, to happily barter human beings for muskets, gunpowder, dry goods, and rum. And if the African sellers often tried to pass off the halt and the lame as sturdy field hands, European buyers just as frequently diluted the liquor and weighed short the goods. It was a sorry business, and had no redeeming features.

The slave trade with the New World began early, and before it ended at least ten million Africans had been transported and countless others had died. Most of those transported went to the West Indies and to South America. But the extent of this forced migration to the North American colonies is suggested by the presence of 697,897 blacks registered in the United States census reports for 1790. In 1714 there had been 59,000.

Just as the chronic need for labor in the colonies provided an incentive for white immigration, so the demand for workers stimulated the slave trade. Blacks appeared early in the North American colonies, the first handful in 1619, and they continued to be brought in through the seventeenth century. But it was not until the end of the seventeenth century that the flow of Africans became heavy, stimulated by the rise of the plantation system in the South where black gang labor proved economically more advantageous than white servant labor, and reinforced in the latter years of the seventeenth century by the official entrance of the English into the slave trade, a trade that increased shipping and provided capital later invested in mines, railroads, and cotton mills.

The unholy character of this involuntary migration was intensified by the horrors of the voyage. The unknown terrors facing the captured blacks—many of whom were convinced that they were being taken to a land of white cannibals—and the incomprehensible loss of the familiar as they were torn from their own shores, drove many to throw themselves into the sea. Others sank into a trance-like immobility, refusing to eat or drink, and dying in a strange state of melancholy. Jammed into coffin-like quarters aboard the slave ships, with little fresh air, often forced to lie in their own excrement, taken on deck for scant exercise and inadequate food, slave women subject to the sailors' lust, the sick thrown callously overboard if the ship were threatened by disease or shortage of rations—the slaves, if they survived, and many did not, arrived in the New World in at best a state of shock. The entire experience was brutalizing and dehumanizing for white as well as black. Crews were maltreated beyond belief, the casualty rate among them higher than that of the slaves themselves. Starved, flogged, beaten, exposed to disease, few ever signed on voluntarily with full knowledge of what they were in for.

Self-Improvement   At the end of the colonial period the pattern of immigration had left its indelible stamp upon American society and culture. We were a mixed bag in race, nationality, and culture, with English predominant. Though the variety was not as great as it was to be by the twentieth century, the mixture by the time of the Revolution was unique in modern times. This diversity was to give us an affinity for those societies that had donated their peoples to America, and yet make it hard for others to understand us. The mixture unquestionably enriched our society and culture and gave reality to the idea that it was possible for people of diverse cultures to live in harmony. Yet it also created a problem Americans have always had to struggle with: how to make diversity productive and fruitful and keep cultural and racial animosities and suspicions at a minimum. It is worth remembering that Benjamin Franklin, the colonial model of common sense and moderation, had by the mid-eighteenth century become perturbed by the presence of so many Germans in his precious Pennsylvania and complained that the colony was in danger of being Germanized. Generations later the Germans were to have similar feelings about the Irish, the Slavs, and the Poles. The tendency of some Americans to suggest that others go back where they came from got an early start.

The pattern of immigration had other effects than increased diversity. The motives and circumstances of migration shaped the social character of American society from the beginning. Except for sons without inheritance, members of the British and European upper classes (though some invested financially in the initial settlements) had no reason for migrating, and thus the aristocratic element was absent from the start in American society. The colonies were founded and continually rejuvenated from the middle and lower classes. It was this fact which was to make America notable as the society of "the common man."

Finally, migration, in the sense of *movement*, left its psychological mark on the American people. Every year, every month, saw the arrival of immigrants, most of whom came believing that they would be better off than they had been at home. In this sense, movement became associated in the American psyche with opportunity and the solution of problems. So the idea that to move is to get a fresh start, a second chance, a new break was part of the American attitude from the first settlements onward. Encouraged by the availability of frontier lands to try for that fresh start again, and yet again if necessary, and encouraged even further in modern times by the continual opening up of new towns, cities, and industries, Americans have always been a people on the move—"on the go," in the unique American phrase.

It is largely this that has made us known as a restless people, rootless even. We seem eternally caught between where we have been and where we are going. The American concept of home has rarely been associated with putting down deep roots, though of course many people did and many more talked of doing so. It is a distinctly American observation that "home is where you hang your hat." And it was the American writer Thomas Wolfe who wrote that *You Can't Go Home Again.* These are conceptions that other peoples in the world have found difficult to grasp in their attempts to understand those strange creatures of an Other World, the Americans.

The Gifts of Europe

The Americans were not, of course, shaped by the experience of immigration alone, powerful though this influence was. Other factors of primary importance contributed to American development.

The first of Europe's gifts to America was the Old World itself. Many of us assume that America was somehow created and built on its own, that the origins of the nation lie entirely within ourselves. We assume this from natural pride in our achievements, but in doing so we forget that this country was, from the beginning, a product of European civilization. We did develop along lines of our own, and by the end of the colonial period were well on toward creating a distinctly American society and culture. Nevertheless it was a society and culture constructed out of basic European materials, though modified by New World conditions and experiences. Our debt, therefore, to the European heritage and experience is very great indeed.

The Political Debt   For example, consider our political debt. It was Great Britain that provided the larger political and governmental framework within which American growth took place in the colonial period. By the time of the initial settlements, Britain had achieved the status and power of a great national state, and it was the power and authority of this state that in large measure guaranteed the successful effort to establish settlements on the edge

Part of the charter of the Massachusetts Bay Company. John Winthrop and other leaders decided to expand the government of the colony by transforming the company into a commonwealth and opening up the right to elect lawmaking representatives to most of the adult male colonists who were members of the Puritan church. Eventually, the entire General Court—deputy governor, council of assistants, and deputies, who were representatives from each settlement—were elected by these "freemen."

of the North American continent. Britain granted the original charters for the first companies of settlement, such as the Virginia Company and the Massachusetts Bay Company, and further provided protection for the budding colonies against the threats of other countries such as France and Spain. And it was Britain that provided the colonists for so long a time with what sense of political unity and identity they had, and even more importantly with a sense of security, the reassurance that they were not alone in the world.

Moreover, the particular forms of political and governmental organization adopted in the colonies, however modified they were to be, closely followed the English model with which the original colonists were generally familiar. Thus the New England town and the Southern county units of government reflected English institutions, and colonial government found its general parallel in British experience: the colonial governor having his counterpart in the King, the colonial assembly in the House of Commons, and the governor's council in the House of Lords. The English experience with representative government, especially local self-government and citizen participation, was not abandoned by the colonists, but refined and strengthened in a new environment. Fundamental political ideas that we associate with democracy in America were ideas put forth, explored, refined, and developed in England, especially in the seventeenth century. The ideas of John Locke on the rights of man were extensively used by the Americans to reinforce and strengthen their own experience. Indeed, the whole political heritage of the ancient classical world and the Renaissance, which formed the bedrock upon which American political and governmental development rested, flowed to America through English channels.

The Economic Debt Of equal significance is the economic debt owed by America to Europe. The American colonies were not only sustained and nourished within the British colonial system, they were woven into the general fabric of European economic life. The colonies were incapable of completely sustaining themselves economically. It was the financial resources of English investment in the form of the joint-stock trading company that first opened up settlement. The Massachusetts Bay Company, though it turned itself into a government in the New World, began as an economic corporation financed by English investors. Moreover, it was Europe that provided, mainly through British trade, the market for the primary resources of the New World—the tobacco, the grain, the timber and other forest products—while at the same time it provided the growing colonies with the manufactured goods they needed for survival and development.

The Cultural Debt Finally, the colonies owed a great social and cultural debt to Europe, and again mainly to Britain. Religion is the most obvious example. The great Protestant Reformation which so shaped the European experience lay behind the predominant influence of Puritanism in New England. Other strands of the same influence stretched to America in the form of Presbyterianism from Scotland and Quakerism and Methodism from England. And behind the rise of evangelicalism in America lay the ideas of the German Protestant sects whose members came to America: Moravians, Mennonites, Amish, Schwenkfelders, and Dunkers. Via the English language the colonists inherited a fully developed literature and a body of scientific thought to nourish mind, heart, and spirit, and along with all this the shape and form of cultural institutions and agencies: schools, newspapers, magazines, and the like. In cultural and intellectual life, as in political and economic life, the colonists could not have survived by their own efforts alone. Life would have been dull, barren, and miserable without the richness of the European heritage to draw on.

The American Environment

The other major factor influencing American colonial development was the environment of the New World, a vast, seemingly endless expanse of relatively free land, basically unsettled and stretching to the distant west. Into this completely different physical setting came the immigrant armed with the European tradition of long-established societies.

Could tradition be transferred intact to a wilderness environment? No;

from the very beginning, modification was necessary. New attitudes and behavior patterns were created; new ideas came into prominence; new institutions and ways of doing things were demanded; old ideas, old institutions, old techniques were altered or took on new meaning in response to the demands of a new environment; and without the natural constraints of an established society, experimentation became easier.

For example, the character of farming was altered almost from the beginning. Products unknown to Europe but domesticated by the Indian greatly determined the colonial farm economy: tobacco, corn, potatoes, pumpkins, and the like. Four-sevenths of our national farm produce today consists of such products. The structure of the farm economy demanded by crops such as tobacco encouraged the plantation system in the South; and the availability of land gave primary importance elsewhere to the small independent farm as the principal form of agricultural production. And the presence of so much fertile land reshaped Old World attitudes toward the land itself. George Washington described the contrast, and his description could have applied to any earlier time in the colonial period:

> The aim of the farmers in this country, if they can be called farmers, is, not to make the most they can from the land, which is, or has been cheap, but the most of their labour, which is dear; the consequence of which has been, much ground has been scratched over and none cultivated or improved as it ought to have been; whereas a farmer in England, where land is dear, and labour cheap, finds it his interest to improve and cultivate highly, that he may reap large crops from a small quantity of ground.

When land is limited, you tend to treat it with as much care as knowledge and skill provide. It's all you've got. In America quite a different attitude developed. So what if tobacco exhausted the soil in a few years? Move on, there's always more.

The incredible abundance of land profoundly affected many of the social and economic ideas brought by the immigrant to America. Many Old World institutions and ideas had developed over a long period of time in an environment in which land and hence wealth was scarce in relation to people. Feudal notions of land tenure, serfdom, primogeniture, and entail—to say nothing of the conception that the world has little to offer to the majority of men except drudgery—simply could not flourish or be maintained in the presence of a vast area of landed wealth. The Puritans, for example, who tried to carry with them to the New World old ideas about a limited and controlled economy, had great difficulty maintaining these in the face of continually expanding opportunity. Moreover, the attempt to transplant the feudal system of land tenure—great estates tilled by peasant tenants—was a failure despite efforts to establish it. The new environment was thus immediately hostile to that Old World institution, the landed nobility.

Such abundance, furthermore, moved the colonists in the direction of economic equality, or more accurately, equal opportunity for economic advancement. Land was there for the taking. Everyone, more or less, had a chance at it.

This fact in turn contributed to the rise of a significant measure of social equality and a relaxation of social convention that defined an established society. In any area where there was a struggle to bring the land under control, this struggle so dominated existence that people had little concern for formalities, rules, convention, and proper forms. In comparison to Europe, all were more or less equal by necessity, and every individual as good as every other. You were judged by what you accomplished, not by who your father was or how gracefully you followed social convention.

The nature of this experience, which so many immigrants went through, created a whole new frame of reference for the individual. The established societies of the Old World defined the place of any individual in the social order. This attitude was transported to the New World, but a much more immediate relationship took primacy over it: the relationship of individuals to the physical environment in which they struggled for survival. Many colonials in consequence came to measure success and position in terms of their encounter with the land, with nature itself. Success and position were determined less by social factors—into what class you had been born, who your parents were, and their position and role in society—and more by the extent of your personal capacity to beat nature to its knees. The effect on a people who have devoured and ground their way across a continent has been obvious. Long in close combat with nature, Americans did not soon feel affection for it. Familiarity here bred antagonism, and the penalty has often been the despoiling of the land itself, an evil apparent even in colonial times.

The New World environment also had a political impact. Transplanted institutions and concepts took on new meaning. In the Old World political authority and power were associated with landed property. The dominant elements of the ruling class in Britain were the landed nobles and the country gentry who owned most of the land and constituted a small fraction of the population. In colonial America, where land was available to almost anyone, political power was no longer, by definition, confined to a small elite, but extended to a far broader segment of the population. The stage was thus set for a very different political atmosphere.

Finally, the psychological impact of vast areas of relatively free land and the economic and social opportunity it offered exerted a pressure upon the imaginations of people that was absent in the more limited Old World where horizons and expectations were precise and restricted. In America the horizon literally stretched westward into the unknown, and opportunity and achievement seemed unlimited. Both reach and grasp expanded, and the optimism generated by a vision of opportunity became an American characteristic. Individuals' imaginations, and the way they saw the future, had no bounds.

So when we think of the colonial era as a whole and seek those broad forces that shaped colonial society and thought—those nutrients giving life and vigor to the roots of our society today—it seems clear that the immigrants themselves, the European heritage they represented, and the New World environment into which they came all combined to produce something new under the sun.

Profile: JOHN WINTHROP

The year 1588 was a good one for both England and nonexistent New England: Drake defeated the Spanish Armada, and John Winthrop—future governor of the Massachusetts Bay Colony—was born.

Raised as a member of the landed gentry in Suffolk, young Winthrop acquired learning and a taste for the pleasures of life at Trinity College, Cambridge. He also acquired there a sense of the trials of the soul, which led him to Puritanism:

> About fourteen years of age, being in Cambridge, I fell into a lingering fever, which took away the comforts of my life: for, being there neglected and despised, I went up and down mourning with myself; and, being deprived of my youthful joys, I betook myself to God, whom I did believe to be very good and merciful, and would welcome any that would come to him, especially such a young soul, and so well qualified as I took myself to be; so as I took pleasure in drawing near to him.

But for Puritans, the drive to cleanse one's soul was not the only way to serve God:

there was also the obligation to purge society of its evil, and it was this duty that was ultimately to take John Winthrop and his fellow Puritans to the New World.

Winthrop had married at seventeen, his wife presenting him with six children before her death ten years later. A second wife died within a year, and then at the age of thirty he married a third time: his beloved Margaret who bore him eight children and gave him comfort for twenty-nine years before her death in 1647, two years before his own. Running the family estate at Groton, maintaining a legal practice in London, and serving as a royal attorney in the Court of Wards occupied much of Winthrop's time and energies. But religious concerns remained in the forefront of his mind.

When James I became king in 1603, he gave cold comfort to those reformers who wished to purify the Anglican Church of its hierarchical authority and popish practices. "I shall make them conform themselves," he said of Puritans, "or I will hurry them out of this land, or else do worse." Under such pressure, the less stalwart might retreat inward with their faith, but Puritans had a profound sense of social responsibility, a conviction that the godly must stand and fight for the salvation of society. This was the true Christian's duty. As Winthrop saw it:

> he which would have sure peace and joy in christianity must not aim at a condition retired from the world and free from temptations, but to know that the life which is most exercised with trials and temptations is the sweetest, and will prove the safest. For such trials as fall within the compass of our callings it is better to arm and withstand them than to avoid and shun them.

Although neither Winthrop nor his friends suffered religious persecution, they did not view the future in England with any assurance as the years went by. And when Charles I dissolved Parliament in March 1629, that future seemed ominous indeed. "I am verily persuaded, God will bring some heavy Affliction upon this land, and that speedily," he wrote to his wife.

Now the plans of those Puritan merchants who had just reorganized the New England Company into the Massachusetts Bay Company for broadened colonization purposes in the New World took on a special significance for Winthrop. But he faced a fundamental problem. True Christians do not flee evil, they fight it. Could moving to the New World be seen not as flight but as continuing the struggle on a new battlefield? It could indeed: successfully creating a truly Christian society in the New World according to God's will would serve as a model for the reform of Christian society elsewhere:

> Men shall say of succeeding plantations: the Lord make it like that of New England: for we must Consider that we shall be as a City upon a Hill, the eyes of all people are upon us.

Such a bold venture could succeed, however, only with a minimum of interference from royal power. When Winthrop learned that the provisions of the charter for the Massachusetts Bay Company made it possible for the company's government to be based not in England but in distant America, all doubt vanished. He made his decision, was elected governor of the company, and threw his talent and energies into recruitment and organization of the Puritan expedition. Sailing in eleven ships, over a thousand Englishmen departed for the New World in April of 1630 under his leadership.

And leader he certainly was, though not always popular. Except for a brief three-year period, Winthrop was governor or deputy governor of the Massachusetts Bay Colony until his death in 1649, and the strength of his personality and the cast of his mind helped to shape the character of the colony for decades to come. Winthrop had told his company on the voyage that their venture into the New World had been undertaken as a covenant with God, like that of the Israelites under Moses, to establish a holy society according to His will. "We must be knit together in this work as one. We must delight in each other, make others' conditions our own, rejoice together, mourn together, labor and suffer together; always having before our eyes our commission." Despite the problems of colonization and rule under new and difficult conditions, this commitment—emphasized again and again by Winthrop—bound the Puritans together in a remarkably stable and cohesive social community.

Winthrop believed that the Puritan commitment to a new holy society could be achieved only under the disciplined guidance of society's chosen leaders who were best able to interpret God's will, and that the colony's charter provided such leadership in the governor and his seven assistants. But Winthrop quickly discovered that those who had embarked with him on the great experiment in the New World believed they were as committed to God's work as he was and hence were entitled to participate in the decisions determining the affairs of the colony. So step by step the oligarchic arrangement Winthrop favored was eroded away: in 1631 the assistants were elected by a newly created body of freemen; in 1632 the governor himself was elected by the freemen, not by the assistants; in 1634 representatives from the towns joined the assistants in making laws; in 1641 a Body of Liberties defining the rights and obligations of citizens was adopted; and in 1644 a two-house legislature was established.

Although Winthrop opposed these changes, his strong sense of realism and his commitment to the Puritan cause prompted him to work with them once they were adopted. He gave no thought to abandoning the holy experiment or to imposing his own views by force. His chief political concern was to maintain respect for authority, without which no community could survive: "So shall your liberties be preserved in upholding the honor and power of authority amongst you." But authority itself was also bound by law. The magistrates, he declared, "shall govern you and judge your causes by the rules of God's laws and our own, according to our best skill." If they fail, they can be voted out, as his own experience of being voted out of office demonstrated. In spite of disagreements and tensions which arose within the colony—over Roger Williams and Anne Hutchinson, for example—the commitment to the rule of law rather than the rule of men provided a remarkable political and social stability within the colony.

It was Winthrop, too, who defined the relationship between the colony and England in such a way as to start the colonies on the long path to independence, though no one foresaw this at the time. For though the charter of the Massachusetts Bay Company had been granted by the King, the Puritans had made a covenant with God to establish a new society, a new nation. Their allegiance, therefore, was to God and his chosen magistrates in the colony, not to the King. Obedience to the King was proper only if it did not conflict with their own divine mission. As far as Winthrop was concerned, it might be politically expedient on occasion to declare allegiance to the King, but in actual fact allegiance was to God and to Massachusetts. Moreover, Winthrop saw danger in having Parliament involved in the affairs of the colony: "if we should put ourselves under the protection of parliament, we must then be subject to all such laws as they should make, or at least such as they might impose upon us; in which course though they should intend our good, yet it might prove very prejudicial to us." And when Robert Childs in 1645 accused the Puritan leadership of violating the charter and maintaining "rather a free state than a colony or corporation of England," Winthrop wrote with unmistakable intent that "our allegiance binds us not to the laws of England any longer than while we live in England, for the laws of the parliament of England reach no further, nor do the king's writs under the great seal go any further." Long after Winthrop's death, Massachusetts was to pay dearly for this view when its charter was revoked in 1684 and a royal governor appointed to rule. But the concept that Winthrop and the Puritan leaders had expressed in the seventeenth century for their own purposes of mission was to be revived in a new form in the revolutionary crisis over a century later.

Winthrop was a hard and determined man, as men with a sense of mission tend to be, and he presided over the founding of New England with a firm hand. The perfect society of God he dreamed of building was not to be, but his impact on American society was strong and lasting, nevertheless.

Chapter 3
LIFE IN THE
COLONIES

The Spirit of the Times
WORK

Before individuals can enjoy the fruits of their labor, they must labor. It is work that makes the world go round, or so Aesop said in the fable of the grasshopper and Benjamin Franklin reminded us in a dozen aphorisms. There can be no harmonious social order, no speculative thought, no good life until economic life is organized and productive; no chasing the bluebird of happiness until the crops are in. The first colonists in America at Jamestown learned that lesson the hard way: those who don't work, don't eat.

Few people really like to work, which may explain why a good part of the Protestant world had work endorsed as a virtue by God out of John Calvin, and why the Catholic Church, though it praised the piety of ascetics who sat on pillars, did not urge the rest of the population to follow their example. But whether work is regarded as a virtue or not, little can be accomplished without it. This was a primary lesson of colonial life.

True, there were always complaints in the colonies about those who didn't work or worked but little. The Reverend Charles Woodmason, carrying the Gospel through the backcountry at the end of the colonial period, noted that the Scotch-Irish of the region would rather sit "hovering over a few embers" than get up and cut firewood.

> They are very Poor owing to their Indolence. They delight in their present low, lazy, sluttish, heathenish, hellish life and seem not desirous of changing it. Both Men and Women will do any thing to come at Liquor, Clothes, Furniture, etc etc, rather than work for it.

But perhaps this critical view was occasioned by the fact that his preaching did not have the effect he intended: "After the Service, they went out to Revelling, Drinking, Singing, Dancing, and Whoring, and most of the Company were drunk before I quitted the spot." Then, too, there were always the bandits and robbers of the backcountry whose plundering and stealing were not regarded by the pious as industrious labor. But even banditry is hard work, as Butch Cassidy and the

An engraving of one of Benjamin Franklin's popular maxims. A mixture of humor and practicality, Poor Richard's Almanack *offered the advice of diligent work to those who sought success.*

Sundance Kid were later to discover. It depends, one must suppose, on what you define as work.

But work the colonists did, because work was the key to survival and the pleasures that come from survival. It was upon the land that most colonials labored. This was where their lives were centered. Captain John Smith noted:

> Who can desire more content, that hath small means or but only his merit to advance his fortune, than to tread and plant that ground he hath purchased by the hazard of his life. If he have but the taste of virtue and magnanimitie, what to such a mind can be more pleasant than planting and building for his Posteritie, gotte from the rude earth by God's blessing and his own industrie without prejudice to any?

And from the scratched-out acres on the frontier, from the small farms and plantations of the South, from the rich farms of the Middle Colonies, from the reluctant soil of New England came a rich and varied harvest: tobacco, rice, corn, wheat, oats, rye, barley, flax, fruits and berries, garden vegetables, sheep, hogs, and cattle.

And from the natural bounty of the land labor brought furs and timber. The colonists also turned to the sea. John Smith had early reported: "He is a very poor fisherman who cannot get two or three hundred cod." So daring men worked the resources of the ocean, bringing to market fish and whales. But people need tools, equipment, clothing: wheat has to be turned into flour, molasses into rum, skins into shoes, ore into iron, trees into lumber, flax into linen. Much of this work was done in the home, at the spinning wheel, the loom, the carpenter's bench—the axe and the saw were as common in homes as fireplaces. But in villages and towns and on plantations skilled craftsmen also made to order furniture, silverware, hats, shoes, and utensils.

And so the colonists labored—on their farms, in the forests, in their shops and homes, on their ships at sea. Work helped to provide purpose to the present and hope for the future. Work was at the center of existence, the key not only to survival but to the pleasures of life.

Not even the young were idle. From a young girl's journal we read these hasty jottings of her day's tasks:

> Fix'd gown for Prude—Fix'd two gowns for Welsh's girls—Carded tow—Spun line—Worked on Cheese-basket—Hatchel'd flax with Hannah, we did 51 lbs. apiece—Pleated and ironed . . . Spooled a piece—Milked the Cows—Spun linen, did 50 knots—Made a Broom of Guinea wheat straw—Spun thread to whiten—Set a Red dye . . . Spun harness twine . . .

Upon their labor rested the society the colonists had created: its social classes, its homes, its churches, its thought, its art, its schools, its pleasures. Nothing could have been done without it.

The Broad View

Colonial society even in the early decades was an intricate pattern of many threads. No institutions, no aspects of life stood alone and separate. Religion was inextricable from family life; social status was reflected in economic achievement and in such matters as the assignment of pews in church; the family was a primary unit in economic life; and so on.

This weaving was complicated by the fact that colonial society changed and developed as the seventeenth century passed into the eighteenth. Life was far more complex and sophisticated in the eighteenth century than in the seventeenth. More varied immigration, the influence of settled communities that had long since passed beyond the stage of frontier struggle, the evolving experience of an expanding economy—such forces made a society marked by change as it moved from early struggles to a much more settled society confident in its ways and acquiring a special identity of its own.

One useful way to understand the development of any society is to separate its basic elements and note their principal characteristics, remembering that none of these elements was isolated but that each was woven into the larger fabric of society.

The Family in Colonial Times

The family was the basic institution of colonial society throughout the seventeenth and eighteenth centuries, not only because it was the focus of economic and social life, but because God had given it primary significance. The early Puritan divine, John Cotton, referred to God's "appointment of mankind to live in Societies, first, of Family, Secondly Church, Thirdly, Commonwealth." Although the circumstances, attitudes, and ideas peculiar to the age naturally influenced family life in the colonies, it by no means seems unfamiliar or unappealing.

For it is obvious that colonial men and women were greatly interested in one another, sought each other's company, fell in love, joined their destinies for better or for worse in matrimony, raised children and worried over them, and generally worked their way with pain and pleasure through that mysterious maze of human intimacy known as marriage.

Children and Youth   Colonial views about children do not appeal much to the modern mind. Children were not regarded as individuals with their own needs, instincts, and intuitions, but as pre-adults to be molded and shaped into proper adults in accordance with society's conception of the adult role. The Puritans believed that children bore the burden of original sin and were therefore naturally wicked and corrupt. As late as the eighteenth century Jonathan Edwards was capable of saying that unrepentant children were "young vipers and infinitely more hateful than vipers"—a condition that required constant discipline as well as instruction in how to avoid the consequences of an evil nature. Children were put to work early, by the age of seven in their own families and especially on farms. In the towns and villages boys were frequently apprenticed by fourteen and sometimes younger, while girls often worked in homes other than their own by the same age. In Puritan New England, young children were sometimes put in the homes of other families by parents who believed discipline could be better enforced by other than the child's own parents.

These circumstances suggest a grim life for the young. Yet diaries and letters reveal the deepest affection between parents and children. Then as now the affection of parents often led them to treat their children harshly "for their own good." Moreover, the sanctity of the family imposed great responsibilities on parents in the care and raising of their children, and law required that parents meet these responsibilities, providing punishment for neglect or maltreatment and in extreme cases removal of children from homes in which they were neglected.

Young people were likely to marry any time from sixteen to twenty-one, and to exercise considerable control in their choice of mate. Parents then as now had a natural concern about the choice, but unless there were special reasons for exercising a veto, they rarely challenged the decision of their children. There was of course concern that one not marry above or below his station, but the record of lamentation on such mismatchings shows that they did occur and not always for the worse. And where family wealth was at stake, most parents were involved in the delicate negotiations that protected their own as well as their children's interests. In a letter crackling with dry wit and revealing the power of choice by children as well as the role of the parent in negotiation, Daniel Parke, a Virginian residing in London, wrote to John Custis, whose son was courting Parke's daughter in Virginia:

> Sir: I received yours relating to your son's desire of marrying my daughter, and your consent if I thought well of it. You may easily inform yourself that my daughter Frances will be heiress of all the land my father left which is not a little nor the worst. My personal estate is not very small in that country, and I have but two daughters, and there is no likelihood of my having any more, as matters are, I being obliged to be on one side of the ocean and my wife on the other. I do not know your gentleman nor have you or he thought fit to send an account of his real and personal effects: however, if my daughter likes him I will give her upon her marriage with him, half as much as he can make it appear he is worth.

Marriage was not a sacrament to the Puritans, and though the family was an institution decreed by God, the ceremony was a civil one for most of the seventeenth century. For this reason, divorce, though unusual, was possible for reasons of desertion, adultery, or absence of a spouse for a number of years. In Virginia, by contrast, divorce was impossible under the Church of England, and the only way out of marriage was death or flight.

Not only the sanctity of marriage but its economic value in a new society led to disapproval of bachelor- and spinsterhood, and in New England bachelors found their lives quite circumscribed by law. William Byrd of Virginia noted that bachelors and spinsters were "as scarce among us and reckoned as ominous as a blazing star." These pressures led to almost immediate remarriage for most of those who had lost a spouse, and because the death rate was high, couples closing out their lives together might each have been married two or three times before.

The Status of Women Despite the prevailing doctrine, both civil and religious, that women were inferior to men and subject to their authority, women were of great practical value in the New World and their status was considerably above that of their sisters in the Old World. In New England dowry rights were protected by law, punishment of wives by striking or beating was forbidden, and on the death of her husband a wife was entitled to a minimum life interest in one-third of his property. Although everywhere married women were subject completely to their husbands and could act only under their authority, single women and widows could own property, contract debts, sue and be sued in courts, and even run their own businesses. A wife was naturally expected to be submissive to her husband. He was her superior, and possessed, so to speak, the divine rights of a husband. He was, as a Boston minister declared in 1672, "the Conduit Pipe of the variety of

The Peale Family. *The renowned American portrait painter Charles Willson Peale captured the warmth and closeness of his own family.*

blessings that God supplyeth." But she was clearly not his slave or servant. When Daniel Ela made the mistake of telling his wife Elizabeth that "she was none of his wife, she was but his Servant," his neighbors reported him to the authorities and he was fined forty shillings. Everywhere in the colonies circumstance as well as law modified the total authority that European tradition and law accorded husbands. By the end of the colonial period, for example, most husbands reserved their valor for battle and generally consulted with their wives before making decisions affecting the latters' property.

Subordinate or no, many women displayed considerable independence of mind. In the marriage of Sarah Harrison to James Blair, when the minister reached that point in the ceremony where she was supposed to promise obedience to her husband, she was perfectly willing to love and honor him but not to obey. She put the assembled company into a turmoil by thrice refusing this sign of submission, and finally the minister left the word out and the ceremony continued.

Hardship Family life, of course, was not easy in colonial America even among the wealthy. The bearing of children was a continual burden for women, rich and poor alike. Having six to eight children was common. But death was the constant playmate of the young, especially after the first half-century, although those surviving to age twenty had a clear shot at reaching sixty. In spite of the consolation that the death of a child had been decreed by God, the agonizing burden of such losses took its psychological toll of mother and father alike.

The dawn-to-dark labor required of a farm wife, moreover, was beyond measure in its impact on body and soul. Such a woman spun the flax and wool, did the weaving and knitting, sewed, looked after the hogs and poultry, milked the cows, made butter and cheese, baked the bread, cleaned the house, and got all the meals, besides bearing and raising the children. Nor was life all leisure even for the wife of a planter. She may have had servants, but it was her responsibility to manage the affairs of the house, see that all tasks were assigned and completed, and plan and supervise the meals, which alone could shake the confidence of a modern restaurateur. She was also responsible for the care of the sick, both white and black. And the burden of child-bearing was as dangerous to her as to her poorer sister in the backwoods. Life was not easy, and none were spared its realities.

Marital Relations Indeed it was down to earth in more ways than one. There were a great many colonial laws dealing with sexual behavior, and numerous court cases invoking these laws. The problems created by a shortage of women, life in over-crowded quarters, the power of masters over servants, and a number of other factors may have made colonial men and women somewhat more aggressive than they might otherwise have been. The presence of so much forbidding legislation, however, did not mean that colonials regarded sex as wicked in itself; nor did the violation of this legislation suggest a perpetual orgy. What seems reasonably clear is that the intent was to confine sex within marriage, the institution where it properly belonged, but for a number of reasons, including the fact that colonists were much like everyone else, this was not always easy to accomplish.

The Puritans, for example, did not regard sex as evil, but as a glorious necessity decreed by the Lord. And for that very reason they preferred to keep it within the institution sanctified by God. Sex was, so to speak, a way to glorify God in the proper setting. A number of Puritan divines were thus understandably moved to give advice on sexual relationships between husband and wife, a move that occasionally backfired. Operating on the premise that sexual relationships on the Sabbath detracted from one's concern for the primary relationship with God, and also under the erroneous medical assumption that children were born on the same day of the week as they were conceived, one overzealous minister firmly and repeatedly made it clear—Never on Sunday—until that bright Sunday morning when his wife presented him with twins.

In the last analysis, what makes the colonial family appealingly familiar is the deep affection that obviously not only prompted but strengthened so many marriages and that, then as now, was ample reward for its trials and tribulations.

Anne Bradstreet wrote love poems to her husband that were marked by great depth of feeling, and the tenderness of sentiment found in the following line from a letter by Margaret Winthrop to her husband abroad in England speaks for itself: "I will not look for any long letters this term because I pity your poor hand; if I had it here I would make more of it than ever I did, and bind it up very softly for fear of hurting it." And look, for a moment, over the shoulder of Theodorick Bland, away from home during one of the colonial wars, a letter from his wife Patsy lying in front of him, and he now writing in response to her:

> For God's sake, my dear, when you are writing, write of nothing but yourself, or at least exhaust that dear, ever dear subject before you make a transition to another: tell me of your going to bed, of your rising, of the hour you breakfast, dine, sup, visit, tell me of anything but leave me not in doubt about your health. . . . Fear not, my Patsy—yes, you "will again feel your husband's lips flowing with love and affectionate warmth." Heaven never means to separate two who love so well, so soon; and if it does, with what transport shall we meet in heaven.

The other side of the marital coin, incompatability, is not so appealing but is still familiar. The John Custises of Virginia continually quarreled, especially over Mrs. Custis' aversion to living at their home in Arlington. Arguing while on a drive one afternoon, John Custis in anger turned their carriage into Chesapeake Bay. When his wife asked where he was going, he said, "To Hell, Madame." Not to be outdone, the unperturbed Mrs. Custis replied, "Drive on! Any place is better than Arlington!"

Regardless of the degree of affection or the nature of personal relations, the family was the main channel through which flowed most of life in colonial times. Since most colonials were farmers, the family was also the basic economic unit in society, all its members contributing in some fashion to the work required. It was also the conduit through which flowed the influence and dictates of the church that held the family responsible for maintaining and promoting the faith. Bible reading, religious instruction, and responsibility for church attendance were all centered in the family.

Both church and state also operated on the assumption that the family had the primary responsibility for educating the young. Children generally were instructed in their letters by their parents, especially the mother; and in New England, where the state early required public education, the authorities specifically placed responsibility for establishing schools upon the families in the villages and towns. In a predominantly agricultural society, the family inevitably was the center of social life and recreation. The family thus provided an intimate, familiar, closely knit, and comforting framework through which individuals approached and dealt with the outside world. It was the indispensable core of colonial life.

Religion and the Church

Human beings are unique in that they are between an immense past and an unforeseeable future: they are aware of their predicament and want to know why they are in it. History suggests that there is a natural human longing to know the reason for existence and the meaning of the universal scheme of things. Religion has always been a prime source of answers to these questions, and in the colonial period, especially in the seventeenth century, the influence of religion and the role of the church were great.

The Seventeenth Century: Puritanism   The most profound religious influence in colonial America was Puritanism. Although more deeply entrenched in New England than elsewhere, the Puritan influence existed in all the colonies. Its strength sprang not only from the intellectual power of Puritan doctrine, but from the Puritan conviction that the spiritual and the secular life could not be separated, and thus the authority of community and state was made part of a major effort to create a society that in all ways reflected the Word of God. It was, therefore, no mere turn of phrase that called Massachusetts the Bible Commonwealth.

Puritanism thus involved both an elaborate system of serious thought and a way of life embodying that thought, which helps explain why sermons were so long and society so carefully directed.

For the individual Puritan, the ultimate goal lay in the next world: salvation, union with God through Christ in "the only marriage which cannot be dissolved," as Increase Mather put it. For Puritan society, the goal was an economic, social, political, and cultural order glorifying God to the degree that that order successfully reflected His will. To Puritans, therefore, life involved an energetic search for evidence of personal salvation, the sign that God had singled them out for regeneration, and at the same time an energetic communal drive to mold the kind of society God wanted for humanity. Yet there was neither certainty nor perfection in attaining these individual and social goals, for the individual since the Fall was imperfect and necessarily corrupt. But both the individual and society must try.

The key to the search for salvation and the creation of the proper society lay in the Bible, which was not mere inspiration or guide, but the source of the fundamental law governing human behavior and relationships, secular as well as spiritual. And so every chapter and verse was minutely analyzed with a zeal unsurpassed even by modern corporation lawyers seeking loopholes in the tax laws. The Puritans differed from other Christians of the time in this overwhelming reliance upon the Bible as the revealed if not always understandable word of God.

And they differed from other seekers after truth in other ways. One was the grim doctrine of predestination. Although general Christian belief assumed the omnipotence of God, a power so all-encompassing that He had already determined the course of existence to the end of time, only the Puritans stressed the idea that since He had already determined the few who would be saved and the many who would be damned, then of course individuals could obviously do nothing to gain their own salvation. Salvation came only through the grace of God. All, of course, were admonished to lead godly lives, and those who had undergone the experience of regeneration were under a special obligation of saintly living, but the godly life in itself gave no assurance of salvation. Only the Puritans believed with such utter conviction that it was the elect, the "visible saints" marked by regeneration, who should rule both church and society. It was this conviction that led them to confine full membership in the church to the visible saints and to attempt to limit political privilege to these same members of the church.

The key element in Puritanism, it would therefore appear—though Puritan thought is not a room one enters by unlocking a single door—was the experience of regeneration, which identified the person favored by the grace of God. It is no wonder that the Puritan divines spent much time explaining this experience to their congregations, so that they would recognize it when it came. Indeed, they outlined the process in great detail. But because the experience was so subjective, as communion with the infinite tends to be, it was not easy to comprehend. As the Reverend Thomas Hooker said, "The mystery is very great." Indeed it was. Those who had been through the experience had difficulty explaining to others what precisely had happened, and those who had not undergone it had difficulty conceiving what it might be like. In this, it was much like going through a battle. Those who have never done so cannot really understand, and those who have find they cannot adequately explain it. The climactic experience of regeneration frequently occurred while listening to a sermon, or perhaps while standing alone at dawn on a hilltop watching the sun rise in all God's glory, or while walking down your own road to Damascus by way of Salem. Suddenly, inexplicably, the whole thing happened. You became one with God, and you *knew.* Yet to be saved it was not necessary to have this experience—it might never come in this form. But all Puritans wanted it to come, looked for it, and searched their lives for other signs that they were of the elect. Those who lived the godly life for themselves and their neighbors, and prospered in the work to which they had been called might well be among the favored.

No wonder the Puritan was so energetic, so intense, so consumed with concern about self and others. They worked hard, tried to do nothing that would make God's will seem trivial or frivolous, were willing to submit to authority, saw nothing wrong in requiring others to do the same, were suspicious of those who did not see God's truth as clearly as they did, and saw no reason to tolerate the presence of unbelievers. It was common for a long time after to tick off in condescension the absurdities and unpleasantness into which their intensity and concern led the faithful. In Massachusetts Bay Colony nineteen "witches" were hanged in 1692, the right to vote was denied to all but a few, five Quakers were put to death for contrary beliefs, the esteemed Roger Williams and the sensitive Anne Hutchinson were driven out, the majority were consigned to the flames of hell, and the arts, dancing, and the theater were denounced. The net impression is of a community of self-righteous killjoys who made life miserable for themselves as

Increase Mather, by Jan Vanderspriet. As a member of the clergy, a politician, and an educator, Mather was involved in such diverse matters as the Halfway Covenant, the organization of a scientific discussion society, the presidency of Harvard, the negotiations with the King for a new Massachusetts charter, and the promotion of the idea of smallpox innoculation.

well as for everyone else. And to a greater or lesser degree, the Puritans were quick to condemn and sharply intolerant of any beliefs but their own.

But to condemn them entirely for this narrowness would be like dismissing the democratic achievements of American society solely because it once tolerated black slavery. In fact, life for the Puritans was often a good life. They were even curiously tolerant in that they recognized the frailties and imperfections to which human beings are naturally prone. Save on matters of faith they were not without humor. They liked their tot of rum, puffed their pipes, relaxed in the satisfaction of fine homes and good dress, and accepted music and the dance—outside the church.

In pursuit of their goals for themselves and society, the Puritans laid down patterns of activity and encouraged attitudes that, separate from their religious purposes, strongly influenced American life and thought.

Influence of Puritanism   The idea of the covenant, which saw salvation as essentially an agreement between God and man to which both were held, carried over into church and civil government. The faithful banded together to form a church and choose a minister and in so doing agreed to be bound by that commitment to the laws of God. Likewise men banded together in communities to create government, and bound themselves thereby to obey its laws. The Puritan church and community were thus ruled by law, not whim, and rulers as well as ruled were bound to abide by the law. The Puritan was no believer in unlimited power.

In other ways as well, the Puritans influenced American life. In seeking aids to understand God's will they had faith in the power of reason and knowledge. Cotton Mather observed that "the light of reason is the law of God." To know the world, which God had created, was one of the ways in which God might be understood. So the Puritans cultivated reason and promoted knowledge. Their reliance on intellect gave them a deep concern for education. And early in the game they made provision for education and laid down requirements for family and community responsibility in educating the young that were unusual in the Western world and that had much to do with establishing the foundations of the educational system of New England and ultimately the country as a whole.

One of the more influential facts about the Puritan experiment is not that it failed, but that the Puritans thought it could succeed. Their firm conviction that they were in the right, and their supreme confidence in their ability to accomplish what they set out to do, became cornerstones of the American character. Certainly two of our more enduring and troublesome traits as a people have been self-righteousness and self-confidence.

At any rate, the Puritan experiment did fail, and for a number of reasons. Problems of rule arose at the outset in the attempt to confine power to the hands of the saintly, who constituted by definition a small minority. Not only did those left out increasingly protest their exclusion, but as population grew and towns proliferated, there simply were not enough of the provable elect, nor had they time to fill all offices and discharge the many responsibilities of public decision making. As a practical necessity the doors to office and responsibility had to be opened to others than church members. Despite the wish to limit involvement in the Puritan community to believers, or at least to those who kept their mouths shut if they disagreed, the urgent needs of a society being created in the wilderness demanded that the standards of admission be relaxed. The labor, skills, and capital of people unwashed by the blood of the lamb turned out to be as useful as those of the elect, and sometimes more important.

All this suggests another cause for the demise of the Puritan experiment. In an expanding society particularly, the affairs of this world are so demanding that it becomes harder and harder to focus your main attention on the affairs of the next. Puritan doctrine itself unintentionally contributed to this distraction. For the Puritan believed that while worldly success was not the road to salvation, it could be a sign of God's favor, and no matter how often you may have been reminded that salvation is not the reward of the prosperous there was a strong human tendency to think the other way, particularly as you became more prosperous.

Finally, despite the attempt to create a society bound by a single commitment and belief, it never really was that way, even from the beginning. The Puritans were continually challenged by equally sincere and committed people who had other ideas, people who not only intruded from the outside, such as the Quakers, but who rose up within their midst. The most powerful challenge came from those who could not believe that only a few had been singled out for salvation, who argued instead that any man could be saved who believed in Christ, and that the good life merited salvation. If you prefer salvation to damnation, this is clearly a more hopeful and appealing view of your prospects. The Puritan divines themselves recognized the harshness of their doctrine, and John Cotton, long before he died in 1652, was arguing that if you sought the gift of salvation God would not deny it to you. And in 1662, the famous Halfway Covenant broke down the earlier rigidity by admitting to baptism the children of pious parents who had not yet had a religious experience.

The presence and steady growth of non-Puritan elements in the colonies, the ever-increasing concern with the practical problems and profits of building a new society that necessarily had to take into account the interests and ideas of most if not all the people, and the challenge of other faiths that struck at the weak links in the armor of Puritan theology—all these combined to blunt the original conviction of the Puritans that they had been assigned by God to build a New Jerusalem as a model for all humanity. Yet the idea of being a model for the world at large was left by the Puritans to subsequent generations to carry on in other ways.

The Eighteenth Century: Changes in Religion

Diversity and Decline In matters of religion and the church the eighteenth century was a very different time in America from the seventeenth. People began to come from many other lands than England, and they brought a variety of religions with them. The great religious revival of 1735–1745 known as the Great Awakening produced yet more new churches, so that the dominant characteristic of American religion became diversity. By the end of the colonial period, the list was astonishing: it included Congregationalists, Presbyterians, Baptists, Quakers, German Reformed, Dutch Reformed, Lutherans, Anglicans, Catholics, Methodists, a multitude of small radical Protestant sects, and within Congregationalism and Presbyterianism a split within congregations between the "New Lights" and the "Old Lights" over revivalism. There came into being, in short, a kind of great religious supermarket in which was displayed a variety and choice such as could satisfy the spiritual taste of anyone. As often happens when so much is available, the tendency was to sample and shop around—a habit of the religiously inclined that has marked many an American ever since—and

Penn's Treaty *by Edward Hicks. Penn brought Quakers to his colony in
the late seventeenth century as a refuge from the persecution they faced from
Puritans. The religious liberty offered by Pennsylvania attracted many
Quakers, but numerous other sects were drawn to the colony as well.*

the minister who failed to provide the nourishment his parishioners wanted
saw his congregation drift off to other counters.

At the same time the choice increased, the influence of religion and the
church declined, and by the end of the colonial period church membership
and attendance were probably at their lowest point in all American history.
One European visitor was stunned by what he regarded as the neglect if not
indeed the total absence of religious belief and sentiment, a neglect noticeable not only in the large numbers unbaptized but in their views as well:
"Many do not even believe that there is a true God and Devil, a Heaven and
hell, salvation and damnation, a resurrection of the dead, a judgment and an
eternal life."

With many colonials the decline of religious interest sprang not from
abandonment of belief as such, but rather from circumstances both social
and environmental. There is little doubt that the opportunities for getting
ahead in America made life in this world a more attractive proposition than it

was in Europe, and thus worth devoting time to for its own sake and not only for the glory of God. And when by dint of hard work people got ahead, the natural tendency was to attribute their success more to their own efforts than to the Lord's.

Deism   Among colonials of a more intellectual turn of mind, the rationalism and the science of the eighteenth-century Enlightenment lessened the impact of religion on life and thought. To the educated, if the universe ran in accordance with certain natural principles and laws as Newton suggested, then comets, earthquakes, epidemics, and the like were natural phenomena, not signs of the wrath of an intruding God. And God, therefore, clearly did not interfere in and daily direct the course of the world and the affairs of His people once He had created them and set things in motion. Thus was shifted the role of religion in people's lives. This new rational attitude and belief, held by an educated minority in the colonial period, was known as Deism, and its main tenets were well exemplified in remarks by Benjamin Franklin shortly before his death in a letter to President Ezra Stiles of Yale College. Basic faith is not abandoned, but Franklin's views would hardly have been accepted by John Winthrop.

> I believe in one God, the creator of the universe. That he governs it by his Providence, that he ought to be worshipped, that the most acceptable service we render him is doing good to his other children, that the soul of man is immortal and will be treated with justice in another life respecting its conduct in this. These I take to be the fundamental principles of all sound religion and I regard them as you do in whatever sect I meet with them.
> As to Jesus of Nazareth, my opinion of whom you particularly desire, I think the system of morals and his religion as he left them to us, the best the world ever saw or is likely to see; but I apprehend that it has received various corrupting changes and I have, with most of the present dissenters in England, some doubts as to his divinity; tho it is a question I do not dogmatize upon, having never studied it, and think it needless to busy with it now when I expect soon an opportunity of knowing the truth with less trouble.

Franklin's celebrated wit did not desert him even on these hallowed subjects.

Revivalism   In spite of the general decline in the influence of religion and the role of the church—perhaps in part because of this decline—the intensity of feeling among the faithful increased rather than lessened, and indeed resulted in further diversity in religious belief as well as church organization. For the mid-eighteenth century was marked by the impact of a religious revival known as the Great Awakening.

Influenced by powerful intellects such as Jonathan Edwards and shaped by traveling artisans of the Gospel such as George Whitefield, Gilbert Tennent, and James Davenport, the revival movement rolled from Georgia up through New England. The preachings of these men brought their terrified audiences

George Whitefield, the controversial and dynamic symbol of the Great Awakening. The son of a tavernkeeper, he came to America several times as a philanthropist and missionary, setting up an orphanage and a church and traveling as a preacher throughout the colonies. His power as a preacher had an overwhelming effect on congregations.

to a pitch of emotional agony in which they recognized their own helplessness and despair before an all-powerful God. Out of this agony emerged conversion, the feeling that they had been saved. The emphasis in the Great Awakening was that the conviction of one's utter dependence upon Christ for salvation, and the sudden realization of salvation stemming from that conviction, were both overwhelming emotional experiences. The whole movement reaffirmed the primary role of emotion in religious experience.

There is little doubt that the Great Awakening was a response to what had happened in religious thought with the decline of Puritanism in the seventeenth century. For by the first half of the eighteenth century the emphasis had shifted from union with Christ "in the only marriage which cannot be dissolved" to the living of a virtuous life shaped by morality and doing one's duty to God, family, church, and society. This was the new road to salvation. This emphasis had strong social and economic implications, for it tended to stress that worldly success defined the moral and dutiful life, thus suggesting that only the successful were "true Christians." That left a lot of ordinary people partially if not completely out. The Great Awakening was not only a restatement of the primacy of salvation achieved only through the emotional experience of receiving God's grace, but an indirect statement of social and economic protest against the upper classes.

It is hardly surprising that ministers of the settled churches tended for the most part to take a dim view of revivalism, finding the emotional fervor more suggestive of hysteria than of Christian virtue. And congregations everywhere found themselves split. Parishioners were not backward in putting pressure on their ministers, and if they found those leaders wanting they did not hesitate either to remove them or to break away from their churches and form new congregations.

The Great Awakening created an atmosphere encouraging those sects—such as the Baptists and later the Methodists—which embraced the new emotional enthusiasm, and all that did so profited greatly in growth as a consequence. Moreover, the Great Awakening set the pattern for subsequent revivals that were to sweep the country periodically and bring the errant back into the fold.

The Impact of Religion   The imprint of the colonial religious experience was deep and enduring. The presence of so many sects established the pattern characteristic of the American religious experience. Although certain churches in the colonial period became "established" by law and practice—Congregationalism in New England and Anglicanism in Virginia, Maryland, and the Carolinas, for example—no hierarchy developed that could force established belief on a community, and even under the broad umbrella of Congregationalism or Anglicanism differences in ritual and belief varied from church to church. Diversity became the American way.

Although colonial ministers exerted social influence with varied success, there was no direct political involvement by a church hierarchy as in England, and ministers were less the rulers of their congregations than their servants, being chosen and dismissed by the lay leaders of the individual churches. By the end of the colonial period, the emphasis on morality and the necessity of the true Christian to "do good" had set the stage for the influence of religion in secular reform, injecting a moral tone into American political life that was to persist from the Revolution to the Civil War. And revivalism became not only a periodic reminder of fundamental belief in an omnipotent God and the significance of personal salvation, but a continual source of new sects and new interpretations.

The Class Structure

Although America was soon known as a society generous and congenial to the common man, which implies a society without class distinctions, from the beginning distinctions did exist and seemed natural to most. John Winthrop remarked that "in all times some must be rich, some poor, some high and eminent in power and dignity; others mean and in subjection"—though it is worth noting that observations of this kind are usually made by those at the top of the social ladder. At any rate, by the end of the seventeenth century there was a well-defined class structure that largely shaped and defined social, economic, political, and cultural life as well as personal relationships. This class structure was different in important ways from that of Europe.

The Upper Class   The upper class in colonial society, numerically small but highly influential, rested upon wealth, and consisted of the great merchants and landowners. Although farming was the mainstay of colonial life, large-scale land holdings were principally confined to the South, where the necessities of production and profit for tobacco and rice, as well as the system of land granting, gave impetus to the growth of great plantations. Energetic men quick to assess the advantages of large holdings and gang labor laid the basis for the rise of the planter class. Many of these men had capital to begin with and thus a head start, but others came up through the ranks. Whatever their origins, as their holdings expanded with each generation and their wealth increased, they came to regard themselves as considerably above their neighbors. Not surprisingly they sought to pattern their lives after the aristocracy of the Old World.

This class tended to dominate the life of the South, and there was, in the position its members came to occupy, much to suggest the landed aristocracy and rural gentry of England. The great planters, quite naturally, did nothing to discourage this presumption, which added to the envy and discomfiture of their less fortunate neighbors, though it probably did not detract from their respect. Politically, the great planters came to occupy positions of leadership in their colonies. They sat not only in the assemblies but also on the governor's council, and thus were guaranteed a dominant voice in public policy. They sat as local magistrates and exerted influence within the county. They were prominent in the local militia, and not as privates in the ranks.

Although they might assume—as did planter William Byrd—that what was good for William Byrd was good for the rest of Virginia, the planters were generally liberal in outlook, well-read, educated their children extensively and often in England, and were generous to a fault. William Byrd II, for example, sat in the House of Burgesses and later became a member of the Council of State. He represented his colony in London, was made a Fellow of the Royal Society in recognition of his scientific contributions, directed a considerable economic enterprise in Virginia, was a colonel in the militia, and read Greek, Hebrew, or Latin every day for most of his adult life. Much of the planters' growing wealth was spent on gracious living: elegant homes, elaborate furnishings, fine clothes, and of course their famed hospitality. Guests were frequent, dinners bountiful, drinks abundant, cards plentiful, dances sprightly. It is not surprising that guests often stayed for days and even weeks.

The other chief element in the upper class consisted of the great merchants, centered mainly in the Middle and New England colonies. This group also was well established by 1700, and its members included those who came with sufficient capital to get a jump on everyone else as well as those who rose by their own energy and ability. These were no mere shopkeepers, but men who had developed extensive holdings and who directed large-scale business enterprises. They had capital invested in wharves, warehouses, ships, real estate, sawmills, and trade. They also lent money at rates of interest that sometimes went as high as fifty percent.

The End of the Hunt, *a popular recreation among the landed upper*
class. By an unknown American artist.

Wealth gave these men a powerful influence in political life, similar to that
enjoyed by the planters in the South. But they lacked the peculiar social and
sporting habits of their Southern brethren, and cared little for being colonel
of the militia or riding to hounds, and did not conduct an extensive social life
at board and gaming tables. They were, however, equally well-read and
interested in education for their children, and their business interests often
demanded diverse knowledge and promoted a certain cosmopolitanism not
found in many members of the planter class.

The Middle Class   Bulking large in the colonial population was the middle class, the traditional backbone of American society, which included the
land-owning farmers, professional people, tradesmen, craftsmen, and other
workers. The overwhelming majority of the middle class were freeholding
farmers. As property owners they came to occupy a position of significant
political influence by the end of the colonial period. Less interested in status
and position than those whose energies drove them to wealth and power,
they were nevertheless hardworking folk who looked forward to improving

Bethlehem, Pennsylvania, 1757, an industrious, ordered, middle-class community.

their condition and that of their children. Working their own acres with the aid of the family and perhaps a servant or a hired hand or two, they were independent and self-reliant, took pride in their accomplishments, and thought themselves as good as any man.

Of significant influence in the middle class were the professional people—the lawyers, doctors, clergy, printers and editors, teachers. In the seventeenth century, particularly in New England, the clergy was probably the single most influential group in society. In Puritan New England, ministers worked closely with magistrates to shape not only the spiritual but the political and social life of their communities. By the eighteenth century, however, the influence of the clergy in the North had waned, and in the South, which suffered a chronic shortage of Anglican clergymen, their influence had never been great. Although lawyers were almost nonexistent in the seventeenth century, by the time the established society of the eighteenth century came into being, they had become indispensable to the economic life of the colonies. And as the century wore on, with its rising tide of troubles between colonies and mother country, lawyers became a potent political influence. With the rise of newspapers in the eighteenth century, printers and editors (generally one and the same) rose to prominence as shapers of public opinion and feeling.

In the lower middle class were the tenant farmers, traveling artisans, dockworkers, fur traders, sailors, fishermen, and the like, leading a hard life and often failing to make a go of it, although their sons and daughters sometimes rose to better positions.

The Lower Classes   At the bottom of the ladder were the two indispensable groups which supplied most of the labor for most of the colonial economy. These were the indentured servants, who were more common in the seventeenth century, and the black slaves who became numerous in the eighteenth century.

Indenture   One of the most powerful forces at work in colonial society was the urgent necessity for workers. Labor was continually in short supply. It was the continual demand for it that encouraged the migration of so many of the downtrodden to the New World. And under a contract system known as *indenture,* selling one's services for a period of years became both a way of getting to America and a solution to the shortage of labor in the colonies. The planter who needed agricultural workers, or the merchant who wanted servants, was more than willing to pay the cost of transportation plus a profit to the shipmaster who brought workers. In return the master was assured the servants' labor for a period of three to seven years. The extent of this system is suggested by estimates that perhaps as many as half the white immigrants to the colonies in the seventeenth century came as indentured servants.

Once these people had served their time, they moved out into society as free citizens with full opportunity to advance as their capacities and desires indicated. Many moved upward quickly, becoming craftsmen, farmers, merchants, planters. In Virginia in 1663, forty-three percent of the membership of the House of Burgesses consisted of men who had once been indentured servants. The position of the servants was defined by the particular terms of the indenture they signed, by the varied laws of the colony they lived in defining the master-servant relationship, and most of all by the temper and personality of the master himself. Colonial laws and the indenture agreement generally provided that servants must receive adequate food, clothing, and shelter, be protected against personal abuse, and be provided at the end of their term of service with certain clothing, tools, and money. Some colonies even granted land to each freedman. Such laws and guarantees were not always followed, since masters naturally had more influence than servants as far as the law was concerned, and many masters were not above stretching the law and their own power if it proved to their advantage. By treating servants harshly shortly before their term was up, for example, some masters were able to persuade their servants to take a few months' early release from their contract in return for which they abandoned their claim on the master for tools, clothing, money, or land.

Servants could and sometimes did seek the protection of the law against abuse, and sometimes won their cases. But masters had exceptional powers. They controlled the marital status of servants, inflicted punishment usually

Woodcuts of runaway slaves. Owners often placed notices in newspapers to seek assistance in finding runaways. A description of the fugitive and sometimes the offer of a reward were printed below the stock woodcut kept by the printer.

by whipping and other corporal measures, and generally ruled their lives from dawn to dawn. The harshness of life as a bound servant is suggested by the large body of legislation dealing with runaways.

Slavery At the very bottom of the class structure was the black slave. Slave labor became important, especially in the South, because it was cheaper and more certain than servant labor. Moreover, black slaves appeared to be more adaptable to work in the rice colonies. In the early years of the seventeenth century, slavery was not a well-defined institution. Some blacks brought in early in the century were bound as indentured servants and hence were ultimately freed. It was this practice that accounted for the small number of free blacks there were by the end of the colonial period. But by the later years of the seventeenth century, when slave labor became more desirable in the South than indentured white labor, legislation establishing slavery as a permanent status went on the books. And what few civil and legal rights the blacks had possessed quickly disappeared.

Only a few peculiar souls were opposed to slave labor, white or black (there were instances of whites sold into slavery in the New World in the seventeenth century), but the institution of slavery simply did not take root outside the South on any significant scale except in New York. Agriculture elsewhere did not require the kind of gang labor demanded by the staple-crop production of the South, nor were there enough tasks on small farms to keep slave labor busy through the year. Few craftsmen, moreover, wanted slave labor in their shops. What slaves there were outside the South tended to be household servants, and these were found in all the colonies and in many communities. The Puritan Cotton Mather was happy to accept a black slave as a gift from his thoughtful congregation.

Although it has often been said that most masters treated their slaves well because they were valuable property, it is worth remembering that when individuals are granted total power over others, they are aware of that power only to the extent that they exercise it. Certainly the record in this regard as far as white servant labor is concerned is not particularly impressive, and if masters were inclined to maltreat white servants they were certainly not going to be averse to doing the same to black slaves. In fact, slaves often tried to follow the example of white servants and run away. The large body of legislation dealing with fugitive slaves and reflecting the fear of slave revolt is indication enough that the lot of the black slave was not a happy one.

Special Characteristics of the American Class Structure The gap between the Virginia planter and the slave was greater than that between an English lord and the tenant farmer. But the class structure in America developed notable differences from that of the Old World. Its most striking characteristic, with the single tragic exception of black slavery, was fluidity of movement. Class lines were neither rigid nor hereditary. Individuals rose and fell within the social structure. The established might resent the intrusion of newcomers, but the process continued all the same. William Byrd's father started as an Indian trader and small-time farmer. Anthony Lamb was transported as a convict in 1742 and became a respected instrument maker with his own shop in New York City. Ex-servants became independent farmers, skilled craftsmen, merchants, and planters.

Nor should it be forgotten that the attempts of the upper classes to set themselves off from their lesser neighbors by legislating humbler dress for the ordinary folk was a pretension that never quite came off. People who felt themselves as good as anyone else were not ready to accept such distinctions. Their unwillingness to do so was reflected in a Massachusetts law of 1651, passed by the better sort naturally, which indicated how far things had got out of hand. The law declared "our utter detestation and dislike, that men or women of mean condition, should take upon them the garb of Gentlemen, by wearing Gold or Silver Lace, or Buttons, or Points at their knees, or to walk in great Boots; or women of the same rank to wear Silk or Tiffany hoods, or Scarfes, which tho allowable to persons of greater Estates, or more liberal education, is intolerable in people of low condition." In the simpler, less sophisticated society of the seventeenth century, distinctions between classes were not as great as they came to be later. But in the eighteenth century there was a greater degree of social fluidity simply because there were so many more economic opportunities.

What the social structure reflected was the role of wealth in colonial society. Family, occupation, and learning helped to define the upper class as society became more established, but it was mainly wealth that opened doors. Impressed by his own family background and reputation, by his own more or less assured and genteel income, and by his own distinguished learning, the aristocratic New Yorker Cadwallader Colden was inclined to complain in 1748 that "The only principle of Life propagated among the young People is to get Money and men are only esteemed according to . . . the Money they are possessed of"—as though it had not been money that put him in the position to make such a remark.

But if recognition seemed to depend so heavily upon possession, and the desire for wealth seemed the obsession of the multitude, yet the social system was open, and ability and ambition alone often determined how high one could rise. This was in notable contrast to a European society in which it was automatically assumed that a carpenter's son had neither ability nor ambition for anything but hammer and saw. While wealth may well become an obsession when the opportunities for making it are great and frequent, it is not the only road to recognition. Benjamin Franklin's status in colonial society did not rest upon his business acumen, sharp though it was.

The atmosphere in colonial society was such that a man who rose to the extent of his ability and desire, even if this did not carry him to plantation or countinghouse, felt he was at least entitled to respect for the distance he had traveled. *The Pennsylvania Journal* in 1756 noted that the people of the colony were "chiefly industrious Farmers, Artificers or Men in Trade; they enjoy and are fond of Freedom, and the meanest among them thinks he has a right to Civility from the Greatest."

Finally, in an open society in which it was as easy to fall as it was to rise—easier in fact—and neither property nor income nor family was preserved and protected by law, there was no such thing as a leisure class. The great planter or merchant worked as hard as his lesser neighbor, and if work often became a blind obsession even more powerful than the wealth it sometimes produced, it was a quality found in all classes and not in one alone. It is of course more pleasant to be rich and work hard than to be poor and work hard; yet that society in which work is equally respected by all is surely more attractive than the society in which leisure is the prerogative of a privileged few, and unrewarded labor the curse of the many. Such a society was bound to be more inclined to cooperation than conflict between classes.

The Colonial Economy

As we know from the grim experience of many impoverished countries in the world today, the establishment of a satisfactory economic life is the prime necessity of human existence, since little else can be accomplished without it. People not only want to survive, they want to be able to enjoy their survival. Such was the goal of the colonists from the time of the earliest settlements.

The Land As it had throughout the world for thousands of years, agriculture absorbed the energies of most people. Ninety percent of the colonists were directly engaged in agriculture, and their lives centered about the seasons of planting and harvest. By the time settlement began in North America, the Indians had long since domesticated a number of plants unknown elsewhere in the world, and colonial agriculture heavily depended upon these. From the Indian came pumpkins, squashes, beans, white and sweet potatoes, tomatoes, and New World cotton among other things. But the two most important Indian contributions to American agriculture were corn and tobacco. Corn became the major food crop—for man and beast alike—and was produced in all the colonies. Corn was nutritious and could

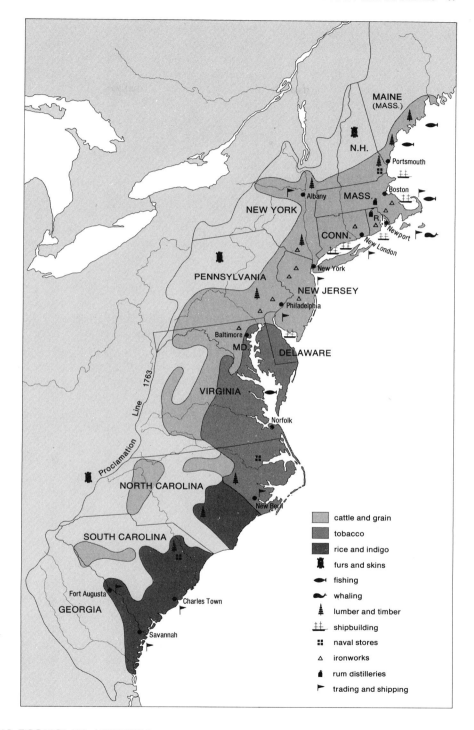

COLONIAL ECONOMIC ACTIVITY

be served in a variety of ways; it could be turned into an easily transportable liquor; and it provided nourishment for livestock. And tobacco was the original moneymaker, the gold everyone was originally searching for. From Europe the colonists brought with them wheat, barley, rye, oats, rice, hops, clovers, forage grasses, garden vegetables, fruits, berries, and farm animals. All this constituted a rich and varied agriculture. Except for special refined products such as sugar, spices, and wine, the colonists were thus able to supply their own food and to live well. Except for the early years of hardship, one of the attractions America had for ordinary people in England and on the Continent was a full table.

Yet farming methods were so primitive that not only was much land ruined, but the richness of the bounty available was never fully realized in the colonial period. Neither long-practiced European methods nor the techniques learned from the Indian were anything but careless and improvident. Advanced agricultural methods appearing in England in the seventeenth and particularly the eighteenth century were largely ignored in America, although here and there some colonial farmers shook off the reluctance to change so characteristic of those who worked the soil. Particularly was this true of many German farmers in Pennsylvania. But by and large farming was primitive and wasteful in technique. From the Indian the colonists learned how to clear the forest by girdling the trees and burning around the roots, as well as how to plant corn, potatoes, and other crops in hills occasionally fertilized with fish. Farm implements remained much as they had been for hundreds of years. Plows were cumbersome and few were iron-tipped prior to 1700. Grain was cut and threshed with tools largely unchanged since Biblical times. The same carelessness and ignorance marked the raising of livestock, which generally roamed free and subsisted on their own. Not until the eighteenth century did improvements in stock-breeding take place.

The type of farming varied widely, depending on geography and climate as well as the systems of land-granting and settlement.

In New England a basic subsistence farming prevailed. A visitor's description of the region suggests why: "the air sharp, the rocks many, the trees innumerable, the grass little, the winter cold, the summer hot, the gnats in summer biting, the wolves at midnight howling." Gnats and wolves, of course, do not dictate the limits of farming, although their presence may indicate why some people preferred the sea to the land. But neither climate nor geography in New England was favorable to large-scale farming. Isolated in the interior by mountains and the absence of navigable rivers, farmers were limited in their ability to ship crops to market. The soil of New England, therefore, was devoted largely to the satisfaction of New England's own needs, although the growth of population by the eighteenth century forced the importation of additional foodstuffs from the Middle and Southern colonies. Corn was a principal crop in New England, and later wheat for a time became significant in the Connecticut Valley. Barley, oats, rye, and flax were also raised. Cattle- and sheep-raising, as well as dairy farming, sustained some and provided a supplementary income for others.

The defeat of the Pequots. As they struggled with the land for survival, so did the colonists struggle with the Indians. During the 1630s settlers organized themselves to combat scattered killings by the Pequots. The Pequot War culminated in the fire set by the colonists which destroyed the Pequot fort and hundreds of Indians trapped inside.

Land for farming was originally granted in New England to groups, usually church congregations under the famous township system, which was influenced not only by social and religious motives but also by the economic solidarity it provided in a land whose agricultural potential was limited. The village thus became a predominant form of settlement with the inhabitants allotted three to five acres in the villages plus fifty to two hundred acres in scattered strips outside the village. Pasture, meadow, and forest lands were held in common. Later, as settlements expanded, small farms dominated. Agriculture, though providing the New England colonists with much of the basic stuff of existence, was clearly not the key to that economic surplus needed for a more satisfying life.

In the South a completely different kind of agriculture developed. Here climate and geography, aided by the wide-open system of land-granting known as the headright system—which allowed individuals fifty acres of land for every person they brought in from abroad or claimed they had—

promoted the growing on large plantations and smaller farms of staple crops such as tobacco. The availability of transport on navigable rivers made possible the easy shipment of such crops direct from plantation to commercial market. It also resulted in widely scattered and isolated plantations and farms rather than the village settlement typical of New England.

Tobacco in Virginia and Maryland, and to a lesser extent in North Carolina, boomed the colonial economy. From a mere 2500 pounds in 1616, production then leaped to 20 million pounds in 1680 and to well over 100 million on the eve of the Revolution. Because tobacco wore out the land within a few years and was best served by a large labor force—at first indentured servants and then slaves—its production naturally favored the rise of the large plantation if profits were to be assured. Tobacco was in such demand, however, that in spite of the fall in price as production expanded, small farmers using no more than five servants or slaves produced almost half the tobacco raised in Virginia and Maryland in the colonial period.

At the end of the seventeenth century rice introduced from Madagascar provided a new cash crop for the South. At first grown in inland fresh-water swamps, the development of irrigation techniques in the 1740s made possible its expansion into the tidal river areas. Most rice was grown in South Carolina, the rest in Georgia. Some 100,000 pounds a year were produced for export by 1700, and by the time of the Revolution over 65 million pounds were grown annually. In the 1740s indigo became an important cash crop in the South. Its production was greatly stimulated by the lure of British bounties, since the dye was crucial to the British woolen industry. Indigo was an ideal supplementary crop since the plant could be grown on high ground not useful for rice, and it was cultivated when slave labor was not needed in the rice fields. Cotton was not a major cash crop in the South in the colonial period.

Between the South and New England lay the so-called Middle Colonies—New York, Pennsylvania, New Jersey, and Delaware. The river valleys of these colonies possessed great fertile lands, and the climate allowed a somewhat longer growing season than in New England. The result was that the region became the commercial breadbasket of the colonies. Crops similar to those of New England were raised, with wheat and wheat products predominating. Oats, rye, barley, and other cereals, as well as potatoes, were extensively grown for export. Yet New York and Pennsylvania wheat exports near the end of the colonial period were nearly seven times the exports of other crops, and it was wheat that made Pennsylvania the richest Northern colony.

In Pennsylvania and New Jersey the headright system of land-granting generally prevailed, and led to the establishment of independent farms of fifty to two hundred acres or more. In New York the practice of granting large-scale holdings to a few individuals that were then leased or rented to various tenants was common enough to hold back somewhat the colony's agricultural development. Renting hardly satisfied the ordinary man's desire for his own land, especially since acquiring it elsewhere was relatively easy.

Everywhere in the colonies livestock were raised. Almost all farms had a few sheep, hogs, and cattle. And in the backcountry the practice developed

A tobacco plantation, one of the foundations of the colonial economy.

of maintaining open ranges for cattle somewhat similar to that which developed later on the plains of the Middle West in the nineteenth century. By the eighteenth century, cattle were being driven to market and fattened for slaughter, thousands, for example, making the long drive from the North Carolina ranges to the markets of Pennsylvania.

The Forest From the very beginning the wildlife of the forest augmented colonial incomes, though as time passed the search for furs and skins had to be extended deeper and deeper into the wilderness; hunters and traders ranged inland as far as a thousand miles by the end of the colonial period. A local fur trade was for a few years a source of extra income for the first colonists in New England. And furs flowed through Massachusetts, New York, and Pennsylvania to both England and the Continent in the eighteenth century, supporting a substantial hat industry abroad and prompting the colonists also to turn to hat production. Deerskins also were important. At the end of the colonial period the amount of deerskin funneled through Charleston from the Southern backcountry totaled over one million pounds.

Shipbuilding, a thriving industry. The colonies were able to capitalize on their rich timber resources as well as the skill of their shipwrights and their ability to produce ships inexpensively to provide a substantial portion of the English trading fleet.

Of far greater importance were the incredible timber resources of the New World that supported a substantial lumber trade, shipbuilding, and the production of naval stores (tar, pitch, turpentine, rosin, hemp), as well as the potash essential to the English textile industry.

The white pine of New England was used for masts and spars. The finest, reserved for the British fleet, were marked by the "King's broad arrow." The white oak of the Middle Colonies was made into ship timbers, barrels, and staves; and the live oak of the Carolinas was especially prized for shipbuilding. From the yellow pine of the South came the tar, pitch, and turpentine so essential to Britain that in the eighteenth century she paid the colonies almost one and a half million pounds sterling in bounties to encourage their production. Out of the forests also came the walnut, red maple, and cherry—the hardwoods needed for the manufacture of the desks, tables, highboys, chairs, and other furniture turned out by the cabinetmaking industry of the eighteenth century.

The Sea   The opportunities for fishing off the Grand Bank of Newfoundland were being exploited by Europe shortly after the discovery of the New World, and New Englanders early saw the resources of the sea as a way of strengthening their economy. New England's fishing fleet competed so successfully with Britain's that by the end of the colonial period it was equalling if not surpassing Britain's total catch in the New World. As early as 1641 over 300,000 cod were being brought into Massachusetts ports alone. By 1664 over thirteen hundred ships were engaged in fishing. Ships were small, generally requiring only the master and a crew of three, who yearly made three trips for cod and mackerel. Salted and dried, cod were a valued product for export as was the oil made from cod liver. By the end of the colonial period at least ten thousand men were engaged in the fishing industry, some five thousand directly and the rest in maintaining the fleet and disposing of the catch.

By the eighteenth century whaling had become a significant ocean venture, dominated by the seamen of New England and New York. By 1774 whalers were operating in some 360 ships from the Arctic Ocean to the southern seas, and bringing in approximately 45,000 barrels of oil each year for soap, illumination, and lubrication. About 75,000 pounds of whalebone a year were made into corset stays. Ambergris from the sperm whale was a key ingredient in perfume, and spermaceti was used for the manufacture of sperm candles.

Manufacturing   The products of land and sea were useful only as they could be turned into something else: wheat into flour, trees into lumber, flax into linen, skins into leather. Most of this manufacturing was done in the home. This was particularly true in the seventeenth century when the colonists had not yet developed the economic capacity to import the finished goods they needed. But even as late as the end of the colonial period most Pennsylvania farmers, for example, were still making their own clothing. Thus the majority of colonial families made most of their own furniture, tools and equipment, household utensils, clothes, and food and drink.

Nevertheless, in the growing towns and villages local manufacturing arose. Here were found carpenters, weavers, tailors, tanners, masons, shoemakers, silversmiths, cabinetmakers, and other skilled craftsmen. These men worked on a small scale. The craftsman not only created his own product, but usually sold it directly to the customer, having made it to order on the customer's specifications.

There also arose flour mills, bakeries, distilleries, glasshouses, brick kilns, saltworks, furnaces and forges, shipyards, sawmills, and many other enterprises. From these efforts came a multitude of products: flour, bread, shipbread, beer, rum, salt beef and pork, dried fish, furniture, ships, and many more. By the middle of the eighteenth century some of this manufacturing was extensive and of great importance to the colonial economy, both local and international. By 1760, for instance, 80,000 pairs of shoes were being made yearly in Lynn, Massachusetts, alone. And by the end of the colonial period, thirty percent of the 7700 ships under the British flag had been built in American shipyards. By the eve of the Revolution the iron industry in the colonies was supporting more blast furnaces and forges and producing more bar and pig iron than Britain: approximately 30,000 tons a year.

Some manufactures were in such urgent need that local communities as well as colony authorities provided incentives in the form of land, tax relief, and subsidies to encourage their development. As one historian has noted, since sawing lumber into planks by hand is such an agonizing job that it probably gave rise to the practice of profanity, little wonder that sawmills were one of the earliest industries to be encouraged.

Commerce and Trade It was commerce and trade that brought to rich fruition colonial labors on the land, in the forests, on the sea, and in the homes and shops, linking the colonial economy together as a productive unit. Simple, limited, and fragmented in the seventeenth century, commerce and trade became extensive and complex in the eighteenth as the population expanded by 1760 to ten times what it had been in 1700. Though only a relatively few were directly involved in trade, its importance was beyond measure. Trade made possible the rise of colonial cities, created an active merchant class, promoted such industries as shipbuilding, allowed the colonists to enjoy the amenities of life, and provided the means for the accumulation of capital necessary for further growth and development.

Trade between the colonies was greater than foreign trade in the seventeenth century. This led to inland trade along the tidewater and between the tidewater and the frontier as the products of different areas found their way into colonial markets and thus stimulated the rise of businessmen in the growing villages and towns. There was also an expanding coastal trade centered in the seaport towns of Boston, New York, Philadelphia, and Charleston, which became bustling centers of commercial activity, transporting the products of one region to another. By the end of the seventeenth century ships leaving Boston with products for other colonies about equalled in tonnage those going to Great Britain.

But in the eighteenth century colonial trade overseas—with England, the Continent, Africa, and the West Indies—became of major proportions. From the ports of New England and the Middle Colonies grain, flour, livestock, dried fish, lumber, and lumber products went to the English and French islands of the Caribbean where they were sold in exchange for molasses, sugar, and slaves. A further link in this chain was the flow of molasses to New England where it was made into rum, some of which was then shipped directly to Africa in exchange for gold and slaves who were transported to the West Indies and the Southern colonies. By the middle of the eighteenth century one-half of the total commerce of the Northern colonies and one-eighth that of the South was involved in one way or another with the West Indies.

And so the colonies prospered. From very humble and limited beginnings, the colonies by 1760 had created a complex, sophisticated, and integrated economy that gave them not only a satisfactory livelihood but an economic surplus enabling them to enjoy the pleasures of life as well.

Indigo processing—Eliza Pinckney's success.

Profile: ELIZA PINCKNEY

Her life spanned much of the eighteenth century—1722 to 1793—from the days of colonial dependency to those of the young republic. Born Elizabeth Lucas, daughter of a British army officer stationed in the West Indies, she died seventy-one years later one of the most respected women of America: developer of a key Southern crop, shrewd businesswoman, and mother of two leaders of the new republic. At his own request President Washington served as a pallbearer at her funeral, providing both personal and official recognition of her accomplishments.

This extraordinary woman had the good fortune to have a father who recognized her abilities and her unusual character and gave them full play. He educated her in England, and through his own library introduced her to writers many colonial men had never read, including such English writers as Milton and Locke and classical authors Virgil and Plutarch. She spoke excellent French and was accomplished in music.

Inheriting property in South Carolina but with duty taking him back to the West Indies, Colonel Lucas turned over the management of his scattered plantation holdings to his daughter, who was then only seventeen. With the naïveté, energy, and imagination of youth, but with the perseverance and practicality of someone far beyond her years, Eliza took over her responsibilities and made a major contribution to Southern colonial agriculture by her successful cultivation of indigo.

The dye made from indigo was essential for English cloth manufacturers, yet the British were compelled to import it from the French West Indies, an economic dependency deplored by manufacturers and government alike. Experiments to raise indigo in the Carolinas had been unsuccessful decades earlier. Rice was South Carolina's principal money crop, but wars in Europe early in the eighteenth century had curtailed that market. Alternate sources of income were needed. With her father's long-distance encouragement, young Eliza sought profitable substitutes for Carolina rice. In 1739 she recorded in her journal "the pains I had taken to bring the Indigo, Ginger, Cotton and Lucerne and Casada to perfection and had greater hopes from the Indigo (if I could have the seed earlier next year from the West Indies) than any of the rest of the things I had tried."

Despite numerous obstacles, including a doublecrossing dyemaker from the French island of Montserrat who deliberately ruined an experimental batch of dye to protect the indigo trade of his own island, Eliza continued her experiments. She brought in a successful crop in 1744, seed from which was sent to England where it was "found better than the French indigo." Eliza distributed seed from the crop to many other planters and the new product soon flourished. By 1747 almost 100,000 pounds of indigo were being exported to England, which then provided a bounty for it. Until the Revolution indigo remained crucial in South Carolina's economy.

The same year Eliza brought in her first successful crop of indigo, at the age of twenty-two, she married Charles Pinckney, a widower almost twice her age. Marriage and a family—she had four children, one of whom died in infancy—did not prevent her from maintaining her interest in agricultural experimentation. On her husband's plantation, for example, she cultivated silkworms and instituted the manufacture of silk on an experimental scale. Her managerial abilities were called to the front years later in 1758 when her husband died, at which time she took over the direction of his various lands. At the time the Pinckney estates were much neglected and barely paying their own costs. "I find," she wrote to a friend, "it requires great care and attention to attend to a Carolina Estate, though but a moderate one, and to do one's duty, and make all turn to account." But under her guidance, conditions greatly improved.

Eliza was much involved in the education of her three children, two boys and a girl. When her first-born, Charles Gatesworth, was only four months old, she wrote a friend in England to send her "the new toy (a description of which I inclose) to teach him according to Mr. Locke's method (which I have carefully studied) to play himself into learning." Modern methods seem dubious by comparison, since a year later Eliza wrote that her son could "tell all his letters in any book without hesitation, and begins to spell before he is two years old." The education of her children continued in London where the family resided from 1753 to 1758 while her husband was commissioner from South Carolina. Her sons remained to study in England after Eliza and her husband returned to South Carolina in 1758 when war broke out with France. The boys remained there until the eve of the Revolution, receiving advice and guidance from their mother, who encouraged them to pursue their own ways. She did well by them. Both served in the Revolution, and afterwards were prominent in public life—Charles serving at the Constitutional Convention in Philadelphia, representing the United States on a mission to France, and being twice the candidate of the Federalist party for president, while his brother Thomas served as governor of South Carolina, minister to Great Britain, and special commissioner to Spain.

Eliza Pinckney: her life was a full one, and she illuminated the century in which she lived.

Chapter 4
THE NEW
COLONIAL CULTURE

The Spirit of the Times
MATURITY

In the seventeenth century, those few colonists who traveled abroad did so because of urgent business for church, state, or trade. Few others had the inclination, means, or motive for setting aside the work of the New World to embark on the long and sometimes dangerous voyage to the Old.

Even in the eighteenth century most colonials confined their travels to the nearest village or perhaps to one of the port cities. But the increasingly complex society of the eighteenth century had a number of people with the means, inclination, and motive for travel to Great Britain and even the Continent. To those reasons prompting travel in the seventeenth century were now added education, health, the pursuit and exchange of knowledge, and the pleasures of enjoying an ancient and cultivated society. Proud as Benjamin Franklin was of the achievements of colonial society, he recognized the greater intellectual and cultural stimulation provided by the mother country: "Of all the enviable things England has, I envy it most its people. Why should that petty island . . . enjoy in almost every neighborhood, more sensible, virtuous, and elegant minds than we can collect in ranging 100 leagues of our vast forests?" And the English painter Joshua Reynolds wrote to the American painter John Singleton Copley: "With the advantages of the example and instruction which you could have in Europe, you would be a valuable acquisition to the art and one of the first painters of the world, provided you could receive these aids before it was too late in life and before your manner and taste were corrupted or fixed by working in your own little way in Boston." In the eighteenth century a large number of colonials made their way abroad. Copley was one of them.

Speedier ships and greater comfort made the voyage across the Atlantic a more endurable experience than it had been in the previous century. Some colonials even welcomed the voyage as a boon to health. Thus Anderson Phillips sailed for England plagued, wrote Cotton Mather, by "some illness which it was hoped the sea would help to cure." But the voyage was still fraught with discomfort and even peril—storms, pirates and privateers, disease, short rations, and the seasickness that curses even the modern traveler. William Samuel Johnson, the Connecticut agent in London, wrote that "the fatigue and danger of the voyage is too great to engage in, merely for the sake of seeing it." And Copley might have taken Reynolds' advice years sooner if he had not been so terrified of the Atlantic crossing. Yet in spite of these difficulties, numerous colonials made not just one trip to the Old World but several.

Probably the most distressing feature of ocean travel was uncertainty about the duration of the voyage. Actual sailing time was not the problem, but the frequent and innumerable delays that might stretch the journey to as much as four months. After boarding ship, passengers might find the sailing delayed for many reasons: storms, waiting for convoys to form, the absence of favorable winds or any at all. The same held true for debarkation. It was not unusual for a ship to beat about the English Channel for days and even weeks before it could dock at London.

Given the fact that the length of the voyage was so uncertain, comfort depended upon the passengers' choice of accommodations and their skill in anticipating their probable needs. While some passengers made the mistake of traveling on ships with no real facilities for passengers—and suffered accordingly—before 1750 ships with attractive accommodations were making the trip between America and Britain. James Pemberton praised his in 1748 as "exceedingly convenient and our fireplace in the cabin we find particularly serviceable."

Sensible passengers made sure to take sufficient provisions, laying in stores of food, beer, rum, and even chickens, goats, and cows to insure a supply of fresh eggs, milk, and cream. Quaker Jane Crosfield did not lack for nourishment on her trip. Her provisions included four dozen bottles of beer, a dozen of "Best Madeira Wine," six bottles of wine from the Canary Islands, half a dozen bottles of claret, three of sack, half a barrel of beer, half of cider, and a keg of rum.

Having reached England and concluded their business, an astonishing number of visiting colonials set out on the tourist trail. Improvements in roads in the eighteenth century made possible the kind of travel unheard of a century before. Colonists took to the road by coach, private carriage or post chaise, or on horseback. Trying to cover as much ground as possible and see as many sights as possible made touring the same exhausting experience it frequently is today. Virginian John Ravenscroft wrote home after a tour of several weeks that "I was so sore—every inch of me—and so tired that I could not well stand or sit."

Colonial agents in London, private individuals who had moved permanently to England, native Britons with American connections and prominent in banking, industry, trade, the arts, the sciences, and publishing—all provided aid, advice, hospitality, and contacts for visiting colonials. As sometimes happens, a few took undue advantage of such hospitality, prompting Charles Carroll to write his son in London that "It might seem to be pride not to accept now and then their invitations, but do it so seldom and in such a manner as not to make yourself cheap."

Many colonists included in their travels a visit to the places their families had come from, tracing their genealogy, looking up relatives, and often then enjoying their hospitality and service as guides to the local sights. Colonial tourists generally took in such attractions as Oxford and Cambridge, Winchester and Salisbury cathedrals, Stonehenge, the famous spa at Bath, the great castles of Windsor, Blenheim, Chatsworth, and Wilton. A surprising number, in the two or three decades before the Revolution, also visited Britain's growing industrial and commercial towns, such as Birmingham, Liverpool, Manchester, Derby, and Sheffield. A number also visited Scotland, particularly Glasgow and Edinburgh.

In the eighteenth century, numerous Americans also toured the Continent, using Britain as their base of operations. Italy, Switzerland, France, and the Low Countries found their delights most often sampled. An occasional colonist of means, such as Arthur Middleton of South Carolina, traveled extensively throughout Europe, everywhere indulging his tastes in literature, music, and painting.

Many Americans maintained their ties abroad through correspondence. Business interests of course prompted much exchange by mail. But other Americans who for one reason or another had traveled abroad often kept up a correspondence with those they had met on their travels. Those with scientific interests corresponded with learned men abroad. Family ties were frequently maintained, and immigrants to the New World wrote to their friends and relatives back home telling of their life in the colonies and learning about those still at home. Some idea of the extent of colonial overseas correspondence is indicated by figures for the Falmouth–New York run from 1755 to 1762, which show that over one and a half million letters were handled by the regular postal service alone, which does not include mail carried separately by ship captains and passengers.

And so, numerous colonial Americans enjoyed the pleasures of the Old World, not the least of which is the reward of all travelers—a greater appreciation of their own country. Dr. Benjamin Rush of Pennsylvania wrote: "I think every native of Philadelphia should be sent abroad for a few years if it was only to teach him to prize his native country above all places in the world." In short, the colonies as a whole were by the middle of the eighteenth century far from being isolated from the interests and ideas of the Western world.

Nor can it be said that the colonies were lacking in other elements of the civilized life, even though most colonists lived on farms and plantations or on the frontier. For by the eighteenth century cities had become vital and central in colonial life, and were contributing substantially to cultural growth and maturity.

The chief towns were New York, Boston, Newport, Philadelphia, and Charleston. Near the end of the seventeenth century Boston with 7,000 people was the largest of these and Charleston with 1,100 was the smallest. By 1760 Philadelphia with 40,000 people was the largest colonial city and ranked among the top four in the British Empire. Newport, the smallest of the five by then, had approximately 11,000. In addition, there were some fifteen secondary cities whose populations ran from around 3,000 to 8,000. These cities seem like miniatures compared to modern cities, and indeed they were small compared to the London and Paris of the eighteenth century. But they were nerve centers of colonial society, and had a vitality, spirit, and sophistication that made them far more interesting and important centers of life than any of the provincial towns of England.

The cities and towns were, of course, primarily commercial communities, and thus the key to the expanding economic prosperity of the colonies. In them was centered internal, coastal, and international trade, and most of the intellectual life of the colonies in science, literature, and the arts. Here the colleges were located and a variety of schools and educational institutions developed. They were the principal points of cultural, social, and political contact between the Old World and the New. It was to the towns that people came to find out what was going on and to establish contact with others. The New England towns developed a new political organization, the town meeting, which proved efficient in the handling of urban problems. The building of these new communities generated a relatively high sense of civic responsibility absent in most European cities. By the eve of the Revolution the towns and cities of colonial America had become remarkable

The flourishing city of New York—a detail from an engraving, 1716–1718. At the time, New York was the third largest city in the colonies.

centers of activity and achievement in many ways. They harbored the political activity that marked the colonial response to the crisis brought about by the British after 1763.

Education in Colonial America

Of great importance to most colonials—as indeed to most Americans ever since—was education. It is true that through most of our history the Americans have had a curious pride in the so-called "self-made man," who with no formal education rose from obscurity and poverty to fame and riches. From Benjamin Franklin to John D. Rockefeller, we have seen self-made men attending "the school of experience" and graduating from "the college of hard knocks." But in spite of our admiration for such people, our concern for formal education has never lessened. In fact, the first thing many self-made men did after they acquired riches was to found a college and thereby insure their fame.

Schools The early colonists respected knowledge and valued education. The Puritan leadership largely consisted of university-trained men. A number of considerations stimulated the concern for education among the Puritans, whose educational achievements were greater than those elsewhere in the country. The most important consideration was religious. How else but through education could one find in the Bible the fundamental meaning of existence? How else could the people be protected from religious error? How else could succeeding generations of ministers be provided? "Ignorance is the mother ... of Heresy," declared one Puritan divine, and Edward Johnson opened *New England's First Fruits* with the assertion that "After God had carried us safe to New England ... one of the next things we longed for and looked after was to advance learning and perpetuate it to posterity, dreading to leave an illiterate ministry in the churches when our present ministers shall lie in the dust." But there was more to the Puritan experiment than theology. They were also building a new society, and they expected education to turn out not only a literate body of civil leaders but an educated community—a great expectation indeed. Finally, the Puritans somewhat more practically expected the young to be trained for a calling of use not only to themselves but to society.

The first legislation on education, the Massachusetts Act of 1642 and its amplification in 1647, reflected these expectations—religious, political, and economic—by requiring town officials to keep an eye on the matter of teaching children "to read and understand the principles of religion and the capital laws of the country," and to write and learn a trade. A number of communities, led by Boston in 1635, had already taken steps to establish schools. The initial responsibility for educating the young, as laid down in the law of 1642, was placed on the family, an institution already heavily burdened with obligations and duties. The difficulties posed by this law resulted in another Massachusetts law in 1648 that extended the responsibility to communities and required that every town of fifty families hire a schoolmaster. Towns of one hundred families were required to institute a Latin grammar school to prepare youths for that university training which would create a supply of future ministers. Religious considerations were also

A — In *Adam's* Fall
We finned all.

B — Thy Life to mend
This Book attend.

C — The Cat doth play
And after flay.

New England Primer. *The Primer first appeared in 1690 and was used for over 150 years throughout the colonies, giving schoolchildren a common heritage in the religious and moral principles used to teach them reading.*

reflected in a subsequent law of 1654 that cautioned selectmen of the towns not to choose teachers unsound in faith. To make sure the unsound did not slip through to corrupt the young, ministers played a key role in screening candidates for the job.

Other New England colonies followed the leadership of Massachusetts, and by 1672 all New England except Rhode Island had some system of compulsory education. These laws were of course sometimes more honored in the breach than the observance. Enforcement was often difficult, towns of less than fifty families had to rely upon instruction in the home, and in frontier settlements even the teaching of reading and writing was generally minimal. Schools rose and fell. In the seventeenth century, there were only about eleven Latin grammar schools of any significance that managed to stay continuously in operation, including the justly famed Boston Latin School, and in many small settlements there was only the dame school, in which a housewife taught small children to read and write. Although town schools required tuition fees from nonresidents as well as a small entrance and expense fee from all students, provision was made for the admission of those unable to pay, for the intent was not to deny schooling because of poverty.

By the eighteenth century, general growth and stability had greatly improved the condition of the schools in New England. In many communities private schools known as academies developed where, besides Latin and the classics, there was more practical study in mathematics, languages, navigation, and accounting. Night schools for apprentices, and even for businessmen out to improve themselves, also became popular. Writing schools to teach penmanship and arithmetic cropped up in various towns.

The Middle and Southern colonies lagged behind New England, and much of the educational effort was handled by the churches. Under the guidance of the Reformed Church the Dutch had developed a fairly good system of primary education, but this was abandoned after the New Netherlands was taken by the English, and private schools controlled by the Anglican Church replaced it. The Quakers in Pennsylvania did not see in education the same intense religious or social significance that the Puritans did. The Quakers were more concerned with the practical economic value of education, and the Governor and Council were early ordered to see that "all children within this province of the age of twelve years shall be taught some useful trade or skill, to the end that none may be idle." Although an early law required parents to teach children to read and write, it was not enforced, and no public school system developed; yet illiteracy among Quakers was rare. Of the various German sects that poured into Pennsylvania, only the Moravians had any real commitment to schools and the promotion of learning, but the Scotch-Irish brought with them to the Pennsylvania frontier and elsewhere a respect for a learned clergy that produced in the eighteenth century an attempt to establish the classical grammar school in the wilderness.

In the South, the weakness of the Anglican Church and the limited number of Anglican clergy combined with the diffusion of the population among plantations and farms to limit the development of church schools. The Anglican Church felt that education which it did not control tended to encourage religious and social dissension, and this attitude hindered the development of schools by non-Anglicans. Some who feared political dissension agreed with Governor Berkeley that "Thank God there are no schools and no printing presses in Virginia and I hope there will be none these hundred years." Things never got that bad, of course, but nothing resembling the school system of New England arose. There were some private schools sponsored by the Anglican clergy and particularly by the Society for the Propagation of the Gospel in Foreign Parts, and a limited number of Presbyterian academies. But these all failed to reach the masses. Tutors provided the main instruction for children of wealthy planters who sometimes were also sent to England for their schooling.

In the towns of the Middle and Southern colonies numerous teaching masters gave private instruction in almost any subject for which there was demand, particularly the more practical subjects and those of contemporary value. In Philadelphia one could study mathematics, bookkeeping, surveying, the rudiments of natural science, drawing, and painting. And there was instruction in English, German, French, Spanish, Italian, Portuguese, Latin, Greek, Hebrew, and Arabic.

Education in the colonies was thus uneven, though it is probably safe to say that by the end of the revolutionary crisis literacy, especially in New England, was exceptionally high—certainly far greater than it had been a century earlier. The frequent complaints about the low level of knowledge did not indicate indifference to the necessity for education. In 1713 in New York the Reverend John Sharpe noted with great distress that "there is hardly anything more wanted in this country than learning." And the records are full of repeated efforts to get schools established and in operation, though many such efforts went for naught. In Maryland, Governor Francis Nicholson proposed to the Legislative Assembly near the end of the seventeenth century that "a way be found out for building of a free school," which, he wrote to the Bishop of London, would instruct "our youth in the orthodox religion, preserving them from the infection of heterodox tenets and fitting them for the service of the church and state in this uncultivated part of the world." Everywhere by the end of the colonial period private schools of one kind or another, itinerant schoolmasters, wandering ministers, and concerned parents filled the gaps left by the absence of public schools. The net result was a literacy rate higher than any then existing in the Western world.

Colleges The most astounding educational achievement of the colonies was the establishment of nine colleges. The striking fact is not that only two colleges came into being in the seventeenth century, but that there were any at all. Proposals were frequently made to get colleges started, including one at Jamestown as early as 1619.

The first college actually established was Harvard in 1636, a mere seven years after the first wave of Puritan migration, when Massachusetts Bay Colony agreed to give some £400 toward a college and John Harvard donated his library and half his estate to its initial support. The institution got off to a somewhat uncertain start under the administration of Nathaniel Eaton, who almost starved the students, misused college funds, whipped the innocent as well as the guilty, and finally took off for Virginia where, according to John Winthrop, he succumbed to vice. After this shaky beginning Harvard set the pattern in curriculum for American colleges. Following Cambridge and Oxford, it stressed Latin, Greek, Hebrew, logic, ethics, and rhetoric, but paid little attention to mathematics and the natural sciences, and none to history or modern languages. Harvard also set the pattern well into the nineteenth century in the motive for its establishment, which was mainly to train ministers and promote sound theological doctrine—although it was also designed "to advance learning and perpetuate it to posterity."

Indeed, of the nine colleges there were by the end of the colonial period all but one had a religious impetus. William and Mary in Virginia was established under Anglican auspices in 1693, and Yale in 1701 because Harvard was considered too liberal and possibly immoral—certainly too secular for the more pious Congregationalists. The Reverend Solomon Stoddard of Northampton remarked in 1703: "Places of learning should not be places of

Harvard College, 1740. Like the other original American colleges,
Harvard was governed by a board of lay trustees of various denominations
although the original purpose of the school was to provide training for
ministers—in Harvard's case, of the Congregational faith.

riot and pride. Ways of profuseness and prodigality in such a society lay a
foundation of a great deal of sorrow. . . . It is not worth the while for persons
to be sent to the College to learn to compliment men and court women. They
should be sent thither to prepare them for public service and had need to be
under the oversight of wise and holy men." Princeton (1746) was Presbyterian; Dartmouth (1769) Congregational; the College of Rhode Island, later
Brown University (1764), was Baptist; King's College, later Columbia University (1754), was Anglican; Queen's College, later Rutgers (1766), was
Dutch Reformed. Only the Philadelphia Academy, later the University of
Pennsylvania (1740), was nonsectarian in origin and control.

Yet motives other than religious also underlay the founding of colleges in
colonial America. A developing and prosperous eighteenth-century society
could and wanted to support higher education, and increasingly regarded it

as a necessity for the training of civil leaders. It is worth remembering that the majority of the leadership in the late colonial period and revolutionary era were college trained, and some eighteen of the signers of the Declaration of Independence were college men.

Enrollments at the colleges were never large. The student body at Harvard in the seventeenth century seldom numbered more than fifty, and by the time of the Revolution averaged only 180. Yale averaged 170, Princeton 100, and the rest below 100. But with academic mortality very low, the number of college graduates increased rapidly, totaling about 5,500 between 1715 and 1775. By the time of the Revolution there were also several hundred young Americans who had been educated in English, Scottish, and Continental universities.

The nonsectarian College of Philadelphia played an important role in shifting the direction of higher education, not only in initiating the trend away from church control but in broadening and liberalizing the curriculum by putting emphasis on foreign languages, history, and the natural sciences. The College of Philadelphia, along with King's College, also initiated medical studies before the end of the colonial period, but for formal training in medicine and law students had to go to Britain or the Continent. Most sought medical training at the University of Edinburgh, while aspiring lawyers studied at the Inns of Court in London.

Other Tools of Learning

But learning is not bounded by the classroom, as any schoolboy knows. Libraries personal and public, newspapers and magazines, the intellectual exchange arising within discussion groups and societies—all these reinforce and extend the promotion of learning initiated in the schools.

An occasional pastime of armchair Robinson Crusoes is to speculate on what key book or books they would want with them if marooned on a desert island. In a very real sense this was the decision faced by many immigrants to the New World, particularly in the earlier years. Such a decision, whether speculative or real, was in part a recognition that we do not live by bread alone. "How hard will it be for one brought up among books and learned men to live in a barbarous place where there is no learning and less civility," Robert Tyece warned his friend John Winthrop in 1629 on the eve of the latter's departure for New England. But civilized people also need practical information on how to get by when thrown upon their own resources without the easy availability of specialists and experts. Winthrop and others were well aware of all this, and the books that formed a vital part of the immigrants' baggage reflected their awareness. So they took books to nourish body, mind, and soul, books to sustain society and civilization in the wilderness. They were as useful as gunpowder, axes, and flour.

Books, in short, were valued for their knowledge, not the status they gave their owners. In this the early Puritans agreed with Henry Peacham, an

English writer the Puritans were familiar with, who observed in 1622 in *The Compleat Gentleman:*

> Affect not as some do that bookish ambition to be stored with books and have well furnished libraries, yet keep their heads empty of knowledge; to desire to have many books and never use them is like a child that will have a candle burning by him all the while he is sleeping.

Books Among the useful books widely read in the colonies were practical works on farming, engineering, military tactics, medicine, and legal procedures. Farmers North and South utilized Gervase Markham's works on agriculture. Laymen drawn by necessity to or before the bench turned in the seventeenth century to Michael Dalton's *The Country Justice,* Sir Edward Coke's *Reports,* or Sir Thomas Littleton's *Tenures* to aid them in dispensing or gaining justice. By the end of the colonial period they were relying on Blackstone's *Commentaries.* The sick and the maimed survived, or succumbed, by following Philip Barrough's *The Method of Physic* or William Vaughan's *Directions for Health, Both Natural and Artificial,* and in the eighteenth century self-treatment might rely on John Wesley's *Primitive Physick.* Highly useful was the extensive information found in the encyclopedias, the most popular in the seventeenth century being Pierre de La Primaudaye's *The French Academy.*

Of a different order of usefulness were historical works, which ranked second in esteem in the seventeenth century to works of divinity. History was regarded as a source of political and moral truths, and by providing a link to the great achievements of the past helped give colonists a sense of the importance of their own mission in human affairs. In a much-quoted sermon of 1668, William Stoughton was drawing upon this sense of historical destiny in the founding of New England when he reminded his Puritan listeners that "God has sifted a whole nation that He might send choice grain over into this wilderness." Stoughton and many others were familiar not only with the classical historians of Greece and Rome but also with the historical writings of their own time. Sir Walter Raleigh's *History of the World* remained popular in the colonies throughout the seventeenth century, particularly with the Puritans because it demonstrated the divine purpose in human affairs. Nor were works on current history neglected. John Rushworth's *Historical Collections* and Bulstrode Whitelocke's *Memorials of the English Affairs* provided accounts of events in the crucial years of controversy between crown and parliament. Classical as well as contemporary historians were read in the eighteenth century, though more for political than moral guidance.

The colonials were also interested in books on the governance of society. *The Commonwealth of England and Manner of Government* by Sir Thomas Smith, a standard Elizabethan work, was common among those suddenly responsible for government. The present-day American who is convinced that American politicians have always been noted for their Machiavellian habits will not be surprised to learn that *The Prince* was widely known. But then so was Sir Thomas More's *Utopia.* For some, at least, among those who recognized that

The trade card of a bookbinder. In addition to importing books from England, the colonies quickly established their own presses, printing the first book, the Bay Psalm Book, *in 1640. Boston, New York, and Philadelphia became the printing centers, producing some German, Dutch, French, and Indian language books as well as English. The types of books printed varied regionally—theology predominantly in New England, law in the South, and literature in the Middle Colonies. But despite its regionality, the colonial press was a powerful force in shaping the colonial mind.*

they were creating a new society in a New World, it was clearly reassuring to have at hand in *Utopia* a model of society and government.

It was not unique that the colonists were concerned about human conduct and relationships. Every society has such concerns. But the desire to maintain normal civilized behavior was strengthened in the early years by the disorder of pioneer conditions, hence the strong colonial interest in books of instruction on everything from table manners and polite conversation to the godly life. While such concern can produce stultifying conformity, the absence of recognized standards of conduct can also lead to the social chaos portrayed in William Golding's *Lord of the Flies*. The colonists were well aware of the disintegrating effect that crude and primitive frontier conditions could have on individual and society, an effect that those who wanted to maintain culture were committed to avoiding.

For instruction on manners, proper conversation, and domestic affairs, the colonists had Stefano Guazzo's *Civil Conversations*, Robert Cleaver's *A Godly Form of Household Government*, William Gouge's *Of Domestic Duties*, and a book called *The Academy of Compliments*. But civilized conduct meant other than witching sweet ladies with soft words and looks. And it was to pious books and collections of sermons that the seventeenth century turned for guidance on living the decent and civilized life. Works on religion and morality were common to all, not to the Puritans alone. The sinner as well as the saint recognized that it was religion that set the standard for the good life. The Carters of Lancaster County, Virginia, were not noted for their piety, yet the inventory of John Carter's library, taken after his death in 1690, indicates that nearly a third of his books were on religious subjects. Many popular devotional works were collections of sermons. Especially in the seventeenth century the sermon was not thought of as a heaven-sent polemical exhortation but as a practical, sensible guide to the successful Christian life. The sermon-essay by the popular English preacher, William Perkins, *A Treatise of the Vocations*, emphasized diligence, thrift, efficiency, and hard work. And while these were clearly virtues in the eyes of the Lord, they were also qualities of great use to a new society a-building in the wilderness.

Neither fiction nor poetry was absent from the reading of the early colonists. Elizabethan and early seventeenth-century poets were popular, including Shakespeare, Spenser, Herrick, Quarles, and the devotional poet George Herbert, who was probably the most widely read poet in the century. Occasionally colonists escaped into the world of romance, and they held Bunyan's fictional allegory, *Pilgrim's Progress*, in high esteem. Yet it is likely that even when they read for escape or esthetic pleasure, most seventeenth-century readers were probably persuaded that they were also getting something morally useful from the fiction and poetry they read.

By the middle of the eighteenth century the impact of the Enlightenment and the interests of a more settled and secular society with a century of experience greatly broadened the reading of the colonists. Their interest in government and society went beyond the simple mechanics of organization and administration to broader questions of who should rule and why, and many read such moral and political philosophers as Voltaire, Montesquieu, Diderot, Harrington, Sydney, and Locke. A shift in interest from the supernatural to the natural found colonists reading in experimental science, or in Lord Shaftesbury's *Characteristics*, which argued that man has an inborn moral sense and a benevolent nature—thus taking issue with the theological concept of innate human wickedness.

Over fifty years ago Professor Thomas Wright of Yale made a study of the books and libraries of colonial New England that is still useful in indicating the extent and breadth of colonial reading as time went on. His representative list for the seventeenth century was based on the one hundred books left by Samuel Eaton to New Haven in 1640, and contained only the following nine books or authors: Plutarch, Virgil, Sandys' translation of Ovid, Dionysius of Halicarnassus, More's *Utopia*, Erasmus' *Proverbs*, Raleigh's *History of the World*, Foxe's *Book of Martyrs*, Heylyn's *Cosmography*. But his list for the eighteenth century, based on a donation of over seven hundred volumes given to Yale in 1714, contained fifty-eight titles, including complete works, which he divided into categories. The collection had the usual theological works, but also most current key books on medicine and philosophy, and representative works of science, history, and literature.

Libraries Some colonials managed to establish significant private libraries. Cotton Mather in Boston had accumulated between 3,000 and 4,000 volumes before he died in 1728, and William Byrd II of Virginia left a library of over 3,600 books at his death in 1744. Many such private libraries became, in essence, circulating libraries, if we may judge by the frequent complaints in letters and diaries about book-borrowing, and particularly about the borrower who failed to return a precious volume or grandly lent it in turn to someone else, after which the original owner lost track of it. No book-loving historian has ever had the pleasure of recording the name of a careless book-borrower guilty of neglecting to return a volume who suffered the same legal penalties as an equally neglectful borrower of a horse—which might suggest that in most societies horses have been more valued than books, or that true justice will always elude us. But it is more likely that there is something about books that suggests a common ownership and use. Attempts were made quite early at organized sharing of books through the establishment of a few town libraries. These were minor efforts and not very successful, and it was not until the eighteenth century that the prototype of the modern free public library appeared in the form of subscription and circulating libraries.

Subscription libraries, in which individuals pooled their resources for the purchase of books and thus had available far more than they could possibly hope to acquire on their own, had their origin in the Library Company of Philadelphia, founded by Benjamin Franklin in 1731. Its first order of books omitted religion and concentrated on classical and contemporary history, geography, grammar, scientific treatises, mathematics, government, politics, agriculture, architecture, and issues of the English literary journals, *The Spectator*, *The Tatler*, and *The Guardian*. Much later, in his *Autobiography*, Franklin remarked about the influence of the kind of reading encouraged by the Library Company:

> This was the mother of all the North American subscription libraries, now so numerous. It is become a great thing itself and continually increasing. These libraries have improved the general conversation of Americans, made the common tradesmen and farmers as intelligent as most gentlemen from other countries, and perhaps have contributed in some degree to the stand so generally made throughout the colonies in defence of their privileges.

The Library and Surgeons Hall in Philadelphia, 1799.

Surviving records indicate that at least sixty-four such libraries existed in the colonies before the Revolution, and the assumption is that there were many more.

As distinct from subscription libraries, circulating libraries had their beginnings very late in the colonial period, and were organized primarily by booksellers and publishers who rented books for a small fee.

Newspapers, Magazines, and Almanacs Another important kind of reading matter for colonial Americans—of whose knowledge Franklin was so proud—was newspapers, which were first published in America early in the eighteenth century. The first successful paper, the Boston *News-Letter*, was founded in 1704. By the time of the Revolution local newspapers in every region provided outlets for public opinion and became an important instrument of public information. Newspapers were generally two to four pages in length, came out weekly, and contained not only local news and political developments but essays on literature and science, foreign news, and advertising. Then as now, their quality ranged from excellent to appalling, their tone from sprightly to dull, their politics from safe to controversial.

Franklin played an influential role in the development of newspapers. He was trained in the printer's shop of his half-brother James who published one of the early New England papers, and in Philadelphia in his own highly successful shop Franklin trained apprentices who left to establish their own shops and papers elsewhere, some backed financially by Franklin himself.

Franklin and other interested publishers attempted to found magazines, but none were really successful. *The American Magazine and Historical Chronicle,* edited by lawyer Jeremiah Gridley of Boston, set the record for longevity, a three-year span from 1743 to 1746, which is not what you could call a winning streak. But local talent already had an outlet in the newspapers, and those interested in more sophisticated critical and contemplative writing were satisfied by magazines and journals from abroad, as the order list for Franklin's Library Company indicates.

Of far greater significance than magazines were the famous almanacs of the eighteenth century, geared to the interests and needs of the farm family whose library was limited to a handful of books at best. The almanacs were practically encyclopedic in their coverage. Frequently saved for many years and constantly reread, they were a portfolio of information and entertainment. They contained jokes and humorous anecdotes, illustrations, practical advice on health and medicine, the planting and harvesting of crops, the weather, the position of the stars and planets in the different seasons, household hints, and political information. The almanacs of highest quality, such as the best sellers put out by Nathaniel Ames and Benjamin Franklin, also contained pieces by well-known European writers, including the English essayists Addison and Steele, and the poets Thomson and Pope whose heroic couplets and appreciation of nature were widely admired. Folk wisdom and maxims of self-help and self-reliance appealed strongly to a people dependent on their own efforts and eager to improve themselves. The pages of the almanacs abounded in such maxims as "Let the Poor be Content with their present Lot, for when they come to make Brick without Straw their case will be yet Worse." Modern Americans disturbed at the presence of poverty in the United States would probably view that homely observation with some skepticism. Yet after totaling the corporate wealth in this country they might well marvel at the foresight in another bit of almanac wisdom, "God gives all things to Industry." Be that as it may, the almanacs were close to the heart of colonial life when they reminded their readers of the virtues of frugality, enterprise, hard work, and self-reliance.

Discussion Clubs Still another important intellectual stimulus and encouragement to thoughtful reading came from the various clubs and societies whose members banded together for discussion. Many of these groups formed the nucleus of various subscription libraries. As early as 1683 Increase Mather and some of his friends created "a private philosophical society" which met bi-weekly for discussions "upon improvements in philosophy and additions to the stores of natural history." The most famous of the discussion societies was that founded by the young Franklin in 1727 when he brought together a small group of Philadelphia artisans and tradesmen of intellectual curiosity who formed the Leather Apron Club, later known as the Junto. Such clubs were not unusual, and this one was modeled after one of Cotton Mather's earlier Neighborhood Benefit Societies.

The Junto held regular meetings at taverns to explore questions of politics, morals, poetry, natural philosophy, and other matters. In Newport in 1730 the wealthy merchant Henry Collins founded the Society for the Promotion of Knowledge and Virtue by a Free Conversation, its twenty-four members meeting in their respective homes every Monday night "to converse about and debate some useful questions in Divinity, Morality, Philosophy, etc." Groups such as these were found in the major towns and even in the villages. There have always been a surprising number of people interested in the excitement of intellectual exchange in the midst of congenial and informal surroundings. It has been so since those distant days when individuals first settled down to less energetic pursuits than hunting and thus found time to speculate on the vanities and vexations of existence.

Literature and the Arts

Colonial Writing The colonists not only read and talked, they also wrote. The fabled hero of Jamestown, Captain John Smith, no sooner put down his sword than he picked up his pen, which he wielded with equal vigor. It is common to dismiss most of the colonial period as unproductive in literature. It had no ranking poets, no genuine novelists, no perceptive playwrights, no thoughtful essayists or literary critics. Of course there are not very many of these talented people in any age in any society, even the most sophisticated. And the odds were certainly against their appearance in a new society lacking the leisure and resources to support them and provide them with audiences. It was not a question of colonial writers being unable to make a living out of their writing. There have always been writers starving in garrets in established and relatively well-off societies who nevertheless wrote without cessation. Rather, colonial society itself could not afford individuals who spent all their time with pen and ink when other work needed to be done and other values had a higher priority. This does not mean that colonials did not write. Quite the contrary. But those who wrote were not professionals. They were people active in work that society urgently needed and who therefore wrote for purposes generally associated with their main practical interests and activities.

Colonials also of course wrote for private purposes. Many kept diaries and journals, an art and interest unfortunately no longer much practiced. Such personal records of daily happenings and private thoughts not only provide important avenues for understanding life in other times but help us to appreciate the universal humanity we share with men and women of the past. It is with wry amusement that we read Cotton Mather confiding to his diary in 1715 his views on the younger generation: "Oh, what a horrible Spectacle have I before me! A wicked, stupid, abominable Generation; every

Year growing rather worse." Mather's *Diary*, Winthrop's *Journal*, the *Diary of Samuel Sewall*, and the *Diaries* of William Byrd II are the most famous of the many that have survived from the colonial period.

Though by no means all that colonials wrote saw print—indeed many were called to their pens but few to the press—yet an extraordinary amount was published on matters of value to a new and growing society making its place in the wilderness. Thus accounts of what was happening or had happened, travel and geographical descriptions, promotional literature, and religious comment poured out in a steady stream.

This began with the first settlement, when John Smith published in London in 1608 his *True Relation . . . of Virginia*, a plain, unvarnished narrative of the events of the first few months at Jamestown. Smith's *Description of New England* (1616), based on his journey there, was a solid account of the region and its natural potential.

Although William Bradford's *Of Plymouth Plantation* was not published in full until the nineteenth century, its realistic and vivid account of the trials of the early Pilgrims marks it as narrative literature of the highest order. The earliest published account of the Pilgrims appeared in London in 1622, written by Bradford and Edward Winslow. Winslow followed this with his *Good News from New England*, and in 1634 William Wood's *New England's Prospects* excited much interest in England. New England writings such as these were designed not only to describe the natural aspects of the country and to emphasize the fruitfulness of the land and its attractions for settlers, but also to make it clear that God was watching over the faithful in this new land and promoting their endeavors. For over a hundred years after the first settlements in New England additional accounts of its founding and development, its trials and tribulations, were ground out, culminating in Cotton Mather's *Magnalia Christi Americana* (1702) and Thomas Prince's *A Chronological History of New England* (1736). Most of these accounts had as their dominant theme the conviction that New England was very high indeed on God's priority list. It was not until the eighteenth century was well along that histories of New England reflected a secular rather than a religious interpretation. William Douglas, for example, put out his two-volume *Summary, Historical and Political*, at mid-century, and Thomas Hutchinson, last royal governor of Massachusetts and more interested in scholarship than theology, brought out the first two volumes of his *History of the Colony of Massachusetts Bay* in the 1760s.

Elsewhere in the colonies accounts of development were not nearly as numerous as in New England, nor were their authors interested in proving God's will at work in the New World. William Smith wrote the only extensive account of New York (London, 1757), and the earliest comprehensive account of Virginia was Robert Beverley's *The History and Present State of Virginia* (1705). Dr. John Brickell published a history of North Carolina in 1737, and in 1741 a group of fugitive settlers from Georgia brought out a satirical view of that colony and its administration entitled *A True and Historical Narrative of the Colony of Georgia*.

The frontispiece of John Smith's The Generall Historie of Virginia, New-England, and the Summer Isles, published in 1624. It was in this book that Smith told the story of his capture by Indians and subsequent rescue from death by Pocahontas. The truth of that tale and Smith's veracity in general were a subject of much controversy, and he gained a considerable reputation for exaggeration.

Of special interest in narratives of life in the colonies was the North American Indian. Daniel Gookin wrote compassionately of the Indians in New England, an attitude not shared by William Hubbard, whose *A Narrative of the Troubles with the Indians in New England* (1677) took the view that the Indian was worthy only of annihilation. This was an attitude shared by Increase Mather and his son Cotton Mather, whose *History of Remarkable Occurrences in the Long War Which New England Hath Had with the Indian Savages from the Year 1688 to the Year 1698* has to be viewed with interest if for no other reason than that it called for the same treatment for invading Quakers as for rampaging Indians. Cadwallader Colden wrote a more objective account than most in his *History of the Five Indian Nations* (1727). And John Lawson's popular and readable *New Voyage to Carolina* (1709), describing explorations and adventures among the Indians, went through three editions. Lawson was burned at the stake by Indians in 1711—which should resolve the controversy about who were the first literary critics in America.

Probably the most delightful narrative of the colonial period was William Byrd II's *History of the Dividing Line Run in the Year 1728*, a title not at all suggestive of the urbanity and humor of its author. Not printed until the nineteenth century, the *Dividing Line* was the journal of an expedition to survey the boundary between Virginia and North Carolina, but Byrd's comments on his associates and the people he met and visited on the way are worldly, amusing, and revealing of the life of the times. Here is the account of his party's encounter in the backwoods with an eighteenth-century Adam and Eve:

> While we continued here, we were told that on the south shore, not far from the inlet, dwelt a marooner, that modestly called himself a hermit, though he forfeited that name by suffering a wanton female to cohabit with him. His habitation was a bower, covered with bark after the Indian fashion, which in that mild situation protected him pretty well from the weather. Like the ravens, he neither plowed nor sowed, but subsisted chiefly upon oysters, which his handmaiden made a shift to gather from the adjacent rocks. Sometimes, too, for change of diet, he sent her to drive up the neighbor's cows, to moisten their mouths with a little milk. But as for raiment, he depended mostly upon his length of beard, and she upon her length of hair, part of which she brought decently forward, and the rest dangled behind quite down to her rump, like one of Herodotus' East Indian pigmies. Thus did these wretches live in a dirty state of nature, and were mere Adamites, innocence only excepted.

Much descriptive writing in colonial America was promotional. The colonists everywhere were naturally inclined to persuade others to join them. This pattern was established early when the Virginia Company subsidized a glowing account of the Jamestown settlement. Even such accounts as Edward Johnson's *Wonder-Working Providence of Zion's Savior in New England* (1654), a history designed to show that the development of Massachusetts Bay rested upon God's special providence, clearly hinted that investment in the colony would be looked upon with favor by the Lord. Daniel Denton turned out a hack effort in 1670 called *A Brief Description of New York*, which was typical of the more obvious promotional pieces in its description of the colony as the proverbial land of milk and honey. And William Penn produced promotional tracts in three languages that convinced many that Pennsylvania was the earthly paradise. He had help from such as Gabriel Thomas and his *Historical and Geographical Account of . . . Pennsylvania and West New Jersey* which characterized Pennsylvania as the poor man's paradise. Thomas told his readers:

> What I have written here is not a Fiction, Flam, Whim or any sinister Design, either to impose upon the Ignorant, or Credulous, or to curry Favour with the Rich and Mighty, but in mere Pity and pure Compassion to the Numbers of Poor Labouring Men, Women, and Children in England, half starved, visible in their meagre looks, that are continually wandering up and down looking for Employment without finding any, who here need not lie idle for a moment, nor want due Encouragement or Reward for their Work.

Among the published writings of colonial America the sermon and other religious essays rank high in quantity, given the zeal and seemingly endless energy of Puritan divines. The father and son team of Increase and Cotton Mather brought out an astonishing six hundred titles between them. Religious controversy must have been cheerfully welcomed by printers since disputants had a tendency to think their arguments were further sanctified

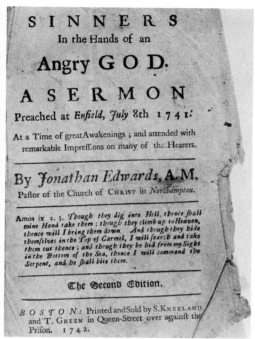

Jonathan Edwards and the frontispiece from one of his sermons. Edwards' interpretation of the experience of regeneration as both an intellectual and a mystical communion with God became the basis for the first revival and formed a powerful New England theology. Unfortunately, his insistence on a "sensible perceiving of the immediate power and operation of the Spirit of God" as the requirement for admission to the church clashed with the opinions of those in his parish who were accustomed to more flexible tests for election, and the controversy eventually concluded with his dismissal.

by appearing in print—a conviction not absent in our time or confined to theologians.

The finest religious writer of the period appeared in the wrong century, the eighteenth. Some people are indeed born too late, and one of these was Jonathan Edwards, who devoted his extraordinary intellect and talent as a writer to a futile attempt to restore, and in effect modernize, the Puritan theology of the early seventeenth century. His most famous pieces were the sermon *Sinners in the Hands of an Angry God* (1741) and the tract *A Careful and Strict Enquiry into . . . That Freedom of Will* (1754).

There was little in the colonies of literature for its own sake, but we do have the devotional verse of Anne Bradstreet, who is more popularly known today for her love poems to her husband, an example of which is the following verse:

> To my Dear and loving Husband
> I prize thy love more than whole Mines of gold
> Or all the riches that the East doth hold.
> My love is such that Rivers cannot quench,
> Nor aught but love from thee give recompense.

which may be a better example of wifely affection than of poetic talent.

Some modern readers might also hesitate to dignify Michael Wigglesworth's incredible best seller, *Day of Doom*, by calling it poetry. His grim descriptions of the fate of the sinner after judgment were designed to terrify the young into repentance:

> With Iron bands they bind their hands, and cursed feet together,
> And cast them all, both great and small, into that Lake for ever.
> Where day and night, without respite, they wail and cry, and howl
> For tort'ring pain, which they sustain in Body and in Soul.

Reading his endless verses and trying to realize the impact of terror he intended, one is reminded of the remark attributed to the Duke of Wellington as he reviewed his grim-visaged veterans before Waterloo: "I don't know whether they'll frighten the French, but by God, Sir, they frighten me!"

At any rate, it is a relief to turn to Edward Taylor (1644–1729), whose devotional poetry was left in manuscript and was not rediscovered and printed until the 1930s. To call Taylor a great poet would be to over-rate him, but he is certainly the one authentic poetic voice in the American wilderness. The first stanza of "The Joy of Church Fellowship Rightly Attended," the last two lines of which are repeated at the end of each stanza of the poem, suggests the depth of his feeling, his rapture, and his love of God:

> In Heaven soaring up, I dropt an Ear
>   On Earth: and oh! sweet Melody:
> And Listening found it was the Saints who were
>   Encoacht for Heaven that sang for Joy.
>   For in Christs Coach they sweetly sing
>   As they to Glory ride therein.

In the eighteenth century particularly a considerable amount of verse found its way into print, though mercifully a lot remained in manuscript. Most of it was clearly amateurish even if its moods were solemn—love of someone fair, death of a friend, pride in one's city. Colonial poetic endeavor climaxed with Thomas Godfrey's *The Prince of Parthia*, which has more historical than literary significance, being the first full-length verse play by an American to be performed professionally in this country (1767). Finally it should be noted that a great deal of the published verse appeared in newspapers, and much of this was simply amusing doggerel written hastily to

Captain Thomas Smith,
Self-Portrait.

make a point, such as the following, which was a response to a published plea for temperance:

> There's but one Reason I can think,
> Why People ever cease to drink.
> Sobriety the cause is not,
> Nor Fear of being deam'd a Sot,
> But if Liquor can't be got.

Painting and the Decorative Arts   Just as there was no literary class in America, so there was no artist class. For the vast majority of Americans, therefore, artistic pleasures were limited and simple. But the urge to see oneself on the wall in something besides a mirror, or to have a record of one's estate more colorful than an account book, is great indeed. Thus by the later seventeenth century, men of social and economic substance were having their portraits painted. The growing prosperity of the eighteenth century saw the practice widespread. Many colonial portraits were done in England by unknown painters who worked from written descriptions. Others were done in the colonies by journeymen craftsmen, engravers, house painters, sign painters, and the like. Occasionally visiting painters from Britain or the Continent, men of some skill if not talent, painted their way through the colonies—sometimes, like the Swiss Jeremiah Theus, settling down to make a living by his brush, as a *South Carolina Gazette* advertisement of 1740 proclaims:

> Notice is hereby given that Jeremiah Theus, limner, is removed into the Market Square near Mr. John Maurens, sadler, where all gentlemen and ladies

Westover, the home of William Byrd. Byrd was one of the most prominent of a group of successful Virginia tobacco planters and traders, and Westover was typical of the enormous and gracious homes they built for themselves along the James River.

may have their pictures drawn, likewise landskips of all sizes, crests and coats of arms for coaches or chaises. Likewise for the conveniency of those who live in the country, he is willing to wait on them at their respective plantations.

Among the upper classes, too, there was a tendency to import paintings both portrait and landscape from England as well as prints and etchings, although the desire to impress one's neighbors, rather than taste, seems often to have governed their selection.

Though art shops were found in the major cities where painting materials, engravings, and prints were sold, and instruction in drawing and painting could be obtained as well, no real professionalism was possible. The two colonials of real artistic talent who appeared on the scene late in the colonial period, Benjamin West and John Singleton Copley, both ended in England where a long-established society and tradition could support and nourish their talents.

The most extensive and enduring colonial achievement in the fine arts came in architecture. There were no professional architects, although in the eighteenth century Peter Harrison of Newport, Rhode Island, came as close to being a professional talent as it was possible to come and still remain a gentleman. His Redwood Library, Jewish Synagogue, Freemason Hall, and Brick Market in Newport, and his Christ Church in Cambridge, Massachusetts, have all been hailed as remarkable achievements.

Design for both private and public buildings was a matter for the gentleman amateur or the master carpenter who acquired considerable skill in use of the various architectural manuals imported from England. The surprising thing is not that monstrosities came from this practice, but that there were so many strikingly handsome residential and public buildings. Following the English lead, design favored an adaptation of the classical style known as Georgian, such as represented by the State House in Philadelphia, or Westover, the home of William Byrd in Virginia.

In the years of transition from the rough, crude days of early settlement in the early seventeenth century to the more established and affluent life of towns and plantations in the late eighteenth century, the construction and design of buildings reflected a combination of environmental conditions, utility, and European example. The first settlements at Jamestown were huts made of boughs, bark, sod, and thatch. Similar shelters were built by the first arrivals in New England, but there severe weather forced settlers to more substantial frame buildings of familiar European design, although clapboard was early added as further protection against the cold. The log dwelling, unknown to the English, was familiar to the Swedes and later to the Germans, and was picked up in the eighteenth century by the Scotch-Irish who saw its practical value and made the log cabin a familiar sight on the frontier. Wood was the chief building material because it was so readily available, although by the end of the seventeenth century brickmaking had become common, and in the towns brick buildings were fairly numerous.

By the eighteenth century houses began to reflect a growing prosperity and sophistication. Windows became larger and of clear glass, doorways were larger and often decorative, fireplaces acquired mantels, walls were often plastered or paneled, and scenic wallpaper made its appearance.

Changing conditions also wrought a change in the useful or decorative arts as applied to furniture and utensils. Throughout much of the seventeenth century, colonials crudely fashioned most of their own furniture and implements, using the wood available everywhere, and on the frontier this continued to be true in the eighteenth century. But town and city dwellers finally protested against meager interiors. Happily a growing prosperity brought into being a body of skilled colonial craftsmen who, using the manuals of famed English cabinetmakers and silversmiths as well as their own imaginations, produced large numbers of beautiful and well-made desks, chests, sideboards, chairs, tables, coffee- and tea-pots, flat silver, and other pieces. Elegant design and fine workmanship gave the best creations of the period a classic beauty and a value that has increased enormously, as anyone knows who has visited any of the major museums of the country where much of this work is now on permanent display.

Although growing affluence made possible the importation of furniture from abroad as well as of woods not native to the colonies, the skill of American craftsmen and familiar American woods answered most of the practical and aesthetic needs of the colonists. And indeed an American, Duncan Phyfe, became one of the greatest furniture designers of the time. Likewise American silversmiths, such as Paul Revere, became so numerous and so skilled that they ended by providing a great deal of the tableware and utensils found in the wealthier colonial homes.

All told, in architecture and the various useful arts, the colonial achievement was considerable. Colonists by the eighteenth century were seeking, if not always finding, aesthetic excellence in their homes and furnishings. Adapting older designs and styles to a new environment, they tended to move in the direction of simplicity and clarity of design that has great appeal to modern eyes. Artistic achievement that reflects the character and belief of the people producing it always carries real conviction. People today, for example, who stand before one of New England's many harmonious churches, or before Westover in Virginia, are unable to escape the feeling that they are looking at something brought into being by individuals who had confidence in themselves and faith in their lives, and that their strength of character and love of beauty surely lie there interred in timber, brick, and mortar.

The Theater   Although behind them in England lay a rich tradition of theater, a gap in that tradition and the absence of a developed urban life in the seventeenth century meant that the performing arts found no fertile ground in which to strike roots. Moreover, the Puritans as well as the Quakers took a dim view of actors and stage plays. But by the opening of the eighteenth century a change in attitude and circumstance began. Strolling players made their first appearance in the colonies, "full of lice, shame, poverty, nakedness, and hunger," as one of them reported. The first theater of record appeared in Williamsburg in 1716 in conjunction with a dancing school. Community and college amateur performances began to appear in the South by the 1730s, and within two decades two professional troupes came to the colonies, the first headed by Thomas Kean and Walter Murray and the second by Lewis Hallam and his wife. These companies frequently encountered difficulties with the authorities in the Middle and New England colonies but found the relaxed atmosphere of the South more congenial. The plays of Addison, Steele, Congreve, Shakespeare, Dryden, and others proved popular with audiences, although people had constantly to be reassured that they would be offered nothing "indecent and immoral."

In New England laws against the performance of plays were evaded by proclaiming them to be moral dialogues, a subterfuge that failed to deceive the pious citizens of Providence, Rhode Island, who attacked the company of Hallam's successor, David Douglas, and were restrained only by John Brown, who rolled up a cannon in front of the theater and threatened to fire if the mob molested the players. In 1766 Douglas built the first permanent colonial theater in Philadelphia, and from this base his company toured the principal towns and assured the theater a place in American life.

Nancy Hallam in the cave scene from Cymbeline. *Miss Hallam was painted by Charles Willson Peale in 1771 during a return engagement to Annapolis, Maryland.*

America and the European Enlightenment

Educated and inquiring Americans were by no means outside the mainstream of Western intellectual development, notably the Englightenment. A number of colonial Americans made important contributions to scientific knowledge. In natural history, Americans played a role in the discovery, description, and classification of the varied and often new flora and fauna of the New World, passing on their findings to the Royal Society in London. There was a steady rise in the number of European publications acknowledging such American contributions. The most respected name was that of the American Quaker, John Bartram. John Frederick Gronovius of Leyden, preparing a new edition of one of his works, wrote to Bartram: "You shall find therein the names of all the minerals and fossils you ever sent me, with . . . thanks of all the benefits you have bestowed upon me." Cadwallader Colden's scientific catalogue of the plants on his New York estate appeared in the transactions of the Academy of Sciences at Uppsala in Sweden, and when the Englishman George Edwards published his *Natural History of Uncommon Birds* in the middle of the eighteenth century, he expressed his debt to colonial studies in ornithology. Americans of a scientific turn of mind studied and sent abroad their descriptions of such diverse phenomena of the natural world as fossils, comets, cyclonic storms, whales, the moose, and the migration of pigeons. When a German bibliographer near the end of the eighteenth century compiled a list of Anglo-American authors of repute, including students of science, the list contained the names of some three hundred Americans, many of them from the colonial period.

A rising interest in science among eighteenth-century Americans was paralleled by an expanding interest in other aspects of the European Enlightenment. The belief in a rational, well-ordered world, capable of being understood by the application of reason and knowledge, affected the thought of those American colonists who read the writings of the great European thinkers. It was rationalism, for example, that led a number of colonial clergymen, including Jonathan Mayhew of Boston, to reject the ideas of predestination and the total depravity of humanity, and to challenge the doctrine of the Trinity itself. And it was rationalism that led Charles Chauncy in his *Beneficence of the Deity* to argue that God was a rational being whose essential goodness was reflected in nature and in humanity. The conviction of enlightened thought that an individual through reason and knowledge could uncover the laws of nature and society led intellectually curious colonists to study not only the natural world but the social, economic, and political worlds as well. For through such knowledge they could better control their destinies and improve themselves and society. It was this conviction that brought about in the eighteenth century a gradual infusion of new studies into colonial college curricula, especially history, economics, and social theory, and prompted considerable American writing on agriculture, trade, taxation, and currency. It is significant that Franklin wrote in favor of free trade as opposed to the then-popular doctrine of mercantilism because it seemed to him a much more *natural* economic system. He wrote in 1766 that "It seems contrary to the Nature of Commerce for Government to interfere in the prices of commodities."

Humanitarian sentiment—the concern for the downtrodden and the unfortunate—was also a part of enlightened belief. If human beings were essentially good and if improvement in individual and social conditions was indeed possible, then such conditions as slavery, the unhappy fate of the handicapped, and the miserable treatment of the wretch in prison were unreasonable and unnatural and need not be endured. The Englishman William Wollaston had written that "There is something in human nature resulting from our very make and constitution, which renders us obnoxious to the pains of others, causes us to sympathize with them, and almost comprehend us in their case." American Quakers particularly, although others as well, responded to this sentiment and were thus found aiding the poor, arguing against slavery, and seeking to ease the harsh criminal code and to improve the treatment of prisoners.

Of the greatest importance in enlightened thought was the philosophy of natural rights. In this view all individuals originally lived in a state of nature, possessing the same natural rights and being governed by the same natural laws—the rights to life, liberty, property, and happiness. But under natural conditions, in which individuals protected their own rights by themselves, the strong would take advantage of the weak. Therefore people banded together to institute government, in the form of the social contract, in order to protect their rights. In doing so they gave up not the natural rights themselves but only the right to protect them individually. Implicit in this concept of the origin of government were the ideas of government by the consent of the governed, popular sovereignty, and the right of revolution. For John Locke had written that if government infringed upon or failed to protect people's natural rights, then

> by this breech of trust they forfeit the power the people had put into their hands ... and it devolves to the people who have a right to resume their original liberty, and by the establishment of a new legislative (such as they shall think fit) provide for their own safety and security, which is the end for which they are in society.

Educated colonists were familiar with this philosophy, and were not averse to referring to it when necessary. It had been used to justify the overthrow in New York of the regime of Governor Edmund Andros in 1689; it was used by John Wise at the beginning of the eighteenth century to defend the traditional Congregational form of church government against Presbyterianism; and it was used by the Reverend Jonathan Mayhew of Boston on the one hundredth anniversary of the execution of Charles I to defend the execution. Mayhew's sermon was to be remembered and reprinted on the eve of the Revolution.

So the American colonists, while not at the intellectual center of the Enlightenment, were familiar with the writings and work of the Europeans who were. Although the average settler was no reader of Newton or Locke, yet the educated colonist who did read them belonged to that group of Americans who constituted the basic leadership of the country. It is also clear that American contributions to the thought of the day, from Mayhew's sermons to Franklin's experiments with electricity and Benezet's pamphlets denouncing slavery, were read by Europeans and provided an image of an America that was far from isolated and provincial.

It must also be remembered that in Europe there was enormous interest in America in general in the eighteenth century, an interest that saw colonial society not as a primitive backwater but as a society of advanced views, with an experimental atmosphere and notable achievement. Europeans flooded their American friends—especially Franklin—with schemes for social and economic reform, with the hope that these could be tried in America "where old prejudices do not exist." The spirit of religious toleration, and the skepticism toward established churches that generally prevailed in the colonies by the eighteenth century, attracted the attention of dissenting and minority sects abroad and stiffened their own resolve. Voltaire made frequent references to Pennsylvania as that "land unique in the world," noted for its civil liberty and toleration; and once he even indicated that he would like to end his days there: "A man can, for a dozen guineas, acquire a hundred acres of very good land; and on these hundred acres he is in truth a king, for he is free and he is a citizen." In short, the colonies as a whole were by the middle of the eighteenth century far from being isolated from the interests and ideas of the Western world. In many ways they had come of age.

Profile: BENJAMIN FRANKLIN

Benjamin Franklin was so rare a man, so broad in his talents, so complex in personality, so varied in interests, so successful in all he turned his efforts to that he has to be approached, as someone has written, not as a single man but as a syndicate: businessman, printer, economist, wit and humorist, writer, civic leader, humanitarian, scientist, inventor, diplomat, and statesman.

Though unusual and even perhaps unique, Franklin was also a representative man. He was representative of the new society in America and by the time of his death in 1790, of a new age in the life of the Western world—the age of merit rather than of privilege. His European friend, Baptiste Le Roy, said of him: "In Paris, that great man under the ancient regime would have remained in obscurity, for how could one have put to use the son of a candlemaker?" So in the age of the democratic revolutions, he served as symbol of a new order in which eminence is based not upon the privilege of birth but upon talent and service to mankind. Franklin once remarked on this as characteristic of the Americans: they "do not inquire concerning a Stranger, What is he? but, What can he do?"

Shrewd, practical, energetic, ambitious, full of common sense, inquiring of mind, Franklin came as a young man to Philadelphia from Boston where he had been born in 1706. Before he was thirty, he was a highly successful printer and the publisher of the Gazette, of books, pamphlets, government documents and money, and of Poor Richard's Almanack. The success of the Almanack rested upon the "Sayings of Poor Richard"—"God helps them that help themselves," "Early to bed and early to rise makes a man healthy, wealthy and wise," "A penny saved is a pound earned"—utilitarian virtues reflecting a society open and fluid in its economic and social opportunities to those who by their own effort could find "The Way to Wealth."

A successful businessman, Franklin did not regard economic advancement as an end in itself but as a means to other goals, and he never accorded to private economic endeavor that divine sanction which gave it precedence over everything else: "Private property . . . is the creature of society, and is subject to the call of that society whenever its necessities shall require, even to its last farthing."

Following his own advice without regret, as few of us do, he retired at age forty-two so that he might, as he put it, live usefully rather than die rich. He passed with honors. His usefulness to Philadelphia, to Pennsylvania, to the colonies, and to mankind was almost beyond measure.

He believed that the best way to worship God was to do good to other men. To keep in condition for such a life he drew up a list of what he called the useful virtues—Temperance, Silence, Order, Resolution, Frugality, Industry, Sincerity, Justice, Moderation, Cleanliness, Tranquillity, Chastity—adding Humility when a friend looked over the list and told him he was too proud of himself. But Franklin humorously noted that he took up these virtues only one at a time for a week each, going through a thirteen-week "course" of self-improvement four times a year.

His interest in the world about him and his desire to put knowledge to work for the improvement of mankind embodied the spirit of the Age of Enlightenment, but few could approach the breadth of his investigations. He studied the nature of earthquakes, discovered that northeast storms on the Atlantic coast moved against the wind, made observations on linseed oil, hemp land, the draining of swamps, variations in climate, the cause of springs on mountains, sea-shell rocks, grass seed, the value of fresh air to good health, the connection between smoke and pulmonary complaints—among other subjects. He introduced various American plants into Europe, brought Scotch kale, Swiss barley, and Chinese rhubarb into America, and familiarized Americans with pulverized gypsum as a fertilizer. And of course in his famous experiments on electricity, his single fluid theory made understandable the phenomenon of electricity and stimulated the experiments of Priestley and others. His urge to make knowledge useful led to such things as the lightning rod, the Franklin stove which circulated heated air, bifocal glasses, and other practicalities. He was a member of the Royal Society of London, the leading scientific organization of the day, and he founded the American Philosophical Society for the exchange of "useful knowledge." His zest for the expansion and use of knowledge led him to make the first suggestions on the value of education in agricultural science, to help found the academy which ultimately became the University of Pennsylvania, to establish the Junto, a society of tradesmen devoted to self-improvement by reading and discussion, to help form the first subscription library, and to teach himself French, Spanish, Italian, and Latin.

Philadelphia, Pennsylvania, and the other colonies had cause to be thankful for his shrewd and speculative mind. He helped found the Pennsylvania Hospital. He initiated projects for the establishment of city police and fire departments. He promoted the paving and better lighting and cleaning of streets, and organized an efficient postal system for all the colonies. Franklin organized the Philadelphia militia and later the defenses of Pennsylvania in the French and Indian War. He proposed in 1754 the most sensible plan for union among the colonies prior to the Constitution, and served for years in London where he explained and defended the colonies in parliamentary testimony, in some 133 articles in London newspapers, and by innumerable reprints of colonial letters and pamphlets which poured out of his office in a stream suggesting a freshman Congressman who has just discovered the delights of the franking system. He wrote learnedly, and in some cases prophetically, on such subjects as paper money, free trade, population growth, and

*Electricity game. Franklin's fascination with electricity began with an
"electric tube" sent to the Philadelphia Library by Peter Collinson. He spent
several months experimenting with the gadget and then reported to
Collinson his extensive results. His later experiments with the Leyden jar
and with his kite established his reputation in the field. In addition to the
serious scientific work being done with electricity there was some whimsy as
well, like this game.*

slavery. "Providence," he once observed, "seems to require various duties of me."
And there was more to come: his service to the Revolution and to the forming of
the new nation under the Constitution.

Arriving in France in December 1776 as agent of the revolutionary government,
he played the crucial role in gaining essential French support for the Revolution.
In the process he became, not only to the French but to much of Europe, a symbol
of America and what it represented. His influence was enormous. John Adams, a
man not given to exaggeration, especially in regard to Franklin, summed up from
personal observation Franklin's impact on France and Europe:

> His reputation was more universal than that of Leibnitz or Newton, Frederick or
> Voltaire, and his character more beloved and esteemed than any or all of them. . . . His
> name was familiar to government and people, to kings, courtiers, nobility, clergy, and
> philosophers, as well as plebians, to such a degree that there was scarcely a peasant or a
> citizen, a valet de chambre, coachman or footman, a lady's chambermaid or a scullion

in a kitchen, who was not familiar with it, and who did not consider him as a friend to human kind. When they spoke of him, they seemed to think he was to restore the golden age.

Nine years later he returned home, older still, revered beyond all others, and his duties not yet over. He was elected governor of Pennsylvania; and in 1787 was sent to the Constitutional Convention. His prestige, his reputation, and his common sense, which never deserted him, aided greatly in the final achievement of the Constitution itself.

No one has better summed up this extraordinary American, capturing so well his breadth and his essential humanity, than the historian Carl Becker many years ago when he wrote:

> Not only was Franklin by temperament disposed to take life as it came, to make the most of it; in addition, fate provided him with a rich diversity of experience such as has rarely fallen to the lot of any man. Rising from poverty to affluence, from obscurity to fame, he lived on every social level in turn, was equally at ease with rich and poor, the cultivated and the untutored, and spoke with equal facility the language of vagabonds and kings, politicians and philosophers, men of letters, kitchen girls, and femmes savantes. Reared in Boston, a citizen of Philadelphia, residing for sixteen years in London and nine in Paris, he was equally at home in three countries, knew Europe better than any American, America better than any European, England better than most Frenchmen, France better than most Englishmen, and was acquainted personally or through correspondence with more men of eminence in letters, science and politics than any other man of his time. Such a variety of experience would have confused and disoriented any man less happily endowed with a capacity for assimilating it. Franklin took it all easily, relishing it, savoring it, without rest and without haste adding to his knowledge, fortifying and tempering his intelligence, broadening his point of view, humanizing and mellowing his tolerant acceptance of men and things—in short chastening and perfecting the qualities that were natively his; so that in the end he emerges the most universal and cosmopolitan spirit of his age. Far more "a good European," a citizen of the world, than Adams or Jefferson, Washington or Hutchinson, he remained to the end more pungently American than any of them. . . . Twenty-five years of almost continuous residence abroad did not spoil Franklin. Acclaimed and decorated as no American had ever been, he returned to Philadelphia and was immediately home again, easily recognizable by his neighbors as the man they had always known—Ben Franklin, printer.

Chapter 5
THE AMERICAN REVOLUTIONARY EXPERIENCE: 1763–1789

The Spirit of the Times
MORE AMERICAN THAN EUROPEAN

By 1763 the population of the thirteen colonies had grown to over 1.6 million, occupying an area far larger than Britain and steadily expanding westward. This population explosion had wrought profound changes in American life. It meant increased production in agriculture, industry, and trade, as well as increased demand for services of all kinds. This greatly increased wealth contributed to the development of culture and a significant urban life. Such changes gave the colonists a confidence and self-assurance absent in the seventeenth century, and provided them in their economic and social life, in their thought, and in the conduct of their political affairs with a maturity and sense of independence they could not have dreamed of a hundred or even fifty years earlier. Thus the colonists entered the last third of the eighteenth century with characteristics, patterns of association, habits of mind, attitudes, and ways of doing things that made them quite different from their British elders. This sense of difference prompted The American Magazine to proclaim in 1759 that "A new world has arisen, and it will exceed the old." John Adams echoed this sentiment when he wrote in 1765 that "I always consider the settlement of America with reverence and wonder, as the opening of a grand scene and design of Providence for the illumination of the ignorant, and the emancipation of the slavish part of mankind all over the earth."

What were the differences that prompted this sense of mission and that underlay colonial maturity? The sense of social equality, which led a British official to observe in 1760 that in America "all mortifying distinctions of rank are lost in common equality," was one such difference. So, too, was the absence of a single

The Capitol in Williamsburg, Virginia, seat of the House of Burgesses.
Established in 1619 and persisting in its function of carrying on the
legislative affairs of the colony despite the continued opposition of the king,
the House of Burgesses was the first representative assembly in the colonies.

dominant established church and clergy, protected by law and enjoying privileges and power. But the major distinctions were political. Abundance had opened wide the door to independent ownership of land, and thus created a large electorate on which rested a representative system that responded directly to the interests of the voters. In Massachusetts, for instance, the practice had developed in town meetings of voting instructions to their representatives in the colonial assembly. As one town wrote to its representative, "It is our inalienable right to tell you our sentiments. . . . We expect you will hold yourself bound at all times to attend to and observe them." In England, on the other hand, the electorate was very small, being confined principally to well-to-do landowners of the upper class, and the members of Parliament could hardly pretend to be elected by or be responsible to all the people of their districts. Thus each member claimed to represent not a particular area but rather the country as a whole. Whatever Parliament did, therefore, was presumably in the interests of the entire nation. The developing British experience was to define the Constitution as the total body of the laws of the land, thus centering all power in the hands of Parliament.

But this constitutional development was not what occurred in the colonies. There, the granting by the King of charters as the legal basis for the colonial governments—a practice paralleled in the early years by the Puritan covenant that bound the members of both church and community together under the laws of God and man—tended to make the Americans regard constitutions as written documents clearly defining the powers of government and the rights of individuals. In the past the colonists had often invoked these charters in their struggles to run their own affairs.

This difference in view was very great. It was noted in 1760 by Governor Bernard of Massachusetts, who wrote to the Secretary of War in London: "In Britain, the American governments are considered as Corporations empowered to make by-laws, existing only during the pleasure of Parliament. In America they claim . . . to be perfect States, not otherwise dependent upon Great Britain than by having the same King." And James Otis of Massachusetts asserted that "To say the Parliament is absolute and arbitrary is a contradiction. . . . The Constitution is fixed; and . . . the supreme legislative . . . cannot overlap the Bounds of it without destroying its own foundation."

In the realm of government, there were other divergences as well. In the eighteenth century Britain moved in the direction of ministerial government in which the executive or cabinet of ministers came directly from the Parliament, thus preventing a distinct separation of powers between the executive and the legislative. In America, no such tradition developed. The executive was the King represented in absentia by the governors, and the colonial experience of struggle between governors and legislatures was to lead later to sharply defined and separated powers for each.

These differences were part and parcel of the maturity that the colonies had acquired by 1763. The central fact of this maturity was that for over a century the colonies had for the most part run their own affairs and made the key decisions that affected their lives from day to day and year to year. Separated by three thousand miles of ocean from a Britain which had long had its hands full at home and in Europe, the colonies passed through a long period of what Edmund Burke was to call "salutary neglect." The colonists compensated for this neglect by doing things for themselves.

On the local level, the town governments of New England and the parish and county governments of the South had long placed in local hands the daily work of government that most affected the lives of ordinary people. Though such government tended to remain in the hands of families who were better off than their neighbors, there was an intimate and confident relationship between people and officials, and the kind of experience acquired in service as a local official often proved a passport to higher office within the colonies.

In all colonies the basic political institution was the colonial assembly. From the beginning, as these legislative assemblies came into being on the model of the British House of Commons, they steadily extended their power and influence. On paper the governors, appointed by the Crown or by the proprietors, had powers much like those of the King. They executed the laws, appointed numerous officials, called the assemblies into session or dismissed them, proposed legislation, and could veto colonial laws. But as the assemblies acquired financial power, including the right to set the governor's salary, and as they acquired a powerful sense of their own interest, they simply overrode any real exertion of authority by the governors.

Moreover, these assemblies, though they tended everywhere to be dominated by members of the upper class, possessed a popular mandate. They were the most democratically constituted in the Western world. Those who served in them had to compete for votes to gain office, and they enjoyed the general confidence of the people in their leadership. In 1774 when Benjamin Harrison was setting out to represent Virginia at the First Continental Congress, a number of his neighbors waited upon him and their spokesman said: "You assert that there is a fixed intention to invade our rights and privileges; we own that we do not see this clearly, but since you assure us that it is so, we believe the fact. We are about to take a very dangerous step, but we confide in you, and are ready to support you in every measure you shall think proper to adopt."

The degree to which the colonial assemblies ran their own affairs is indicated by the fact that only five percent of colonial laws were vetoed by the British government. Moreover, the assemblies saw their political tie to Britain running directly to the King, and not to Parliament; they were the parliaments for the colonies. As early as 1759, Andrew Burnaby, a visitor from England, had observed of Virginia's rulers: "They are haughty and jealous of their liberties, impatient of restraint, and can scarcely bear the thought of being controlled by a superior power. Many of them consider the colonies as independent states, unconnected with Great Britain, otherwise than by having the same common king and being bound to her with natural affection." This observation applied with equal validity to other colonies.

While the colonists developed their own bodies of power, the British had no parallel institutions of rule and authority in the colonies. The British official class in America was small, its members wished to get along in their jobs, to enjoy the pleasures of office and of association with the local aristocracy, to make money, and to return home. The armed forces were small and scattered, and their presence was rarely felt, often to the considerable annoyance of colonists who wondered where the troops were when rampaging Indians were about. British colonial administration in London was scattered, decentralized, and unspecialized—there were no offices or civil servants trained in and dealing solely with American affairs. The vast majority of the colonists, therefore, lived out their lives untouched in any visible way by British authority, and it was only natural that they should turn to their own leaders and expect them to handle the practical problems of land, Indian troubles, currency, trade regulations, taxes, and the like. And this they did, in the towns and counties and in the colonial assemblies.

The importance the colonists attached to running their own affairs, to their political life as the key to all other areas of life, was best expressed by John Adams as the colonists entered upon the course of Revolution:

> I must study politics and war, that my sons may have liberty to study mathematics and philosophy, geography, natural history and naval architecture, navigation, commerce and agriculture, in order to give their children a right to study painting, poetry, music, architecture, statuary, tapestry and porcelin.

It is clear that by 1763 a new and mature society had come into being in the New World constructed out of basic English and European materials but, under the impact of its own experiences, now more American than European.

The Coming of the War

By 1763, at the close of the great war for an American empire that the British had won against the French, the British set out to reorganize their vast possessions, to provide for their orderly administration, and to put their finances on a sound footing. They provided for a standing army in North America of ten thousand troops, set up governments for Canada, Florida, and their new territories in the Caribbean, retained for the Crown all lands

An allegorical representation of the surrender of Quebec. The verse celebrates the victory of General James Wolfe over the Marquis de Montcalm during the siege of Quebec during the French and Indian War. The war lasted from 1754 to 1763, originating with hostilities between the French Canadians, who built Fort Duquesne on the Ohio River, and the Virginia colonists, who had claimed that territory as their own. The conflict eventually developed into a struggle between France and Britain for control of the continent.

west of the Alleghenies and closed them to settlement and unlicensed trade, extended to all colonies the ban on paper currency, and ordered customs officials to enforce the laws and the Royal Navy to support them.

Irksome New Regulations   In 1764 Parliament passed the Sugar Act, which taxed many items besides sugar, and was designed to provide at least half the revenue needed to support the foregoing measures. In 1765 it passed

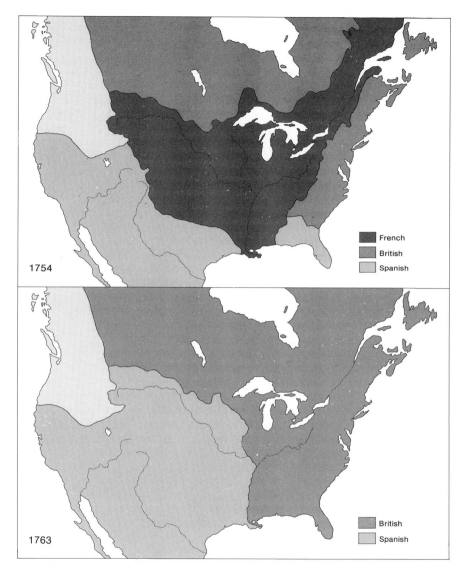

1754

French
British
Spanish

1763

British
Spanish

COLONIAL POSSESSIONS

the Stamp Act to raise the rest of the needed revenue. This act required the purchase of stamps for public documents and transactions of all sorts—liquor licenses, wills, advertisements, contracts, and the like. These taxes struck at every colony, affecting particularly the articulate and influential in each.

The colonists saw these new measures and the taxes designed to support them as a threat to their established way of doing things. To many the proposals seemed designed to halt colonial growth, to reverse the process of political maturity, and to erase those characteristics that identified the colonists as American—particularly since these proposals came from a Parliament accused of corruption and decadence and dominated by a nobility and clergy who were hostile to the equality, tolerance, and liberty that the colonists saw as their natural style.

Protest to the Stamp Act was widespread and often violent. Andrew Oliver, who had been appointed stamp distributor in Boston, was burned in effigy, his office was destroyed and his home wrecked, and he preserved his own good health only by fleeing to the sanctuary of the royal fort in Boston Harbor. Similar actions elsewhere, or the threat of them, brought the resignation of those appointed in the other colonies. The colonists refused to buy the stamps, and nearly a thousand merchants signed nonimportation agreements which struck heavily at the pocketbooks of British merchants as trade fell off sharply. The British repealed the act in March of 1766, but on the same day made clear where they believed authority rested by passing the Declaratory Act, which asserted that Parliament could pass any law it pleased "to bind the colonies and people of America . . . in all cases whatsoever."

Reflecting this belief, the government on the advice of Charles Townshend, the new Chancellor of the Exchequer, then levied new taxes on a variety of goods imported into the colonies—glass, tea, paint, lead, and paper. These duties were designed not only to raise revenue, but to eliminate smuggling, and these provisions weakened colonial authority and rights. A special resident Board of Customs Commissioners for America was established with responsibility for the collection of duties and the enforcement of trade laws. Special courts were set up in key ports to try those accused of violating the new acts and to do so without a jury or the normal protection of common law. General search warrants were authorized as aids to enforcement. Revenues derived from the duties were to be used to pay the salaries of governors, judges, and other officials. This measure effectively broke the financial, and hence political, hold of the colonial assemblies on the royal governors.

Subsequent opposition and protest encouraged by the Massachusetts legislature prompted the British to dispatch two regiments of troops to Boston. Their presence, as sometimes happens when soldiers are set down amidst civilians, led to a series of incidents that in March of 1770 culminated in a clash known as the Boston Massacre. At the same time the British government repealed all the Townshend duties except that on tea, which was still in effect in 1773 when the government, faced with another problem in its far-flung empire, decided to save the East India Company from bankruptcy by allowing it to bypass both British and American wholesalers and sell its tea directly through its own agents in the colonies. This decision gave a legal monopoly to a single company, and suggested that if the British could do this with one product they could do it with any other. The colonial response was the famous Boston Tea Party in which a group of disguised colonists boarded three tea ships and dumped their cargoes into Boston Harbor. This act of defiance followed by only a few months the affair of the *Gaspee,* a British naval vessel that had run aground in Rhode Island while chasing a suspected smuggler and had then been set upon and burned by an irate band of colonists.

British troops landing in Boston, 1768, a line engraving colored by Paul Revere.

The Intolerable Acts These illegal actions broke the back of British patience, and prompted the government to retaliate with the so-called Coercive, or Intolerable Acts, designed to bring the colonies to heel once and for all and to settle the matter of who ruled America. "The die is now cast," said the King. "The Colonies must either submit or triumph." The Coercive Acts were directed only at Massachusetts, but they created outrage everywhere, rallied the other colonies to her support, brought into being the First Continental Congress, and led directly to war and independence.

The Coercive Acts included the Boston Port Bill, which threatened the very livelihood of the city, cutting off all trade except supplies for troops and such food and fuel as was approved by customs officials, and the Quartering Act, which allowed private homes to be commandeered for soldiers. But the most significant act in terms of revealing British intentions was the Massachusetts Governing Act, which reordered the entire government of that colony and so altered its machinery and processes that the colonists were no longer able to run their own affairs. The act was a fundamental challenge to the institutions that had been developed by the colonists over several generations. The governor's council, previously elected by the lower house, would now be appointed by the King. On recommendation of the governor, so would the judges of Massachusetts' highest court. All judges, in fact, including justices of the peace, were to be appointed by the governor. So too the attorney general and the sheriffs. The sheriffs, now controlled by the governor, would summon juries and thus control their composition. Except

America in Flames, *1774, a wood engraving depicting the Intolerable Acts fanning the flames of American dissent.*

for the annual town meeting electing local officials, town meetings were forbidden. Additional ones could be called only with the governor's approval and could deal only with matters to which he had given his approval. The power of Massachusetts men to run their own affairs was flatly denied. By destroying the old charter of 1691 with this act, Parliament had made it clear that it did not regard such charters as the foundation of government and the rights of citizens in the colonies. It was only natural for those in other colonies to feel that if this was Massachusetts' fate today, it could be theirs tomorrow.

Indeed, to many it appeared that Parliament was bent on reversing the very course of government in the colonies, an opinion many colonists believed to be substantiated by Lord North's remarks that "the democratic part" of the Massachusetts charter was too strong. Lord George Germain had been even more blunt: "I would wish to bring the constitution of America as similar to our own as possible."

On the same day that the Massachusetts Governing Act was passed, Parliament also passed the Quebec Act, another disaster in the view of the

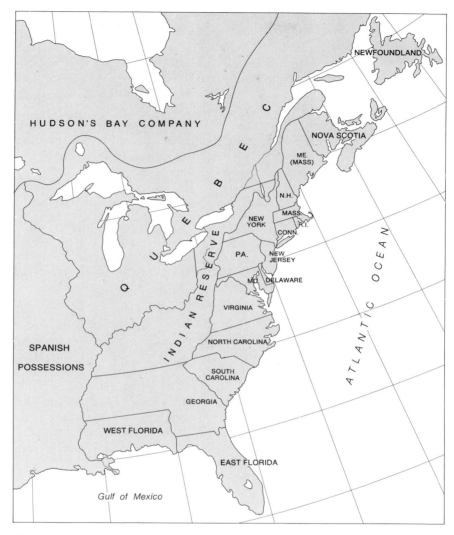

BOUNDARIES ESTABLISHED BY THE QUEBEC ACT

American colonists. The Quebec Act was not properly a part of the Coercive Acts, but was so regarded by the colonists. Intended to define the government of that part of Canada won from the French, the act recognized the Catholic Church and retained the basic pattern of French government. This meant an appointed rather than elected legislature, trials without jury in accordance with French civil law, and French feudal land-tenure laws. What shocked the American colonists was the definition of Quebec's boundaries to include the Old Northwest, that frontier territory comprising what is now Ohio, Indiana, Illinois, and Michigan. For this action not only challenged claims by various colonies to this territory as set forth in their charters, but turned over an important area of the western frontier to settlement and control by a government and a state-supported church under procedures hostile to the colonial tradition of land settlement and development.

These acts were accompanied by the dispatch of additional regiments of British troops to Boston and the appointment of General Gage as Governor of Massachusetts. In effect, Massachusetts had had its government abrogated and was under martial law.

These developments do not of course tell the full story of the growing crisis between mother country and colonies. But they indicate that if the British were to have their way, government and society in America would be turned away from their democratic course, and Old World aristocratic and authoritarian influences, heretofore largely absent, would dominate the scene. The colonists were already too far down the road to let this happen without a fight. In the face of such challenges to their way of doing things, the final choice was to submit or to rebel. And so came the Revolution.

The Way to Victory

The American Revolution was not a sustained war but a sporadic series of strikes and sieges, raids and forays, that covered the seven years from 1775 to 1781. Starting in Lexington and Concord, Massachusetts, it moved slowly southward, its epicenter moving from Boston to New York to Philadelphia, and it finally came to an end with the surrender of the British under Cornwallis at Yorktown, Virginia. The forces involved were never large. When the British took New York in 1776 they had as many as 33,000 men, and the Continentals 18,000. At its lowest ebb the colonial army numbered as few as 3,000, and during the cold and perilous winter of 1777–1778 at Valley Forge, it was largely the miracle of Washington's personal force and powers of leadership that held it together as an army at all.

British Problems   But while the Continental Army had a precarious hold on existence, the task facing Britain was insurmountable. This was no typical European war in which major armies clashed, one was defeated, the war ended, and if the victorious force was the invader it went home. Rather, Britain had to conquer a continent and reestablish her authority over it.

But she lacked the necessary military and political resources to do so. The British army was a highly capable professional fighting force. It won practically every battle in which it faced the American regulars. But it was inadequate to the larger task confronting it. It was far too small to occupy a continent. There was no draft or conscription upon which it could rely to increase its forces, and limited additional forces were obtained only by hiring German mercenaries. The army, therefore, had only the capacity to take what its commanders regarded as strategic areas—a city, a stretch of coast, a valley. Given the size of the country, this was utterly unproductive. Such "conquests" constituted no defeat of the colonial cause. In the European

1. The Detachment of the Regulars who fired first on the Provincials at the Bridge. 2. The Provincials headed by Colonel Robinson & Major Buttrick. 3. The Bridge. A. Doolittle Sculp.

The engagement at the North Bridge in Concord, April 19, 1775, from an engraving by Amos Doolittle, a Connecticut militiaman. After a brief conflict at Lexington Common that left eight dead, seven hundred British regulars marched to Concord to destroy ammunition stores. At North Bridge the minutemen attacked and as the British attempted to retreat to Boston thousands of Americans pursued and harassed them.

experience the loss of a nation's capital would end a war, but the Americans lost their capital, Philadelphia, without suffering more than a momentary drop in morale. The government simply moved elsewhere. Moreover, British forces were so limited that in order to take one area the army was sometimes forced to give up another.

The Royal Navy was no asset either. Its size had been reduced after the victory over the French in 1763, and incompetence characterized the leadership of the First Lord of the Admiralty as well as that of numerous admirals. While these limitations were not so great that the Americans could successfully challenge Britain on the high seas, they were enough to keep the British from effectively blocking the flow of supplies from overseas and to permit the French navy to aid the Americans in the crucial battle at Yorktown near the end of the war.

British political leadership was also inept. The King and many of his key ministers, such as Lord North, lacked the organizing ability essential to conducting a distant war, and failed to provide field commanders with flexible instructions freeing them from constant reliance upon London.

Of equal importance was the lack of broad popular support for the war at home. A significant part of the English press as well as influential public and private figures not only opposed the war but supported the Americans. The attempt to crush the Americans was seen as an insidious move against British liberties as well as those of the colonists. Whigs fearful of the rising power of the King perceived the American crisis as a part of their own struggle against the revival of royal prerogative and ministerial despotism. Lord Grafton declared in 1775: "I am perfectly convinced that the liberties of America once gone, those of this country will not long survive her." Richard Price, who prominently displayed the Declaration of Independence in his home, supported the American cause in his *Observations On Civil Liberty* (1776) which sold over sixty thousand copies within a year. The government was further embarrassed by the actions of private citizens who collected money for the widows and orphans of colonials killed at Concord and Lexington, by officers who resigned their commissions rather than serve in the American war, and by newspapers that supported the Americans. One paper, for example, suggested that "The prevailing toast in every company of true Englishmen is Victory for the Americans and the re-establishment of the British Constitution."

Colonial Problems Few governments have ever deliberately undertaken a war with such handicaps. The problems facing the Americans, however, were also considerable. While they had great potential resources, it proved impossible to draw upon them in an effective and organized way. The manpower was there, but Congress had no power to conscript. Wealth was there, but concentrated in land and not easily translated into military supplies, especially in a country without adequate transportation or industrial capacity. The absence of a strong centralized government forced Congress to rely upon the individual states for funds, which were often late in coming and often in depreciated currency. Lacking the money to get recruits, both Congress and the states relied upon such inducements as grants of western land and even slaves. This helped, but did not provide soldiers with food, clothing, weapons, and ammunition. When Nathanael Greene took over the army in the South in 1780, he reported to Washington that "Nothing can be more wretched and distressing than the condition of the troops, starving with cold and hunger, without tents and camp equipage. Those of the Virginia line are literally naked, and a great part totally unfit for any kind of duty. . . ." This was all too frequently true throughout the war. Although enough powder was soon being produced, muskets and cannon had to be imported from France, purchased through French and Dutch loans. These weaknesses made it impossible for the Americans to field a regular army strong enough to challenge the British on equal terms.

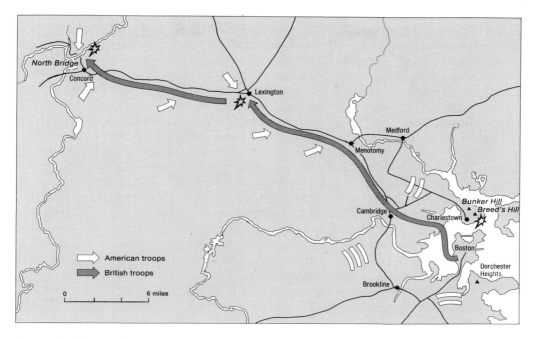

MASSACHUSETTS 1775

American Advantages But the Americans had several advantages. True, there was no professional officer class whose experience could be drawn upon, and civilians had to do the job. And there were many inept commanders, but a surprisingly able officer corps arose out of civilian life, with fine leaders such as Nathanael Greene, Henry Knox, and Francis Marion among them. Their talents were augmented by a number of able officers from abroad who volunteered to help the American cause: Lafayette from France, for example, and Baron von Steuben from Germany. Of the greatest importance was George Washington, the Commander-in-Chief, who had an extraordinary capacity to inspire loyalty and devotion to duty. Not technically a great general, he was personally a great leader. The weakness of the central government placed enormous responsibilities on Washington, who was compelled to do much that civilian authorities normally handle in wartime. But his great self-discipline, his unfaltering devotion to the cause, his vast integrity, and his unrelenting pursuit of victory undeterred by any defeat, made him the key ingredient in the success of the Revolution.

A major advantage was the entrance of France on the American side. French money and supplies had been available for two years before the treaty of alliance signed in February 1778. Now, additional millions of French livres in the form of muskets, cannon, uniforms, and munitions proved indispensable to American troops. And in the battle at Yorktown, Virginia, in 1781, some seven thousand French troops and the French fleet off Chesapeake Bay proved crucial to the American victory.

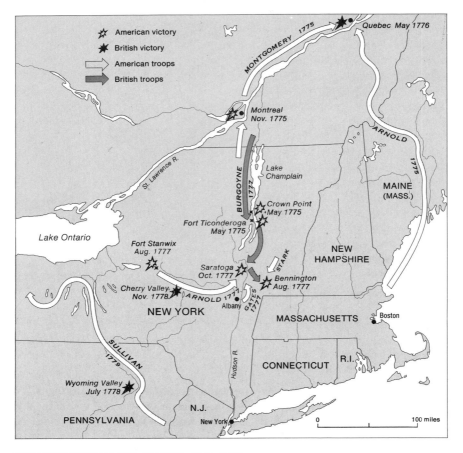

THE NORTHERN CAMPAIGN 1775–1778

The Strategic Pattern   Strategy on both sides was dictated as much by weakness as by strength. The British goal was two-fold: to meet the American army and decisively defeat it, and to occupy key cities and regions. The assumption was that either achievement would bring victory: that was the European experience. The American goal was to keep a regular army of sufficient size in the field so that the British would continually worry about its existence, and to bring to bear against the British at every opportunity the numerical weight of local militia. Conceding cities and key points to the British, the American assumption was that their tactics would keep most of the country unoccupied and in the long run wear down British arms and British will. And this proved to be the case.

Washington's forces were frequently beaten both in the North and in the South, but they were never destroyed. In 1776 and 1777 the British were able to take New York and Newport, Rhode Island, and to capture Philadelphia. But the attempt to isolate New England by a force moving down from

THE CENTRAL CAMPAIGNS
1776–1778

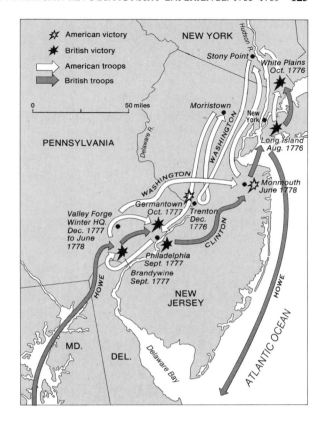

Canada under General Burgoyne failed. The British were cut off in the interior far from supplies, and confronted at every turn with thousands of militiamen whose overwhelming numbers forced Burgoyne to surrender at Saratoga. In 1778 the frustrated British commander, Major General Sir Henry Clinton, abandoned Philadelphia, returned to his main base in New York, and planned a southern campaign in the hope that the South could be cut off from the rest of the colonies. His decision was perhaps influenced by the fact that he could think of nothing else to do. Forces diverted from New York took Savannah, Georgia, in December 1778, and Charleston, South Carolina, in May 1780. The British commander in the South, General Cornwallis, established garrisons everywhere and began a long march north to Virginia.

The Americans continually harassed Cornwallis and his garrisons of loyalist militia with regular troops sent south by Washington and with southern guerrilla fighters. By 1781 South Carolina and Georgia had been liberated and the British limited to Savannah and Charleston. Cornwallis ended at Yorktown, where he could be reinforced and resupplied, but there he was trapped by the French fleet and by American and French troops brought south by Washington from New York. Joined with American forces

THE SOUTHERN CAMPAIGNS
1778–1781

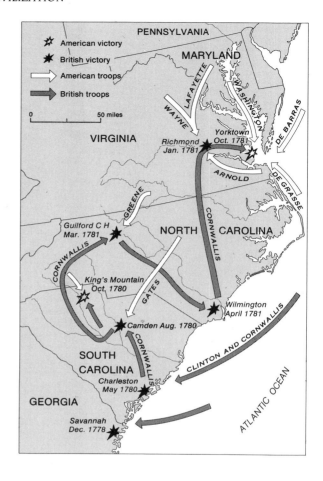

already in Virginia and additional French troops landed from the fleet, the army confronting Cornwallis was twice the size of his own, and he had the French fleet at his back. Cornwallis surrendered on October 17, 1781. It was a major victory in the classical European tradition, and hence decisive. Five months later Parliament resolved "to consider as enemies to his Majesty and the country all those who should advise or by any means attempt to further prosecution of offensive war on the continent of North America." Peace negotiations were begun, and almost two years later a peace treaty was signed at Paris. The long road to victory had been traveled. Independence had been won.

The Price of War

Wars always disrupt life, introducing uncertainty, postponement, neglect, deprivation, social and personal strain. The American Revolution was no exception.

The surrender of Cornwallis at Yorktown. In this French interpretation of the victory, the French fleet and officers dominate the successful siege of the city.

Personal Suffering The absence of husbands, sons, and lovers who went off to the fighting was an unhappy affair for their families and the neighbors who worried about their fate. A soldier's pay was so small that absence often worked severe hardship on those left behind, and wives and children were compelled to take up the peaceful tasks the men had abandoned. Although many soldiers were later to receive grants of land for their services, compensation rarely balanced the economic loss at home as a consequence of absence. As the town of Ashfield, Massachusetts, reported in 1778:

> Even the best friends of the cause are unwilling to enter the service because of the likelihood that their pay would be worth nothing when they return home, and they would leave their families at home in hunger and cold.

If a colonial family lost none of its men, it surely knew of a family that had, and grief for the fallen in battle is always strong and never lessened by the conviction that they died in a good cause. Total military casualties were only around 10,500 for the Americans—not much by modern experience in a seven-year war. But especially in frontier areas where the Indian allies of the British were turned loose, there were substantial civilian casualties. At any rate, those maimed in battle came home, and the sick who never recovered. Such tragedies within families were to be found from one end of the colonies to the other, and the families so affected were never to be the same again.

Those who stayed at home had their difficulties as well. Although there were areas untouched by the fighting, where it did occur pillaging British and Hessians were not averse to seizing a farmer's horses, cattle, poultry, and pigs, even his daughters. Shops were looted and burned. American troops were not of course equally disposed to plunder their own countrymen, but foraging parties did requisition cattle and grain, pay off in generally worthless currency, or simply carry off needed supplies without even a gesture toward payment. Colonial troops, moreover, did not think it criminal to force known Loyalists to hand over supplies, and occasionally burned their houses or barns to emphasize the point.

Personal sufferings were accentuated by larger social disruptions. The financial demands of the war meant less could be spent to repair roads, support schools, and maintain other public services. In areas that received an influx of refugees from British occupation or from fighting, the burden of support put a serious strain on local resources and often created resentment.

Scarcity and Inflation   Everywhere the country suffered scarcities and inflation. The war clearly pointed up the dependence of the colonies on outside markets and sources of supply. Normal channels of trade were disturbed or destroyed. British subsidies for naval stores and indigo were naturally cut off, as was the market for fish, rice, lumber, flour, and other raw materials. New England fishermen were barred by the British navy from the Grand Banks of Newfoundland and often from waters close to home. And intercolonial trade via coastal waters was frequently disrupted. Many items formerly imported became scarce: coffee, tea, sugar, molasses, wine, glass, paper, ironware, and clothing. Improvisations occurred everywhere. With the importation of wool cut off, farmers raised more sheep. Sweet syrup from a grain called sorghum was substituted for the sugar molasses formerly brought in from the West Indies. Local gun factories were set up, and in some areas saltpeter and sulphur for powder became common articles of home manufacture. The shortage of ammunition, particularly in the early years of the fighting, forced the Massachusetts Assembly to pass a resolution asking people to melt down their leaden window-weights and even their pewter dishes, and cast them into bullets. Many women, in the hours they could spare from other chores and duties, made clothing and blankets for the army.

In any time of disruption, there are people who take advantage. There were charges of graft and corruption, particularly against those supplying shoddy or polluted goods to the fighting men. One soldier bitterly complained in a letter home that "We many times have drawn such rotten stinking meat that the smell is sufficient to make us loth the same." The desperate need for soldiers prompted the offering of cash bounties for enlistment, and scoundrels and others desperate for cash often traveled to a strange town, enlisted under a false name, collected their bounty, and then promptly disappeared. At Springfield, Massachusetts, one young girl dressed in men's clothing tried this, but before she could collect her bounty "the want of a beard and the redundance of some other matters" aroused suspicions and gave her away.

As always in wartime there was profiteering and a thriving black market, many government contractors made small fortunes, and American merchants willing to run the British blockade to Europe or the French West Indies could lose one ship out of every two and still become wealthy. The Cabot brothers of Beverly, Massachusetts, made enough to move to Boston and join the aristocracy. There were frequent complaints among soldiers about civilians getting rich without hardship or danger. Despite attempts at price and wage controls, people attempted to sell their goods as high as possible and to demand higher wages. Inflation, prompted by scarcity and the issuance of paper currency, was a serious problem until somewhat eased by the influx of French and Spanish hard money near the end of the war.

All these disruptions in normal life created problems of morale. Desertion and the overstaying of leaves were common, and war weariness affected large numbers. Newspapers defying the British, and ministers promising heavenly rewards to fighting men, found it hard to keep enough spirit among the populace to sustain the war effort.

Effects on Culture   Cultural and intellectual life was disrupted. War took many away from intellectual pursuits. David Rittenhouse, the famed colonial astronomer, supervised the manufacture of saltpeter. The elderly Franklin, vainly longing to return to the tranquillity of his scientific studies, found himself serving as minister to France.

Education was affected. Rural schools were often closed, and in the towns schoolwork was hindered or crippled by lack of funds and teachers. New York had no schools at all from the British occupation to the end of the war. College attendance dropped, academic study was restricted, and financial difficulties plagued all. Dartmouth was reduced to "nakedness and want." Some college buildings were used to quarter troops rather than scholars. Study abroad was impossible, and contact between American and European men of learning was greatly reduced.

Some libraries, so painstakingly built up in the colonial period, were looted or destroyed. "The pilfering hand of the British . . . carried on war not only against men but against learning," sadly commented one observer. Publishing also suffered. The import of books from England was cut off, and there was a serious shortage of paper for print. Not one newspaper in existence during the Revolution was able to publish without interruption at one time or another.

The Loyalists   Those who were loyal to the King had a difficult time. Some sixty thousand were compelled to leave the country, fleeing to Canada or to Great Britain, and their property was confiscated. Those who did not flee but chose to stick it out were abused and threatened and their lives made miserable by hostile neighbors. Among those who fled the country were a number of learned men, including Miles Cooper, head of King's College, and naturalist Dr. Alexander Garden. The permanent departure of such men temporarily weakened American cultural life.

All told, the disruption caused by the war was extensive and serious. Life was made uncertain and uncomfortable, but American colonials had endured hardship and distress in the past and their essential self-reliance enabled them to continue.

Political Achievements: Democracy and the Constitution

The Revolution confirmed and extended democratic tendencies, gave fresh vitality to the ideas behind them, provided the impetus for the development of new democratic procedures and techniques, and committed the new nation to the first great experiment with democracy in modern times.

No one would claim that the Revolution created or guaranteed a completely democratic society and political system. The rights of some were violated or ignored; past injustices and arrogance continued; skepticism if not outright hostility toward popular sovereignty was found even among revolutionary leaders; many expressed contempt, not tolerance, of those with opposing views; vituperation in public discussion seemed often more prevalent than sweet reason; there was deep disagreement over the meaning of what was happening and what should be done, and all the ugly behavior such disagreement often gives rise to. Yet the astonishing thing is the extent to which the Revolution made it possible for democracy to prevail. What was accomplished, not what remained to be done, gave the Revolution its enormous significance.

Popular Sovereignty The democratic achievements of the Revolution were primarily political. The Revolution was first and foremost an assertion of the sovereignty of the people, of the principle that public power must arise from those over whom it is exercised—in short, that the people are the ultimate source of power. By 1763 the colonists had already moved a considerable distance down this road, but the Revolution committed them to the rest of the journey.

It was the Declaration of Independence that formally committed the Americans to the proposition that the people are sovereign, declaring that to secure the inalienable rights of life, liberty, and the pursuit of happiness "governments are instituted among men, *deriving their just powers from the consent of the governed,* that whenever any form of government becomes destructive of these ends, it is the right of the people to alter or to abolish it."

Yet this proposition was already public property, as it were, given the extent to which the colonists by 1763 believed the existing instruments of government to be representative of their interests. More than a decade before the Declaration, a town meeting in Connecticut, in response to the Stamp Act, had asserted that "every form of government, rightly founded,

The Signing of the Declaration of Independence, *by Trumbull. The Second Continental Congress convened in 1775 to assume responsibility for the war effort, although some delegates still hoped to reconcile the differences with the king through the Olive Branch Petition. When George III rejected the petition and war intensified, the Congress was still reluctant to commit itself to the cause of independence that had originated in the colonial assemblies. It was not until Thomas Paine's pamphlet* Common Sense *created enormous sympathy throughout the colonies and individual assemblies began making their own declarations and instructing their delegates to Congress to support the move that Congress finally appointed a drafting committee. After considerable debate, all the colonies except the abstaining New York voted to adopt the Declaration.*

originates from the consent of the people," that the people set the limits to government and when these are ignored "the people have a right to reassume the exercise of that authority which by nature they had before they delegated it to individuals." Popular belief in this proposition was also evident in the unanimous support of the following resolution by a town meeting in Westminster, Massachusetts, in 1778 during the public discussion on a proposed state constitution:

> The oftener power returns into the hands of the people the better, and when for the good of the whole the power is delegated it ought to be done by the whole. . . . Where can the power be lodged so safe as in the hands of the

people and who can delegate it so well as they, or who has the boldness without blushing to say that the people are not suitable to put in their own officers—if so why do we waste our blood and treasure to obtain that which when obtained we are not fit to enjoy, or if but a selected few only are fit to appoint our rulers, why were we uneasy under George?

It was the revolutionary experience, stretching from the initial crisis on through the final formation of a new government under the Constitution, which institutionalized this belief. How this happened may be noted in a number of ways.

Popular Leadership   The first thing that strikes one about the role of the Revolution in developing and consolidating the principle of the sovereignty of the people was the rise of a body of men of recognized ability who were thrust into revolutionary leadership by their talent and by the consent of their compatriots. Washington, the Adamses, Jefferson, Richard Henry Lee, Robert Morris, Patrick Henry, John Dickinson, Franklin, Hamilton—these and many other unusual men became the leaders of the revolutionary generation. It has sometimes been argued that "the people" were ahead of their leaders and forced them to take actions they did not want to take or believe should be taken. But even if true this would only illustrate that society and government had so developed that no leader could go his own way and the public be damned. It is significant that many leaders recognized and responded to the general opinion—whether reluctantly is not the point—and where they did not accept the idea of popular sovereignty, new men came to the fore.

Some of the revolutionary leaders came from the upper class, some did not; some were familiar, some unknown. In 1763 John Adams was an obscure lawyer, Samuel Adams a Boston tax collector, Samuel Chase the son of a poor parson. Many of the revolutionary leaders disagreed with one another. Some were cautious and conservative, some more radically inclined; some represented the past ruling establishment, some did not. But all rose out of a political environment that recognized merit, rewarded talent, and saw the people as choosing their own leadership rather than having it imposed upon them by tradition, force, or fear.

These leaders, and their supporters, did not abandon familiar political techniques and practices. They used that experience to the fullest. The organized opposition to the succession of British measures after 1763 came out of the existing representative institutions and relied upon representative techniques. It was the colonial assemblies and the town and county meetings, for example, that passed the resolutions condemning British action and proposing alternatives. In the crisis the colonies *elected* delegates to the Stamp Act Congress and the Continental Congress as well as the local committees formed to enforce the nonimportation agreements. In the tumult of 1775–1776, at a time when royal officials had fled, resigned, or were unable or unwilling to act, and when revolutionary state governments had not yet

The leaders who negotiated the peace treaty with Great Britain. From the left, John Jay, John Adams, Ben Franklin, Henry Laurens, and Franklin's grandson and aide, William.

come into being, local committees elected by the people took over in the towns, counties, and villages. And where colonial assemblies were unable to meet, provincial congresses organized along the lines of the assemblies were elected to function in their place. None of this would have occurred if the colonists had not had a significant commitment to the idea that it is basically the people who rule, not kings or lords. Nor would it have occurred if they had not had substantial experience with representative institutions to back up their commitment.

Developing Forms of Democratic Government   Indeed, when the break with Britain finally came and the colonies were thrown on their own, this could clearly be seen in the new governments that were established. By 1780 all states had adopted new constitutions with the exception of Rhode Island and Connecticut, which simply continued under their old charters. These constitutions created nothing new. Yet the impact of the Revolution could be seen in the degree to which they reflected a strengthening and extension of democratic government. In most states, many important officers were popularly or legislatively elected. The old governor's council, which had been associated with the executive branch, was separated and made into an upper legislative house, elected by the people or by the lower house. Governors, whose powers were viewed with suspicion on the basis of colonial experience, had their powers curtailed and now faced election by the people or by the legislatures. In many states public officials had to face the scrutiny of the voters annually. Although property qualifications for holding office were retained in all states, in most the average owner of a hundred-acre family farm qualified for at least the lower house of the legislature.

The right to vote, already broad because of the widespread ownership of property, was only slightly extended. No state abandoned property requirements of some kind although New Hampshire, Pennsylvania, North Carolina, Georgia, and later Vermont admitted all poll-tax payers to the vote. These requirements left disenfranchised large numbers of adult males in the cities, but prevented few in predominantly rural America from exercising the right to vote. Perhaps more important was that various inequalities in popular representation were eliminated by the end of the colonial era. As population moved westward, the new western parts of the colonies had little or no representation, particularly in Pennsylvania and South Carolina. But the most serious of these inequalities were corrected by the states in their new constitutions.

Only six states sought authority from the voters for the existing assemblies to draft a new constitution, and in only two states was there a measure of popular ratification of the constitutions drawn up. Yet it was difficult everywhere to ignore the wishes of the people. In most states, town and county meetings produced instructions, advice, and recommendations that the assemblies found it wise to consider. The sense that the people were involved in this whole process, that the authority for creating new government came from them, was present everywhere.

The experience of Massachusetts, one of the two states seeking popular ratification for its constitution, illustrates the sense of a sovereign people at work. Its first state constitution, drawn up by the old house of representatives and the council under popular authorization in 1778, was defeated when submitted to the voters. Thereafter in a special election all towns chose delegates to a state constitutional convention, which accepted with slight modification a constitution mainly drafted by John Adams. This constitution was adopted in 1780 by a two-thirds majority in a popular referendum that included all free adult males. The vote itself was light, suggesting that there was little controversy.

Adams, in his version of the preamble, had written: "We, therefore, the delegates of the people of Massachusetts . . . agree upon the following . . . Constitution of the Commonwealth of Massachusetts." Significantly, the convention amended the preamble to read: "We, therefore, the people of Massachusetts . . . agree upon, ordain, and establish . . ." *We the people ordain and establish.*

The Constitutional Convention   The Massachusetts experience fed into the Philadelphia convention that created the Constitution of the United States. Indeed, it was here that the Americans brought to its fullest expression a unique political invention, the constitutional convention. The idea was that a convention, chosen for the specific purpose of setting up institutions of government, drafts a constitution that defines the powers and functions of government and declares the basic rights of citizens. If the people by popular vote ratify that constitution, the convention disbands and government comes into being under the constitution. Having created the higher law of the constitution that only they could make or amend, the people put their sovereign power into storage, so to speak, and come under the statutory law of the government that they have brought into being. This turned out to be a very useful way of creating government. It is all very well to talk about popular sovereignty, government by consent of the governed, representative institutions, and the social contract. The practical point is how do you actually put all this into operation, how do the people institute a new government? The Americans, by and large convinced of the sovereignty of the people and long experienced in representative institutions, struck upon the device of the constitutional convention. Used experimentally by some states during the Revolution, it came into full use in Philadelphia in 1787. The delegates completely bypassed existing government and submitted their work to the people for ratification through state conventions elected specifically for the purpose. The delegates at Philadelphia may have disagreed on many matters, but all accepted the assumption that the people, in Madison's words, are "the fountain of all power," or if they did not, they removed themselves from the convention. Where, Madison asked, are we to locate the source of power if not in the people? In kings, in a privileged class, an economic interest? All agreed that it had to be in the people themselves.

The Limitation of Power

Checks and Balances   A second major political impact of the Revolution lay in the development of practical political ways by which power could be limited. The Americans never believed in unlimited power, even for the people themselves. They were, in fact, highly suspicious of power—whether exercised by the few or the many, the rich or the poor, the ignorant or the intelligent. The idea of institutionalizing a limitation on power was something new in the political affairs of man, and it had been developing for some time in America as a consequence of colonial experience with the abuse of power.

First in the revolutionary state governments and then in the new federal government, the Americans relied upon two ways to insure that power was limited and restricted. The first separated and divided power and set up an accompanying system of checks and balances. Building on the colonial experience, the state constitutions divided their governmental functions into

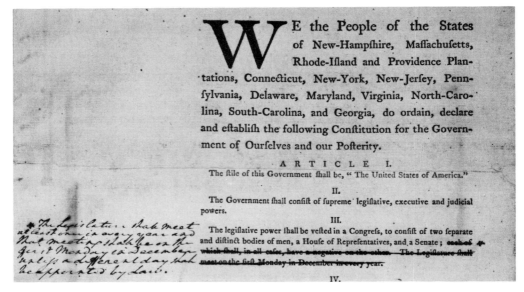

W E the People of the States of New-Hampſhire, Maſſachuſetts, Rhode-Iſland and Providence Plan-tations, Connecticut, New-York, New-Jerſey, Penn-ſylvania, Delaware, Maryland, Virginia, North-Caro-lina, South-Carolina, and Georgia, do ordain, declare and eſtabliſh the following Conſtitution for the Govern-ment of Ourſelves and our Poſterity.

ARTICLE I.
The ſtile of this Government ſhall be, " The United States of America."

II.
The Government ſhall conſiſt of ſupreme legiſlative, executive and judicial powers.

III.
The legiſlative power ſhall be veſted in a Congreſs, to conſiſt of two ſeparate and diſtinct bodies of men, a Houſe of Representatives, and a Senate ; each of which ſhall, in all caſes, have a negative on the other. The Legiſlature ſhall meet on the firſt Monday in December in every year.

IV.

A copy of page one of the first printer's draft of the Constitution, received from the President of the United States on March 19, 1796, by Timothy Pickering, Secretary of State.

legislative, judicial, and executive, each with its own defined functions and powers. In all states except Georgia and Pennsylvania there was a further division of the legislative branch into two houses.

The Constitution of the United States restricted power by similar divisions and its own ingenious system of checks and balances among the executive, legislative, and judicial branches. The President had power to veto an act of Congress, but he could be overridden by a two-thirds vote of both houses. The Senate had authority to confirm appointments and ratify treaties, the House to initiate appropriations bills, and Congress to declare war and vote monies for the armed forces.

The Bill of Rights   Fear lest power in government threaten or destroy individual freedoms found expression in bills of rights, which declared certain liberties to be beyond the reach of such power. Virginia's famous Declaration of Rights of 1776 provided a precedent for the Declaration written by Jefferson, and was closely followed in the Declaration of Rights in the Massachusetts constitution of 1780. Other states had similar declarations, which led the men at Philadelphia to feel that a national declaration of rights in the Constitution was unnecessary. But some people, including Jefferson, feared that such rights and liberties needed also to be protected from abuse by national authority, and those favoring ratification promised a series of amendments to the Constitution guaranteeing these rights. This promise was kept, and one of the first acts of the new government was to adopt ten of twelve recommended amendments which constitute the Bill of Rights. These amendments provided that Congress should make no laws infringing freedom of speech, religion, or the press, and that the people should have the right to assemble and petition for a redress of grievances. Right of trial by jury was guaranteed, and no one could be compelled to testify against himself in a criminal case or be subject to unreasonable search and seizure, or cruel and unusual punishment. Finally, no one could be deprived of life, liberty, or property without due process of law. The Tenth Amendment, not strictly a part of the Bill of Rights, left to the states or the people all power not specifically delegated to the United States or denied to the states by the Constitution.

The significance of these amendments in strengthening democratic development in America is beyond measure, for they assert that there are some rights so central to the definition of a free human being that they must not be open to invasion by any authority, that indeed it is the responsibility of government to protect them. If government fails in that responsibility, then the people have the right to abolish or alter it and institute new government that will accept that responsibility.

The major political achievements of the Revolution, then, consisted of putting the twin principles of popular sovereignty and limited power on a practical political basis reflected in the instruments of government and embodied in the law of the land.

Social and Economic Gains

The revolutionary era also saw a number of social and economic developments associated with a rising democratic society. Religious toleration and the separation of church and state had long been essential if not fully established facts of life in colonial America. Though the details varied from state to state, the trend was toward strengthening religious toleration and separating church and state. For all practical purposes, complete religious liberty was attained in the Middle States. It already existed in Delaware and Pennsylvania, where there had never been any genuine established church. New Jersey also had no established church, and its 1776 constitution forbade that church attendance or support of any particular denomination be required. The New York constitution of 1777 ended the dominance of the Anglican and Dutch Reformed churches, which had never been strong. In New England, except for Rhode Island, Congregationalism remained favored by law, although greater recognition was given to dissenting sects. In the South, where the Anglican church had been the legal establishment, it had never had popular support and was rather easily disestablished. Jefferson's famed Statute of Religious Limitations of 1786, which provided for complete religious freedom and complete separation of church and state, was an important legal statement, but only put into law what had long been developing in fact.

A similar fate befell the few remnants of feudalism that had reached American shores. Quitrents, the payment of fees to proprietors or king, had long been slight and often ignored. Primogeniture, which required that inheritance of land pass to the eldest son, and entail, which allowed the owner of property to prevent his heirs from disposing of it, had not been widely practiced in colonial America. Now all three were either abolished or so modified as to be meaningless. These laws, geared to the maintenance of large estates in Europe, smacked of aristocracy, and encouraged the existence here of great estates rather than the family-sized holdings that most Americans favored.

Indeed, the consequences of the Revolution for landholding by the ordinary individual were vital, in terms not only of economic democracy but of political democracy as well. Since voting and officeholding both still depended on ownership of land, the availability and distribution of land for the ordinary settler was significant. Here the effects of the Revolution were great. Hundreds of millions of acres passed from the hands of the Crown and of various lords into the hands of the people of the United States or of the various states. The states themselves ceded their claims to western land to the central government, and under the ordinances of 1785 and 1787, these lands were thrown open to settlement on a democratic basis, providing equal economic opportunity to all who sought it, and also easy access to full political status, given the relative ease with which land could be acquired. In the Southern states, as well as in New York and Pennsylvania, land belonging to the Crown or to proprietors was taken over by the states and disposed of liberally. Much of it was offered in bounties to encourage enlistment in the revolutionary armies, and most of it quickly found its way into private hands. The final step in democratizing land ownership was confiscation and resale of the estates of landowners loyal to the Crown. Soon after independence the states by law provided for the seizure of loyalist property. Many estates were involved. In New York alone more than two and a half million acres, including some of the best land in the state, were taken from fifty-nine loyalists. Much of this passed into the hands of speculators and wealthy men who were themselves large landowners, but much of it eventually came into the hands of small landowners.

Although there were no specific laws about social equality, the developments noted above, and indeed the whole revolutionary atmosphere, reinforced the sense of social equality long developing in colonial society. All laws that struck down privilege in any form contributed naturally to the sense of social equality. So did the revolutionary environment itself, which brought together in common cause people of all means and station. An experience of Colonel Thomas Randolph, Virginia aristocrat who fought for the Revolution, will illustrate. Entertaining a captured British officer in his home, he was interrupted by three farmer neighbors who came in to talk business. They made themselves quite at home, removed their boots, put their feet up on the furniture, and generally took their ease. After they left, Randolph observed to his guest that "the spirit of independency was converted into equality, and everyone who bore arms esteemed himself on a footing with his neighbor. No doubt," he said, "each of these men conceives himself, in every respect, my equal." Randolph may have thought himself superior to his neighbors, but in a society which had rejected privilege and had recently declared that "all men are created equal," would-be aristocrats were on the defensive, and if they held high opinions of their own worth they did not broadcast them.

The Revolution also saw some advance in humanitarian sentiment and achievement. There was some prison reform and an easing of the harshness of the criminal code, notably a reduction in the number of crimes punishable by death. But unfortunately the revolutionary era left the institution of slavery intact to plague the future. The Constitution itself gave legal recognition to the institution through the three-fifths clause, which counted a slave as three-fifths of a person in determining the population basis for representation in Congress, as well as in the fugitive slave clause recognizing the right of owners to the return of runaways. And the agreement at the Convention to allow any state to reopen the African slave trade for twenty years unhappily was taken full advantage of by Georgia and South Carolina.

The Containment of Slavery Nevertheless, the process began that was to limit and confine slavery and make it regional rather than national, a fact of great importance. Whereas before 1776 slavery was accepted everywhere as a matter of course, outright abolition or a provision for its abandonment began in the Northern states. In Massachusetts, for example, the constitution of 1780 declared all men free and equal, and the courts held that this declaration abolished slavery. State after state fell in line, so that by 1830 less than one percent of Northern blacks remained slaves.

In 1787 Congress in the famed Northwest Ordinance decreed slavery illegal in the upper Western territories, an áction that was to keep the institution out of Illinois and Indiana and prevent its gaining support in the Midwest. Then in 1807, at the request of Jefferson, Congress took advantage of the opportunity afforded by the Constitution to abolish the African slave trade. The long-run effect of this decision was to drive slavery deeper and deeper into the South. With the African supply closed, the new Southwest was forced to draw its slaves from the older areas, thus reducing both slavery and the commitment to it in the border area stretching from Delaware through Maryland and Kentucky into Missouri. The ultimate consequence of this was that by the time of the Civil War slavery remained secure in only eleven of the fifteen slave states. Finally, the humanitarian sentiment of the revolutionary era against slavery further weakened it in the border states through the voluntary freeing of slaves by their owners. In Maryland, for example, there were 103,000 slaves and only 8,000 free blacks in 1790; but there were 87,000 slaves and more than 84,000 free blacks in 1860. In short, if slavery had not been limited and confined through both the actions and the sentiments impelled by the revolutionary experience, it would have remained national and not become regional, and the American future would have been very different indeed.

Disappointments of the Revolution   Yet it cannot be denied that for those vast numbers in bondage, the Revolution seemed to mean very little. The high hopes of many slaves that the Revolution would mean their freedom were doomed to disappointment, as the elderly slave Jupiter Hammon wrote in 1787.

> That liberty is a great thing we know from our own feelings, and we may likewise judge so from the conduct of the white people in the late war. How much money has been spent and how many lives have been lost to defend their freedom! I must say that I have hoped that God would open their eyes, when they were so much engaged for liberty, to think of the state of the poor blacks, and to pity us.

In other areas, too, little or no progress was made. Women, though their status in America had long been much improved over that of their European sisters, did not see the Declaration's eloquent assertion of equality applied to them. Abigail Adams wrote to her husband John: "By the way, in the new code of laws which I suppose it will be necessary for you to make, I desire you to remember the ladies and be more generous and favorable to them than your ancestors." But neither John Adams nor any other revolutionary leader espoused major changes in the position of women. Nor did the Revolution bring about any change in the laws of indenture, though a number of indentured servants assumed that the Revolution entitled them to their freedom and accordingly abandoned their masters and took off. Though most revolutionary leaders saw the importance of an educated citizenry if a democratic republic were to survive, and Jefferson proposed an elaborate scheme for free public education for all, this sweeping proposal too was to be postponed.

Yet though much remained to be done, the Revolution promoted democracy, building upon the substantial achievements of the colonial past. Historians have debated whether the Revolution instituted democracy in America or merely confirmed a democracy already achieved. It would seem that it did both. It turned thirteen dependent colonies under monarchy into one independent republic and legalized the considerable independence they had already developed. It ended the separation of colonies already developing a community of interest, and it brought into being a unified nation under federal authority. It extended many democratic institutions and techniques developed earlier, and fully institutionalized control by the people of their own government on all levels. It laid down in the Declaration of Independence principles by which the new nation should be guided in the future, principles with which the colonists had long been familiar. It limited the exercise of power to public authority under the Constitution and the Bill of Rights, thus establishing in law what the colonists had long been striving for. And it strengthened in law, custom, and habit of mind the slowly rising sense of equality and liberty that had marked the colonial experience. In short, the Revolution opened wide a door to the future that had been only partly opened before.

The Role of Ideas   Toward the ideas of the Enlightenment that underlay the remarkable achievement of the Revolution, the ideas by which the Americans justified their actions and reinforced their own experience, most people today have a skepticism born of knowledge beyond that possessed by the Founding Fathers. Patrick Henry may have said to the Continental Congress, "Government is dissolved. . . . We are in a state of nature." But we are well aware that the origin of government does not really lie in the decision of individuals living in a state of nature to enter upon a social contract with one another. We know, too, that people are as much moved by the forces of passion, pride, and prejudice as by intelligence and reason. We may question the assertion that all individuals are equal and that they possess certain rights derived from nature. But who could deny that belief in these ideas contributed to the creation of a remarkable body of working institutions? For Americans then or now to say that they will try to regard people as equal, that they will try to protect and promote certain rights as though they were inalienable and from the hand of nature and of nature's God, that they will try to base their government on the general consent of the governed and that government exists to serve its citizens—to say all this is to set an ideal for the nation that is as noble and as decent a goal to spend our lives pursuing as we are likely to find.

The Impact of the Revolution Abroad

The American Revolution was a momentous event not only for America but for Europe as well. Many Europeans saw the Revolution and its consequences as a climax to the Age of Enlightenment, proof that it was possible to put into practice the ideas of equality, popular sovereignty, the rights of man, religious liberty, and freedom of thought and speech. Among those Europeans who for decades had been arguing the case for these ideas only in the courts of their own imagination, the American Revolution caused great excitement. For the first time, they had an example of the vitality of these ideas in a people willing to hazard their lives, their fortunes, and their honor to defend them. Condorcet noted, "It is not enough that the rights of man be written in the books of philosophers and inscribed in the hearts of virtuous men; the weak and ignorant must be able to read them in the example of a great nation. America has given us this example."

The American Revolution thus helped to introduce into Europe a feeling that great changes were about to take place and a new era about to begin. The Dutch patrician, Van Hogendrop, after a trip to America in 1782, reported this impact of the American example:

> In Ireland a revolution is going on without civil war and even without astonishment. In France, I am assured, there is much agitation. The Germans bear the yoke of an arrogant nobility with impatience. In the United Provinces power is taken from the hands to which it was entrusted. A British vessel in

the Mozambique Channel, finds the native inhabitants in revolt against their Arab masters, and when they ask why they have taken arms, are told: "America is free. Could not we be?"

And Edmund Burke was to observe that "A great revolution has happened.... It has made as great a change in all the relations and balances and gravitations of power as the appearance of a new planet would in the system of the solar world."

News of the American Revolution was brought to Europeans through a variety of channels. The great expansion in the European press in the last half of the eighteenth century saw hundreds of newspapers and magazines appearing, all of which carried information and discussion about the crisis in the New World. Many books were published on America, and politically oriented reading clubs and Masonic lodges found the American revolutionary crisis a stimulus to heady discussion of political and social affairs. European soldiers who fought in the Revolution, notably the French but also Poles, Swedes, and those Germans who fought for the British, often carried back favorable views of America, marking well the contrast with life in Europe. Wrote one French officer of the New Englanders:

> Their education is very nearly the same; so that a worker is often elected to their assemblies, where there is no distinction, no separate order.... The country farmers all own their own land. They plow their fields themselves and drive their own oxen. This way of living, this sweet equality has charms for thinking men. This life would suit me pretty well.

The Continent was also flooded with propaganda favorable to America, sponsored by such Americans in Europe as Franklin and by sympathetic Europeans.

In the quarter of a century of the revolutionary era—from 1763 to 1789—there developed in many parts of Europe a belief that the American Revolution was a great turning point in history that would give "greater scope to the Enlightenment, new keenness to the thinking of people and new life to the spirit of liberty."

In a number of countries the American Revolution seemed to give the green light to abortive movements for reform, change, and even independence. It helped stimulate the radical movement and an unsuccessful call for parliamentary reform in England in the early 1780s; it generated Irish pressure for short-lived economic and political concessions from Britain, leading one Irish leader to make the premature announcement that "it was on the plains of America that Ireland obtained her freedom"; in the 1780s it provided inspiration for the abortive revolution in the Dutch provinces against the House of Orange and the regent oligarchs known as the Patriot movement; and in the late 1780s it strongly infected the political atmosphere in Belgium and produced an unsuccessful revolt against Austrian rule.

Elsewhere in Europe—in Switzerland, Italy, Poland, Sweden, Germany, and even Russia—the Revolution provided a focus for discussion about reform and change, especially among young people, intellectuals, writers, and a number of European nobles. It seemed to contribute in these countries to a

The Tennis Court Oath. In 1789 the third estate met to commit itself to the creation of a new French constitution.

rising political awareness, a conviction that new things were in the making, and that America was pointing the way to the future. All this was summed up by the Swiss Isaac Iselin, who wrote to his friend Peter Ochs that "I am tempted to believe that North America is the country where reason and humanity will develop more rapidly than anywhere else."

Influence on France The American Revolution struck a responsive chord throughout Europe, but its effects were to be most deeply felt in the only truly revolutionary endeavor on the Continent in the eighteenth century—that which took place in France.

From the beginning of the American Revolution it was in France that the greatest enthusiasm was shown and the most extensive discussions occurred. The public imagination identified the American cause with forces long at work in France and with ideas long held but not put into action. The Count de Ségur, in Spa in the summer of 1776, recorded in his memoirs the outbreak of revolution:

> In that little town of Spa, where there were so many tourists, accidental or voluntary deputies, as it were, from all the monarchies of Europe, I was particularly struck to see burst forth in everyone so keen and universal a sympathy for the revolt of a people against their king.

This sympathy and enthusiasm for America swept every class in France, produced a seemingly endless flood of books, articles, poetry, and drama about America, and promoted extensive discussion of revolutionary ideas: liberty, equality, republicanism, constitutions, popular sovereignty, and all the rest. Franklin was incredibly popular when he arrived in France in December 1776. The reception accorded him was directed as much at the new nation he represented as to him. Visitors and invitations poured in upon him; his portrait was painted again and again; his likeness appeared on clocks, medallions, snuffboxes, rings, watches, vases, dishes, handkerchiefs, and pocketknives. The Comédie Française gave special performances of two of Molière's plays because Franklin had been heard to remark that he had never seen them. He had access to the highest social and intellectual circles through his presence in the salons of Madame d'Houdetot and Madame Helvetius and by his acceptance into the Masonic Lodge of the Nine Sisters and the French Academy of Sciences, where at a dramatic meeting he embraced Voltaire. His own writings were already enormously popular, and he now inundated the country with political literature on the Revolution, indcluding its key documents. He became a symbol not only of America, but of a new spirit in France itself.

Today, after many decades of more recent revolutions, the world is accustomed to seeing individuals of humble origin raised to high positions, and so we tend to overlook the significance of Franklin's reception in France. But he was something remarkably new to the European concept of men of power and influence. He was no mailed warrior, no conqueror with his foot on the throat of the world; no man of ancient lineage with the imperial nose testifying to his ancestry. He was simply an old man with white hair, a cane, a fur cap, and the gout, who had risen from obscure beginnings to show the world how to bring both arbitrary nature and arbitrary rulers under control. The society that created such a man, that allowed him to rise and express his talents, must indeed be extraordinary. In a sense Turgot must have been thinking that all Americans were Franklins when he wrote in 1778 that "They are the hope of the human race; they may well become its model"—a remark few Frenchmen would be prone to make today.

The pro-American feeling in France during the American Revolution increased through the 1780s. Politicians and intellectuals, including men who were to dominate the National Assembly at the outbreak of the French Revolution, continued to read and discuss events in America. On the popular level, a sentimental, romantic vision of America was kept before the populace in novels, plays, poetry, and prints. In the years before the French Revolution increasing emphasis was laid upon the United States as a practical demonstration of democracy, with its guarantees of person and property, representative government, separation of powers, legal and political equality, and all the material and social benefits which flow from a society so constructed politically.

Then, with the meeting of the Estates General in 1789, America overnight became a political as well as a social model for France to follow. This is not to suggest that French revolutionaries worked from American blueprints, but particularly in 1789 and 1790, the United States was regarded as a source of political inspiration and action. What have been regarded as the two most significant events in the inauguration of the French Revolution owed much to American precedent: the establishment of the National Assembly through the Tennis Court Oath, and the Declaration of the Rights of Man.

The idea of constituting government through the people, of having a constituent assembly or constitutional convention, came to France from the United States. The very word *convention* entered the French language from America, as Brissot's "Plan of Conduct" of 1789 for the deputies who were about to meet illustrates. In arguing that only a constitutional assembly could draw up a new constitution for France, he asked where the idea came from. "We owe its discovery," he wrote, "to the Free Americans, and the convention which has just formed the plan for a federal system has infinitely perfected it." Moreover, he added, "this device or method of the Free Americans can perhaps be very easily adapted to the circumstances in which France now finds herself." It is worth remembering that the work of the National Assembly in abolishing the old order in the late summer and fall of 1789 was carried on under the leadership of those who had for years been pro-American in outlook. Lafayette, who had rallied the young nobles and was regarded by many (not excluding himself) as the French Washington, Brissot, J. J. Mounier, and many others had helped to create the American image in France and were deeply committed to it. It was they who consulted a number of Americans in Paris on the formation of a constitution and a declaration of rights, turning particularly to Jefferson.

The other significant event setting the French Revolution on its irrevocable path was the issuance of the famed Declaration of the Rights of Man and Citizen. The historian R. R. Palmer has called this a political act of the first magnitude in that it raised, as did the American Declaration of Independence, a visible standard for the nation, providing Frenchmen with a map, so to speak, of the road ahead. It was both "the death certificate of the old regime" and "the birth certificate of the new," in the phrasing of two modern historians. It is clear that the idea for issuing such a declaration was suggested by the various American state and federal bills of rights, and an examination of the French Declaration and the Virginia Declaration of Rights shows a remarkable parallel.

The French Revolution, of course, went its own way and was to exert a profound influence not only on France but on all of Europe. But the American Revolution provided encouragement to the French to initiate their own. At the time, certainly, few Frenchmen would have denied that America was the source of their inspiration. The poet André Chénier, for example, wrote:

> Liberty, shining on American shores,
> kindled a fire in fraternal French eyes.
> And soon shall faithful accounts
> announce to our models
> the fruits of their example and our glorious achievements.

In a letter to the State of Pennsylvania, the National Assembly declared in 1791 that it would strive to "transplant and defend in the Old World the inestimable gift of liberty received from the New World. . . . Long live France! Forget not all she owed to your example." Brissot, who was to be virtual head of the French government in 1792, said bluntly that "The American Revolution was the mother of the French Revolution," and no one took issue with him.

The impact of the American Revolution upon Europe has best been summed up by R. R. Palmer:

> The effects of the American Revolution, as a revolution, were imponderable but very great. It inspired the sense of a new era. It added a new content to the

conception of progress. It gave a whole new dimension to ideas of liberty and equality made familiar by the Enlightenment. It got people into the habit of thinking more concretely about political questions, and made them more readily critical of their own governments and society. It dethroned England, and set up America, as a model for those seeking a better world. It brought written constitutions, declarations of rights, and constituent conventions into the realm of the possible. The apparition on the other side of the Atlantic of certain ideas already familiar in Europe made such ideas seem more truly universal, and confirmed the habit of thinking in terms of humanity at large. Whether fantastically idealized or seen in a factual way, whether as mirage or as reality, America made Europe seem unsatisfactory to many people of the middle and lower classes, and to those of the upper classes who wished them well. It made a good many Europeans feel sorry for themselves, and induced a kind of spiritual flight from the Old Regime.

If the story of the American Revolution had closed with its impact upon the people of the eighteenth century, it would remain an impressive story. But in an important sense, the Revolution has never ended. Its effects have continued, reaching into every corner of the globe, threatening old orders, inspiring movements of protest and revolt, and today even challenging the country of its origin to reexamine her own traditions.

Profile: THOMAS JEFFERSON

One of the chief authorities on Jefferson, Julian Boyd, has written that "mathematics was his favorite branch of study; music his chief art; architecture his joy; mechanics his useful pastime; agriculture his sustenance of body and soul; politics his duty—and his greatest achievement." Yet Jefferson's interest and study extended into every field of knowledge: law, government, history, medicine, languages and literature, music, education, philosophy, religion, and almost every branch of natural science from astronomy through zoology. In his letters he can be seen occupying himself with such matters as gardening, gunnery, rice, olives, fortifications, medicine, weaving, foundries, Greek and Latin grammar, weights and measures, the distillation of sea water, Indian languages, silk culture, spinning machines, steam engines, sulphur, tides, sawmills, sheep, meteors, plows, coinage, canals, almanacs, and torpedoes.

Yet Jefferson for all his learning did not live only in the scholar's study; he took his knowledge and thought out into the world of men and put them to practical use. He was that rare and happy combination, the man of thought and the man of action. He applied his knowledge to such diverse matters as designing a more efficient mold-board for a plow, transplanting seeds from Europe to New World soil, designing and building his own home, creating a university from the ground up. Most important of all, armed with his knowledge and understanding of political life—liberty, self-government, toleration, freedom of conscience—he entered the world of politics and government. As delegate to the Continental Congress, revolutionary governor of Virginia, minister to France, Secretary of State, Vice President, and President of the United States, he turned his thought into action in the Declaration of Independence, the statute on religious liberty, counsel to the revolutionaries in France, the creation of a new political party, the Louisiana

Purchase, and the sending of a scientific expedition to explore that vast territory. Few men ever had such opportunities or made so much of them.

Seeing him in this light, it is easy to understand why President John F. Kennedy, in greeting a distinguished company of American Nobel Prize winners, remarked: "This is the most distinguished company ever gathered for dinner at the White House, except possibly when Thomas Jefferson dined here alone."

Faced with such a distinguished personage, the range and scope of whose thought and action were so great that he seems a combination of the Encyclopædia Britannica and the major Greek gods—a phenomenon, not a man—it is easy to lose sight of Jefferson the human being. Jefferson himself occasionally had the same sensation, which is comforting to know. Sometimes he longed for rest from it all. "Let Adams have it," he said wearily when urged to be a candidate for President in 1796. He would be happier at Monticello "with the society of friends and neighbors, friends and fellow workers of the earth."

Jefferson the man comes through in his years in France from 1784 to 1789, which were perhaps the happiest of his life. We see him vacationing in the south of France in the spring of 1787, delighting in his solitude and reflecting in his room at a roadside inn that "a traveler . . . charmed with the tranquillity of his little cell . . . finds how few are our real wants, how cheap a thing is happiness." He communed with the ancient past, entranced by the Roman ruins at Nimes: "Here I am . . . gazing whole hours at the Maison quarree, like a lover at his mistress." The enchantment of being free, if only for a time, from the strains of public life, moved him to think that "If any person wished to retire from their acquaintance, to live absolutely unknown and yet in the midst of physical enjoyment, it should be in some of the little villages of this coast, where air, earth, and water concur to offer what each has most precious." Who in our time, backed to the wall by the pressures of a different world, would not for a few brief moments, at least, enjoy this form of happiness?

And let us not forget Jefferson, the forty-three-year-old widower in Paris who fell in love with Maria Cosway, wife of the English painter who was so busy with his own work that he did not object to Jefferson escorting his wife about. This was the Jefferson who, on a walk with the beautiful Mrs. Cosway, apparently tried to leap over a wall to demonstrate his virility, but fell and broke his wrist. Anyone who has ever been in love can understand this Jefferson.

And there is Jefferson the slave owner, a less attractive figure to many twentieth-century eyes, but no less human for that. We are all victims as well as beneficiaries of our own times. Jefferson was no exception. Ambivalent about slavery, he opposed the institution and feared its effects in the future, but along with the prevailing sentiment of the times felt no strong compulsion to free his slaves. Recent reexamination of an old story about his personal involvement with Sally Hemings, a quadroon and one of his slaves, suggests the possible truth of a story scholars have tended to dismiss as scurrilous: that for many years after the death of Jefferson's wife, Sally Hemings was Jefferson's mistress and bore him several children. The evidence is a web of circumstance, however, and the truth will never be known.

Yet even if the story were proved beyond all doubt, it would not detract from the Jefferson we know best, except for those who demand unattainable perfection and consistency in their leaders.

Jefferson's greatest contribution to America, and to the world, was his illumination in his extensive writings of a complex of ideas that constitute the clearest statement on democracy ever produced in America. His basic concern was to prove that a free society, government by consent of the governed, was practicable and sound; his basic hope was that the success of the American experiment would be a model for others. A few days after his inauguration as President, he wrote to John Dickinson:

> A just and solid republican government maintained here will be a standing monument and example for the aim and imitation of the people of other countries: and I join with you in the hope and belief that they will see from our example that a free government is of all others the most energetic; that the enquiry which has been excited among the mass of mankind by our revolution and its consequences, will ameliorate the condition of man over a great portion of the globe.

No one has ever spoken more clearly or with greater faith on the subject of democracy than Thomas Jefferson. Let him, therefore, speak for himself.

On self-government:

> Every man, and every body of men on earth possess the right of self-government. They receive it with their being from the hand of nature. Individuals exercise it by their single will: collections of men by that of their majority; for the law of the majority is the natural law of every society of men.

On the common sense of the people:

> I have such reliance in the good sense of the body of the people and the honesty of their leaders that I am not afraid of their letting things go wrong to any length in any case.

Where the people are well-informed they can be trusted with their own government; whenever things get so far wrong as to attract their notice, they may be relied on to set them to right.

On freedom of thought and press:

Our liberty depends upon the freedom of the press, and that cannot be limited without being lost.

I join you [he wrote to a young lawyer] in branding as cowardly the idea that the human mind is incapable of further advances. This is precisely the doctrine which the present despots of the earth are inculcating . . . and applying especially to religion and politics. . . . But thank heaven the American mind is already too much opened to listen to these impostures; and while the art of printing is left to us, science can never be retrograde; what is once acquired of real knowledge can never be lost. To preserve the freedom of the mind then and freedom of the press, every spirit should be ready to devote itself to martyrdom; for as long as we may think as we will and speak as we think, the condition of man will proceed in improvement.

On freedom of conscience and religious toleration:

Religion is a matter between every man and his maker, in which no other, and far less the public, has a right to intermeddle.

The rights of conscience we never submitted, we could not submit. We are answerable for them to our God. The legitimate powers of government extend to such acts only as are injurious to others. But it does me no injury for my neighbor to say there are twenty gods or no God. It neither picks my pocket nor breaks my leg.

And there is the Jefferson who speaks to every generation; the Jefferson who believed in change, that nothing human was permanent or immutable except the rights of man; the Jefferson who speaks to each generation as it takes its place upon the stage, who said "The earth belongs . . . to the living . . . and the dead have neither powers nor rights over it"; the Jefferson who wrote in 1816:

Some men look at constitutions with sanctimonious reverence and deem them like the ark of the covenant, too sacred to be touched. They ascribe to men of the preceding age a wisdom more than human, and suppose what they did to be beyond amendment. . . . I am certainly not an advocate of frequent and untried changes in laws and constitutions. . . . But I know also that laws and institutions must go hand in hand with the progress of the human mind. . . . As new discoveries are made, new truths disclosed, and manners and opinions change with the changes of circumstances, institutions must advance also and keep pace with the times. . . . Each generation . . . has the right to choose for itself the form of government it believes the most promotive of its own happiness. Nothing, then, is unchangeable but the inherent and inalienable rights of man.

Thus Thomas Jefferson, the master spokesman of democracy, whose great concern was freedom—freedom for the whole individual, for the spirit and the mind, who wrote as his epitaph: "Here was buried Thomas Jefferson, author of the Declaration of Independence, of the statute of Virginia for religious freedom, and father of the University of Virginia."

Keeping himself alive in his last months by sheer power of will, so that he might live to the fiftieth anniversary of the Declaration of Independence, he died in the early hours of July 4, 1826. In distant Massachusetts, his old friend John Adams died a few hours later, whispering "Thomas Jefferson survives." And so he does.

Part Two

THE NEW NATION

Chapter 6
THE UNITED STATES BECOMES A NATION: 1789–1865

The Spirit of the Times
NATIONALISM

It is not easy to become a nation, as many a new nation in Africa and Asia can painfully testify. Yet despite the difficulties, nationalism has been one of the most powerful forces in the modern world. Jefferson, a citizen of "the first new nation," may have been entertaining a certain sophisticated cosmopolitanism common to educated men in the eighteenth century when he grandly proclaimed France to be his second home. Yet he breathed a sigh of relief when he returned to American soil after his long service there. Most Americans today react the same way after even a short vacation abroad, and there is more to their relief than a conviction that they are returning to the perfect society, the land of perpetual bread and honey. They are coming <u>home</u>.

Even though you may disagree violently with your country's policies, detest its current leaders, and curse its reluctance to do what seems to you sound and sensible, it remains, after all—and the phrase has more meaning than appears at first glance—the country you love to hate. Thousands of young American men in the 1930s signed the Oxford Peace Pledge never to fight in war, but after the disaster at Pearl Harbor on December 7, 1941, they hastily applied for the privilege of getting shot in the defense of their country. In more recent times, harsh critics of American society have often been asked by exasperated defenders of the status quo why they simply did not depart for other shores if they found American life so unattractive; and almost invariably the response was that they did not wish to leave because they "love this country." It is because people become deeply identified with their own nation that they are able and willing to expend such energy upon it, in defense as well as in criticism. Few Americans ever spend as much time defending or criticizing other nations as they do their own. Fewer still ever go into

John Woodside's painting of a sailor free of his shackles and crushing a crown underfoot reflects the importance of freedom of the seas to the young nation. It was to become the justification for the War of 1812 as a principle necessary not only to the economic viability of the nation but to its sovereignty as well.

exile with any real pleasure or success, and when they do the pull to return is very strong. When Richard D. Bucklin, who went AWOL from the U.S. Army because of his opposition to the Vietnam War, returned in late 1973 from four and a half years of exile in Sweden, he told the press that he expected to spend time in prison for his desertion. But, he added, "it's a small price to pay to be home again."

What this suggests is that nationalism is essentially a matter of deep identity. It not only provides purpose and meaning to the life of a people as a whole, but to the lives of its individual citizens. So deep is this identity that most attempts to induce people to accept other identities, and loyalties that go beyond the confines of the nation, have failed. Cries of "Workers of the World, Unite," usually end at best in uniting only the workers of a particular country. Christian pronouncements that all people are part of the human family and should love one another get everyone's approval until the chips are down in a dispute, say, between the United States and Germany, and then there is a quick and easy shift to the assumption that only Americans are really your family, not Germans. Such is the power of national identity, and it has an equal grip on all nations.

Nationalism is complex and elusive, and few understand it fully. But it may be partly defined in the following ways.

To begin with, nationalism depends upon the political independence of a people grouped within a definable geographic territory. That is to say, such a people assume the right to decide their own affairs and work out their own destiny without interference from without or disruption from within. Major goals of any nation, therefore, are to provide for its own survival and security as an independent political unit. Although a nation may rely upon a number of techniques to accomplish these goals, survival and security finally come down to the nation's ability to defend itself. Hence the compulsion, even among the smallest and poorest nations, to acquire armies, navies, and air forces. Even if a nation can field only a battalion of infantry, a thirty-year-old gunboat, and a Piper Cub armed with a Gatling gun, these at least indicate the nation's determination, if not its ability, to preserve itself.

But there is more to it than this. No nation has any reasonable assurance of survival and security without unity. There must be a common and accepted political, economic, social, and cultural framework within which the life of the nation takes place. If there is not, the nation is weakened in its capacity to direct its own affairs without interference, and in its ability to avoid fragmentation. This unity, and the loyalty it implies, rest upon a sense of identity growing from shared experiences, of being more alike than different, and of feeling that the fate of each is bound up in the fate of all. In any people the sense of nationalism grows from these shared experiences (or history), from common goals and objectives (or the anticipated future), from attachment to the land they live on, and from the society and culture they share: the religion, art, culture, political experience, education, and language.

Finally, nationalism implies for any people that their nation, its society, history, culture, destiny, and way of doing things are special and superior. At the least, there is pride or desire for pride in the nation individuals call their own, so that even criticism and demands for improvement are a part of nationalism.

Any people seeking to become a nation are thus found working hard to preserve and protect their independence, to build unity, to create and promote a common identity, and to emphasize the special quality of that identity.

So it was for the Americans in the great period of nation building from 1789 to 1865. In fact, almost everything that took place in America in this period can be understood in whole or in part by the concept of nationalism as it has here been defined.

Problems of American Nationalism

The course of nation building, like that of true love, never runs smooth, and there is always someone around to say it will not work. There were those both at home and abroad who were skeptical about the chances of the new

United States. In 1790 the Englishman Josiah Tucker scoffed at the whole idea: "As to the future grandeur of America and its being a rising Empire under *one* head, whether republican or monarchical, it is one of the idlest and most visionary notions that was ever conceived even by writers of romance."

Strong words, but it is easy to see why some people felt that way. Look at the odds. In 1789 the population was small, less than four million people, somewhat smaller than the new African state of Ghana when it gained its independence in 1957. This limited population was scattered over an area larger than that of any state in Europe except the empires of Austria and Russia. It was thus difficult to bind the American people into a cohesive unit, a difficulty compounded by the shortage of transportation and communication. In the 1790s it took four days to travel from Washington to New York, and four weeks from New Orleans to Washington. And large as they were, the new United States occupied but a fraction of the continent that they shared with four major powers: Britain and Spain as of 1789, France in 1800 when it secured Louisiana from Spain, and Russia, whose presence was of no consequence until later. Moreover, for all its previous economic growth and unquestioned potential, the American economy was weak and undiversified. Overwhelmingly agricultural, it lacked manufacturing capacity, and its markets were essentially local. Such weakness posed problems of survival, as the Revolution clearly showed.

Political survival was precarious also because the new nation was embarking upon a new experiment in government. The question was not only whether it could withstand threats from without, but whether it could keep from fragmenting under the pressure of forces within. The Constitution was, after all, untested, and the national authority it provided was neither fully understood nor completely defined. Indeed, that authority was to be questioned time and again in the period of national growth, culminating in the great challenge of civil war.

In terms of the unity provided by a common cultural identity, the Americans faced problems of equal seriousness. As the nation began its first decade, isolation hampered cultural interchange and made it difficult for Americans to think of themselves as an identifiable cultural unit. Moreover, the Americans had no common art, literature, science, or scholarship, and no organized and developed sense of their own past. The simple fact was that in the main areas of cultural life they were heavily dependent upon Europe. It was with a certain sense of shock if not humiliation, for example, that in building his University of Virginia Jefferson discovered that he was compelled to seek abroad for its first faculty.

How, then, were these problems of national security, unity, and identity dealt with?

National Security

The presence of major European powers on the North American continent, or even in the Western Hemisphere, was a matter of concern to those responsible for the security and preservation of the new republic. The British held Canada and claimed joint occupancy of the Oregon Territory. Spain possessed the Floridas, the Southwest, the Pacific coast, and for a while the vast interior of the country known as the Louisiana Territory. France returned at the opening of the nineteenth century when Spain ceded the Louisiana territory to Napoleon. She attempted to return again at the time of the Civil War when French troops put Maximilian on the throne in Mexico. Russia had been in Alaska since the 1780s and in 1821 claimed a hundred miles off shore as far south as the fifty-first parallel, suggesting an interest in pushing the southern boundary of Alaska deep into Oregon country.

The American Response: Expansionism

The American response to all this was simple: to ignore no opportunity to take possession of as much of the continent as possible, preferably all of it, and in the process to push the European powers out. When it proved necessary, the Americans were prepared to turn on their own neighbors within the hemisphere, even though in a series of revolutions after 1810 these neighbors threw Spain out of Central and South America and set up their own independent republics in flattering imitation of the United States. Such was the case in the war with Mexico, when that chaotic country had the misfortune to possess the last great territories standing between the United States and the Pacific.

The story of American expansionism, therefore, is the story of growth at the expense of everyone else, in the process acquiring natural security against threats from the outside. From 1789 to 1867, the Americans talked, fought, threatened, bullied, bluffed, cajoled, plowed, schemed, drove, walked, and purchased their way across the continent in one of the most extraordinary cases of nation building in history. At the end, the original thirteen states on the eastern seaboard had expanded beyond the most grandiose vision, certainly far beyond Jefferson's concept of what would satisfy the Americans for a thousand years.

In its expansion, every step of which reduced the threat of foreign powers and made more irresistible the succeeding steps, the United States relied upon war, the threat of war, diplomacy, and the judicious use of money. Behind these instruments of expansion, and giving them weight, was a surging population rapidly expanding through natural growth and immigration. The population exploded eight-fold from under 4 million in 1790 to 31.5 million in 1860, and it steadily and aggressively pushed across the continent, even before the land had become part of the United States. It was a simple matter of arithmetic, or so Representative Kennedy of Indiana told the Congress in 1846: "Our people are spreading out with the aid of the American multiplication table. Go to the West and see a young man with his mate of eighteen; after the lapse of thirty years, visit him again, and instead of two, you will find twenty-two. That is what I call the American multiplication table." Less able to appreciate the mathematics of the situation, the British, Spanish, and Mexicans were more inclined to call it greed.

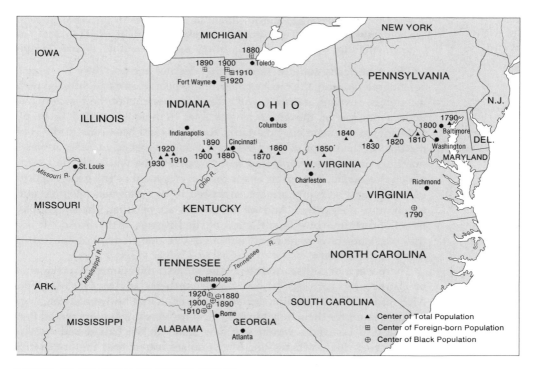

SHIFTS IN CENTERS OF POPULATION

Manifest Destiny   The employment of these national instruments of expansion was justified in the public mind by the widespread conviction that it was the destiny of the United States to acquire and dominate the continent: from 1800 to 1860 nationalistic newspapers, politicians, and private citizens made the point in language ranging from the ridiculous to the absurd. The New York *Evening Post* declared in 1801 that "It belongs of right to the United States to regulate the future destiny of North America." Two decades later another fervent expansionist put God on the side of American destiny: "The great engineer of the universe has fixed the natural limits of our country, and man cannot change them. . . . To that boundary we shall go; peaceably if we can, forcibly if we must . . ."

As time went on the Almighty apparently had become even more generous. In the 1840s, a toastmaster of vision breezily proposed these "limits" to the United States: "The Eagle of the United States—may she extend her wings from the Atlantic to the Pacific, and fixing her talons on the Isthmus of Darien, stretch her beak to the Northern Pole!" This may seem heady brew, but it was mild compared to the prospect which Congressman Davis of Mississippi placed before the House of Representatives in 1859:

> We may expand so as to include the whole world. Mexico, Central America, South America, Cuba, the West India Islands, and even England and France

the United States might annex without inconvenience or prejudice, allowing them with their local Legislatures to regulate their local affairs in their own way. And this, Sir, is the mission of the Republic and its ultimate destiny.

The Americans could believe in this destiny because they were, in their considered opinion, the most extraordinary people on earth, blessed with the mission to develop, transmit, and extend the benefits of their society over as wide a portion of the globe as possible. If there happened to be a few Englishmen, Frenchmen, Spaniards, Russians, and Mexicans in the way, no matter. As the editor of the *Democratic Review* asserted in 1850, it was "our manifest destiny to overspread and to possess the whole of the Continent which Providence has given us for the development of the great experiment of liberty and self-government entrusted to us." Herman Melville put it a touch more poetically: "And we Americans are peculiar, chosen people, the Israel of our times; we bear the ark of the liberties of the world." It is clear that the Americans were amply supplied with one element of nationalism, a sense of superiority.

There were, of course, doubts. Some felt that the country was big enough, or claimed territory too far away and worthless anyway. In 1843 Senator McDuffie of South Carolina declared of Oregon that he "would not . . . give a pinch of snuff for the whole territory." Some New Englanders feared that the purchase of Louisiana would add new states to the Union and reduce the influence of their own region. Abolitionists feared that the annexation of Texas would spread slavery. Some legalists argued that the acquisition of new territories was unconstitutional. And there were those who doubted our mandate to save the world. The Boston *Advertiser* in the 1820s asked in some exasperation: "Is there anything in the Constitution which makes our Government the Guarantor of the Liberties of the World?"

But all such doubts were swept aside. By 1867 the territory of the United States had grown to its present size, except for a few islands in the Caribbean and the Pacific.

The Major Acquisitions   The major acquisitions are well known. The first and probably the easiest was by the Louisiana Purchase, which came about more or less by accident. Evidence now indicates that Napoleon was probably planning some kind of adventures in the New World. But reverses in his attempts to reassert French control in the Caribbean, especially in Santo Domingo, plus a broadening of his campaign plans for Europe, caused him to reconsider, and he suddenly made the decision to unload. Jefferson's agents in Paris, there to negotiate for the purchase of New Orleans, suddenly found themselves faced with the greatest real estate deal in history. The outcome was that for $15 million the United States was doubled in size. A few years later in 1810 American settlers, who had pushed into the Spanish-owned lands along the Gulf of Mexico known as West Florida, simply seized control of the region and handed it over to the United States. The rest of Florida was acquired by negotiation in 1819 as part of a larger settlement with Spain. The western boundary of the Louisiana Territory had never been

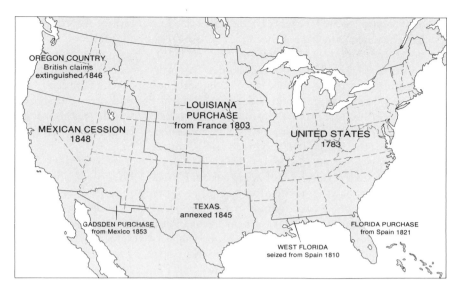

OREGON COUNTRY
British claims
extinguished 1846

MEXICAN CESSION
1848

LOUISIANA
PURCHASE
from France 1803

UNITED STATES
1783

TEXAS
annexed 1845

GADSDEN PURCHASE
from Mexico 1853

FLORIDA PURCHASE
from Spain 1821

WEST FLORIDA
seized from Spain 1810

TERRITORIAL ACQUISITIONS

clearly defined, and the line between it and Spanish Mexico was open to question. Fearful of losing the rest of Florida anyway, Spain agreed to give up Florida in return for an American assumption of the claims of American citizens against Spain (amounting to $5 million) and for a firm boundary commitment as far east of the Rio Grande as possible. In the treaty of 1819 that boundary now followed the Sabine, Red, and Arkansas rivers to the Continental Divide and the forty-second parallel to the Pacific which, though preserving Spanish Mexico for Spain, meant that Spain ceded to the United States its claims to the Oregon Territory.

The American appetite, however, remained insatiable. In the following decade and a half, large numbers of American settlers moved into the northern portion of Mexico and by 1835 were powerful enough to engage in revolution against the Mexican government and to establish the new republic of Texas in 1836. Ten years later, Texas was annexed to the United States. War with Mexico over this act and the disputed southern boundary of Texas followed a year later. Victory over Mexico yielded to the United States one of its biggest expansionist prizes—those vast areas now encompassing the states of California, Nevada, New Mexico, Arizona, Utah, and of course Texas. The final piece of territory from Mexico came to the United States in 1854 in the Gadsden Purchase. A large area now comprising the southern portions of Arizona and New Mexico lay in the path of a proposed southern route for an American transcontinental railroad. After negotiation, it passed to the United States for $10 million.

Meanwhile, at the time American relations with Mexico were slipping into war, the United States was trying to settle the matter of the Oregon Territory held jointly by the United States and Britain. Thousands of American settlers had migrated into the southern part of the Oregon country and, not surprisingly, the Americans quoted the ancient dictum that possession was nine points of the law. There was a great deal of hard-nosed talk about fighting for the entire territory if necessary. But both countries had already offered several times to compromise the issue, and in the end common sense prevailed. In 1846 by treaty the forty-ninth parallel, which was the northern boundary of the Louisiana Purchase, was simply extended as the dividing line from the Rocky Mountains to the Pacific.

The last great acquisition of American territory came after the Civil War in 1867 with the purchase of Alaska from Russia. This project, however, was different in that the acquisition was not originally proposed by the Americans. Although American ignorance of Alaska at first produced considerable opposition to the purchase, once the word spread about its great resources, and the possibility that in the future the area might fall to Britain, the opposition faded. For $7 million the land passed to the United States, and Russia departed from the New World.

At the end of it all, after six and a half decades, from 1803 to 1867, the United States stood dominant on the North American continent. The nation stretched from sea to sea and had grown in size from 888,811 square miles to 3,615,211 square miles. The new lands were a reservoir of unbelievable wealth. The vast territories gained by the Louisiana Purchase and the war with Mexico contained some of the richest grain-producing lands in the world, extensive grazing for a future cattle industry of major proportions, endless forests of diverse timbers, and staggering deposits of copper, iron, lead, zinc, gold, silver, oil, uranium, and other valuable minerals. Alaska possessed great resources of fish, fur, timber, gold, and on the North Slope one of the world's great reservoirs of petroleum, a dividend not known until the 1960s.

The resources were America's main economic strength and hence its power as a great nation. Yet no one at the time had any firm concept of the real wealth represented by these lands, nor did the United States have the means to exploit that wealth. Indeed, throughout the process of expansion, the Americans had more land than they had any need for. As late as 1820 there were still unsettled acres in the original thirteen states, and many counties were underpopulated. Parts of existing states were still frontier at the time Americans were pushing to acquire additional lands.

When the process of expansion was completed, there was no foreign threat to the United States on this continent; that goal of American nationalism had been reached. To reinforce its intention to reach that goal, the United States in 1823 asserted that the entire New World was no longer to be considered a site for European colonization. Talk by some European powers of regaining for Spain its New World lands lost in the Latin American revolutions of 1817 to 1822 led to the Monroe Doctrine, embodied in President James Monroe's annual message to Congress in 1823: "The American continents by the free and independent condition which they have assumed and maintain, are henceforth not to be considered as subjects for future

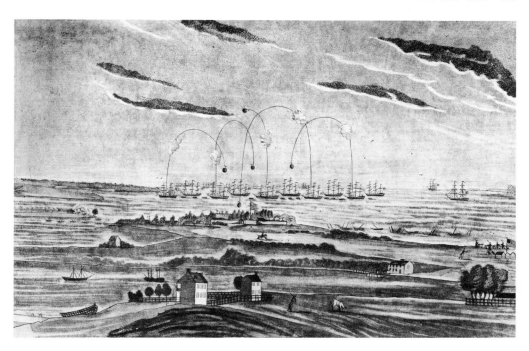

A View of the Bombardment of Fort McHenry. *The United States was unprepared and ill equipped for the war declared by President Madison in 1812 and suffered a series of defeats and humiliations in the early stages of the conflict. But in 1814 this small fort on the outskirts of Baltimore withstood twenty-five hours of bombardment and prevented the British from landing.*

colonization by any European powers." Attempts to do so, said Monroe, would be considered a threat to the "peace and safety" of the United States. Any European plans to regain Spain's lands in the New World were checked more by British opposition than by Monroe's statement. But if in 1823 the United States had no real power to enforce its manifesto, it later acquired the power, as Napoleon III recognized in 1867 when he withdrew French troops from Mexico where they had been sent to place the young Austrian, Maximilian, on an uncertain throne, and as Khruschev discovered almost a century later when he withdrew Russian missiles from their equally uneasy base in Cuba.

One vaguely pursued goal of American expansionism—Canada, the acquisition of which would have removed the British completely from the North American continent—was never attained. Though a desire for Canada played no part in the development of the clash with the British, the War of 1812 did offer an opportunity to seize Canada. And after the war began a number of Americans talked in these terms. But the total failure of the

American expeditionary forces against the British in Canada killed that possibility. The war, however, did serve the interests of American expansionism in other ways. It marked the final elimination of the Indian barrier in the Northwest, a process already underway before the war under the relentless pressure of western frontiersmen and General William Henry Harrison, governor of the Indiana Territory. The war also opened a new era of amicable relations with the British. Shortly after the war the basis for favorable trade relations was laid by agreement at a commercial convention, commissions were established to settle boundary disputes between Canada and the United States, although the completion of the task took years, American fishing rights off Newfoundland and Labrador were settled, and demilitarization of the Great Lakes and ultimately the entire border was achieved. After the war, therefore, Britain no longer seemed a threat to American national security. Canada itself was to develop at a slower pace than the United States, and was never seen as a threat. In fact, Canadian development was so much influenced in subsequent years by the United States that to most Americans Canada bore little resemblance to a foreign nation, and indeed seemed so natural a part of the United States in an unofficial way that expansionists throughout the nineteenth century confidently assumed that sooner or later Canada would voluntarily become one of the United States. Hence there was no need to spend money, force, or diplomatic effort to gain what would eventually fall "like a ripe plum" of its own accord. This assumption was, of course, resented by the Canadians, and ironically stimulated a determined Canadian national sentiment.

Such was American expansion, surely one of the big success stories of all time. Yet living as we do today in a world that has seen the most calamitous results stem from national aggression and expansionist desires, a world that has grown weary of the dangerous and extreme lengths to which nations are apparently willing to go to protect their security, we are often tempted to damn the more aggressive aspects of American expansion. In retrospect these seem a kind of prologue for the worst to come, the sort of bad example no one wants to admit having been. But there was an innocent exuberance about American expansionism that bears little resemblance to the calculated and threatening national assertions that have marred the twentieth century.

The clash with Mexico—a hemisphere neighbor, not a European power—was a distressing event and one that upset many Americans at the time. But the territories acquired from Mexico, which had inherited claim to them from Spain, were vast and had been little populated or developed. Those who argue that it would have been better had the Americans not taken their neighbor's property have, however, to reckon with the realities of the westward movement. As the experience of Texas showed, American settlers would have moved in anyway. Half of Mexico would have been dominated by Americans. Given their political and economic aggressiveness and sophistication, the Americans would have become a powerful, possibly dominant element in the life of all Mexico. The real tragedy in national expansion westward sprang from its impact on Indian life and culture—a story to be discussed later.

PLUCKED:
OR,
THE MEXICAN·EAGLE BEFORE THE WAR!   THE MEXICAN EAGLE AFTER THE WAR!

A cartoon from the New York weekly Yankee Doodle. *The question of war with Mexico, developing over the immediate problem of the annexation of Texas in 1845 but encompassing the much broader issue of manifest destiny, was a subject of bitter dispute between Whigs and Democrats. This pro-war cartoon was typical of Democrat opinion.*

The motives behind American expansionism may seem in retrospect to have been selfish and greedy, and the rationale as naive at best and hypocritical at worst. The rhetoric of expansion was crude and its tone embarrassing to modern ears, but proclamations that the American drive from coast to coast would best promote and extend the blessings of liberty to themselves and their posterity were accepted at face value by most Americans. Their national life was in fact highly influenced by the desire to improve and extend democracy among themselves as well as to promote it elsewhere by their successful example.

The Americans seriously believed that the exclusion of European nations would promote national security. Expressing sentiments to be repeated time and again in other instances as well, Niles' *Weekly Register* in 1819 observed of the Spanish-held Floridas that their possession by the United States "was found by experience to be indispensable to the safety of our citizens—they had been to us as an enemy's country . . . and . . . ought to have been seized upon many years ago." Certainly a United States hemmed in by foreign territories and sharing the continent with major European powers could have faced an uneasy future, and its subsequent history would have been radically different.

National Unity

The security of the new nation rested on more than rapid expansion across the continent. In fact, its rapid growth posed serious problems. For no nation is safe if its lands are not connected, if its people remain isolated, if it is not economically secure, if its authority among its own people is not defined, recognized, and accepted: if it is not, in short, united. Much of American development in this period led to the achievement of this unity.

Economic Developments   Of primary importance to national unity was a secure and dynamic economy. It is satisfying to the ego to strut across the world's stage, but if at the same time you are deep in debt, have a dubious credit rating at home and abroad, and find your economic activities largely of one kind, then prospects are not exactly encouraging. Independence under such circumstances is more imaginary than real. Many an underdeveloped new nation in the world today has had to face the same painful experience, and with far fewer advantages than had the new United States.

Hamilton's work as secretary of the treasury in the 1790s put the United States on a secure financial footing (see the Profile). Two important tasks remained if the nation was to have the economic security and independence Hamilton believed to be essential to its survival. The economy had to be unified, and it had to be diversified. Two economic revolutions developing in the first seven decades of the young republic's existence made possible the achievement of these goals and each as it occurred reinforced the other: an astonishing growth in transportation and communications, and the equally impressive building of an industrial establishment.

A number of factors fed and nourished these economic revolutions. Of major significance was the flood of inventions and new technological processes that washed over the Western world, some of which sprang from Yankee ingenuity and others from European expertise. Regardless of the source, the Americans proved eager and willing to put them to rapid use. Eli Whitney set the pattern with the invention of the cotton gin in 1792, which not only expanded Southern agriculture by giving it a new crop—upland cotton—but made possible the rise of the cotton mills of New England. Of even greater significance was Whitney's use of interchangeable parts in manufacturing—the basic idea in mass production—which he worked out in a limited way while under contract to produce muskets for the government. In later decades the system of interchangeable parts allowed such things as clocks, watches, hardware, sewing machines, and other items to be produced

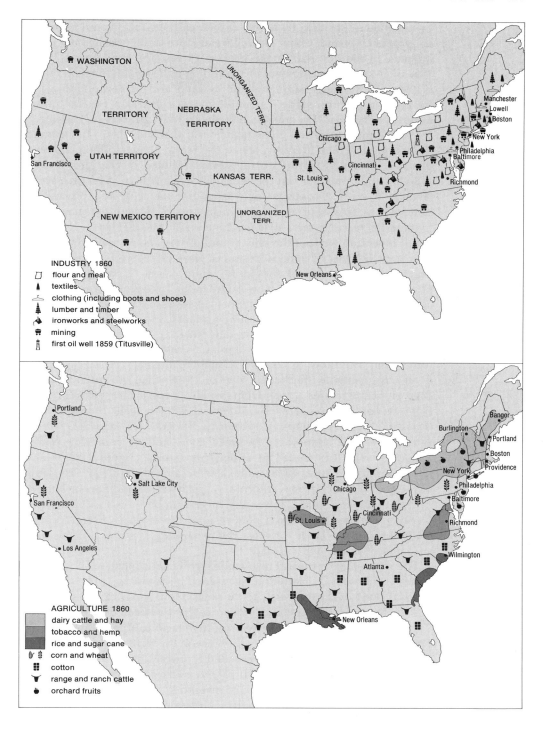

INDUSTRY 1860
- ☐ flour and meal
- ⬧ textiles
- ⚓ clothing (including boots and shoes)
- 🌲 lumber and timber
- ⚒ ironworks and steelworks
- ⚖ mining
- 🗼 first oil well 1859 (Titusville)

AGRICULTURE 1860
- dairy cattle and hay
- tobacco and hemp
- rice and sugar cane
- 🌾 🌾 corn and wheat
- ⬛ cotton
- ⬥ range and ranch cattle
- ● orchard fruits

MANUFACTURING AND AGRICULTURE, 1860

by machine rather than by highly skilled workers turning out each individual product by hand. Other technological innovations speeded the growth of industry in the first half of the nineteenth century. For example, after the War of 1812 the development of the rolling mill simplified the manufacture of sheet iron formerly hammered out by hand, and the new puddling process for refining pig iron made it possible to use cheap coal for fuel instead of expensive charcoal. The invention of the cylinder process for making paper led to the mechanization and expansion of that industry. The invention of the sewing machine literally created the ready-made clothing and shoe industries. Cyrus McCormick's inventions resulted in the farm machinery industry and brought about the enormous expansion of Western agriculture. And so it went. Dozens of new machines, devices, and processes, and hundreds of small but useful improvements in design and manufacturing method helped to bring a new machine world into being.

But invention was not the only stimulus to economic development. Every year new deposits of natural resources were discovered and exploited. For example, the opening of the Sault Sainte Marie Canal in 1855 made it possible to move the rich iron ore found in the Lake Superior region by water and rail to the bituminous coal districts of western Pennsylvania and eastern Ohio, where coke furnaces, puddling furnaces, and rolling mills were linked together to turn out finished iron rails for the railroads. Capital, too, supported the revolutions in transportation, communication, and industry, and came from a number of sources. Commercial wealth first flowed into industry, for example, during the War of 1812, when the conflict cut off the flow of manufactured goods from Britain. Capital also increasingly came from the profits generated by industrial growth itself. Foreign investors increasingly poured funds into America. By 1839, for example, British citizens alone held somewhere between $110 million and $165 million in American securities issued to underwrite internal improvements such as canals and roads. After 1848 capital also became available as a consequence of the gold discoveries in California. A greatly increased flow of immigrants in the 1840s and 1850s, especially large numbers of unskilled Irish and German workers, provided a pool of poor but eager workers, from which could be drawn a labor force for the expanding factories and for the construction of canals and railroads.

The national government also made significant contribution to these economic revolutions, as Hamilton had argued it should. In 1816, when the first postwar flood of cheap British goods poured into America and threatened to destroy those struggling young industries that had been built during the war, Congress passed the first openly protective tariff to shield American manufacturers from foreign competition. A rise in the tariff also occurred in 1824, 1828, and 1832, as Congress responded to increasing pressure from American manufacturers. Congress also passed a series of patent laws, beginning in the 1790s, to protect the work of inventors.

These were the factors that nourished the economic revolution in America from 1789 to 1860. What were the achievements that were wrought by these revolutions?

Transportation and Communication

Roads and Bridges Beginning in the last decade of the eighteenth century came the first extensive building of roads and bridges. Existing roads were for the most part little more than trails, impossible for heavy wagons and dangerous to those on horse and foot. Rivers and streams had to be forded, often a risky venture, or crossed on ferries of uncertain schedule and operation. By 1820, roads and bridges were everywhere improved, linking North and South and tying the nearby interior to the coastal cities. State and local governments did the building or chartered private companies to do the job, the latter getting their return by toll charges. Most charters provided that after a specific period roads and bridges were to become public and toll-free. The national government became involved in the process by constructing a major east-west road from Cumberland, Maryland, to central Illinois.

Canal Building Useful as roads were, transportation by land was slow and expensive. It cost $70 to ship a ton of goods by road from Pittsburgh to Philadelphia. This situation resulted in the boom in canal building, which began soon after the War of 1812. Within twenty years over 3,300 miles of canals linked rivers and lakes into a vast network binding together the interior and the seaboard. The first and most successful of the major canals was the New York Erie Canal, constructed at a cost of $7 million and returning to the state a profit within a few years, one of the few times that happened. Connecting the Hudson with Lake Erie, the canal provided unbelievably cheap transportation, cutting the cost of hauling goods from New York City to the Great Lakes by ninety-five percent. Canals in the interior, in Indiana, Ohio, and Illinois, tied that region to the Atlantic ports by way of the Great Lakes and the Erie, or to the Gulf through the Ohio and Mississippi rivers. Canal construction took place everywhere, even where geography prevented complete linkage. Pennsylvania, Maryland, Virginia, New Jersey—no state was immune to the fever. Some states, dazzled by the financial success of the Erie, overextended and lost heavily, as did the investors in their bonds. Some sixty percent of the $200 million that went into canal construction came from the public funds of the various states—which was Hamiltonian subsidizing with a vengeance.

Although canals, together with rivers and lakes, made possible cheap transportation by boat, water transport remained slow, and upstream traffic was impossible on any large scale. Technology solved this problem and made possible the full use of the rivers of the interior by the invention of the steamboat. It was the river steamboat that opened up a new era of economic development in the West.

The Railroad Important as these developments were, the appearance of the railroad was far more so. Its worth already demonstrated in England, the railroad was first introduced into America in the late 1820s. There were a few years of experimentation, but in less than three decades the railroad had

THE EXTENT OF THE RAILROADS, 1860

revolutionized American life. By 1860 there were thirty thousand miles of track, linking areas of production to areas of consumption, making possible the exploitation of the country's natural resources, creating a national market, and bringing into being a truly national economy. The railroad could carry more goods to more places in a far shorter time at less cost than horse-drawn vehicles, canal barges, or steamboats.

As some canal builders learned to their sorrow, you can't build canals just anywhere, nor can you change the course of a river or shift a lake to accomodate a steamboat. But the railroad engine could darken any sky. And building upon the considerable accomplishments of canal, road, and steamboat, the railroad stimulated economic development and opened up the country beyond what anyone had thought possible at the beginning of the century. In the single decade from 1850 to 1860, for example, the shipments of western corn to the East rose from 3.6 million to 19 million bushels, of western pork from 300,000 barrels to 900,000. In the same decade the population of Illinois doubled. It was the railroad that made the crucial difference.

It is significant that the railroad—wherever it came into being, not just in the United States—created a new concept of space, the space of national unity. No one was interested in laying track to link the United States to Mexico or to Canada. But it is worth remembering that even during the terrible crisis of the Civil War, the initial steps in construction of the first transcontinental line were taken to bind the east coast to the west. With the arrival of the airplane and the rocket ship in the twentieth century, we have been brought face to face with still another new concept of distance, sweeping far beyond the confines of national space as these were defined by the railroad of the nineteenth century, a new concept of unity whose implications we have yet fully to grasp and respond to.

The Telegraph Accompanying the railroad in its march across the country were the lines of the telegraph, an invention that rounded out the nineteenth-century revolution in transportation and communication and made it possible for words to travel far faster than either people or their goods. In 1852, only eight years after Morse transmitted the first message from Washington to Baltimore, there were 23,000 miles of telegraph lines in operation. Since it was both easier and cheaper to string wire than to lay track, the telegraph crossed the continent well ahead of the railroad. On October 24, 1861, the President of the United States received a telegram from the head of the Overland Telegraph Company:

> I announce to you that the telegraph to California has this day been completed. May it be a bond of perpetuity between the states of the Atlantic and those of the Pacific.

The telegraph made it possible for the railroads to operate more efficiently, but more important, it greatly improved business communications, allowing businessmen to learn within hours instead of days or weeks the latest details on prices, goods, and services in all parts of the country so essential to the conduct of their affairs.

Industrial Growth The other major achievement that turned into reality Hamilton's dream of one great American system—an indissoluble Union—was the rise of industry, which went hand in hand with the revolution in transportation and communication.

It is customary to mark the beginnings of American industry with young Samuel Slater, an English immigrant with factory experience, who in 1790 was spinning cotton thread by machines operated by a handful of children. By the opening of the nineteenth century there were a number of small mills and factories in operation, many of them precarious ventures. As has been

View of Lowell, Massachusetts. The city was a center of the textile industry in the early nineteenth century and the site of several important technological innovations.

noted, the War of 1812 saw a rise in the number of factories as many commercial men put money into factories to produce the goods no longer imported from Britain. Many of these failed after the war, but by the 1820s and 1830s the manufacture of goods by machines was put on a sound basis. In the 1820s, for example, the number of cotton spindles in New England factories increased from around 190,000 to 1,200,000.

By the 1840s and 1850s the factory system had hit its stride, and the major industries had been established. By 1860 the total value of manufactured goods produced in the country was almost $2 billion. One state alone, Massachusetts, was by 1855 producing yearly nearly $300 million worth of goods, far more than the entire country four decades earlier. The census of 1860 revealed that there were 140,000 manufacturing establishments in the nation, and approximately 1,500,000 workers in industrial enterprises. The ten major industries in America on the eve of the Civil War were, in terms of the value of their products, the flour and meal business, cotton goods, lumber, boots and shoes, men's clothing, iron, leather, woolen goods, liquor, and machinery, eight of which relied upon agriculture for their raw materials. Over a century later, the leading industries in America in terms of the value of their products included the automobile industry, steel and iron, communications equipment (including radio, TV, telephone and telegraph), petroleum, publishing, aircraft (including engines and parts), machinery (excluding electrical), pharmaceutical products, lumber and wood products, and ordnance and accessories (including missiles)—and not one of these relied on agriculture for its raw materials. Though a majority of the labor force in 1860, somewhat less than sixty percent, was still employed in agriculture, a great change was taking place. The capital invested in industries, railroads, commerce, and city property already exceeded in dollars the value of all farms and plantations from the East coast to the West.

This economic revolution, for a nation that had been so overwhelmingly agricultural only a half-century earlier, was considerable and widely recognized. By 1850 the United States led the world in the production of goods requiring the use of precision instruments, and the display of these and other products of American industry at the Crystal Palace Exhibition in London in 1851 astounded viewers. Prizes for originality of design were won by the Borden "meat biscuit," the Dick engine tools and presses, the Bond device for observing astronomical phenomena, Goodyear India rubber, and the McCormick reaper. The working demonstration of McCormick's farm machinery under adverse conditions in the field literally dumbfounded observers. The London *Times* remarked that "Great Britain has received more useful ideas, and more ingenious inventions, from the United States, through the exhibition, than from all other sources."

Punch put the case for American superiority to the British in a different fashion:

> Your gunsmiths of their skill may crack;
> But that again don't mention;
> I guess that Colt's revolvers whack
> Their very first invention.
> By Yankee Doodle, too, you're beat
> Downright in Agriculture,
> With his machine for reaping wheat,
> Chaw'd up as by a vulture.

More practically, the British government was sufficiently impressed to send commissions to the United States to study American manufacturing techniques and practices, and ended ordering equipment and hiring technicians to establish an arms factory in England. One of the pleasant ironies of American achievement was that the London *Times*, which delighted in denouncing American political institutions, ran its tirades on rotary presses that came from the United States.

The effect of these economic revolutions was dramatic. When the nineteenth century opened, markets were local, production was limited, and most things were done by hand. Americans wore homemade clothes turned from the raw wool of their own sheep into a finished product by the women of the household or a local artisan. A nearby tannery produced leather that went to a village shoemaker who produced boots and shoes on order. Guns were handmade by the village blacksmith, and tools and farm equipment were made by a local blacksmith or the farmer himself. Travel was on foot or by wagon. But by 1860, markets were national, production was steadily expanding, and much of the work of America was being done by machines.

Samuel Colt's first patent. Colt designed the first practical revolving firearm, but was unsuccessful in his first attempt to market it because he could not persuade the army and navy to purchase it. Unable to sustain itself with sales to individuals, the business failed in 1842 and Colt lost his patents. But with the outbreak of the war with Mexico came an order from the federal government for a thousand pistols. Colt's business was re-established and his success was guaranteed.

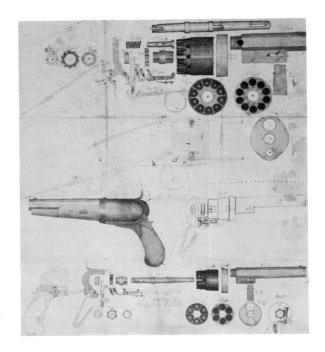

Americans were using factory-manufactured cloth and wearing factory-made clothing and shoes. Their weapons came from Colt factories, and their fields were furrowed by manufactured plows. When they traveled, more likely than not they went by rail.

By 1860, in short, the United States had achieved through major developments in transportation, communications, and manufacturing the kind of economic strength, diversification, and unity that seemed to suggest that the country was indeed one nation. It was not quite that, because these developments did not apply uniformly across the country. But what Hamilton had in mind for America was well on the way to full realization.

Political Unity

Yet economic bonds alone were not enough to make a nation. Political strength and unity were also essential. The new nation had to establish the authority of its government under the Constitution. The question was whether that authority could be defined and exercised in a manner acceptable to the American people—few of whom, then or now, have been noted for their acceptance of authority unless it served their own self-interest.

For the most part, however, this national authority was accepted without question, a fact that suggests that it did indeed serve the interests of most people. The Constitution quickly became a highly revered document. But it could be construed over a wide range of interpretations. And in cases of dispute, disagreement, and doubt the Supreme Court and the Presidency played the major roles in asserting and establishing the authority of the national government.

The Supreme Court and John Marshall   The Supreme Court, in the early crucial decades of national development, was dominated by John Marshall, who served as Chief Justice from 1801 to 1835. Marshall believed in a strong national government, and few men did more than he to define the supremacy and authority of that government. Judicially, Marshall laid the foundations for American political nationalism by his insistence that the Constitution sprang from the authority of the people, not from any compact of separate sovereign states as Calhoun argued. He held that the national executive (the Presidency), legislative (the Congress), and judicial agencies (the courts), established by the Constitution were supreme, and that it was this condition that constituted the nation as a political unit. It was this interpretation, not that espoused by Calhoun, that was ultimately to prevail.

During Marshall's long years on the Court legislative acts passed by more than half of the states were declared unconstitutional. One of the most important of the cases defining the authority of the national government was that of *McCulloch v. Maryland.* After the War of 1812, various state-chartered banks sought legislative aid in curtailing the powerful competition they faced from the United States Bank. A number of states, including Maryland, had passed legislation requiring any bank not chartered by the state to pay a tax for the right to issue notes. McCulloch, the cashier of the Baltimore branch of the Bank of the United States, refused to pay the $15,000 tax and was promptly sued by the state of Maryland. Speaking for a unanimous court, Marshall declared that the Maryland law was unconstitutional since Congress had a perfect legal right to create the United States Bank. Although, of course, the Constitution itself did not provide for the creation of a national bank, its legality was implied in the many powers specifically granted to Congress, which must have "discretion," said Marshall, in deciding how its powers "are to be carried into execution." Through this and similar decisions it gradually became established that federal law takes precedence over state law.

Five years later, in *Gibbons v. Ogden* in 1824, Marshall made the same point and further strengthened the doctrine of the implied powers in the Constitution. Ogden held a New York state-granted monopoly for steamboat navigation on the Hudson. Gibbons, holding a federal coastal license, set up a competing line, and was sued by Ogden, who argued that Gibbons could operate on the New Jersey side of the Hudson but not in New York state waters. When the case came before the Supreme Court, Marshall decided in favor of Gibbons, thus destroying New York's monopoly on navigation. Marshall argued that a state could regulate commerce that began and ended within its own territory, but when the transaction involved crossing state lines then national authority took precedence. "The act of Congress," he wrote, "is supreme; and the law of the state . . . must yield to it."

John Marshall

In an earlier case, in 1821, *Cohens v. Virginia*, the Marshall court had reaffirmed in strong language the power of the federal courts to review state-court decisions, making unmistakably clear that state courts could not be separate from but were subordinate to federal courts. In so doing, it also made clear what was meant by political nationalism:

> That the United States form . . . a single nation has not yet been denied. In war we are one people. In making peace we are one people. In all commercial regulations we are one and the same people. In many other respects the American people are one, and the government which is alone capable of controlling and managing their interests in all these respects, is the government of the Union. It is their government, and in that character they have no other. America has chosen to be, in many respects, and to many purposes, a nation; and for all these purposes her government is complete; to all these objects it is competent. The people have declared that in the exercise of all the powers given for these objects it is supreme. It can, then, in effecting these objects, legitimately control all individuals and governments within the American territory. The constitution and laws of a state, so far as they are repugnant to the constitution and laws of the United States, are absolutely void. These states are constituent parts of the United States.

In major decisions handed down while he was Chief Justice of the Supreme Court, John Marshall did more than any other one man to assert and establish the sovereignty of the national government over the states. While this principle was to have its final test in the titanic struggle of the Civil War, it is possible that the union might have been fatally weakened or perhaps even dissolved before that great event if separatist states' rights tendencies rather than John Marshall had had the firmer hand.

The Whiskey Rebellion   Fortunately, the Executive as well as the Judiciary helped strengthen the young nation's unity. The day-to-day exercise of authority by the President, acting as the chief executive of the nation, also slowly and steadily strengthened the sense of political unity in the country. But two situations in particular illustrate the unifying effect of Presidential action. At the very beginning of the young republic there occurred an incident which became known as the Whiskey Rebellion. To help pay the cost of assuming the state debts, Congress in 1791 placed a tax on whiskey. This greatly angered western farmers who, in a time of totally inadequate transportation, found it easier to transport alcohol to market than the bulky grain from which it was made. In the summer of 1794 serious rioting broke out in western Pennsylvania as backcountry farmers made known their displeasure. The federal courts were prevented from operating, the houses of federal officials were burned, the mails were looted, and in August a rabble of protestors, loaded with rifles and their own whiskey, even marched into Pittsburgh.

The response of the President was prompt and decisive. Washington called up an army of twelve thousand militiamen and sent it westward. There was no fighting. The rebels quit and went home. National authority was not only maintained, it had been asserted in unmistakable fashion by the President. The tax itself was henceforth collected peaceably until repealed in Jefferson's administration.

The Nullification Crisis   The second major challenge to the political authority of the nation came almost forty years later, during the Presidency of Andrew Jackson, in the form of the Nullification Crisis of 1832. The high tariff law of 1828, designed to protect infant industries against foreign competition, greatly disturbed many Southerners, for whom it did nothing except raise the price of English goods they imported. And when the tariff law of 1832 failed to lower duties as much as Southerners desired, it was argued in South Carolina that the acts of 1828 and 1832 should be declared null and void. The question, in terms of political nationalism, was whether a state could refuse to obey a federal law, whether a member of the Union was more powerful than the Union itself. In 1828, in reaction against the high tariff of that year, John C. Calhoun had written an essay entitled the *South Carolina Exposition and Protest*. In it he had argued that the states had made the Constitution, therefore a state could pass on the constitutionality of an act of Congress and nullify within its borders any such act that it thought violated the Constitution. Such a violation of the original agreement—the Constitution—also cancelled the obligations of the states to the Union, from which they were then entitled to withdraw.

These were the arguments now heard in 1832. But Jackson would have no such challenges to the political integrity and unity of the nation. The Constitution had been created by individuals, not by states; the Union was indestructible. He warned the Nullifers that they could "talk and write resolutions and print threats to their hearts' content. But if one drop of blood be shed there in defiance of the laws of the United States, I will hang the first man of them I can get my hands on to the first tree I can find." No idle threat this, as all knew who recalled Jackson's summary execution of two Englishmen during his invasion of Florida in 1818. Yet in November 1832 a special convention was elected in South Carolina that passed an Ordinance of Nullification prohibiting the collection of tariff duties in the state after February 1, 1833. The state legislature followed up by authorizing the raising of an army.

Jackson responded with military preparations of his own, while indicating at the same time his willingness to compromise on the tariff, and issued his own proclamation declaring that the assumption by a state of the power to annul a law of the United States was "incompatible with the existence of the Union, contradicted expressly by its spirit, inconsistent with every principle on which it was founded, and destructive of the great object for which it was formed." Secession was treason, and he warned that he would act accordingly.

Jackson's iron commitment to the nation, plus his willingness to agree to a face-saving compromise for South Carolina on the tariff, prevented a showdown. South Carolina backed down, the Union was upheld, and national political unity, though not guaranteed, took on new strength.

The Emergence of National Identity

Important—crucial even—as were the processes of uniting the new nation economically and politically, they could hardly have succeeded were not the Americans developing a powerful sense of social and cultural identity, a self-conception as a distinct people enjoying a common past, sharing a common present, and working toward a common future. Every new nation, and the United States was no exception, is strongly motivated to be independent of alien, outside influences. It has an intense desire to be independent of other cultures. Noah Webster had put the case early, telling his fellow Americans:

> Unshackle your minds and act like independent beings. You have been children long enough, subject to the control and subservient to the interests of a haughty parent. You now have an interest of your own to augment and defend . . . a national character to establish and extend . . .

Every nation, in short, wants to be seen as special, unique, different. It seeks to identify those traits that differentiate it from others; its people remind

*Fourth of July celebration, 1819. The first anniversary of the Glorious
Fourth was limited to the major cities but after the adoption of the
Constitution the celebration became more widespread. Fireworks have been
present on the Fourth since the beginning but other aspects of the festivities
have evolved with the times. The time once reserved for the sermon, for
instance, is now filled by the political oration.*

themselves of what they perceive to be their special qualities, emphasize the
virtue of their achievements, point with pride to their own geography, and
often assign themselves, as the Americans did, a special role in the affairs of
humanity.

Except under the most unusual conditions, however, such desires are
rarely fully realized. Countervailing forces are always at work, and they certainly were with the United States. As a nation founded on the cultures of
other societies, for example, America could never escape its common heritage with Western Europe, and in the last analysis who would want to? Few
Americans have ever felt that they were abandoning their own nation by
reading and admiring Shakespeare. At the other end of the scale were internal forces challenging the concept of a single national identity. Americans
everywhere took pride in their locality and the life they lived there. Massachusetts men were as convinced of the superiority of life and society in the

Bay State as South Carolinians were of theirs. As time went on a growing sense of sectional distinction threatened the idea of national identity.

Yet in spite of, and indeed in part because of, these countervailing forces, the impulse for national identity moved through American life.

Discovering the American Past   Of primary importance was the American past, the achievements of colonial and revolutionary times. Through the first few decades of the new nation Americans were reminded in biographies, histories, and public speeches of the extraordinary achievements against insurmountable odds—"trials of wandering and exile, of the ocean, the winter, the wilderness, and the savage foe"—of their colonial and revolutionary forebears. To make sure that the young grew up knowing and venerating that past, Massachusetts in 1827 became the first state to require the teaching of American history in the public schools. Other states made haste to follow.

Helping to develop a record of the American past were historical societies, of which at least thirty-five came into being between 1830 and 1850. Compilers of historical documents, such as Peter Force and Jared Sparks, sought to preserve the record, and Force persuaded Congress to purchase the papers of some of the Founding Fathers to protect them for future generations.

National holidays, monuments, and symbols provided an equally potent if less bookish awareness of origins. The great annual celebrations were the Fourth of July and Thanksgiving Day, binding Americans in respectful observance of the trials of their colonial ancestors. Monuments such as the obelisk at Bunker Hill, statues such as that by Horatio Greenough of Washington, and paintings such as "Washington Crossing the Delaware" reminded Americans of their common past. Symbolic gestures, such as hoisting the flag over the schoolhouse, though not general until 1860, or the singing of the national anthem, served the same purpose.

Shared Experiences   Shared experiences, present and past, were also important in establishing an American national identity. Of particular significance were the experiences of the frontier, immigration, and religion, in all of which the Americans saw something which marked them off as different from other peoples.

Not all Americans moved west and helped to turn wilderness into settled country. But in the early decades of the republic, just as for almost two hundred years before, many did directly confront the challenge of the frontier and all were conscious of this element in American life. The stories, the institutions, the values, the myths, the way of life in the wilderness were part and parcel of the being of every American whose own locale, earlier or later, had once been wilderness too. Many Americans of cultivated taste who lived in established areas of the country may have been appalled by the crudity and primitiveness of much of the life in the West as they saw or read about it. But ordinary men who left eastern farms or shops and headed westward were united in the conviction that it was the West which offered opportunity for a better life for themselves and their families. Moreover, the experiences of taking up land, house-building, combatting the elements, starting communities, and a hundred more activities associated with the settlement of the West, were duplicated over and over again, forming a reservoir of experience and memory held in common by many and identified by them as peculiarly American.

Another major element in American life both past and present that fed into the pool of common experience was immigration. All Americans were conscious of the fact that the country's origins literally rested on the migration of peoples from abroad, and few were unaware of the continuing role of the immigrants in this period of national growth. Some six million immigrants entered the United States between the founding of the Republic and the Civil War. In proportion to the country's population, this was the heaviest tide of immigration in the nation's history. Indeed, in 1855 fifteen percent of the population had entered the country only within the previous ten years. With the exception of the South, which did not attract many from abroad, these immigrants were found everywhere—in the city and on the farm, in the East and in the West. A significant element of the population thus shared the experience and the rest were well aware of it. By the 1840s and 1850s, it is true, some feared that national identity might be threatened by hordes of illiterates from abroad who were ignorant of the nation's traditions and who professed a Catholicism alien to the Protestantism of the past. But for the most part, immigrants were welcomed—indeed solicited by many states and localities—not only for their role in building an expanding national economy but because their presence seemed to document the long-held American conviction that alone among the countries of the world America offered a home to those fleeing oppression. James Russell Lowell spoke for many when in 1861 he characterized the American nation as

> She that lifts up the manhood of the poor,
> She of the open soul and open door,
> With room about her hearth for all mankind!

Until the advent of Irish and German Catholics in the 1840s and 1850s the religious experience of Americans also served to strengthen national identity. Indeed, Americans were so overwhelmingly Protestant in their religious convictions and beliefs that this new migration produced a powerful anti-Catholic movement. Part of the problem stemmed from the fact that the Catholic Church was the only church in America that had not cut its ties with Europe after the American Revolution, and its presence therefore was viewed by some as an alien institution directed by a foreign power and as such a threat to the American nation. This problem was not lessened by the attitude of the leading prelate, Archbishop Hughes of New York, who proclaimed in 1850 that "the object we hope to accomplish in time is to convert all Pagan nations, and all Protestant nations . . ." Yet the dominant American attitude toward religion remained what it had always been, acceptance of

Immigrants Landing at the Battery, *a painting by Samuel B. Waugh.*

diversity. And most Americans were united in the conviction that this tolerance was not only a major strength of the nation but one of the characteristics that distinguished it from other nations.

Another factor that reinforced the American identity was language. Although the heavy tide of immigration brought a variety of languages to the
United States, none rose in competition with English. The initial establishment of American society by English-speaking people made English the
language of politics and government, trade and commerce, education and
learning. Foreign-speaking immigrant groups often held tenaciously to their
native tongue, seeking to retain it in their churches, their local schools, and
their families. But the basic life of the nation was conducted in English, and
however much first-generation immigrants might cling to the old and garble
the new, their children quickly discovered that English was the passport to
getting ahead in America. The disunity that might well have come from a
babel of languages was thus avoided. This is not to say that English remained
pure and unchanged in the new republic. Indeed it was modified considerably in America, not only in the spelling and meaning of many words, but
also in the many adaptations that came from the Indian and the variety of
languages imported by the immigrants. As a matter of fact, some proponents
of a distinct American nationality hoped for a language quite separate from
English, one clearly American in identity. Jefferson himself in 1813 declared
that "The new circumstances under which we are placed call for new words,
new phrases, and for the transfer of old words to new objects. An American
dialect will therefore be formed." Many Englishmen would doubtless agree
with George Bernard Shaw that the Americans have indeed achieved this
goal of Jefferson's, that English hasn't been spoken here for years.

The enormous pride Americans took in their natural environment, even as they were engaged in the process of destroying it, was also a part of their identity as a people. They were united in the conviction that nowhere on earth was nature more varied and awe-inspiring. On a visit to Europe in the 1840s, Elkanah Watson blithely observed that "What are called mountains in Europe are hills in America; rivers are reduced to mere brooks; trees to bushes; and lakes to ponds." This attitude of amused disdain toward the landscape of other countries still prevailed almost a hundred years later. In the first World War, a young American soldier wounded in France in a crossing of the Ourq River—a somewhat misdesignated shallow stream a few yards wide—refused a drink of water from the canteen of a buddy. "Give it to the Ourq," he said, "it needs it more than I do." With less humor but equal confidence, the editor of *The Scenery of the United States,* published in 1855, had remarked that "Nowhere else on the globe is Nature lovelier, grander, less austere and more varied and picturesque than upon this continent." Thus even the Himalayas and the Amazon must bow to the Appalachians and the Ohio when they are backed by national pride.

A National Culture   It is easy to see that the Americans had a great deal going for them in their quest for a national identity, but in one area their lack of distinction was painfully apparent: in literature, learning, and the arts. Throughout the early period of national development there were not only frequent calls for American creativity but strident defenses of what Americans had presumably already achieved in these areas. The exaggerated and almost frantic nature of this call to arms suggests how important it is that a nation have its own self-created culture. William Ellery Channing, in his celebrated *Remarks on National Literature* (1830), observed that "A country, like an individual, has dignity and power only in proportion as it is self-formed." Many a spokesman for a nation new on the world scene in the last twenty-five years and sensitive to his nation's former colonial status, has echoed those words.

The American predicament was bluntly described by the English writer, the Reverend Sydney Smith, in a famous article in the *Edinburgh Review* in 1820:

> In the four quarters of the globe, who reads an American book? or goes to an American play? or looks at an American picture or statue? What does the world yet owe to American physicians or surgeons? What new substances have their chemists discovered? or what old ones have they analyzed? What new constellations have been discovered by the telescopes of Americans?— what have they done in mathematics?

The answer, unfortunately, was: not many, not much. William Ellery Channing in 1830 was one of the first who raised the call for an American literature that would strengthen the nation:

> Literature is plainly among the most powerful methods of exalting the character of a nation.... Do we possess indeed what we may call a national

literature? Have we produced eminent writers in the various departments of intellectual effort? We regret that the reply to these questions is so obvious. . . . The more we receive from other countries, the greater the need of an original literature. . . . A foreign literature will always, in a measure, be foreign. It has sprung from the soil of another people, which, however like, is still not our own soul. Every people has much in its own character and feelings, which can only be embodied by its own writers.

Few went so far as Melville, who asked that America prize, cherish, and glorify her own writers and artists over those of all other nations even if the Americans were mediocre. But it was argued by many writers and editors that there were themes aplenty for American writers to deal with in terms of their own land—"subjects, scenes, places, and persons to be found in our own fine and native country"—rather than "the great, the remote, the romantic, what is doing in Italy or Arabia." As early as 1819, Thomas Upham listed some worthy themes for American writers:

The character and civil habits, the piety and magnanimity of the first settlers, the sufferings and devotedness of the missionaries, who penetrated into dreary forests and abodes of savages; the adventures of the first explorers of the country; the seclusion, devotions, and sufferings of frontier villages.

Other cultural nationalists demanded that American writers "be inspired by the magnificent scenery of our own world," but Longfellow took a somewhat broader view in recognition of the varied cultures contributing to American society. "Vast forests, lakes, and prairies cannot make great poets," observed the author of *Hiawatha* in an unconscious but supremely accurate comment on his own work. "They are but the scenery of the play and have much less to do with the poetic character than has been imagined. . . . We have, or shall have a composite [literature], embracing French, Spanish, Irish, English, Scotch and German peculiarities. Whoever has within himself most of these is our truly national writer."

Charles Ingersoll in a brilliant defense of American culture in 1823, his *Discourse Concerning the Influence of America on the Mind,* perhaps was overgenerous in his appraisal of American cultural and intellectual achievements, but he noted shrewdly and with some justice that the uniqueness of the American achievement lay in the fact that "the average of intellect, and of intellectual power in the United States, surpasses that of any part of Europe." Moreover, he emphasized what was to be the main unifying theme in the call for a distinct American culture when he declared that America would "prove to the world that the best patronage of religion, science, literature, and the arts, of whatever the mind can achieve, is SELF-GOVERNMENT." This theme was to be repeated again and again. The *Democratic Review* argued, for example, that "the vital principle of an American national literature must be democracy." American writers, it declared, must in their work "breathe the spirit of our republican institutions." More than anything else it was the awareness of this principle and this sense of mission that gave the United States unity and a sense of national identity.

Profile: ALEXANDER HAMILTON

Born in the British West Indies in 1755, and killed by Aaron Burr in a duel in 1804, Hamilton in his relatively short life exerted a powerful influence on the new American nation. He was one of the brightest and the best of the young men of the revolutionary era. In 1774 and 1775 at the age of seventeen he defended the colonial cause in three pamphlets whose brilliance gained him entry into New York ruling circles. He became an officer in the colonial forces where his extraordinary ability brought him to the attention of Washington, who made him his aide-de-camp. The alliance struck here was to bear fruit in later years. In the last three years of the war Hamilton's activities were energetic, to say the least: he married Elizabeth Schuyler, who came from one of New York's most distinguished families; he studied law and was admitted to practice in New York; he prepared an analysis of the financial problems of the government; he was elected by New York to the Continental Congress; he managed to share in the victory over Cornwallis at Yorktown; and he wrote a series of articles for the New York Packet arguing for a strong central government. When peace came, Hamilton was only twenty-eight years old. His most important work lay ahead.

Although a delegate to the Constitutional Convention, Hamilton's major influence came after the work of the convention was finished. His own views on what the new government should be had been so conservative as to be unacceptable, but Hamilton was a realist if he was anything. He recognized that the proposed Constitution would establish the kind of strong central government needed to insure the survival of the new nation. It was he who conceived the idea of a public defense of the Constitution during the debate over ratification, an idea which took shape as The Federalist Papers, among the most influential writing in the revolutionary period and now a classic in political literature. Hamilton wrote two-thirds of these essays; the others were by James Madison and John Jay.

It was a stroke of good fortune for the new nation that when its first government was formed under the Constitution with Washington as President, the first secretary of the treasury was Alexander Hamilton. For Hamilton recognized with a clarity possessed by few that if American independence were to be a reality the United States must have a truly national economy. No single person did more than he to get the new nation moving in this direction. His intent was clear:

> Let Americans disdain to be the instruments of European greatness. Let the thirteen states, bound together in a strict and indissolu:ble Union, concur in erecting one great American system, superior to the control of all transatlantic force or influence and able to dictate the terms of the connection between the old and new world.

The "one great American system" he had in mind was the development of a self-sufficient and diversified economy promoted, stimulated, and encouraged by the national government. How did he propose to bring this about?

First, Hamilton's Report on Public Credit, accepted by the Congress despite strong opposition, proposed that the United States government pay off at face value the debt it owed both to foreigners and to its own citizens, totalling over $50 million, and that the government should also assume and pay off at face value the remaining debt owed by the various states, amounting to some $21 million. As Hamilton saw it, capital was needed to develop America's resources, and he argued that investors would be more inclined to channel funds into economic development in America if the record showed that the United States honored its obligations. His argument was sound. The consequence of funding the debt was a sharp rise in the credit standing of the United States and the beginning of that heavy flow of foreign capital into the country which was to become in the decades ahead an important factor in American economic growth. In fact, such investments in the succeeding century were to involve billions of dollars and to make economic development far less painful in both human and economic terms for the American people than would otherwise have been the case. Today, fears of "economic imperialism" have made many new and underdeveloped nations cautious about taking this road to national strength and independence, and ironically much of this caution stems from fears of the undue influence that might accompany investment from the United States, the first underdeveloped nation of the modern world.

Hamilton's next step was to secure the establishment of a national bank chartered by the Congress. Although the government would own some twenty percent of the stock in the bank and appoint one-fifth of its directors, the majority of the stock, and hence control, went to private individuals. Nevertheless the bank was designed to play a vital national role. It was to serve as a financial agent for the government, but more importantly it could issue bank notes that were much needed in an economy traditionally short on specie. The bank thus made it easier for business enterprises to raise capital for new ventures, and in turn stimulated the establishment of various state-chartered banks that had in their areas much the same economic impact.

Hamilton's vision, and his ultimate influence, were also apparent in his famous Report on Manufactures, in which he proposed encouraging the development of manufacturing enterprises to make the United States economically independent of other nations. A strong manufacturing interest would also help bind the country together, he argued, by providing farmers with goods formerly purchased abroad and by absorbing in turn the products of agriculture. He suggested that manufacturing be promoted by protective duties on goods from abroad that might compete with new American manufacturing, by subsidies and bounties, by prohibiting the export of raw materials needed for American manufacturing, by the development of an adequate transportation system, and by various other measures. His Report was rejected by Congress and the President, although some of his specific proposals on duties were adopted.

More importantly, in the long run, he set the tone of persuasion and argument for the need to diversify the American economy and the essential role of government in promoting diversification. Others were to take up his arguments and to expand upon them. Economic thinkers such as Daniel Raymond, Matthew and Henry Carey, Fredrich List, and political leaders such as Henry Clay with his American System, built and expanded upon Hamilton's ideas in the first half of the nineteenth century, arguing for a self-sufficient and unified national economy whose promotion was a responsibility of the government.

Hamilton's view that men of property should have greater influence in society than others was antithetical to the views of men such as Jefferson, but this did not detract from the essential soundness of his economic proposals. Nor did his skepticism about democracy weaken his argument for a strong central government.

Had Hamilton been alive in 1860, the economic condition of the United States would have provided complete vindication of his proposals—an experience rare for a politician and almost unheard-of for an economist—for much of the nation's history in the half-century after his tragic death involved the transformation of Hamilton's ideas into reality. In shaping the new United States into a nation few had a more lasting influence than he.

Chapter 7
THE BROADENING
OF DEMOCRACY

The Spirit of the Times
FREEDOM AND THE COMMON MAN

All observers of the United States in the first decades of the republic were impressed by a sense of movement, vitality, experiment and change, excitement, a feeling that momentous events were under way. The French observer de Tocqueville remarked in the 1830s that "No sooner do you set foot upon American ground than you are stunned by a kind of tumult; a confused clamor is heard on every side, and a thousand simultaneous voices demand the satisfaction of their social wants. Everything is in motion around you." That was a comment on the continuous impact of politics in America, but it held true in every other aspect of life as well. Change was the order of the day. "The American has no time to tie himself to anything," wrote de Tocqueville. "He grows accustomed only to change, and ends by regarding it as the natural state of man. He feels the need of it, more, he loves it; for the instability, instead of meaning disaster to him, seems to give birth only to miracles all about him."

Excitement, change, momentum, yes. But where was it all leading? Foreign observers could not agree whether the Americans were bound for hell on a roller-coaster or were on the high road to paradise. One thing <u>or</u> the other, it's always been that way with America in the eyes of the rest of the world. Earthly paradise or worldly hell—only the images have changed: the noble savage rivaling the virtuous of the Golden Age, or the cannibalistic devil lusting after Christian flesh; the sturdy yeoman farmer reading Latin as he walks behind the plow, or the vulgar, tobacco-spitting, illiterate backwoodsman; Wilson the spokesman for the rights of man and nations, or Babbitt the symbol of vulgarity and money-grubbing; the dream of science and technology as the happy servants of humanity, or the air-conditioned nightmare of a world dehumanized.

Although European visitors were fascinated by all aspects of American life—food, travel, houses, dress, personal habits, attitudes toward women, child-rearing, and a score of others—what drew the most attention was the attempt of the new nation to establish itself as a social, political, and economic democracy. On this subject, as on all others, reaction split. Was the American experiment a boon or a

Election Day, 1816. The tumultuous character of American politics—from polite discussion to rowdy argument—is depicted in this painting by John Lewis Krimmel.

disaster for humanity? An article published in 1784 bore the title, "Has The Discovery of America Been Useful or Hurtful to Mankind?" In 1960 the Oxford (University) Union carried on the tradition by debating the motion, "That this house holds America responsible for spreading vulgarity in Western society." America's experiments with constitution-making, with universal suffrage, with a free press, with a free public school system, with the disestablishment of religion and the separation of church and state, with social reform—were these the hope or the terror of the future?

Thus, by humanitarians and liberals America was looked upon as the defender of the common man, who in his new dignity and general elevation in society marked the triumphant test of democratic institutions. For John Bright in England, America defined the society of the future: "a free church, a free school, free land, a free vote, and a free career for the child of the humblest born in the land." Anthony Trollope wrote of the Americans that "They walk like human beings made in God's form. If this be so . . . should not such knowledge in itself be sufficient testimony of the success of the country and of her institutions?" And the radical <u>Reynolds' Weekly Newspaper</u> summed up for Englishmen the meaning of the much-used word, Americanization:

> Americanized, as far as we are able to make out, means that the working classes should be made free citizens of the country enriched by their toil and defended by their

courage—that they should have a voice in the making of the laws which they are bound to obey—that every child born in the country should have the means of a moral, a mental, and a physical education placed within its reach—that every worker should be amply remunerated for his work—that every man, woman, and child in the land should have plenty of wholesome food to eat and plenty of comely and comfortable clothing to wear—that no able-bodied pauperism should be permitted to exist—and that no man or woman should be compelled to resort to criminal courses for the preservation of life.

Europeans who wanted to change the nature and structure of their society tended thus to view America as the hope of the human race.

But the view was different from the other end of the telescope for those who had no wish to see their secure world shattered and reordered along lines laid out by the American experiment. That defender of the old order, the Austrian Count Metternich, wondered "what would become of our religious and political institutions, of the moral force of our governments, and of that conservative system which has saved Europe from complete dissolution" if America's "evil doctrines and pernicious examples" were to triumph. The French novelist Stendhal's hero, Lucien Leuwen, complained about the lack of humanity, the lack of dignity that sprang from the evil doctrine of the free vote: "Universal suffrage rules as a tyrant—a tyrant with dirty hands . . . men are not weighed, they are counted." Beaumont, who travelled to America with de Tocqueville, saw a deadening impact from America's vaunted equality: "Don't seek in this country," he wrote, "either poetry, or literature, or beaux arts. The universal equality of conditions exhales on the whole society a monotonous hue. No one is ignorant of all things, and no one knows too much; what is more lusterless than mediocrity?" And the conservative journal <u>Young England</u> ridiculed the hypocrisy of an America that proclaimed itself the land of the free and the home of the brave in blatant disregard of slavery, that "cancer in the root of the seemingly fair and flourishing plant . . . which corrupts and destroys."

The only comfort for those who viewed America with distaste and alarm was the consoling thought that the experiment could not possibly last: America had no king, no hereditary aristocracy, no established church; it preached the illogical idea that individuals were free and equal; it elevated backwoodsmen to the Presidency and made legislators out of common tailors; it undermined respect for authority by the mob violence of lynchings and by fisticuffs in its deliberative assemblies; and it had come into being in the first place on the once-in-a-million success of the foolhardy notion that a people's army could defeat professionals.

Commitment to Democracy

Every leader from Washington to Lincoln proclaimed that the American destiny was to prove to the world that democracy was possible. Washington in his first inaugural declared that "the preservation of the sacred fire of liberty and the destiny of the republican model of government are presently considered . . . staked on the experiment intrusted to the hands of the American people." John Adams had written that the fate of the American experience would be decisive for all humanity. Madison had remarked on the universal value of the Republic in "proving things before held impossible." Jefferson was certain that if America held true to the Declaration of

Independence, this nation would inspire the rest of the world to the democratic pursuit of happiness.

At both the opening and the closing of his career as President, Jackson felt compelled to remind his fellow countrymen of their responsibilities as the custodians of freedom for people everywhere. This sense of destiny was equally felt by those who might disagree with Jackson on other matters. "We are charged by Providence," said Calhoun,

> not only with the happiness of this great people, but . . . with that of the human race. We have a government of a new order . . . founded on the rights of man, resting on . . . reason. If it shall succeed . . . it will be the commencement of a new era in human affairs. All civilized governments must in the course of time conform to its principles.

And Abraham Lincoln at Gettysburg defined our great fraternal strife as a struggle fought so "that government of the people, by the people, for the people, shall not perish from the earth." The American destiny was therefore clear: to preserve and strengthen democracy at home, and by their successful example to promote it in the rest of the world. Though leaders differed on how to go about this task and just how far to go, no other factors played a greater role in uniting the American people, in giving them a sense of common purpose, than this concept of their future.

To modern ears weary of the noisy rhetoric of those who claim to hold the light, this may smack of arrogance. But the Americans of the early republic, even up to the Civil War when their world collapsed about them, were less arrogant than proud and confident: proud of the experiment that offered hope to all, and confident that they could demonstrate its power.

The Need to Adapt and Change   And so the period was marked by the American effort to maintain, improve, and extend the democratic experiment.

Their chief point of reference was a general commitment to the basic ideas of "life, liberty, the pursuit of happiness"—which they saw as being timeless and universal. But society changes, and the way we translate these ideals into the realities of daily life must also change. Jefferson saw this when he wrote that "as new discoveries are made, new truths disclosed, and manners and opinions change with the change of circumstances, institutions must advance also, and keep pace with the times." Nothing then is unchangeable, he noted, "except the inalienable rights of man." Lincoln, looking back upon the work of the Founding Fathers, likewise grasped this truth when he declared:

> They meant to set up a standard maxim for a free society, which should be familiar to all . . . constantly looked to, constantly labored for, and even though never perfectly attained, constantly approximated, and thereby constantly spreading and deepening its influence and augmenting the happiness and value of life to all people . . . everywhere.

Thus democracy becomes a perpetual striving, a never-ending evolution. It was this dynamic that faced the Americans as a democratically-inclined people in the first decades of the republic. The conditions that had marked its emergence came under the impact of powerful forces of change, and new institutions, new techniques in political, social, and economic behavior were called for. It was this necessity that lay behind the great democratic movement of reform in the first half of the nineteenth century.

Political Changes and Reforms

An important instrument of change in the period was that unique American political invention, the constitutional convention. By 1860 the original thirteen states had expanded to thirty-four, and each of them had held at least one convention, and sometimes two or three, for the purpose of revising and updating their constitutions. Some states also provided for revisions by a council established for that purpose or by legislative action. By the 1850s all new constitutions, as well as revisions and amendments, were routinely submitted for approval to the people.

Extension of the Suffrage   One of the most important political reforms was the abolition of all restrictions on the right to vote, chiefly the requirements that a voter must own property and pay taxes. At the time of the Revolution, land holding was so common that most adult white males were qualified to vote. But as industry grew, as cities filled with workers—many of them recent immigrants—who did not own property, and as pioneers moved west and had not yet taken up new holdings, there were huge numbers of men who were not qualified to vote according to the old rule. At first the older states abolished their property-holding regulations and instead set up liberal tax-paying qualifications. But these new regulations came under fire and were shortly abandoned. In the new western states the move toward "universal" suffrage was just as strong. No state entered the Union after 1817 with either a property or a tax-paying restriction on the right to vote. And many granted immigrants the right to vote even before they were naturalized. Wisconsin entered the Union with a constitutional provision which gave immigrants the right to vote if they simply filed a declaration of intent to become citizens.

The Printed Ballot   The idea that the way a man voted was his own affair was reflected in another change, the appearance of the printed ballot. In the colonial past and early decades of the republic voters openly declared their choice at the polls by voice. In small and closely-knit communities in which qualified voters by their very qualification tended to be free of undue pressure from others, such a method seemed the natural and honest way of

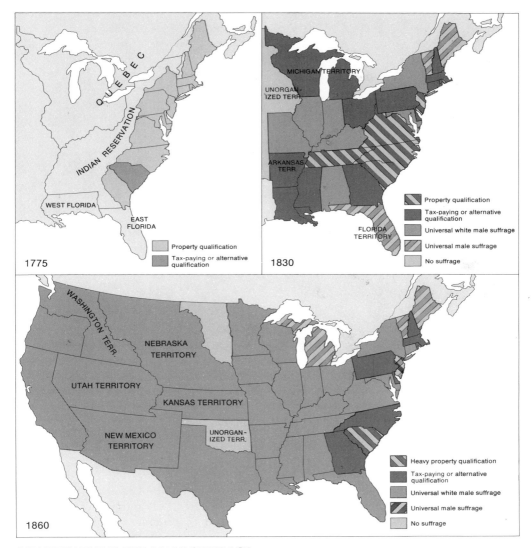

QUALIFICATIONS FOR MALE SUFFRAGE

voting and satisfied most people. But it was a method open to abuse as
society changed and more and more people occupied dependent economic
positions in which they were vulnerable to undue influence from those to
whom they were indebted. The printed ballot, while it did not eliminate
abuse by influence, did allow much greater privacy than before, hence freedom of choice. By 1830 the printed ballot, a common goal of political reformers, was widely used, although open voting long continued in some
localities and did not disappear in Virginia and Illinois until as late as 1860.

Stump speaking *by George Caleb Bingham. A popular Missouri artist, Bingham created an energetic record of life there, often turning to his avocation of politics as a subject. He himself ran twice for the legislature and stump speaking was as much a part of his life as it was a part of his art.*

Increase in Elected Officials   Other political changes also appeared. One of these was the steady drive to extend the number of public officials chosen by popular election. By 1860 governors and other state officials, sometimes including even the judiciary, were elected by popular vote. And in every state except South Carolina, presidential electors were now chosen by popular vote rather than by the state legislature. Everywhere there was a move toward shorter terms for officeholders, to provide constant accounting to their constituents as well as to make officeholding more open to candidates. By 1860 representation in state legislatures had been more equitably reapportioned in most states, correcting imbalances that had seen rising urban areas denied adequate representation.

The Nominating Convention   Political reform on the national level included the appearance of the nominating convention, which was widely used on the state and local level, but was of particular importance in the selection of presidential candidates. In the past, members of Congress had banded together in caucus to select candidates, and since Congress had been elected by the people this seemed a reasonable procedure. But as political parties appeared and consolidated their positions, it became clear that the rank-and-file members of the parties had no voice in the selection of candidates. By the Jacksonian era, there was dissatisfaction with this situation and the nominating convention, composed of delegates chosen by local party organizations, came into use as a more democratic way for ordinary people to take part in the selection of candidates. Other developments on the national scene also brought people into closer contact with their government. Among these were open sessions of the Senate, the opening of the House gallery to the press, and the recording and publication of the proceedings of the Congress, all instituted early in the life of the republic.

The Spoils System   Particularly as defined by Andrew Jackson, the "spoils system" meant removing large numbers of officeholders appointed by the previous administration and replacing them by supporters of the new administration. The practice of filling offices with one's own supporters was not in itself an innovation, and Jackson probably did not remove more than twenty percent of the government work force. But he argued that in a political democracy the practice of rotation was right and proper. "In a country where offices are created solely for the benefit of the people, no one man has any more intrinsic right to official station than another," he said. Rotating public jobholders, he declared, enabled more citizens to participate in their own government and lessened the danger of creating an entrenched bureaucracy indifferent to the public interest. To those who argued that trained personnel would thus be replaced by the untrained with inefficiency and confusion as a result, Jackson replied in language typical of the rising democratic faith of the time that "The duties of all public officers are . . . so plain and simple that men of intelligence may readily qualify themselves for their performance." Jackson's idea of the uses of the presidency to express the aspirations of the whole people also broadened the possibilities of that office as a tool of democracy. (See Profile on p. 221.)

Leveling Effect of the Frontier   Finally, the nature of settlement in many areas of the West was a stimulus to political democracy. Most new settlement in earlier colonial times, throughout New England for example, was by organized groups with an established leadership possessing recognized qualifications in religion, education, and wealth. In the Old Northwest, however, in the early decades of the republic, settlement was mostly by individuals and families, and even if by groups all tended to be people outside the established leadership in the areas they had left behind. But after initial settlement in the West, when population began to increase, the area had to organize politically, and in the process ordinary men were drawn into government in large numbers. Townships and counties were organized from

President Jackson astride a pig wallowing in political misdeeds. There were those who disagreed with Jackson's use of the spoils system, as this Whig cartoon indicates. When he took office, Jackson's critics assumed he would make a clean sweep of all positions and make new appointments on a partisan basis. In fact, he removed no more than previous presidents and it was his Whig critics, taking office after him in 1841, who actually made the clean sweep.

scratch, and positions had to be filled. There were no incumbents; there were many offices and someone had to fill them. So the extent of participation was considerable. For example, the first election in Lawrence Township, Ohio, involved the selection of two justices of the peace, one clerk, one school examiner, three trustees, two overseers of the poor, two fence viewers, two appraisers of property, three supervisors, two constables, and one lister of taxables. Ordinary men with no political experience except voting found themselves holding office, and from that experience frequently came the firm conviction that in a political democracy the ordinary individual counts and can do something. Indeed the whole process of creating new communities—establishing schools, building churches, seeking new business, constructing roads and bridges, providing civic services, and founding government—required a degree of public decision making and a trust in the goodwill as well as the abilities of one's neighbors that served to spread the idea and the practice of democracy.

All of these developments represented a change from the old concept of limiting political leadership mainly to meritorious members of the economic and social elite, a practice challenged by the ideas of the Revolution but now broadly implemented by new techniques and experiences that more directly involved ordinary people in the processes of local politics and government.

Yet these achievements by no means constituted a portrait of perfection. Women were left outside the political arena, and in only a handful of states were free blacks allowed to vote, and then generally under restricted conditions. Large numbers of qualified voters neglected to exercise their right except for a particular candidate or issue. Politicians sometimes less able than ambitious sought power and took personal advantage. Votes were bought and sold, officials were bribed, politicians were distracted from the main issues, and some things got out of hand. But all told, the American political experiment worked and served the people fairly well. Americans themselves were convinced of its virtues, and observers abroad were often impressed. In England in the 1830s the radical William Carpenter, writing in the *Political Magazine,* declared:

> I know of no nation that might not exchange its constitution and condition for those of the United States with considerable gain. I have no pertinacious inclination to the form of monarchy or of republicanism . . . but that country will ever be the most prosperous and happy, where the interests of the people have the greatest influence on the conduct of the legislature; and it is almost superfluous to declare that by a democratic ascendency is this benefit the most extensively secured.

Social Reforms

The first half-century of the republic, particularly the decades from 1820 to 1860, were strongly colored by social ferment and reform. A list of even the major reform movements of the time is long enough to suggest that the country was full of bitter, angry, and unhappy people bent on remaking American society. Some caught up in the reform impulse seemed out of touch with the practicalities of life; in 1856 the Reverend Joseph Nicholson, with a certain fervor of his own, wrote that reformers are "the disorganizers of civilization, the foes of liberty, the vampires of high toned morals and chivalrous deeds." And *The Southern Messenger* a few years earlier had sharply reminded reformers that "all movement is not progress" and that "to innovate is not to reform." But by and large the reformers of the time were strong and confident, and had an enthusiasm and a faith in human perfectibility that was exhilarating and inspired confidence.

Free Public Education   One of the most far-reaching reform movements of the period was the drive for a free, tax-supported public school system open to all. It saw education not only as the general key to progress, but essential to the survival of American democracy and the nation. Washington in his Farewell Address had warned that a government resting on the consent of the governed required knowledgeable citizens:

> Promote then as an object of primary importance, institutions for the general diffusion of knowledge. In proportion as the structure of a government gives

force to public opinion, it is essential that public opinion should be enlightened.

Jefferson, remarking on the prospects of democracy, had noted that "If a
nation expects to be ignorant and free . . . it expects what never was and
never will be." Others later argued that social equality could be achieved
only when all children regardless of background had equal opportunity for
knowledge, when the son of the poor man sat alongside the son of the rich in
the same classroom. "Free schools," wrote an Ohio educator in 1822, "lessen
the distinction, which fortune makes, between the children of the rich and
poor." Education, wrote Horace Mann, "beyond all other devices of human
origin . . . [is] the great equalizer of men. . . . It does better than to disarm the
poor of their hostility towards the rich, it prevents being poor." In 1841,
Mann also wrote that his goal was to show that "education has a market
value; that it is so far an article of merchandise that it may be turned to a
pecuniary account; it may be minted, and will yield a larger amount of
statutable coin than common bullion." Thus began a utilitarian view that has
influenced American education ever since, not always for the better. Education was also seen as essential to American nationalism, particularly in view
of the rising tide of immigrants, often illiterate and always unfamiliar with
American ways and the American heritage.

Such arguments were needed because, despite a host of good intentions,
there was a large gap between respect for the idea of education and the facts
of achievement. In fact, by the first decades of the nineteenth century schools
actually declined from what they had been in the middle of the eighteenth
century. They were often physically neglected; teachers were ill-qualified,
underpaid, and hard to get; discipline was poor; the curriculum was kept to a
minimum; attendance was low; terms were short. There were charity
schools, schools supported by lottery, and here and there good tax-supported schools. But most of the common schools were so-called rate schools
which levied a charge upon the parents of children attending while passing
themselves off as publicly supported.

The first educational reformers instituted probing actions in the 1820s and
launched a full-scale assault in the 1830s and 1840s. Led by reformers and
educators like Horace Mann, Caleb Mills, Henry Bernard, and Calvin Wiley,
and public men such as DeWitt Clinton and Thaddeus Stevens, the movement spread across the country.

In the marshalling of effort, educational reform was typical of many reform movements of the day. Advocates organized societies on the local,
state, and national levels, such as the Society for the Promotion of Public
Schools, to plan, publicize, and exhort. They established magazines and
journals, such as the *Common School Journal,* to discuss ideas on all aspects of
educational life. They turned out pamphlets, brochures, and reports by the
ton—Mann's *Reports,* issued from his office as Secretary of the Massachusetts
Board of Education, were best-sellers and became influential throughout the
United States, Latin America, and Europe. They lectured wherever they
could get an audience, and used the platforms of the lyceums, the popular

mutual improvement societies of the day. They poured petitions into state legislatures, testified before committees, and supported candidates who agreed with them.

Their extensive demands were to change the entire institution of education and to influence all of society. They wanted strong state boards of education to improve and enforce school laws, raise qualifications for teachers and provide for their training and to improve school buildings and equipment. They demanded minimum attendance laws, and would remove all sectarian doctrine from public schools. They sought to ban the diversion of state funds to church schools. And they demanded compulsory support of public schools by taxation. There were also to be changes in pedagogy and a broadening of the curriculum. In Massachusetts, a leader in educational reform, these demands were all translated into law between 1827 and 1842. Although, as we know from our own time, there is often a gap between law and achievement, the road now lay open for the development of a powerful democratic social institution in America. By the 1850s tax-supported public elementary schools open to all were accepted in principle and were being translated into fact in every part of the country except the South.

The Antislavery Movement   Education provides a classic example of the successful reform movement. The abolition movement was another story. Early assumptions that slavery would die a slow and quiet death for want of economic nourishment proved false as the cotton gin (after its invention by Whitney in 1792) gave the South a new crop and a new need for slave labor. Instead of dying out, therefore, the institution acquired a new lease on life with the spread of the cotton economy throughout the Old Southwest. Even so, it would appear at first glance that abolition of slavery was a certainty, the wonder being that it had not already taken place, since slavery was so blatantly contrary to the nation's democratic ideas, as foreigners were always pointing out. John Stuart Mill, from his sanctuary in England, rebuked the United States as "a country where institutions profess to be founded on equality, and which yet maintains the slavery of black men." But abolition became the most controversial issue of the time, and ended as a classic example of failure in reform.

In many respects abolition was a typical reform movement. Societies were formed, such as the Massachusetts Antislavery Society and the American Antislavery Society. Publications were founded, such as Lundy's *The Genius of Universal Emancipation* and Garrison's famed *The Liberator.* The movement had talented and dedicated leaders, such as Benjamin Lundy, Lewis and Arthur Tappan, Theodore Weld, James Birney, C. G. Finney, and William Lloyd Garrison. They held meetings and lectured, seemingly nonstop. Weld, by one account, "held increasing audiences at fever pitch, with his flashing eye, his clarion tones and marvelous eloquence, without manuscript or note, for sixteen successive evenings." Petitions poured into Washington like a flood, 225,000 signatures in a single Congressional session. Abolitionists also entered the political arena: Birney ran for President on the Liberty Party ticket in 1840 and polled 7,000 votes. By 1850 the various antislavery societies may have had as many as 200,000 members, and many more silent supporters. The moderate position, which represented the majority view, relied after 1840 on local societies and concentrated on such practical goals as the end of the slave trade in the District of Columbia and opposition to the expansion of slavery in the territories. Moderates clearly hoped to chip away at the problem, contain slavery, and bring about an enlightenment of opinion leading to a moral revulsion against slavery that would result in its eventual abandonment.

But abolition was not typical of nineteenth century reform in other ways, especially in the reaction to it up to the early 1840s. Speakers were mobbed, jailed, abused, pelted with debris, and prevented from speaking. William Lloyd Garrison was dragged through the streets with a rope around his neck. Publication offices were stormed and burned. Elijah Lovejoy was killed trying to defend his abolitionist press against a mob in Alton, Illinois, and the jury freed the members of the mob who had been charged with his death. The movement was denounced as this "miserable fanaticism that has commenced to walk abroad in our land." With a peculiar logic we have seen applied to the civil rights movement in our own time many people objected not to the violence directed against abolitionists, but to the antislavery propaganda that presumably brought about the violence, thus seeing the argument against slavery as more threatening to peace, order, and decency than the institution of slavery itself.

Abolitionism was also atypical in that it contained a minority, led by Garrison, so extreme that it hampered rather than promoted the enlightenment of public opinion necessary to any democratic solution of the slavery problem. This group held that slavery was so monstrous an evil that anyone associated with it in any way was also evil. In recent times this attitude about the contaminating effects of evil has prevailed among elements in such diverse movements as those opposing communism, promoting civil rights, and opposing the Vietnam War.

At any rate, Garrison, from the founding in 1831 of *The Liberator*, argued that government, politics, and society were all corrupt because of the existence of slavery; therefore emancipation must come *now*. "I am in earnest. I will not equivocate—I will not excuse—I will not retreat a single inch—and *I will be heard.*" And he and his followers were heard, if not exactly appreciated. The South heard him characterize their Congressmen as "desperadoes" outside "the pale of Christianity," so wicked that he for one would prefer to be governed by "the inmates of our penitentiaries." All Southern whites were villains, all blacks were saints. While one extremist declared that "Slavery and cruelty cannot be disjoined, consequently every slaveholder must be inhuman," Garrison was declaring with the finality of revelation that the life of a slaveholder "is but one of unbridled lust, of filthy amalgamation, of swaggering braggadocio, of haughty domination, of cowardly ruffianism, of boundless dissipation, of matchless insolence, of infinite self-conceit, of unequalled oppression, of more than savage cruelty."

The Alton Riot. Abolitionist Elijah P. Lovejoy was the editor of the Alton Observer *and used his paper in the war against slavery to advocate immediate emancipation. He faced increasing opposition as he more and more openly defended the cause of abolition in the pages of the* Observer. *The repeated destruction of his press failed to silence him and ultimately convinced a group of his supporters to assemble with guns to protect a new press that had arrived at an Alton warehouse. An angry mob of antiabolitionists stormed the warehouse, were repulsed by the armed guard, and tried to set fire to the building. In his attempt to save the press, Lovejoy ran out in front of the mob and was killed.*

The North heard equally interesting language from Garrison and his followers, who were willing to see the Constitution junked and the nation permanently divided if only slavery were ended. Since slavery found legality in the Constitution, that document was "a covenant of death and an agreement with hell," better abandoned than preserved. A Union which permitted slavery within its borders was better off amputated. "No Union with Slaveholders" ran the slogan, while Garrison declared "Accursed be the American Union." No price was too high to pay, and in the view of these men the scrapping of the Constitution and the dismemberment of the Union would be only minor sacrifices, for as abolitionist James Redpath proclaimed:

> if all the slaves in the United States—men, women and helpless babes—were to fall on the field or become victims of vengeance . . . if only one man survived

to enjoy the freedom they had won, the liberty of that solitary negro . . . would be cheaply purchased by the universal slaughter of his people and their oppressors.

As a democratic reform movement, abolition failed. Both moderates and extremists antagonized the South—the moderates by their arguments, the extremists by their inability to recognize that it is possible to have a certain respect for the opposition as human beings even though you may disapprove of their ideas. For there were decent Southerners who agonized over slavery. Gustavus Henry admitted to his wife that "I sometimes think my feelings unfit me for a slaveholder," and a Southern woman after the Civil War recalled that she had viewed the freeing of the slaves with relief—"The great load of accountability was lifted," she said. Yet as a whole, the South responded to such attacks with a defense of slavery as a positive good that was as strident, contemptuous, and extreme in its claim to the truth as any of Garrison's proclamations, a defense that not only closed off discussion of the issue in the South by democratic methods but ultimately extended to the unconditional demand for the right of slavery in the western territories, an unmistakable challenge to the authority of the Constitution and the Union.

The abolition movement also failed as a democratic reform movement because its supporters failed—except for a handful like Garrison—to recognize that slavery was only one side of the coin, the other being the presence of racial prejudice in America, North as well as South. At best, most Americans outside the South might agree with Lincoln when he remarked that the negro "is not my equal in many respects—certainly not in color, perhaps not in moral and intellectual endowment. But in the right to eat the bread, without leave of anybody else, which his own hand earns, he is my equal . . . and the equal of every living man." Abolitionists, therefore, did not engage in any effort to enlighten public opinion on racial equality, a commitment to which lay at the heart of the future role of the black in American society.

The culminating irony of the abolitionist movement was that slavery was finally to be abolished in the course of a war brought about by circumstances and conditions influenced and shaped by the institution of slavery, but fought not to destroy slavery but to preserve the Union and the Constitution. The goal of the abolitionists—the destruction of slavery as an institution—was indeed achieved, but not as a direct result of the democratic process.

Humanitarian Reform   There were a number of other reform movements in the first half of the nineteenty century, but none had the sense of fatefulness for the future of the republic as the abolition movement and the drive for free public schools. Yet they indicated the spreading concern that a democratic society must reflect in all its aspects the ideas that underlie its faith: respect for the dignity and integrity of individuals, their lives, their liberty, their right to happiness. Thus the movement for prison reform attracted attention with its emphasis upon rehabilitation rather than punishment. Today, absurd as our contemporary prison system is, the experiments

The March of Death, *from the literature produced by the temperance movement.*

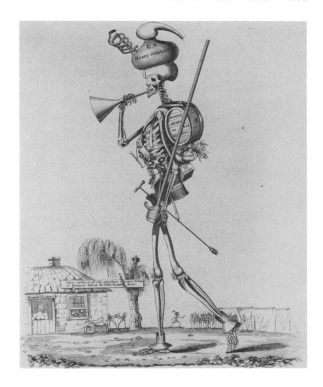

in New York and Pennsylvania based on total silence and complete isolation seem inhumane even though the treatment was accompanied by moral and religious instruction. But the genuine intent of these methods was to reform individuals and to return them fit members to society. Classification of prisoners also made its appearance under the instigation of prison reformers, resulting in the practice of segregation of women prisoners, the removal of the insane to asylums, and the transfer of juvenile offenders to separate institutions. Related to penal reform was the drive to abolish capital punishment. In a number of states, penal code reformers had by the 1830s and 1840s succeeded in getting reduced the number of offenses punishable by death, eliminated some public executions, and gained support for abandoning the death penalty. Michigan in 1847 was the first to abolish capital punishment, followed by Rhode Island in 1852 and Wisconsin in 1853.

The period also saw a rising concern for the handicapped—the deaf, the blind, and the insane. "Every creature in human shape should command our respect," said Dr. Samuel Gridley Howe, who devised for the blind a book with raised letters. "The strong should help the weak, so that the whole should advance as a band of brethren." Such views also motivated Dorothea Dix, who devoted thirty years of her life seeking improved care, treatment, and facilities for the insane. By 1860, such efforts had produced improved conditions in a dozen states. Equal concern was reflected in the establishment of special schools for educating the deaf, such as the American Asylum at Hartford, Connecticut.

Another abuse attacked by determined reformers was drink. Although this may hardly seem to fall under the scope of democratic reform, many concerned people, especially church people, saw in the consequences of excessive drinking a degradation of life and human dignity, a deprivation of human opportunity. There can, at any rate, be little doubt that there was excessive drinking. Grogshops were everywhere and in great number; small children could buy a penny's worth of liquor at the corner grocery store; the farmer downed his glass in early morning thinking it gave him strength and endurance and protection from the chills; liquor was served on all social occasions from christening to funeral; much of the economic and political business of the day, if Daniel Webster was any example, was conducted in what may only be called an atmosphere of alcoholic vapors. The Reverend Lyman Beecher described the scene as "a river of fire . . . rolling through the land, destroying the vital air, and extending around an atmosphere of death"—a description sounding for all the world like nuclear holocaust.

The temperance movement, eventually taken over by those calling for total abstinence by legal prohibition, added a new twist to reform movements when in the 1840s it introduced giant parades enlivened by bands, floats, banners, marching societies, and the Cold Water Army composed of boys and girls who had taken a pledge never to indulge. The movement made strong use of reformed drunkards whose accounts of their terrifying experiences dramatized the cause. The most famous of these was John Gough who in the midst of one of his crusades was found drunk in a New York brothel. His explanation that his soda water had been drugged was viewed with some skepticism. But laws were passed, despite Gough's slip from the wagon, first local option laws, then state-wide enactment. By 1855 some thirteen states had prohibition. But subsequent court decisions and popular referendums began a reversal as dramatic as the original achievement, and by 1868 only Maine remained dry.

The Peace Movement   No view of the great ferment of reform in this period can ignore the peace movement whose goal cannot exactly be said to have become one of the world's great achievements but which has nevertheless managed to survive in men's desires ever since a peace society was first formed in Massachusetts in 1815. It may seem ironic that Americans founded the international peace movement, for they were certainly not averse to the use of force in their personal and public affairs. Many a citizen feeling himself injured or insulted tended to rely upon his guns or fists for satisfaction rather than the law. And banded together, the Americans presented an equally impressive picture. They lynched blacks, attacked abolitionists, burned convents, rioted against banks, beat up actors, chased gamblers and prostitutes out of town, wiped out Indians, raided the Canadians, and fought the British and the Mexicans. Nevertheless, as an English advocate of peace noted, there was something in American institutions "more favorable to the progress of pacific principles" than characterized the institutions of other countries, including his own.

The American Peace Society was founded in 1828 at the instigation of William Ladd and had such close contacts with the London Peace Society as to make the two virtually the same organization. Speakers and writers put forth such measures as disarmament, outlawing of war, a Court of Nations to codify international law, and a Congress of Nations. In the 1840s the American Elihu Burritt founded the League of Universal Brotherhood, an international movement whose members took a pledge of peace. The Americans played a key role in various international peace conventions at Brussels, Paris, Frankfort, and London in putting forth proposals for international machinery to promote and maintain peace. Of particular significance was the idea of using arbitration, originated by Judge William Jay, president of the American Peace Society, an idea that found its way into the Treaty of Paris after the Crimean War. The American Peace Society lost many potential supporters when in 1837 it abandoned the view that a defensive war was justified. Many other Americans were unsympathetic with the New England Non-Resistance Society which opposed not only war but all use of force, even by government in preserving law and order.

Peace movements, unfortunately, suffer from a common human failing. When there is no war, it seems of little moment to be concerned about peace. When there is war, most people tend to be so swept up in it that peace organizations have little fruitful ground to till. No major foreign war threatened in this period, and near its end the passions of dispute between North and South overrode thoughts of peaceful resolution of problems.

Women's Rights   Another important reform movement of the period before the Civil War was that seeking to improve the status of women. Although the role and status of women in America was traditionally regarded as much improved over that of their European sisters, changing social and economic conditions in the first half of the nineteenth century forced a serious new look at women in American society. It was no coincidence that the formal organization of the women's rights movement occurred in 1848, by which time the rise of industry and the growth of cities had begun to affect the traditional family structure in the United States. The old self-sufficient farming family found its identity being altered under the impact of a rising urban and manufacturing environment which offered a degree of independence not heretofore available to women and made many women more conscious of a role for themselves in society outside the confines of the family itself.

Although women got some help from men in initiating demands for change, the embryonic women's rights movement rested primarily on the energies of women themselves, not so much those exploited by the new environment—the mill or shop girls—or those seeking relief from traditional male dominance in their daily lives, but from those who grasped the significance of the changing nature of American society and wished to have greater equality in society's affairs. It is not surprising, therefore, that women who became concerned about their own status in society were those who had been drawn into the larger reform impulse of the day. Yet convention severely limited the role they could play in the reforms that interested them, such as temperance, education, and the abolition of slavery. Women activists were not permitted to speak to mixed audiences, or to sit as delegates equal to men in the conventions of reform societies. Moreover, the denial of the right to vote or to hold office naturally limited their effectiveness in the political activities upon which so much reform depended for success.

The humiliations many women underwent in their involvement in reform activities got a number of them to thinking as much about their own disabilities as those suffered by slaves, by uneducated children, or by the insane whose condition they were trying to improve. What they thought about were the legal disabilities wives endured: they had no right to make deeds, sign contracts, draw wills, or sue in courts without their husbands' consent. They thought about their exclusion from the political process: they could not vote, hold office, or share equally in political party activities. They thought about social restrictions: they were not admitted to institutions of higher learning or the professions. And the more they thought, the angrier they became. Women laboring energetically in the antislavery movement, for instance, wondered why people could not see that women too, in a significant sense, were slaves. It is worth noting that today also the new and vigorous demand for the liberation of women has followed closely on the heels of the black civil rights movement of the post-World War II era.

No one spoke more powerfully from the heart on the matter of women's rights than Sojourner Truth. An ex-slave, unable to read or write, she stunned the crowd at a woman's convention in Akron, Ohio, in 1851 with these words:

> Well, children, where there is so much racket there must be something out of kilter. I think that 'twixt the negroes of the South and women at the North, all talking about rights, the white men will be in a fix pretty soon. But what's all this here talking about?
>
> That man over there says that women need to be helped into carriages, and lifted over ditches, and to have the best place everywhere. Nobody ever helps me into carriages, or over mud-puddles, or gives me any best place! And ain't I a woman? Look at me! Look at my arm! I have ploughed and planted, and gathered into barns, and no man could head me! And ain't I a woman? I could work as much and eat as much as a man—when I could get it—and bear the lash as well! And ain't I a woman? I have borne thirteen children, and seen most of them sold off to slavery, and when I cried out with my mother's grief, none but Jesus heard me! And ain't I a woman?
>
> Then they talk about this think in the head [referring to a previous speaker who had asserted that man had an intellect superior to woman] . . . What's that got to do with women's rights or negro's rights? If my cup won't hold but a pint, and yours holds a quart, wouldn't you be mean not to let me have my little half-measure full?
>
> Then that little man in black there, he says women can't have as much rights as men, 'cause Christ wasn't a woman! Where did your Christ come from? Where did your Christ come from? Where did your Christ come from? From God and a woman! Man had nothing to do with Him!

*Sojourner Truth. Born a slave, Isabella, in
New York, she took the name Sojourner Truth
after New York freed its slaves in 1827 and
she involved herself in religious revivalism. She
eventually became an active abolitionist and a
powerful leader of the movement.*

Women activists, of course, were frequently charged with being exhibitionists, with seeking to destroy the gentle and dependent character given them by God. Editor James Gordon Bennett, in fact, suggested that Lucy Stone, a crusading woman reform lecturer, should be treated in an insane asylum to cure her of her antic behavior. Yet despite such opposition, the movement acquired momentum and considerable success. By the time of the Civil War, women had gained the right of greater participation in public activities on a more equal basis with men; in a number of states, wives had achieved legal success in controlling their own property and in being granted joint guardianship over children; they had broken the coeducational barrier with admission to Oberlin, Antioch, and the University of Iowa, and seen the establishment of a number of women's colleges as well; the Blackwell sisters had defied tradition and become medical doctors, and Antoinette Brown had become an ordained minister.

Utopian Communities   All reform movements in this era, with one exception, focused attention on more or less specific problems and specific solutions. The exception was the communitarian movement: an attempt to demonstrate by model communities how society could be completely reorganized on the basis of new principles, how a new and more attractive life style could be developed if people worked for the benefit of the whole rather than for the individual. Arising primarily in response to the new economic order coming into being and influenced almost entirely by European ideas, the communitarian movement resulted in the establishment in the United States in the first half of the nineteenth century of over one hundred secular

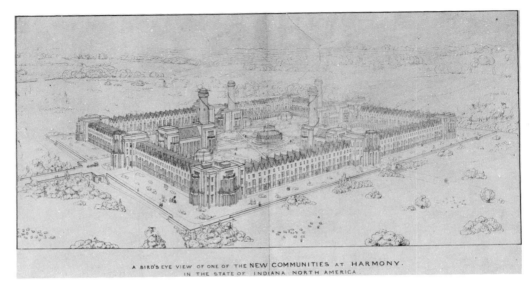

A BIRD'S EYE VIEW OF ONE OF THE NEW COMMUNITIES AT HARMONY.
IN THE STATE OF INDIANA NORTH AMERICA

*New Harmony. An architect's drawing of Robert Owen's plan for the
community, which included public buildings, living quarters, and a botanical
garden. It was Owen's intention that the structure be "regulated by a
careful attention to the most important discoveries and facts of science, as to
form a new combination of circumstances, capable of producing permanently
greater physical, moral, and intellectual advantages to every individual,
than have ever yet been realized in any age or country."*

and religious communities whose objective was to demonstrate that individuals could live more happily under new principles of association than those which characterized contemporary society. Most of these ventures were utopian in outlook, their supporters believing that the perfect society could be created on the basis of successful small-scale experiments, the first units of the society of the future. The majority of these new communities were established in the West, on the assumption that institutions there were not yet fixed, that the social and economic environment was still flexible and open to new ways of doing things. Yet failure was drastic and sharp in the West, and those communities established in the older sections of the country lasted longer. The West did, indeed, offer opportunity, but as much if not more to individuals than to associations.

An example of these characteristics of communitarianism was the experiment of Robert Owen. Owen was a successful English manufacturer with a deep concern for working people. Believing it possible to build a new social order upon the rational principles of socialism rather than competition, he decided America was a more fruitful field for proving his theories than England. His successful business background got him a respectable hearing in the United States—he even addressed Congress—and he purchased an old

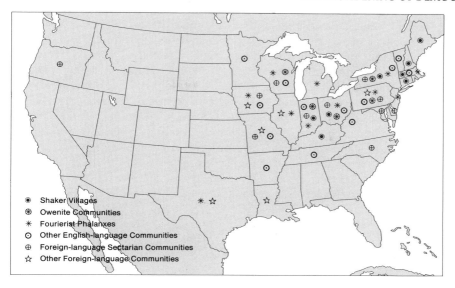

Shaker Villages
Owenite Communities
Fourierist Phalanxes
Other English-language Communities
Foreign-language Sectarian Communities
Other Foreign-language Communities

STATES IN WHICH UTOPIAN COMMUNITIES WERE
ESTABLISHED

Rappite settlement in Indiana in 1824, the site, ironically, of an earlier communitarian experiment. Naming his community New Harmony, Owen attracted from Europe and the United States about one thousand settlers—
intellectuals and would-be intellectuals, farmers and would-be farmers, mechanics and would-be mechanics, rascals and would-be rascals. The community was misnamed, for harmony did not prevail either internally or in
relations with the surrounding populace, who did not take kindly to Owen's
talk about the virtues of free love and atheism. Economically the experiment
was a costly failure, for some had no will to work and others were unwilling
to support the lazy.

More important were the communities established under the influence of
the French socialist, Charles Fourier, who proposed that society be reorganized into cooperative units called phalanxes. His ideas were popularized in
America by Albert Brisbane in the *Social Destiny of Man* published in 1840.
Converts to the cause also included such important journalists as Horace
Greeley of the New York *Tribune* and Parke Godwin of the New York *Evening
Post*. In the 1840s, numerous Fourierist phalanxes were established, the
longest-lived being the one at Red Bank, New Jersey, which was established
in 1843 and survived for some thirteen years by truck farming for the New
York City market. Although Fourierists did not challenge conventional beliefs on sex and religion, their communities consistently failed when their
members discovered they could do better economically on their own than
they could in joint ventures that rarely proved as cooperative as their
founders hoped.

Inspired by the special revelations of their leaders which might, for example, transform celibacy from an earthly aberration into a divine virtue, or

by the belief that society should be organized according to the "communist" principles of Jesus Christ, or by the conviction that the millennium was at hand and individuals should prepare to meet their Maker, a number of religious communities also came into being—the Rappites, the Shakers, the Amana Community, and others. Few flourished, although a number of small communities, particularly those of the Shakers, survived for several decades. When the millennium failed to arrive, or when celibacy forced growth to depend solely upon recruitment, individuals lost heart and communities tended to stagnate. One may admire the faith of those who believe in the imminent second coming of the Savior, or marvel at the fortitude of those who abstained from sex, but few have the capacity to follow their example. Any reform of society that depends upon divine intervention or the denial of human instinct faces adverse odds.

The first half of the nineteenth century in America was thus notable for the tide of social and humanitarian concern that swept much of the country and saw numerous Americans committed to the task of closing the gap between their ideals and social reality. Some were motivated by romantic sentiments of pity and sympathy for the downtrodden, some by moral commitments to the higher law of God, some by practical and rational ideas which stretched back to the Enlightenment about how society could best be organized. Others thought specifically in terms of adjusting a changing society to the ideas upon which the nation had been founded. Whatever the influences, or in whatever combination they played upon the consciences of Americans, such influences were among the forces that fed the democratic heritage of the nation.

The result was both failure and success. Continuing change in America naturally cast its shadow across reform experiments, often leaving them outmoded and inadequate to their task. The idea, for example, that prison should be an experience in rehabilitation, had by the Civil War been smothered by an expansion in the prison population that came from increased urbanism and its problems, and as a consequence prisons became more than anything else simply a place of incarceration where society for its own convenience and security isolated disrupters of law and order. In some instances, society had not yet undergone those broader changes that would propel forward reforms now only partially underway, as with the women's rights movement. When zeal for reform spilled over into the moral compulsion to dictate proper behavior, as in the temperance movement, it was soon discovered that individuals whose habits were the object of reform would much prefer to make such choices on their own, and such reforms ground to a halt.

By and large, however, the achievement was considerable. To many Americans, as well as to observers from abroad, it seemed clear that the extent and variety of reform provided proof of the advantages of a democratic society, that it was more concerned about the lives of ordinary people, more willing to recognize social inadequacies and abuse, more open to experimentation, better qualified by virtue of its political institutions to respond to and implement proposals for social change.

Economic Opportunities and Problems

To many people, then, American political and social life seemed marked by an active commitment to the spread of democratic practices. At the same time, the capacity to provide opportunity for ordinary people, native and immigrant alike, to gather to themselves some of the material blessings of this world, extended democracy economically. At a time in the western world when many people lived lives of quiet economic desperation, this was the bread-and-butter appeal of America.

The Public Lands And it was the land—vast, fertile, and more easily available than elsewhere—that underwrote this economic opportunity. For despite the rise of urbanism and industrialism, it was the land that absorbed the major energies and attention of the American people up to the Civil War.

Opportunity is a key word here. Americans were in no way committed to equality in the possession of property, land or other, but rather to equality in the opportunity to acquire it. This meant that land should be open and available to the person of little resources. Central to economic democracy in America, therefore, was the process for making land available to ordinary people.

It was the national government that controlled the disposition of the vast public domain acquired by the new nation at independence and later extended as the nation absorbed the new territories to the West. Under the influence of Hamilton, the national government at first viewed the disposition of the public domain primarily as a means of raising revenue. But from the beginning there was a rising demand for policies that would make land easily available to the ordinary settler.

The first Land Act of 1796 was not, however, geared to the resources of ordinary settlers. Land was to be sold at auction either by whole townships or by sections of 640 acres, with the minimum price set at $2 an acre and credit for one year. Even speculators found this largely unattractive. Within four years, the minimum purchase was therefore reduced to half sections, with a grant of four years' credit for three-quarters of the purchase price, but the price remained $2 an acre. This act of 1800 also provided for a land office in each land district that reduced the complaints of common people opposed to the expense and inconvenience of attending auctions at distant places. But this act still did not take into account the fact that the first settlers in any area were almost invariably poor and therefore needed small tracts at a price they could afford to pay and on credit terms within their reach.

By 1804, therefore, the minimum purchase had been reduced to one-quarter of a section or 160 acres. Not only was this still too large for many, but the price and inadequate credit provisions left many purchasers unable to pay off their debt to the government. By 1817 land debts had risen alarmingly to about $17 million. Numerous relief measures were passed, but there were many forfeitures of land nevertheless. In 1820, therefore, in a major move, the credit system was abolished, relief measures were instituted

Scenes from the Road West. *Joshua Shaw apparently made his sketches
as he himself moved West, capturing the pilgrim quality of that journey
made by his fellow travelers.*

to clear up debts, the price was reduced to $1.25 an acre, and the minimum
purchase was now set at a manageable 80 acres.

By 1830 Congress had also adopted the preemption system which granted
the right to settle on unappropriated government land and then buy it later
without competition at the government's minimum price. Such a policy not
only responded to the needs of the small independent purchaser but also to
the demands of the numerous squatters, people who had simply moved out
onto the frontier and taken up land on their own without regard to any
formalities of ownership. This had been a common procedure from earliest
colonial times, and the government now legalized the practice.

Thus the trend in land policies moved steadily in the direction of encouraging settlement by ordinary people with limited means, rather than allowing the land to pass into the hands of great landowners and speculators. This
is not to say that land speculation did not occur, but the government favored
the small farmer rather than the speculator. Moreover, the squatters themselves often took up the more attractive locations and simply squeezed out
the speculator. In addition, many early territorial legislatures in the West
aided in the process by imposing high taxes on unimproved land held by
nonresidents, forcing speculators to unload quickly or go broke, which many
did.

The final step was the policy of free land, achieved in the Homestead Act
of 1862 which provided that any head of household over twenty-one years of
age could get 160 acres of the public domain simply by residing on the land
for five years and paying a small registration fee. The demand for free land

for the common people stretched back to the early 1840s, to George Henry Evans and his National Land Reformers among others, but a lingering desire for some revenue from the public domain, and fears that free land would depopulate eastern cities of workingmen, postponed this step until the Civil War.

While there was abuse and exploitation in the disposal of the public domain, nevertheless as the government's policy rapidly became increasingly liberal, it opened wide the door of settlement in the West to vast numbers of the common people, immigrant and native alike, giving them a new chance at economic security and advancement.

Government land policy, moreover, not only promoted opportunity for the would-be farmer, but by doing so also provided it to those in the villages and towns that sprang up everywhere as settlement advanced: the tradesmen, merchants, printers, doctors, lawyers, teachers, mechanics and others who followed the settlers and furnished the services they were ill-prepared to provide for themselves.

Influence on Canada   The successful economic growth of the West that followed from a liberal disposal of the public domain was used with telling effect by reformers in Canada, who saw their own western settlement restricted by narrow British policies providing large land grants to the church and favorites of the government. In sharp criticism of British policy which hampered the opportunity of the ordinary settler, the Quebec *Gazette* in the 1830s invoked comparison between the Canadian and American experience:

> The Upper Canadian sees the southern banks of the great River and Lakes which are known to have been a wilderness when the Upper Canadian Settlements were so far advanced that the first settlers on the American side depended upon them for a supply of provisions, and he beholds them now, surpassing the Canadian Inhabitants in all the necessaries and comforts of life, secured, contented, and satisfied with their own government.

It was this contrast in land policy that so impressed Lord Durham and that he recorded in his famous report on Canada after the abortive Canadian rebellion of 1837. Among other recommendations he suggested that the British government should follow the American policy of disposal of public lands for settlement.

Work in an Expanding Economy   While it was the land of the great West that formed the main arena for economic opportunity, expansion of the whole economy offered opportunity for work to all. There was work in the construction of roads, canals, and railways, of private and public buildings in the expanding older cities and in the rising new towns, in the extension of trades and crafts, in the demand for farm help and household servants, and in the rising mills and factories.

The net result was that to many Americans and foreign visitors the United States was, as Emerson put it, "another word for opportunity." Rufus Eaton, member of the Missouri territorial legislature, in a letter to a friend in 1816 described the fruits of that opportunity in terms of the lands of the West:

> There neither is, nor, in the nature of things can there ever be, any thing like poverty there. All is ease, tranquillity and comfort. Every person, however poor, may with moderate industry, become in a very short time a landholder; his substance increases from year to year; his barns are filled with abundant harvests; his cattle multiply; . . . and his children, active, vigorous and enterprising, seem destined to sustain and extend the respectability of their parentage.

The English Chartist leader, Feargus O'Connor, declared that in the United States "Land is cheap, and the people of America have in greater abundance the necessaries of life than the people of any other country." The English traveler, Alexander Mackay, wrote that "It is extremely seldom that the willing hand in America is in want of employment"—an observation echoed by a Norwegian immigrant in 1835 in a letter home to friends: "We have gained more since our arrival here than I did during all the time I lived in Norway." In urging his friends to follow, he added, "Those who are willing to work will not lack employment or business here. It is possible for all to live in comfort and without want." The Austrian visitor, Francis Grund, described the attractive homes of the skilled mechanics:

> On entering the house of a respectable mechanic in any of the large cities of the United States, one cannot but be astonished at the apparent neatness and comfort of the apartments, the large airy parlors, the nice carpets and mahogany furniture, and the tolerably good library, showing that the inmates are acquainted with the standard work of English literature.

No wonder that another visitor to America ended up describing the United States as "the empire of the working man."

None of this is to say that economic life was a pleasant romp for the common people, that the fruit of one's labor was easy picking. Equality of opportunity often meant an equal chance to break your back on the railroad, shrink your lungs in a stifling mill, or die of pneumonia on an Indiana farm. But to many, the chance for any work at all, for a place of one's own, for three square meals a day, was a glowing opportunity compared to life in the Old World. The records of visitors' impressions are filled with constant references to adequate food, as though this were something unusual. The English visitor Harriet Martineau, made an observation recorded time and again when she wrote that "I saw no table spread, in the lowest order of houses, that had not meat and bread on it." And French observer Michel Chevalier told the story of the Irish immigrant writing home to his family in the old country that he ate meat three times a week, even though he actually had it three times a day. For the contrast between Ireland and America was so great that his family would not have believed him had he told the truth.

Life was often hard in America, but people believed that those willing to work hard had an equal chance to get ahead, to live like human beings. And the records indicate that for many this faith was justified, especially for those who went West. An immigrant working as a hired man for 75 cents a day on a farm in Wisconsin in 1860, for example, could by saving half his wages for 200 days' work have enough to buy 40 acres of land at $1.25 per acre and also pay the expenses of a trip to file for the land. Thus Peter Larson emigrated with his family from Norway to Wisconsin in 1857, working as a rail splitter for 50 cents a day and also as a farm laborer. In 1860 he laid claim to 160 acres in Trempealeau County, and in spite of initial hardship prospered, a few years later selling his farm to his son and buying another for himself. Most such people as Peter Larson had no grand ambitions. They were content to avoid want, to leave something to their children, and to lay the foundations for those other pleasures of life which only economic security can bring. They were willing to work hard and took pride in their labor. No one who reads the records of those looking back upon these experiences and summing up their lives can fail to be impressed by their sense of the worthiness of what they had done. Cornelius van der Meulen, a leader of Dutch immigrants to Michigan, looking back in 1872 upon what they had all achieved in twenty-five years, summed it up as follows:

> We have grown up in this country; we have multiplied; our cattle have increased by the thousands; our forests have been converted into fruitful acres. Thus it has gone in every aspect of our progress. . . . What a transformation in 25 years! It is hardly to be believed. Those who among our people today are regarded as the most prosperous in the beginning were drivers of oxen, men who carried on their business in Grand Rapids, making that trip a couple of times a week. No longer do we need oxen to carry our products to distant market, for now the train daily transports goods and passengers eastward and westward. In one hour we are in Grand Rapids, and in a few hours in Chicago, and in ten minutes in Holland [Michigan] where we have our college, a school where instruction is imparted in all branches, under at least seven professors who prepare their pupils in many scientific matters, for school, for church, and for society. Furthermore, let us note our numerous organized school districts for the upbringing of our youth . . .

Such people were not plagued by doubts at the end of their lives about what they had wrought and had no fears that they had sold their souls for a mess of pottage, but believed that their accomplishments marked an advance in human dignity and welfare. And who today would deny them their pride?

Growth of Urban Poverty Impressive as all this may have been, it was not the whole story. For, just as the record of American social democracy was marred by the presence of black servitude, so was the record of economic democracy tarnished by the rise of a kind of hopeless and depressing poverty that began to appear in the United States in the 1840s and 1850s under the impact of industrial and urban growth. The factories, mills, and slums of the rising new economic system seemed made to order for exploitation and endless misery. Hard work in such circumstances opened no doors to security, dignity, and well-being, but to degradation, ill health, and early death.

A New England shoemaking factory, 1840. With the development of mass production techniques came the widespread use of children in the labor force.

In the early stages of industrial development in the United States, few found themselves trapped in a dead-end of misery. The early factories of New England, rising in the countryside alongside the streams which supplied their power, relied heavily for labor upon farm girls who lived in pleasant company-sponsored dormitories and stayed only long enough to earn enough money for a dowry. In other areas, entire families hired out together, carrying over from the farm the tradition of the family as an economic unit. Some towns relied on child labor, but the pace of early factory life was slow and the conditions of labor really not more oppressive than the work farm children often did at home. In the small semirural communities of the early nineteenth century, many craftsmen and mechanics had subsidiary sources of livelihood in their gardens and in fishing, and thus had a degree of independence and security reassuring in slack times.

But by the 1840s things had changed. Hundreds of thousands of immigrants poured into the country, many of them poverty-stricken and without the resources to take up land. This was particularly true of the Irish. Such people desperately needed work, and were willing to accept meager wages and endure the pace of factory work. By the time of the Civil War Irish workers made up more than fifty percent of the labor force of the mills of New England. And the girls who remained were city girls—tending twice as many looms as before, working at a faster pace for longer hours at less pay and not enjoying the social life and literary discussions that had made early dormitory life so attractive. Moreover, journeymen craftsmen found they were now working for a wage—selling their labor, not their product—with the degrading suggestion that they were selling themselves. Many craftsmen found their skills taken over by machines manned by unskilled workers. And in the exploding cities there was now no space for workers to have their gardens, their pigs, and their cows.

Although expanding industrialism meant prosperity at large, and high profits for owners, workers in the new industrial system did not share equally in the wealth being created. Wages for certain skilled workers advanced, especially in the building trades, but wages for factory operatives, shoe makers, clothing workers, printers, cabinet workers, hatters, iron workers, and handloom weavers declined in relation to the rising cost of living after 1840. Day laborers in New York City in 1846 could earn about $200 a year if they were lucky enough to get work four days a week. Thousands of women earned less than $1.50 a week. The New York *Daily Tribune* reported in 1845:

> A great number of females are employed in making men's and boys' caps. By constant labor, 15 to 18 hours a day, they can make from 14 to 25 cents. We are told by an old lady who has lived by this kind of work for a long time that when she begins at sunrise and works until midnight, she can earn 14 cents a day. . . .

Moreover, wages could often be collected only by the purchase of goods from company stores, where prices were so marked up as to equal a twenty-five to fifty percent reduction in wages.

In addition, brief periods of depression created large-scale unemployment and all the accompanying miseries: prostitution, reliance upon inadequate charity, hunger marches, begging, malnutrition, disease, and crime.

And poverty produced deplorable living conditions unknown to an earlier America. City slums arose whose horrors were nightmarish. In 1850 the New York *Daily Tribune* reported that one in twenty of the population of New York City lived in cellars, a condition not uncommon in cities elsewhere. In Boston, an investigator found one house occupied by a store and twenty-five different families totalling 120 persons. In a single room were found two families, one of ten persons with four boarders. In Boston in 1849, an investigating physician found a house whose triple cellar was occupied as follows:

> The first cellar from the street was occupied in one corner by a bar . . . and served as a kitchen and a parlor. The second . . . served as a family sleeping-room, whilst the third, a dungeon six feet square and the same in height, with no aperture for the admission of air save the narrow door . . . served to accommodate boarders.
>
> The landlord said the tide came through the floor of his rooms but rarely! One cellar was reported by the police to be occupied nightly as a sleeping-apartment for thirty-nine persons. In another, the tide had risen so high that it was necessary to approach the bedside of a patient by means of a plank which was laid from one stool to another; while the dead body of an infant was actually sailing about the room in its coffin.

There were those abroad, hopeful of finding flaws in America as the great model for democracy, who with somber pleasure pointed out that America could not maintain itself as a democracy in the face of these changing economic and social conditions. English conservatives argued that only America's supply of unoccupied land held back the rise of popular discontent and tumult. Democracy, argued the editors of the conservative *Blackwood's Magazine,* was fit only for a rural society, for "dwellers in forests;" it was utterly unsuited to an urban and manufacturing society. As the Americans will learn, warned *Blackwood's* in an ominous analysis, to establish democratic institutions in such a society "is not to extend the basis of freedom, but give the signal for its destruction; not to induce a pacific and stable order of things, but begin the strife which can terminate in nothing but the government of the strongest." The urban poor, equipped with the vote, would in their despair strike out blindly against society and bring it crashing down in ruins. So ran the alarm from abroad, but even at that distance a fair enough warning under the circumstances for the future of democracy in America.

Most Americans, distant from urban centers and engaged in other tasks, seemed unaware of this cancer in their midst. Some who were aware were indifferent to the problem. Others, including the workers themselves, were disturbed by the plight of the worker and the fate of the poor and were moved to action. The problem for the urban worker, skilled and unskilled alike, was not only to use existing institutions but to find new avenues to a decent life, material security, and economic well-being. The period before the Civil War therefore became a time of experiment, of seeking new instruments of economic and social justice, new solutions to the workers' problems.

Working Class Movements   Not surprisingly in a political system in which they possessed the vote, workers took to political action. They formed working men's parties, such as those which appeared in the cities of New York, Pennsylvania, Ohio, New Jersey, and Delaware in the 1820s and 1830s—running their own candidates and endorsing others who supported their demands. Helped by reformers with humanitarian sentiments, they flooded state legislatures with petitions, such as those in Massachusetts in the 1840s demanding the ten-hour day, which led to hearings and studies by investigating committees. Seeking to educate both workers and others to conditions and demands, they established newspapers representing labor's interest, the *Voice of Industry* being a leading example. A few, lured by the communitarian dreams of the Fourierists and others, thought the workers' problems would disappear if society were reorganized completely. Some felt that the only answer lay in rejecting the industrial system and returning to the soil, and these joined reformers such as George Henry Evans in his call for free and equal distribution of land. Others, among them the shoemakers

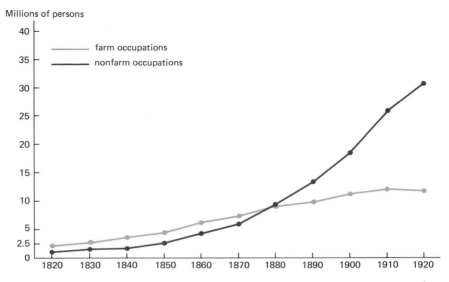

Millions of persons

DISTRIBUTION OF WORKERS

of Lynn, Massachusetts, tried both producer and consumer cooperatives. Finally, at an accelerating pace, beginning in the 1820s, the workers turned to union organization and the weapon of the strike. By the 1830s at least five crafts—the shoemakers, printers, combmakers, carpenters, and handloom weavers—were holding national conventions, and strikes were becoming frequent. Between 1833 and 1837 at least 173 strikes are known to have taken place.

How successful was all this? The record was not particularly impressive. The most notable achievement probably was the increasing move toward a ten-hour working day, stimulated by Van Buren's executive order for a ten-hour day for federal employees in 1840, given added impetus by state legislation, and reinforced by strikes for a reduction in the working day. By the eve of the Civil War many skilled workers had achieved a ten-hour day, and the day in many factories had been reduced to eleven if not ten hours. While this may seem to have been genuine progress, and indeed was for some workers, many day laborers worked far longer hours, and everywhere the six-day week was common. Minimum hours of work were sixty a week, not a happy prospect for the faint of heart and the weak of back.

Success was similarly dubious in the matter of wages. Factory owners granting the ten-hour day frequently reduced wages accordingly. For skilled workers whose wages actually improved, the prosperous expansion of the American economy was probably the major cause, though many skilled workers successfully used the strike to prevent a reduction of wages in bad times and to gain an increase in better times. But a rise in the cost of living in this period prevented the unskilled laborer and the factory worker from improving their economic condition, and their wages improved little or not at all. Everywhere economic insecurity remained a fact of life for those struggling to find a place in the new economic order.

One major achievement was the testing of union organization and the strike. The unions of the period all failed to survive, it is true. They had inadequate financial resources. Confusion and dispute over their own purposes and goals led to internal division, and they were repeatedly crushed by hostile employers. But they got experience and they learned from failure. Unions were beaten in strikes, defeated in the courts, and saw favorable labor legislation dissipated by evasion and lack of enforcement. But they won a number of strikes, and they achieved a legal triumph in Massachusetts in 1842 in the case of *Commonwealth vs. Hunt* in which Chief Justice Shaw asserted the legality of unions and declared that a strike to enforce the closed shop was not unlawful if conducted peaceably. And workers saw the potential political power of their numbers reflected in the passage of legislation that, however weak, was a response to labor interests. If these accomplishments did not constitute a precise road map to the future, they did make it clear that improvement lay not in utopian schemes or workingmen's parties but in political pressure through established parties, strong legislation, and the power of their own unity.

For the poor and the unskilled this was no testing period, except of their capacity to endure. Untouched by political or judicial concern, neglected by union organizations, ignored by skilled workers, the urban poor remained unorganized and miserable, their fate alleviated only by limited private and religious philanthropy.

Yet while economic distress had appeared as a new and threatening challenge to American society by the time of the Civil War, those truly deprived of opportunity were only a fraction of the American population. The immense reserves of land and the expanding economy made the hope of a better life a genuine reality for many whose economic condition was the wonder and the envy of much of the Western World.

Violence   One aspect of American society periodically drew the attention and concern not only of conservatives in America but of foreign commentators as well. This was social violence. At least one thousand people were killed in riots in the decades before the Civil War, and considerable property was damaged. Racial, ethnic, religious, economic, and moral tensions were inevitable in a rapidly changing society, and too easily could explode into violence in a society where firearms were readily at hand and law enforcement practices were weak. Conservatives often feared that such disturbances threatened the collapse of their well-ordered world; foreigners hostile to America believed they revealed the inherent weakness of democracy—the mob in action; and foreign admirers were embarrassed and confused.

The presence of tensions in America certainly made it obvious that there was no such thing as the perfect society, and the violence that sometimes sprang from such tensions illuminated the truth of James Madison's observation that men are not angels. Social violence revealed a problem that has faced American democracy ever since. If power resided in the people, then the individual—whose rights, interests, and happiness were the central concerns of a democracy—had the right to participate equally in society and the equal right to decide what was best. Though the Americans have always been a strong "law and order" people, they have also tended to believe that the individual, alone or in concert with others of similar mind, has the right to punish and correct wrongdoing if the institutions of justice fail to do so, whether or not society approves. Not surprisingly, they developed a taste for heroes who, firm in the right as God gave them to see the right, stood not really against or outside the law but above it in order to right some social wrong. In this the social good and the individual will merged. Such an individual was not threatening society, but protecting it. Turning reality into myth, we have run the gamut of admiration for such men, from Andrew Jackson and Henry David Thoreau to Gary Cooper in *High Noon* and Humphrey Bogart in *The Maltese Falcon.*

In our own time this problem was restated by those in the anti-Vietnam War movement who believed that violence was a morally justifiable instrument to achieve peace in a war that contradicted in so many ways the democratic values of American society. Clearly, this justification ran in a reasonably straight line back to Francis Grund who wrote in 1837 that lynch law "is not properly speaking an opposition to the established laws of the country . . . but rather . . . a supplement to them—as a species of *common law.*"

In this sense, those who defended the incidents of social violence erupting in the period before the Civil War believed they were enforcing justice, not challenging it. The fact that violence was often directed against minorities who were helpless—blacks, nuns, Mormons, for example—demonstrated the tragedy of self-righteous identification of individual will with general social good. The problem has not been resolved, as demonstrated in some reactions to the civil rights movement of the 1960s and school integration in the 1970s.

The Democratic Nation and the World

What the United States accomplished in the decades from the founding of the republic to the Civil War was the creation of a society unique in the Western World. Far from crumbling under the impact of change, the nation was securely established on the continent and in the hemisphere, had prospered and developed economically, and had formulated a commitment to democratic ideas which gave society a flexibility in coping with change.

There were serious problems, but the Americans had a confidence in their ability to deal with change and with the problems that flowed from their commitment to democratic ideas. They were neither passive, indifferent, nor despairing. Despite failures and difficulties they remained confident—probably too much so—that their institutions were powerful and flexible enough to deal effectively with problems and to make the good life possible for those who wanted it.

There was nothing in the world quite like this new democratic nation, and the admiration it aroused in others placed it under the spotlight on center stage in the Western World. No discussion, no debate on revolution or reform in this era took place without some discussion of the United States. America was the model, and as a new nation and a democratic society, it offered a new concept that attracted those tired of their own past and desiring a better future.

For three-quarters of a century those who sought change in reform, revolution, and national independence found the path lit by what many called the "beacon" of America: the unsuccessful Canadian revolt of the 1830s, the Latin American revolutions which drove the Spanish from the New World, the demands of the early Australian colonists for more control of their own affairs, the ill-fated Decembrist Revolt of the 1820s in Russia, the Reform Bill of 1832 and the Chartist Movement in England, social reform in the Scandinavian countries, the revolutions of 1848 in Europe, the drives for German and Italian unity—even a partial listing is a long one. Some succeeded, some failed. The American example loomed large in some, smaller in others. But its presence was felt in all.

The Americans could be and were proud of their achievements and proud of their prestige in the eyes of so many. But pride, as was noted a long time ago, sometimes goes before a fall. And the Americans, who had created the first new nation, who tried to show the world how to make democracy work, were to find both their nation and their democracy challenged and threatened, not from the outside by those who feared their success, but by themselves in a great Civil War.

Profile: ANDREW JACKSON

Unlike the colonial and federalist leaders who preceded him, Andrew Jackson looked like the essence of the common man who rose from the ranks and made good. From frontiersman to aristocrat, poor lad to wealthy planter, humble boy-soldier in the Revolution to General and hero of the Battle of New Orleans, ill-educated youth to successful lawyer, farmer to gentleman, log cabin to White House—Jackson went the route. He was not a typical American but his life seemed to the typical American to exemplify what was possible in a society that emphasized talent and competitiveness rather than privilege.

His career was marked, but not marred, by a youthful taste for gambling, horses, and cock-fighting; by slave holding; by being tough on those who owed him money; by a hot temper which led him to the early-morning duel; by business failure; by an inclination to judge many matters on the personal basis of friendship or animosity rather than on public considerations; by a stern disciplinary and moral code.

But he was a natural leader, a man of integrity, and as he matured and his career advanced, he was capable of impressing people with his gentleness and gravity of manner. He was at ease in forest or mansion, could be as gracious with the ordinary citizen as with one of more exalted status. He commanded popular respect, and as often happens in such cases he naturally developed in his turn a respect for the general good judgment of the people.

Political rewards came to him early and in quick succession. He was United States Attorney at twenty-three, in the House of Representatives in Washington at twenty-nine, the United States Senate at thirty, and on the Tennessee Supreme Court at thirty-one, although in none of these positions did he acquire a national reputation. That reputation came to him through his military ventures at the Battle of New Orleans and in Florida against the Indians. And, given the American political taste for victorious generals, these achievements were to thrust him into the national spotlight and on to the Presidency.

Nothing in his career, until the Presidency, marked him as the man who was to give his name to an era—the Age of Jacksonian Democracy. But he had risen through all positions of status and wealth; he had lived most of his life in the West where people tended to judge individuals on the basis of merit, not on family or place in the social hierarchy; he had participated in and observed the democratic process at work from constitution-making to constitution-interpreting. He had, as some do, an instinct for democracy. He was not, like Jefferson, an intellectual and a political activist. He was a gut democrat; the feeling for democracy did not come to him, as it did to Jefferson, through the mind and through involvement in political creation, but by the nature of his life, the society he operated in, and the responsibilities he assumed.

Jackson's importance as President came from the fact that he made the Presidency a positive instrument of both nationalism and democracy. He intuitively grasped the idea that the President is the main symbol of the nation and of national unity. "The President is the direct representative of the American people," he told the Senate. No President since has avoided being judged on his capacity to reflect these two Jacksonian concepts.

The support Jackson managed to generate in his bid for the Presidency, his election, and his re-election came from all sections of the country and from all classes, and convinced him that he represented the people as a whole, that the President is necessarily identified with the nation, not with a state, a section, a class, or an interest.

He had a deep faith in the nation as the framework within which democracy would develop and flourish, believing that it was the Union which provided the people with prosperity, happiness, and freedom. Therefore, he could not abide challenge to the nation and the democracy it made possible, and in his farewell address he reminded the American people of this belief:

> But in order to maintain the Union unimpaired, it is absolutely necessary that the laws passed by the constituted authorities should be faithfully executed in every part of the country, and that every good citizen should at all times stand ready to put down with the combined force of the nation every attempt at unlawful resistance under whatever pretext it may be made or whatever shape it may assume. Unconstitutional or oppressive laws may no doubt be passed by Congress, either from erroneous views or the want of due consideration; if they are within the reach of judicial authority, the remedy is easy and peaceful; and if from the character of the law it is an abuse of power not within the control of the judiciary, then free discussion and calm appeals to reason and to the justice of the people will not fail to redress the wrong. But until the law shall be declared void by the courts or repealed by Congress, no individual or combination of individuals can be justified in forcibly resisting its execution.

Jackson thus emphasized a democracy of obedience to law. As President he used troops to quell rioting in 1835, and he wrote to a friend that "This spirit of mob-law is becoming too common and must be checked or, ere long, it will become as great an evil as servile war, and the innocent will be much exposed." He believed that democracy involves the fundamental decencies, that its foundations "must be laid in the affections of the people; in the security it gives to life, liberty, character, and property, in every quarter of the country; and in the fraternal attachment which the citizens of the several States bear to one another as members of one political family, mutually contributing to promote the happiness of each other." Jackson tried to merge individualism and social responsibility, a task Americans have faced ever since with greater or lesser success.

Chapter 8
SOCIETY IN THE NEW REPUBLIC

The Spirit of the Times
AMBIVALENCE TOWARD EUROPE

Secure in the expanding bastions of nationalism and democracy and convinced of their own superiority, the Americans in the early decades of the republic threw themselves into the task of building a life distinct from all others, waving the big farewell to the follies of their European relatives across the seas. In the New World humanity was embarked upon a new adventure.

It was natural, therefore, for the Americans to look down upon Europe. A common if dubious way of bolstering oneself is to criticize others, and the Americans have always been skilled practitioners of this art. But it is not as simple a process as it sounds. Sometimes people are attracted by what repels them, and the line between love and hate is hard to draw. So, at any rate, it was for many nineteenth-century Americans in their attitude toward the lands of their origin. Envy and admiration were mixed with contempt. What they thought about Europe tells us more about them than it does about the Europeans.

The dominant, almost official, view was embodied in phrases used to describe Europe and America. Europe was the Old World—decadent, corrupt. America was the New World—fresh, vigorous, innocent. Typical American stereotypes were Liberty, Happiness, Innocence, and Simplicity on the one side, and Despotism, Misery, Corruption, and Sophistication on the other. The goal, therefore, was clear: keep contact to a minimum or America will be contaminated.

Jefferson, who wanted no imitations of Europe in America and who saw Europe "loaded with misery, by kings, nobles, and priests," was thankful that three thousand miles of ocean lay between America and the Old World. Indeed, he wished it were "an ocean of fire." Little wonder that he warned of the dangers that lay in wait for the unwary virtuous American setting foot for the first time on European soil. For the benefit of a young American friend contemplating a trip abroad, Jefferson warned that he might fall victim to such things as "European luxury and dissipation," "the privileges of European aristocrats," and "female intrigue"—a recital that might well have tempted many young men to set sail as soon as possible. Jefferson concluded ominously that "It appears to me, then, that an American coming to Europe for his education, loses in his knowledge, in his morals, in his health, in his habits, and in his happiness."

Jefferson's concern, of course, was with a Europe based on a rigid social hierarchy, monarchy, nobility, established churches, where the masses were exploited by the few who ruled. He never tired of denouncing the pernicious influence of such a society, referring to its rulers as fools, idiots, and degenerates.

But the irony was that Jefferson in many ways loved Europe and drew much from it. And he was to recommend the advantages of a European tour from which an intelligent American might return home "charged like a bee, with the honey gathered on it." As for himself, so far from being corrupted by Europe, he wrote from France: "Were I to proceed to tell you how much I enjoy their architecture, sculpture, painting, music, I should want words." His collection of European books, pictures, and sculpture, all of which he brought home to America from France, left him and his friends not corrupted but enriched. Jefferson's love for classical architecture, which he developed in France, found expression at home in such things as the dome of Monticello, modelled on the Hotel de Salm in Paris, and the noble rotunda he designed for the University of Virginia.

The American scholars, writers, and artists who, up through the 1850s, were to journey to Europe did not have Jefferson's deep concern for political differences that shaped his suspicions of Europe. But they did carry with them a vision of a Europe that contained dangers for the good American. George Ticknor, George Bancroft, Edward Everett, and Joseph Cogswell, who were among those who went abroad to prepare themselves for scholarly careers at home, were convinced that America was purer in heart than Europe and ought to remain so. Bancroft and a fellow American student at Göttingen celebrated the Fourth of July with the toast: "My countrymen, we are Americans. The arts and sciences of Europe cannot make us forget it. Thank God we are Americans." They all thought Goethe's private life a scandal; Ticknor was shocked by the French theatre; and Bancroft wrote that German literature would be much improved if grafted onto the American tree of "high moral feeling."

Nevertheless, in spite of his disapproval of European decadence, Bancroft exclaimed in a letter to his mentor at Harvard, Andrews Norton, that "I have come to the pure fountains of wisdom that I may drink of her unpolluted waters and be refreshed"—a sentiment that shocked the pious Norton whose worst fears for his student set loose amid the temptations of Europe were confirmed when Bancroft on his return home greeted his old teacher with a continental kiss on both cheeks, thus abruptly ending their friendship. Ticknor too, after three European trips totalling eight years abroad, seemed unsullied by his many associations with European scientists, poets, and even royalty. Even a private audience he and Cogswell had with the Pope in Rome did not cost them their American souls. And Ticknor, Cogswell, and Everett all sought to introduce into American academic life the results of their European learning.

Romantic writers such as Irving and Longfellow managed to bypass the dominant view of a decadent Europe hostile to American republican virtues by entertaining their large reading public with nostalgic views of "the shadowy grandeurs of the past," of an older Europe so distant in time that it was possible to view it as Longfellow did the famed castle of Alhambra in Spain—like "the memory of a gorgeous dream . . . a ruin wonderful in its fallen greatness." Dreams are no threat to American purity, nor are fallen ruins. By describing, too, the charms of the old English countryside amid scenery "associated in the mind with ideas of order, of

The Arch of Titus. *George P. A. Healy, Frederick Church, and Jervis McEntee were typical of American artists who studied in Europe.*

quiet, of sober well-established principles, of hoary usage, and revered custom," Irving and Longfellow gave American readers vicarious enjoyment of those very qualities of life absent in their own fast-moving, changing society. It would seem that the Americans were so committed to change, to the future, that the only past they could afford was a second-hand one, the past of Europe.

Most perceptive writers who travelled and lived in Europe, such as Cooper and Hawthorne, could not shake off the conviction that America was by nature of her republican institutions and democratic ideals superior to Europe. But their conviction was tempered by the realization that Europe had much of value. Cooper was disdainful of European aristocracy, writing in his journal that it took "a good deal of faith and more ignorance to entertain a very high respect for what is called an ancient family." Hawthorne was shaken at the sights and sounds of the debasement of English working-class life, and he was repelled by the Rome that was dominated by "a priesthood, pampered, sensual, with red and bloated cheeks, and carnal eyes," and corrupted by "an indolent nobility, with no high aims or opportunities but cultivating a vicious way of life as if it were an art." Yet the splendor of Rome and the social freedom enjoyed by writers and artists in Europe entranced him, and both he and Cooper felt that Europe had a "real reverence for letters, art, or indeed cultivation of any kind," which was absent in America.

Too intelligent and too sensitive to the values of Europe to accept the traditional view of it as all bad and America as all good, Hawthorne in The Marble Faun sounded the new transatlantic theme in American literature by suggesting that contact with evil, in the form of Europe, was a necessary experience if innocence were to be transformed into maturity.

Few Americans would have seriously considered abandoning the New World for the Old, and fewer still had any wish to see Europe's institutions transported to America. But the immense popularity among Americans of travel books and novels with European settings, the reception accorded distinguished European visitors to the United States, the Victorian fad which broke out in America when the Queen came to the British throne in 1837—all these attest to American fascination with a Europe that was in so many ways the opposite of their own society. The Americans may have preferred the prospects of their own future to the contemplation of the grandeur of Europe's past, but there is no doubt that the latter gave them some kind of satisfaction their own society could not provide. America may have been dynamic, challenging, exciting in many ways, but it also lacked glamor, color, and the reassuring signs of human permanence. There may have been a challenge, for example, in moving west, but on the passage there were no ancient ruins to give one a sense of humanity's past accomplishments. Moreover, America was too busy at the workaday task of satisfying material needs to provide much nourishment for the mind and the senses. For the more serious, Europe, for all its faults, was a treasurehouse of cultural riches for mind and sensitivity, and its very existence called attention to a cultural poverty in America that was to be deplored despite the virtues of republicanism and democracy.

Women and the Family

There were in the first decades of the republic isolated attempts to alter radically the traditional framework of the American family: the polygamy of the Mormons; the group marriage and eugenic approach of John Humphrey Noyes and his followers at Oneida, New York; an occasional celibate community automatically geared to self-destruct; a handful of so-called free-love experiments. Whether these had any merit, they had no effect on the family as the primary unit in American society. What did occur in the first half of the nineteenth century, under the impact of new social and economic forces, was the beginning of a shift in attitude toward the relationships among family members and the appearance of new views of their roles, responsibilities, and duties. Yet many Americans were largely untouched by these new currents until the end of the nineteenth century and the opening of the twentieth.

Marriage the Norm   The traditional marriage was still the norm. If failure to marry was not viewed with the same stern disapproval as in colonial times, yet those who stayed single were looked upon with the same pity as the physically handicapped and the mentally distressed. As with so many failures to comply with society's standards, men suffered less than women. Occasionally there were suggestions that bachelors should be specially taxed—particularly to make sure they helped pay for the education of the young—but by and large the assumption was that men who did not marry were simply indulging a personal preference. From the more serious-minded, this elicited more sympathy than pity. Those inclined to view such matters lightheartedly had tongue-in-cheek reactions of envy at the good fortune of such men. For women, however, the failure to marry, to center one's life in a home, somehow indicated failure. A handful of daring women rejected all this as so much nonsense. The writer Gail Hamilton even boasted of her unmarried state:

> I'm not married and I don't think I shall be. I can't afford the time, and besides, the men ought to be given to the women who can't get along without 'em. I can support myself, and so I think I'd better do it. Besides, I have a greater "run" among the men themselves than if I were married. Now I am independent and every man is my "humble servant." If I were married I would be dependent upon the caprices of one. An unmarried woman has an immense advantage over the married woman.

And married or unmarried, Margaret Fuller made such a strong case for the independent woman as to prompt the wry observation from Edgar Allan Poe that humanity was divided into men, women, and Margaret Fuller. She was the first woman editor of an important magazine, the *Dial.* She shot rapids in the West in an Indian canoe and lived to write about it. She broke the sex barrier at the Harvard College Library, wrote a column for the New York *Tribune,* was the first woman professional literary critic in the United States, the first woman foreign correspondent, took an Italian revolutionary nobleman as her lover though he was ten years younger than she, and in 1845 wrote the best book on women's rights published in America, *Women in the Nineteenth Century.* She wrote: "We would have every path laid open to Woman as freely as to Man." She frightened practically everybody.

Attitude Toward Divorce   The attitude toward divorce also suggested the serious-minded view of marriage as the destined common estate of men and women alike. By the eve of the Civil War, divorce no longer required a special act of the legislature, and general divorce laws came into being which

Margaret Fuller. One of her first accomplishments was a course she offered to women in Boston which she called "conversations," turning her skill as a speaker into an occupation and providing "a point of union to well-educated and thinking women . . . ." These proved immensely successful and became the foundation for her book as well as established her reputation among the intellectuals of the time.

recognized such grounds as bigamy, desertion, impotence, adultery, and extreme cruelty. Enough divorces were granted under such laws so that by 1850 one observer commented that "dissolving the marriage tie had got to be a sort of fashionable mania." But divorces were few and most were among the wealthy and the socially emancipated classes. Unhappy marriages generally had to be endured, though some people ran away from them. The records show a number of attempts to find disappearing husbands in order to gain support for wives and children left behind, and an occasional advertisement showed that some women had taken this escape route themselves: "Whereas, Nancy, my wife, has left my bed and board without provocation, this is to forbid all persons from harbouring or trusting her on my account from this date for I shall pay no more debts of her contracting."

Conventional Views of Women   Marriage, therefore, remained the desired goal and the common condition. For the average woman—as opposed to the man, who presumably had more serious matters requiring his attention and energy—marriage was the supreme experience of life. Her upbringing at home, her education, her reading, her religious experience, all proclaimed that marriage and motherhood were the main roads to the fullest expression of her being and the only channels through which she could influence society as a whole. Under such circumstances, it is not surprising that young girls were practically drowned in advice on how to get a husband and what kind of a choice to make.

Although some argued that a girl in her teens was too young and inexperienced for the "responsibilities and cares" of marriage and children, the more romantic and popular view was that sixteen was the ideal age: physical maturity combined with youthful innocence, both sure to fade with age. These attractions, noted one observer, are a girl's "stock in trade, which she must invest while the market is brisk"—an interesting and revealing analogy. Young girls were steeped in the sentimental notion that "first love is the only passion which lingers in the heart," and at the same time they were exhorted to search carefully for young men who did not swear, gamble or drink, who helped little old ladies and children across the street, and who were devoted to God. Love would follow. Both forms of advice seem equally unrealistic.

Once married, wives were no more immune from advice than before. The literature of the time made clear their duties toward their husbands. The family remained, as it had always been, patriarchical, the Almighty having implanted "the instinct of protection in man and the instinct of dependence in woman." But it was also assumed that somehow women were more spiritual and pure than men—a curious contradiction of the old Biblical assertion that woman was the source of original sin—and that marriage would improve the character of men. To the surprise of numerous wives, this frequently did not turn out to be the case.

The assumption of the spiritual superiority of women applied also to the raising of children, whose character was the responsibility of the mother. Fathers were supposed to be the supreme arbiters, but their preoccupation with the responsibilities of earning a living meant that, especially for small children, the mother was "the center and lawgiver in the home of the New World," as the Swedish novelist and visitor Fredrika Bremer observed.

Child-Rearing The goal in rearing children was still the same: obedience. Obedience to parents, to the laws of society, to the laws of God. But new and more liberal ideas about how to achieve these goals did make their appearance. With the disappearance of the older Calvinist belief in the natural depravity of children, responsibility for success in raising children now rested more with parents than with the will of God, and the pressure upon parents increased. Under such circumstances, advice flowed fully, much of it sensible, much of it nonsense. Concern for the child's health was the center of much advice, and given the high infant death rate, it was long overdue. While the axiom that a sound body possesses a sound mind and a sound morality may not have much validity—as the presence of many able-bodied thugs attests—yet sensible suggestions for improved diet for children and recognition of the value of exuberant play were an advance over earlier ideas. The belief that loving and affectionate parents were the best means to developing an obedient child was also an advance over the older technique of physical punishment by a vengeful father. Enough of these ideas took hold so that visitors to the United States frequently remarked how "spoiled" American children were, and one in 1856 deplored "the reign of children." Many of these new ideas, to say nothing of their implementation, reached only the urban middle and upper classes who had access to the books and magazines in which these new ideas were expounded.

Attitude Toward Sex   In the matter of sexual relations, moralists took the view that the main purpose of marriage was the production of children. Holding to such an ideal under the circumstances in which most married couples found themselves—cold room, double bed, unrestrictive nightgown and nightshirt—must have been difficult. Complicating the matter was the belief that women, at least good women, did not possess sexual passion, although men did. The nature of the relationship then, was "the unreasoning and inordinate indulgence of animal passion on the part of the man, and the affectionate submission on the part of the woman." Knowing what we now know about the human animal, such views must have prompted secret and terrified searches into the heart of many a woman as to just what kind of creature she really was. The acknowledged presence in American society of illegitimacy, abortion, a variety of sexual abnormalities, and prostitution clearly indicate that many Americans did not live according to the advice of the moralists. A handful of advanced thinkers suggested that sex was healthy and normal, and a handful of books, ignored by the press, discussed birth control and contraception. But many of these ideas originated in Europe, especially in France, and everyone knew how immoral the French were. For most Americans, the only method of limiting birth was abstention. The net result was successive pregnancies for most wives, summed up in John Pendleton Kennedy's observation of one that "She is a fruitful vessel, and seldom fails in her annual tribute to the honours of the family." If private letters and diaries are any indication, however, many women resented this annual call to duty.

The bearing of numerous children was not easy, and the death rate for both mothers and children was high. Delivery was almost always at home and done with the aid of a midwife rather than a doctor, which was perhaps all to the good since most medical men were badly misinformed about such matters. Indeed, doctors examined women only if it was absolutely necessary and then often in a darkened room with a minimum of exposure by the patient.

Women and Work   A prevailing belief in the first half of the nineteenth century was that women should not work. Since maintaining a house was often a sentence to hard labor, what was actually meant by this was that women should not work outside the home. Yet the census of 1860 showed some 271,000 women employed in manufacturing alone. The census-takers also found women working as clerks, stenographers, florists, farmers, telegraphers, wigmakers, barbers, postmistresses, postal clerks, mint employees, steamboat clerks, and canal boat operators. But few married women were gainfully employed: the female work force was made up of farm girls acquiring a dowry before marriage, unmarried immigrant and black women,

Portrait of an American woman who posed with the implements of her work.

and single girls from the lower-class poor. The married woman who worked did so, as one observer noted, because she preferred working to starvation—widows, women whose husbands had deserted them, or whose husbands had become crippled and handicapped.

Although women were as a whole excluded from the professions, there were two major exceptions: teaching and writing, acceptable because association with adult males was not a hazard of either job and both were regarded as expressive of female instincts—the care of children and moral elevation. By the time of the Civil War, women dominated in elementary teaching, although there were a few in secondary or higher education. Their presence in the world of authorship was remarkable. By 1820, it has been estimated, a third of all novels published in America were written by women, and observers noted in the 1850s an "alarming avalanche of female authors." Since the principal readers of novels were also women, it is not surprising that the sentimental story of domestic bliss or tribulation which bore little resemblance to reality, had become standard fare by mid-century. Women also wrote for magazines and newspapers, and became editors, especially for fashion magazines and gift publications.

But for the majority of American women it was the home, not the office or the factory or the writer's desk, which formed the center of their lives. Here they did indeed work, and work hard. The *North American Review* in 1860 observed that "Women are naturally more industrious than men, and work more diligently. To them, steady, useful employment is the great necessity of life. There is and can be no assurance of happiness without it." If this be so, there must have been a lot of happy women.

The Farm Family Since so much of America was still rural it was the farm that shaped the life of the typical family. Hard though life may have been in the pioneer years, it was not greatly eased even after the stage of survival had passed, and the efforts of all members of the family were drawn into the tasks at hand. So demanding was labor on the farm that young farm girls going to work in Lowell, Massachusetts, enjoyed the mills because the work was less arduous. The man not only worked his fields from planting through harvest time—hard work even with machinery—he frequently built his own home and later added to or improved it, and helped his neighbors do the same. He often made the tables, chairs, stools, benches, beds, and cupboards that were his furniture. Fences had to be built and repaired, and in the early years hunting and fishing were not for sport but for survival. In timber country, cutting trees to clear fields, or splitting wood for fuel and rails, was backbreaking labor. Outbuildings had to be constructed: hay barns, corn-cribs, smoke and spring houses. Farmers made much of their own equipment and tools: gates, carts, barrows, ox yokes, shovels, hay forks, tool handles, barrels, wagons, and many others. Livestock had to be cared for, often by wives and children when they weren't helping the husband in his other tasks.

Farm families often raised their own wool and flax, and wives and daughters labored over the looms and spinning wheels and produced much of the family's clothing. Looking back years later, one woman recalled her mother's incredible labors at these tasks alone:

> In the early years of married life, my mother not only helped in the farm work, but took in spinning on shares, and in this way her family were supplied with all the necessary woolen garments for winter wear, from the woolen socks and stockings to the dresses, coats and pants, besides the all wool home-made blankets and sheets for the beds. In 1842 her brother-in-law, being a carpenter, made her a loom, and with this for more than twenty years she provided many comforts for her family of four daughters and a son; besides, in this way laid up money to help build a new house, never from the beginning falling short of weaving upwards of 1,000 yards, and going as high as 1,800 or 2,000 yards in some years. . . .

Wives and children had other tasks as well. Butchering was a major event in farm life. They helped in the hog killing, cleaning the "innards," cutting, cleaning, and preserving the meat. They did the milking, made the butter and cheese, and raised the beans, pumpkins, potatoes, cabbages, cucumbers, rhubarb, radishes, lettuce, tomatoes, peas, turnips, and other garden crops. They planted and took care of the herb garden, and preserved fruits and

*Barn raising on the farm of Jacob Roher in Massillon, Ohio—work is over
and the celebration is about to begin. There were few how-to-do-it books for
building barns, and neighbors generally pooled their talents and their tools
to produce a structure of simplicity and soundness and an occasion for
socializing and relieving the loneliness of survival on the frontier.*

vegetables for winter use. They made the candles and the soap, a long-drawn-out process. The wife and mother was also the guardian of medicine and the dispenser of treatment. In the rural West doctors were rarely consulted except for the most serious cases.

Most American families were close-knit, bound together in the task of conquering the land, a task that left little time for brooding about the wishes of any individual member or the rights of one as opposed to another. The welfare of all depended on the labor of each. Dissatisfactions there were, many perhaps simply out of the weariness of it all, but these often disappeared with time. Indeed, one of the most striking facts in the reminiscences of those who grew up in these years is the idealization of family life. The primitiveness, the crudeness, the pain of work, the discomforts—all were put into the background.

> I recall my pioneer days as the happiest of my life. Coarse food and rough diet were the regimen of those days, but every cabin was a tent of refuge and relief from want. . . . There existed social reciprocity, a general spirit of charity and free giving. . . . It appears to me that the people lived happier and had more real enjoyment then, than they do at present. . . .

The American family in general seemed to foreign visitors to be satisfied, indeed happy, perhaps partly due to the more easy-going and open relationships. Lines were not rigidly drawn between family members as in Europe, and husbands were observed, as one visitor noted, to do "a considerable part of the slip-slop work:" making the fire in the morning, emptying the slops, getting breakfast. "Even among the trading classes who have private dwellings, it is quite common to see the men bringing parcels from the market, the grocer's, fishmonger's, or butcher's, for the morning meal." De Tocqueville remarked on the respect accorded women despite the fact that they were so "confined within the narrow circle of domestic life:"

> If they hold that man and his partner ought not always to exercise their intellect and understanding in the same manner, they at least believe the understanding of the one to be as sound as that of the other, and her intellect to be as clear. Thus, then, whilst they have allowed the social inferiority of women to subsist, they have done all they could to raise her morally and intellectually to the level of man; and in this respect they appear to me to have excellently understood the true principle of democratic improvement.

The Slave Family   The slave family occupied a position apart from normal family life in America, circumscribed as it was by the conditions imposed by slavery. There was no legal recognition of slave marriages. "The relation between slaves is essentially different from that of man and woman joined in lawful wedlock," said the North Carolina Supreme Court, since "with slaves it may be dissolved at the pleasure of either party, or by the sale of one or both, depending upon the caprice or necessity of the owners."

Slaves were usually permitted to choose their mates within guidelines laid down by their masters, and ceremonies sanctioning the event were almost always performed. Masters imposed rules and regulations on family behavior and heard disputes between husbands and wives in the manner of a domestic relations court. Divorce was at the discretion of the master who might be lenient or rigid.

Within this framework the slave family developed, by and large, as a stable and strong institution. Planters had no motive to do anything but encourage this, since it not only paid off economically but provided a compensatory factor of satisfaction for the condition of slavery. Life for the slave thus centered as much on the family as it did for most Americans. It formed the basic housing unit, the administrative unit, the disciplinary unit, and was the main instrument for procreation and child-rearing.

Not surprisingly, deep "faithfulness, fidelity, and affection" marked the relation between slave couples, as one Georgia master noted, and the open agony at separation by sale "must be seen and felt to be understood," one ex-slave remarked. The bond of affection, too, between mother and children was as deep as that between any other mother and child. Ex-slave Fredrick Douglass recounted the story of the overseer who was stoned by the children of one slave mother as he tied and whipped her while the children screamed "Let my mammy go!"

The slave family faced circumstances clearly not encountered by white families, and it was a tribute to its members that it did not disintegrate but became the principal reservoir of black culture and strength.

Religion and the Church

During the first seventy-five years of the republic, religion remained a vital force in the lives of most Americans and the church remained a major institution. Despite the reports of some foreign visitors that the Americans were so materialistic as to have no interest in spiritual affairs, Americans were essentially a religious people. De Tocqueville wrote that "There is no country in the world in which the Christian religion retained a greater hold over the souls of men than in America. . . . Religion is the foremost of the institutions of the country."

Religion in the Home   Family routine commonly included morning and evening prayers. Grace was said at mealtimes. The schools, despite the banishment of sectarian doctrine from the public classroom, gave general religious instruction. Religious value entered into all kinds of social considerations, including courtship. One young girl, writing about her beloved, remarked: "I found on analyzing my regard for him that I loved him. . . . He has made an exposition of his character to me. So simple. So pure. So just what Jesus loved." Religious sentiments and gestures dotted letters, speeches, novels, poetry, editorials, conversation. One skeptical English visitor with a touch of sarcasm commented that "Grog parties commence with prayer and terminate with benediction. Devout smokers say grace over a cigar, and chewers of the Nicotean weed insert a fresh quid with an expression of pious gratitude."

Mothers prayed over and with their children. Bible reading was often the first and sometimes the only contact the young had with the printed word. Sunday was set aside for special celebration. Everyone was expected to go to church, though ministers complained as often about attendance as farmers did about the weather. No one was supposed to work on Sunday, except for absolute essentials such as milking the cows. Food should be prepared the day before. There was to be no reading, no writing, no social activities. The day should be spent in meditation and prayer. With all these restrictions it is little wonder that one small boy, when told by his pious mother that Heaven was like an eternal Sunday, was not at all reassured: "Oh dear, what have I done that I should go where there is an eternal Sabbath!" Often these requirements laid down by the godly were more honored in the breach than the observance. In the West, especially, one could always find saloons and stores open, even theaters and dance halls. Everywhere trains ran on Sunday, the mail went through, factories and mills repaired machinery, parties were held, odd jobs were done about the house and barn. Even for those who complied with the demand for Sunday inactivity, it may be that after working six days a week from dawn to dusk the simple joy of sitting and doing nothing had a satisfaction quite apart from any religious benefits to be gained from it.

But this is not to say that religion was not a significant part of American life, that the church was outside the main currents of American society. Quite the contrary. De Tocqueville was right: religion was intricately interwoven into almost every major aspect of American development. It became identified, through Protestantism, with American nationalism. It provided divine sanction for the work ethic. The power of the Christian ethic helped to stimulate reform. Churches played a vital role in taming the West and serving as instruments of social control everywhere. Dominations were influenced by the tides of immigration. Crucial social issues affected church organization and relationships. And views toward foreign states and peoples, especially Catholic, were affected by religious beliefs.

Diversity of Sects and Denominations   The diversity that characterized the religious scene by the end of the colonial period increased in the first half of the nineteenth century. New sects came into being, small ones grew, and the long-established churches grew and even divided over doctrinal disputes.

Among the younger denominations, the Methodists attained the greatest growth. Only some fifteen thousand strong in 1785, by 1844 they were the largest Protestant denomination in America, claiming over a million members. The Baptists, also few in number at the end of the colonial period, became second only to the Methodists. Of major importance, because it began the process of alteration in the American religious makeup, was the rise of Catholicism in what was essentially a Protestant nation. Roman Catholics numbered only about twenty-five thousand when the republic was founded. By the time of the Civil War, fed by the heavy Irish and German immigration, and particularly the former, the Catholic Church with three million members was the largest in the country. The older established churches—Congregational, Presbyterian, Anglican (now Protestant Episcopal)—grew, but in no such dramatic fashion as the once-ignored Methodists, Baptists, and Catholics. And the existing Protestant churches suffered splits and divisions, often over doctrinal matters, with new congregations cropping up everywhere. Presbyterians split between the Old School and New School, largely conservative and liberal respectively. The Baptists divided into the Regulars, the Separates, the Two-Seed-in-Spirit Predestinarians, and the Anti-Missions. The Methodists divided into the Republican Methodists, the Methodist Protestants, and the Free Methodists. Episcopalians split between high- and low-church. Even the gentle Quakers, whose influence was far

A Mormon family in front of their Echo City home. The Mormons were a close-knit community who put the interests of the group ahead of individual concerns. It was this cohesion that helped them to face the persecution of those who could not understand households like this one, with its five wives.

greater than their numbers, engaged in dissension when Elias Hicks divided the Society of Friends ideologically with his proposition that Christ was human and not a divine part of the Trinity.

There were many new small sects, some with only a handful of followers and a leader with eccentric views. Some were communally organized, some tied to a single religious view clear only to its believers. Among them were the Shakers with their celibate communities, John Humphrey Noyes and his religion of Perfectionism, William Miller who preached that the end of the world and the day of judgment would arrive on March 21, 1843, and had people on the rooftops waiting the great event.

Dissatisfaction with Presbyterianism by Thomas Campbell and his son, Alexander, led ultimately to the Disciples of Christ, a powerful denomination centered in the Midwest with some 500,000 members by 1865. Campbell, guided by the simple principle, "Where the Scriptures speak, we speak; where they are silent, we are silent," originally hoped to unite all Christians.

The Mormons The Mormons, or Church of Jesus Christ of Latter-day Saints, unlike the followers of Thomas Campbell, saw themselves as having created a new religion under instructions from God. Informed by a messenger from God of a mysterious book written in a strange language on golden plates, Joseph Smith with the aid of special mystic stones or glasses translated the Book of Mormon. Converts flocked to the cause, many impressed by the assertion that Smith was in direct communication with the Almighty. The Mormon church, which was tightly organized economically and politically, was first established in Palmyra, New York, and later moved to Ohio, Missouri, and Illinois. Its economic success plus rumors of polygamy aroused public feeling against its members and resulted in Smith's murder and the removal of the Mormons to Utah. Under the leadership of Brigham Young, and nourished by converts, many of whom came from abroad, the Mormon community flourished. The practice of polygamy, however, shocked the rest of the country, and it was not until it was renounced in 1890 that Mormonism became acceptable and respectable.

The Unitarians   Another new denomination was Unitarianism, which came formally into being in 1825, although the Unitarian philosophy had long been present in New England Congregationalism. Its major spokesman was William Ellery Channing, who rejected the Calvinist doctrine of man's natural depravity, and emphasized the goodness and rationality of God and the belief that individuals through their own minds can understand God. Because the Unitarians preached that individual regeneration was impossible without a larger social regeneration, they assumed that Christians were responsible for reforming society, and the Unitarian influence in the reform movements of the day was considerable. But the Unitarians could not escape dissension any more than other groups. Emerson, Theodore Parker, and others rejected Channing's reliance upon Scripture and ended by challenging the divinity of Christ, their views composing what became known as the transcendental approach: the concept that God, nature, and humanity are all part of the same order, and that the "divine spark" dwells in every person. Though its numbers were small, the Unitarian church was highly influential, exercising a liberalizing effect and softening the strict discipline of American Protestantism. Little appreciated by steely-eyed moralists, Unitarians were brushed aside with this condemnation: "With music and feasting and dancing they drive all religion away during the week, and then they go to meeting to thank God that they are not bigoted, superstitious fanatics."

Revivalism   The growth of old and new sects and denominations was based upon the great religious revivals that washed over the country during these years, beginning after the opening of the nineteenth century with the Second Great Awakening and followed by periodic renewals of faith in succeeding decades. The evangelical movement was particularly active in the West, and denominations able to respond to Western conditions and needs were guaranteed success. Most Westerners had no taste for formal religion and ceremony, little interest in complex doctrine. They wanted preachers who were people like themselves, who spoke their language, lived their lives. They wanted salvation if they repented, and this is what the Methodists, the Baptists, and the Disciples provided. Their ministers lacked formal education and training, but they could paint in the language of the common man

Religious Camp Meeting *by J. M. Burbank. Frontier religion provided*
an acceptable emotional release, as people reacted in frenzy to the vivid
exhortations of the preacher.

the tortures awaiting them in hell. The circuit riders of the Methodist ministry had no formal church, but rode throughout the countryside for
hundreds of miles, staying with their parishioners, eating their food, sleeping
in the loft or in the barn, and helping to promote the establishment of
churches.

Part of the drama of religious growth in the West lay in the famous camp
meetings, drawing hundreds and sometimes thousands from miles around
for several days of preaching, repentance, and conversion. Drawing heavily
upon the emotions, camp revivals were as much noted for the physical signs
of response as for spiritual ones: people jerked, barked, rolled on the ground,
danced, yelled, wept, screamed, foamed at the mouth, and collapsed unconscious to the ground. At night with the scene lit by pine torches, even casual
observers sometimes got swept up by the mass emotion evoked in the

audience. A participant in one early meeting described the experience in the following way:

> We arrived upon the ground and here a scene presented itself to my mind not only novel and unaccountable but awful beyond description. A vast crowd . . . was collected together. The noise was like the roar of Niagara. The vast sea of human beings seemed to be agitated as if by a storm. I counted seven ministers, all preaching at one time, some on stumps, others in wagons. . . . Some of the people were singing, others praying, some crying for mercy in the most piteous accents, while others were shouting most vociferously. While witnessing these scenes, a peculiarly strange sensation . . . came over me. My heart beat tumultuously, my knees trembled, my lip quivered, and I felt as if I must fall to the ground. A strange supernatural power seemed to pervade the entire mass of mind there collected. I became so weak and powerless that I found it necessary to sit down.

Rowdy elements were frequently attracted to such gatherings, and it proved difficult to keep liquor out of camp meetings, even for the Methodists who held the most meetings and had them tightly organized and controlled. Other activities went on as well, prompting the observation that as many souls were begot at camp meetings as were saved there: "When the mind becomes bewildered and confused, the moral restraints give way, and the passions are quickened and less controllable. For a mile or more around a camp-meeting, the woods seem alive with people; every tree or bush has its group or couple, while hundreds of others in pairs are seen prowling around in search of some cosy spot."

The more conservative churches may have been horrified at such goings-on, but camp meetings and circuit preachers assured many frontier souls that in the isolation of the wilderness God had not forgotten them. The denominations that successfully moved into the West and settled there played a major role in civilizing frontier life, setting at least minimum standards of conduct. They laid down strict rules of behavior, and the church records are filled with the punishments imposed on the drunk and disorderly, gossips and slanderers, the quarrelsome and those who gambled, fought, or fornicated.

National Religious Movements   But it was not just personal conduct that more conservative people were worried about. America in the first half of the nineteenth century was marked by rapid change. The democratic atmosphere created a kind of free-wheeling, wide-open environment, within which new forces and experiences swirled and twisted like tornadoes—the upheaval of westward migration; the flood of immigrants from abroad all of whom were scrambling to find a place for themselves; older cities expanding and new ones on the rise with all their attendant problems; factories appearing, calling into being a new kind of labor force. All these things made not just for change, but disruptive change; and brought not only benefits but problems as well. Many staid conservatives in the long-settled East recoiled in alarm, and wondered what kind of hell the country was headed for. They were shocked by the rising power of the West, as seen in the election of Andrew Jackson, and horrified by what would happen when the nation was turned over to the control of uncouth ruffians from the frontier. They were upset that ignorant immigrants were exploited by unscrupulous city politicians. They were disturbed at crime and vice, mobs and riots, which seemed to characterize the expanding cities into which crammed thousands of workers and the poor. Something had to be done to bring peace and tranquility or the republic was doomed to rack and ruin.

The general belief in the steadying effects of religion gave rise to a national movement for the promotion of Christian thought and influence. Between 1816 and 1826, many Presbyterians and Congregationalists, joined by smaller numbers of Methodists, Baptists, and Episcopalians, founded five major interdenominational societies for this purpose: the American Educational Society, which provided financial aid to future ministers attending colleges and seminaries; the American Home Missionary Society, which helped pay the salaries of pastors of poor congregations and also supported ministers sent out to new settlements; the American Bible Society, which distributed millions of copies of the Bible, its goal being one in every home and public place; the American Tract Society, which by 1861 had distributed almost 200 million pieces of religious literature; and the American Sunday School Union, which sent out missionaries to establish Sunday schools and provide students with lessons and books on religious and moral matters.

Although ministers appropriately served on the boards of all these organizations and were deeply involved in much of their work, most of the five hundred officers who served in the organizations from their founding to 1861 were lay people of economic and social status: industrialists, merchants, bankers, lawyers, financiers, men who naturally saw in the disruption and tumult of the time a potential threat to their own interests.

In their view political democracy would work and social order prevail only under the steadying influence of religion. Christianity, declared the Reverend Franklin Vail of the Tract Society, would help to bridge "the dangerous chasm between rich and poor; so that instead of . . . mobs and outbreaks destroying . . . life and property, there will be between these two great classes a reciprocation of confidence and good feeling." And in 1847, Emory Washburn, lawyer and later governor of Massachusetts, supported the work of the Bible Society with the declaration that a Bible in every home and school would cure all of America's social ills. These efforts were to have more influence in introducing a moral tone into American political rhetoric than in affecting the kind of social stability their sponsors desired.

The Class Structure

Given the fact that in colonial America there was an astonishing equality of opportunity as well as flexibility in social status, it is natural to assume that when the new republic embarked upon its democratic career the social structure would become even more equal, open, and flexible.

The Wealthy   De Tocqueville in the 1830s wrote that "In a democratic society like that of the United States, fortunes are scanty" since "the equality of conditions that gives some resources to all the members of the community . . . also prevents any of them from having resources of great extent." As in colonial days, few were poor, few rich, many were adequately provided for, and the opportunities to rise were wide open to all. Or so he assumed.

The contrast to Europe was great, in the sense of a more open society, greater economic opportunity, and a more general sense of equality. Whether this meant that America was a society in which there were few rich, for example, and they possessing wealth of small amount compared to Europe, is another matter. Logic alone suggests that in a rapidly expanding economy of immense resources and few restrictions, some people are going to make a killing—a point de Tocqueville failed to grasp.

Indeed, by the time the new nation was only a half-century old, in the expanding cities there were hundreds of families who had acquired vast fortunes based upon commerce, manufacturing, insurance, finance, shipbuilding, landholding, speculation, and the professions. Mainly centered in the cities of the Northeast, the great fortunes of the Astors, the Binghams, the Masons, the Whartons, and many others were truly impressive, and far from being paltry by European standards, were equal to or greater than the long-established fortunes of European aristocrats. John Jacob Astor's wealth was close to that of Nathan Mayer Rothschild, generally regarded as the richest man in Europe, and dozens of American families had fortunes equal to those of the Duke of Bedford and Sir Francis Baring in England. Herman Thorn, a wealthy New Yorker who lived in Paris in the 1830s, dumbfounded French society with his "princely splendor," yet there were almost a hundred families in New York alone whose wealth surpassed Thorn's. At a time when one could live lavishly on $10,000 a year, John Jacob Astor was probably worth fifteen million dollars or more. And there was no income tax.

In city after city, the one percent at the top of the economic heap possessed somewhere between forty and fifty percent of the wealth. And the top ten percent owned from eighty to ninety percent. This wealth was largely not the creation of those who had been poor, but of those whose families already had considerable resources. There were, of course, self-made men of humble origins, but in an expanding economy those who had money made money. And once they had it they rarely lost it.

Thus there arose in America a wealthy urban upper class which could live not just well but extremely well. Their great houses were run by small armies of servants, were filled with elaborate furnishings and works of art, and had extensive wine cellars and fine libraries. The wealthy enjoyed their summer homes, yachts, parties, balls, and trips to Europe—luxuries beyond the reach of most Americans.

When the New York speculator, Leonard Jerome (who was to become the American grandfather of Winston Churchill), built a new home for his wife, it was a six-story red brick mansion trimmed with marble, with a white and gold ballroom accommodating three hundred people, a private theater seating six hundred, and an elaborate stable for his horses which was three

The Tea Party *by Henry Sargent. The controlled ambiance of social gatherings among the well-to-do was a distant world from the exuberance of the frontier revival.*

stories high, thickly carpeted, and paneled with black walnut. Men such as Jerome and the great banker, August Belmont, had, to the distress of their families, a fine eye for the ladies—a prerogative of the rich which also had its pitfalls. Jerome and Belmont once found themselves competing for the favors of Mrs. Fanny Ronalds, a celebrated beauty and a divorcee. Years after a famous ball given by Mrs. Ronalds, Jerome asked Belmont if he recalled the event. Belmont noted that he could hardly forget it since he had paid for it. "Why, how very strange," replied Jerome, "so did I."

If such families dominated the urban Northeast by 1860, a parallel situation existed in the South. There the great planters, who owned the majority of the slaves and the best lands and some of whom were involved in commercial and financial enterprises, formed the other major element in upper-class America. A planter of consequence owned fifty or more slaves, and such men constituted less than three-fourths of one percent of the free population of the South. They also received the major share of the income. The annual income of the top 1,000 families in the South has been estimated at approximately $50 million, while the other 666,000 families divided the remaining $66 million. The investment of the wealthy in land, slaves, and property often ran into hundreds of thousands of dollars. Bad times sometimes meant losses and debts, but the plantation economy was basically profitable.

The great planter lived extremely well, although neither his income nor his splendor matched that of his Northern counterpart at the top of the economic heap. The plantation mansion itself usually contained about fifteen rooms set off by a row of white columns and surrounded by gardens of trees, shrubs, and flowers. Few equalled John Hampden Randolph's "Nottaway," his plantation home on the Mississippi, with its fifty rooms and great ballroom, decorated with plaster mouldings, marble mantels, and bronze and crystal chandeliers. Some plantation homes were plain, bare, and even shabby, if visitors' accounts were accurate. Nevertheless, all had their house slaves who served the needs of the master and his family. The tradition of hospitality prevailed as of old, sometimes at a high cost. Edmund Ruffin complained that the economic difficulties of the lowlands of Virginia sprang from the extensive generosity of the hosts of the region:

> Such effects are certainly not produced merely by the meat and liquor consumed by friends and visitors; but it is our custom to give up to all our visitors not only the best entertainment but also the time, the employments and the habits of the host—and this not only to friends and visitors . . . but for every individual of the despicable race of loungers and spongers which our custom of universal hospitality has created.

The great planters hunted and rode, and when bored visited the cities and resorts of the region, frequently taking their families on a tour of the spas to avoid the heat of the summer and to enjoy a more extended social life than was possible on an isolated plantation. Sometimes, as did James H. Hammond of South Carolina, they travelled to Europe, developed fine libraries whose books they read, and purchased European sculpture and paintings. By the mid-nineteenth century, however, the planter class as a whole no longer reflected the cultivated and learned atmosphere associated with the planter class of the colonial period. Their interests had become increasingly provincial and self-centered.

Recognizing the value of protecting their interests, the upper class, both urban North and rural South, sought representation in the seats of power. The Northern elite did not always seek major offices themselves, but relied upon others to represent them, including lawyers such as Daniel Webster. But a surprising number appeared on city councils, presumably to protect their property interests from undue taxation and other interferences. The great planters preferred the more direct route and were frequently in their state legislatures and the national Congress, the argument being that their presence would be more directly felt. And it was—sometimes a little too bluntly, as when Congressman Preston S. Brooks of South Carolina entered the Senate chamber one day in 1856 and beat Massachusetts Senator Charles Sumner into insensibility because he had spoken intemperately against Brooks's uncle, Senator Andrew Butler. "Toward the last," boasted Brooks, "he bellowed like a calf. I wore my cane out completely but saved the head which is gold."

The Middle Class Neither factory nor commercial house, neither bank nor plantation, represented in the first decades of the republic the dominant life of America. In 1860 only one-sixth of American society was urban. Most Americans lived on small farms and in small towns and villages. Although the city contained significant numbers of those who worked in banks, offices, and stores, in the professions, and in skilled labor—people whose incomes generally enabled them to get by satisfactorily without deprivation and often with many amenities—the great middle section of American society was found in the countryside.

The farmers of the South, including those who owned ten or fewer slaves, were the most numerous class of that region. These were the people who by and large owned their own land and worked it themselves, their holdings generally below one or two hundred acres. Most of them engaged essentially in subsistence farming, raising their own food, providing for their own needs, and perhaps producing a small staple crop for cash sale. But the cash crops such as cotton, rice, tobacco, and sugar cane were mainly the produce of the plantations.

There was considerable variation in the lives of these Southern farmers. Some lived more ordered and prosperous lives than others, some used slave labor although the majority did not. Some had easier access to markets than others and hence greater economic opportunities. The main body of Southern farmers were an independent lot nevertheless, little interested in the conveniences and comforts that influenced their Northern counterparts, much influenced by their aristocratic plantation neighbors with whom they had an easy-going familiarity. The average farmer read little—indeed illiteracy among the white population in the South was over twenty percent and in some areas as high as thirty. His behavior was often marked by hard drinking, hard swearing, and violence. His social diversions tended to hunting, political rallies, camp meetings, and attending court when it was in session. His home was frequently a crude log cabin with barn, granary, and springhouse near by. The life may have been independent, but the standard of living was not high. By and large, the farmers of the South deferred to the planting aristocracy in political leadership, although far less in the states beyond the Appalachian barrier (except for Louisiana) than in the older states on the seaboard. They held, too, the same views toward slavery as did the planter class, operating on the assumption that they might well rise in the world and join the planters, as indeed some did.

Elsewhere, in the long-established regions of the New England and Middle Atlantic states, farmers remained a significant element in the population although their numbers decreased as the urban population increased and

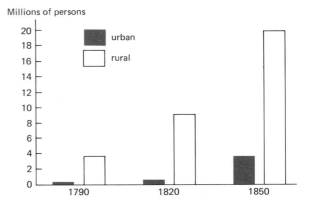

Millions of persons

URBAN/RURAL POPULATION

marginal farmers moved west. In these areas farm production switched to the cash crops of potatoes, dairy products, and fruit and vegetables for the rising urban markets.

But with the growth and expansion of the nation, the great body of farmers was ultimately to be found in the upper Mississippi valley, in the Old Northwest, raising the cash crops of corn, wheat, and pork on a typical 160 acre family farm. In the earlier years of pioneer settlement, farm families here raised their own food and lived off a land rich in wild game, fish, and fowl as well as a great variety of wild nuts and berries. Shelter was the crude lean-to or small cabin. But the desire for better things was strong, and improvements were quickly sought. So rapid was the growth of the West that a prosperous farmer with a brick house and outbuildings often had as neighbor a newcomer living in a cabin or lean-to. The rapid development of transportation facilities made possible the steady, prosperous growth of the farmers of the Old Northwest and in Illinois, Iowa, Wisconsin, and Missouri, which by 1860 dominated the nation's production of corn, wheat, and hogs. Although one could find in the West by 1860 the well-to-do farmer with numerous hired hands and perhaps a thousand acres, who lived in an elegant brick house with fine furnishings, such people did not constitute a special class to which others deferred. The farmer of the West tended to be independent-minded, out to improve himself, and politically active.

Rounding out the middle class were those merchants and tradesmen, lawyers and doctors, printers and teachers, land speculators and promoters who followed the farmer westward and put together the small towns and villages which sometimes grew into cities and which served as political, economic, and social centers for the farming community. If such towns did well, their business and professional people prospered and became members of a local aristocracy, living in the finer homes, setting social standards, controlling the local economy, often dominating politically, and supporting the promotion and development of education and the arts. Their wealth and power in no way matched that of the upper class in the great cities, although it might have been difficult to explain the difference to the communities that they dominated.

The Lower Classes   Low on the social ladder of American society were various categories of people. Here were the unskilled who labored in the factories, mills, and shops of the cities, who worked on the construction of roads, canals, and railroads, who toiled on the riverboats and on the ships at sea, who handled the cargoes at the dock, whose pay was meager, whose life was harsh and often short, who lacked status and often drifted from one place to another but always sideways, never up. Here were the poor whites of the South, poverty-stricken, living on poor soil, often squatters, though some owned their own land. These were mainly hunters and fishermen rather than farmers. Looked down upon even by slaves, they suffered from feelings of inferiority but had a pride that made them refuse to do menial labor. Suffering from poor health and illiteracy, the poor whites were ignored except at election time.

Black Americans   At the bottom of the pile in American society were the free blacks and the slaves, the latter constituting, as Lincoln was to note in the Second Inaugural, "a peculiar interest," an element of enormous influence in shaping the future of American society.

There was by 1860 a considerable body of free blacks in the country—some 250,000 in the South and almost as many elsewhere. North or South, free blacks suffered extensive economic, social, and political discrimination. A few became independent farmers and skilled artisans. Some of the more prosperous of these in the South even owned slaves themselves. But by far the vast majority were confined to the more menial and laborious tasks: serving as porters, messengers, shoeshine boys, domestic servants, and laborers on construction jobs. They were deeply resented even in northern and western cities, where they tended to be cut off from established community facilities if not completely segregated. In Cincinnati, for example, in the late 1820s, fear of the increase in the black population stirred up antiblack sentiment which resulted in a riot. Though the city's better citizens opposed the action, and even though officials and public spokesmen later condemned the incident, the damage was considerable. Hundreds of free blacks left the community, and the incident revealed how thin was the line between decency and intolerance in the attitude of the white community toward the blacks even in the free states.

But it was the slave, not the free black, who constituted "the peculiar interest" and whose condition defined the status of the great majority of blacks.

By 1860 there were some 3.5 million slaves in the southern states. Approximately half a million of these lived in cities and towns or were employed in nonagricultural work. Plantation owners often found it profitable to hire out slaves; some employers outside agriculture owned slaves and also hired free labor; and some hired out inherited slaves for whom they had no use themselves. Slaves, therefore, worked as woodcutters and lumberjacks; in sawmills, gristmills, quarries, and fisheries; they helped mine gold, coal, salt, iron, and lead; they were deckhands and firemen on riverboats; they

Black quarters at Drayton's House, Hilton Head, South Carolina.

helped to construct and maintain roads, bridges, canals, and railroads. In the cities and towns they served as domestic servants in homes and hotels; they were store clerks and dock laborers; the skilled among them were barbers, blacksmiths, cabinetmakers, and shoemakers; they labored in the small manufacturing enterprises of the South: in tobacco factories, iron mills, and textile factories. A number of slaves, almost all skilled artisans, acquired the privilege of "hiring their own time"—working on their own, paying their own living expenses, and turning over a set sum to their owners, keeping what was left for themselves.

But the bulk of slave labor was on the land, on the plantations and the small farms. On plantations slaves served in the house and often on skilled tasks, but most labored in the fields. The pace of work was slow and leisurely on a few plantations, just enough to give rise to the myth that life was a pleasant merry-go-round for slaves who chuckled and sang their way through the day while the scent of magnolia blossoms filled the air. But for the vast majority the pace was steady and long—from "day clean" to "first dark," dawn to dusk. And this was true on small farms as well as large plantations. One Arkansas master described the typical work day as follows:

> We get up before day every morning and eat breakfast before day and have everybody at work before day dawns. I am never caught in bed after day light nor is any body else on the place, and we continue in the cotton fields when we can have fair weather till it is so dark we cant see to work, and this history of one day is the history of every day.

On both moderate-sized (sixteen to fifty slaves) and large plantations (over fifty), which together held over half the slaves of the South, a great deal of the supervision and direction of production was actually in the hands of slaves. Five out of every six overseers on moderate-sized plantations and three out of four on large plantations were slaves, as were most drivers and gang foremen. Slave labor so directed seemed successful, in part because slaves apparently worked more efficiently under direct black supervision. But it also stemmed from the work incentives moderate and large plantations could afford: gifts of cash or goods, holidays, year-end bonuses, and the like.

Recent studies indicate that most slaves were not deprived of the basic necessities of food and shelter to the point where health was seriously affected. Life expectancy was four years shorter than that of white Americans, but on plantations the infant death rate was about the same as for Southern whites and the mortality rate in child-bearing somewhat less. Both food and shelter for plantation slaves were equal to or perhaps better than for northern industrial workers, although it is difficult to judge what this really means in terms of quality. Neither contemporary accounts nor logic suggest starvation levels for slaves whose work efficiency was a matter of concern to planters, but they don't imply living high off the hog either. A Louisiana physician claimed that on most plantations the diet of slaves was "mostly salt pork, corn bread, and molasses—rarely . . . fresh meat and vegetables." Yet it also seems clear that owners often supplied supplementary fruits and vegetables or allowed slaves to grow them.

As for shelter, contemporary accounts describe the cabins on some plantations as "neat and well-made externally as the cottages usually provided by large manufacturing companies in New England to be rented to their workmen," as one traveler in Louisiana reported. But an Alabama doctor recorded that "One of the most prolific sources of disease among negroes is the condition of their houses. . . . Small, low, tight and filthy; their houses can be but laboratories of disease."

Even if slaves lived well, the *condition* of slavery, the fact of human bondage, was a psychological, social, and physical deprivation of major proportions. Although the slave codes of the Southern states recognized the slave to be persons as well as a piece of property, recognition of their humanity was subordinate to their chattel status. The slave could be bought, sold, transported, forfeited for the debts of the master, wagered on the gaming table, mortgaged, inherited, auctioned, offered as a lottery prize. The law defined the slave's condition as one of "absolute obedience," and in every state laid restrictions upon slave movements and activities in order to attain that subordination necessary for absolute obedience. A slave needed a pass to be away from home; no more than five could assemble away from home for any purpose; no one could teach a slave to read or write or give a slave a book; slaves could not beat drums, blow horns, or possess firearms; they could not practice medicine, possess liquor, or own animals. In many localities, the law spelled out in minute and absurd detail what slaves could not do: in Charleston, for example, the law forbade a slave to walk with a cane.

Punishment for violation of any of these laws was usually by whipping. Penalties for slaves (and also free blacks) were far more severe than for whites committing the same offenses. Every Southern state also had patrols which could stop slaves, search quarters, and administer punishment.

All these laws governing the conduct and behavior of slaves were at one time or another ignored by masters who taught slaves to read and write, allowed them time to work on their own and earn money, deeded them property, overlooked such offenses as hunting with guns or gathering in assemblies. But such masters were few.

It is true that southern slave codes also sought to protect the slave as a human being. A number of state constitutions required their legislatures "to pass such laws as may be necessary to oblige the owners of slaves to treat them with humanity; to provide for them necessary clothing and provisions; to abstain from all injuries to them extending to life or limb." While some masters were called to account for violating these laws, there were few convictions, even in cases of murder.

Although the law proclaimed and southern opinion held that the black's natural state was slavery, it is clear from the presence of so much legislation defining the institution that it was far from natural. This could also be seen in the ways by which masters sought the state of absolute obedience that supposedly defined the ideal slave, none of which would have been necessary had slavery been a natural state. Masters thus sought continuously to implant in the minds of slaves the idea of their own inferiority, to heighten their sense of dependence, to instill fear in their hearts of the power of whites. Though there were masters who opposed the practice, many allowed conversion to Christianity in the belief it would help instill notions of obedience and passivity. Some even contended that "the surest and best method of managing negroes is to love them." One Georgia planter wrote that "We know . . . that if we love our horse, we will treat him well, and if this treatment has this effect upon all the animal creation . . . why will it not have the same effect upon slaves?" Some slave owners relied on rewards: gifts of money, a small plot of land, allowing slaves to sell the produce they raised themselves, gifts at Christmas time, payment for extra work done at night or on Sunday, passes to visit other plantations, entertainment and feasting on holidays. But when brotherly love and material rewards failed, the master fell back upon punishment, which could take many forms: the withdrawal of rewards, humiliation—as when one planter forced a slave to eat the worms he had failed to pick off a plant—time in the stocks, the wearing of chains and irons, and the use of the whip. Occasionally sadistic measures such as beatings, burnings, mutilations, and other brutalities were employed.

Nothing more fully indicated the unnaturalness of slavery than the slaves' response to it. On the surface, the common impression given was satisfaction with one's lot. But below the surface it was a different matter entirely, as almost all masters well knew. For in a thousand ways slaves continuously protested against their position. They never relented, never gave up, which is probably why one North Carolina planter wearily referred to slaves as "a troublesome property."

Some lucky ones were able to purchase their freedom, others were freed by their masters. But for most the only way of expressing the desire for a freedom beyond their reach was to be as "troublesome" as possible. And troublesome they were.

They repaid those masters who had stolen their freedom by stealing the master's property, anything they could get away with. Field hands stole and killed livestock; house hands took liquor, jewelry, trinkets. Some slaves systematically stole on a large scale, not just for personal consumption but for sale and exchange. Arson was a frequent form of revenge. A cotton-gin house was burned, a farm building set afire, even crops went up in flames. Slaves slowed the pace of work when away from the immediate eye of the overseer or master. They damaged plants, dropped and broke tools, pretended to be ill and developed ruses of all kinds to simulate sickness. The letters and journals of slave owners were filled with cries of frustration at the extent of slave resistance.

Some slaves resorted to self-mutilation and even to suicide as a last gesture of protest. Others struck not at themselves but at their masters, from insolent defiance to the extreme of attacking and even killing a master or overseer. Every year thousands ran away, although their chances of escape were slight. A few managed to get away and lived undetected in the South for years as free blacks. Others headed North, to Mexico, or to the Caribbean. In 1855 it was estimated that up to that date approximately sixty thousand escaped slaves had fled the South. Most runaways were quickly caught, but some tried again and again.

The ultimate resistance was the one Southerners feared most: revolt. There had been slave revolts since the beginning, and the first half of the nineteenth century was marked by enough attempts so that many Southerners constantly lived on the edge of fear. The most frightening revolt was the Nat Turner rebellion in Virginia, led by a slave whose treatment had apparently been good and whose manner had always been docile and obedient. Yet Turner apparently came to believe that he was destined to be the divine instrument of deliverance for his fellows. Persuading several others to join him, he began his crusade on August 22, 1831. Some sixty whites were killed, including the family to which Turner belonged. White reaction was swift and vicious. Within forty-eight hours the revolt had been crushed, and not only the rebels but scores of innocent slaves were killed. Others were brought to trial for supposedly aiding or sympathizing with the revolt, and several were executed. Turner himself was caught two months later, and was promptly tried and hanged. The rebellion produced panic in many parts of the South, resulting in the arrest and execution of many slaves. Fear of revolt was periodic thereafter.

The Social Structure   The social structure of American society in the years from the founding of the republic to the Civil War was in some ways similar to that which had developed in colonial times. But there had been changes. New and significant classes had appeared: an industrial elite and an

Nat Turner and His Confederates in Conference. *Turner used his influence as a lay preacher to organize a group of followers for his revolt.*

industrial working class. There were far greater gaps between wealth and poverty as a small but immensely rich upper class developed in the rising cities and a small but poverty-stricken urban lower class came into existence, each living lives beyond the comprehension of the other. There clearly seemed to be less flexibility and less mobility than in earlier days, particularly as the room at the top seemed open to only a few. Yet there remained remarkable opportunity for many. The question, perhaps, was not so much could everyone become a merchant prince or a captain of industry or a mighty planter, but rather did most people have an opportunity to get ahead, to do better than they had, to rise somewhat. For many Americans, native and immigrant alike, that was indeed true in those years. The one crucial exception was the slave population, deprived not only of freedom but of opportunity. The condition of the black in American society was to have profound effects.

Profile: LUCRETIA MOTT

Born 1793, died 1880. A long full life, that of a dutiful daughter, loyal wife, devoted mother, faithful servant of the Lord. She quickly learned a woman's lot: up early to help her mother, setting the table, bringing water from the neighborhood pump, washing dishes; helping tend the shop her mother ran while her father was away at sea; mending, darning, making over garments, candle-dipping; learning to cook—Indian pudding with milk and eggs, codfish, berry pudding, the "pig sauce" of Nantucket Island where she was born and spent her childhood; acquiring by hard work with broom, brush, and cloth a respect for "a clean hearth" and an ordered household; her education ending at seventeen; learning to read and write in one of the Dame or Cent Schools on the island where pupils paid for their instruction by leaving a penny on the teacher's desk, then a year in Boston public schools, and finally her formal learning completed at the Quaker Nine Partners School outside Poughkeepsie, New York.

Girls were taught the proper virtues of the home in those days, and their place therein, and these lessons followed her all her long life. Theodore Parker, as late as 1853, when Lucretia Mott was sixty, referred to her as a woman who "adorns her domestic calling as housekeeper, wife, and mother" with "womanly dignity and sweetness." In a letter she herself recorded a list of typical family duties:

> Gathered and shelled ½ bushel peas today and a peck yesterday—so many men consume so much, also cauliflowers, southern potatoes. . . . Large wash dried today—partly ironed—sorry for the soiled counterpane on guests' bed—all clean now—up early, move out parlor furniture, ready for the man to take away the carpets and shake . . .

And this at a time when she maintained a comfortable home and had help available. She was never idle at home and never wanted to be. A relative once told how Lucretia, while sitting with her close friend Mrs. McKim, saw a feather floating above her head: "Without a pause in her conversation . . . Lucretia captured the piece of down, took scissors, needle and thread from a reticule at her waist, unstitched a seam of the cushion on which she was seated, tucked in the feather and repaired it."

She knew, as did all nineteenth century women whether talented or not, the condescension of the male. Richard Webb said of her that "She is proof that it is possible for a woman to widen her sphere without deserting it, or neglecting the duties which appropriately devolve upon her at home." Or the remark made by Daniel Neall when he introduced Mrs. Mott to the singing Hutchinsons who used their talent to promote the antislavery movement: "This is Mrs. Lucretia Mott and her daughters. . . . I thought you should know one another. Mrs. Mott's a great abolitionist, but she's a fine cook too." Lucretia suggested that the young Hutchinsons should go to England. It is not known where she suggested Mr. Neall should go. She endured also the commonly held view of the time that it was dangerous for women to engage in the same intellectual activity as men. Her own sister, on the occasion of an illness of Lucretia's in the 1820s, wrote in a family letter that "I am convinced that Sister L's dyspepsia arises from too much mental exercise."

Mrs. Mott suffered the usual sorrows of the nineteenth-century family in which death struck often and close. Her father died when she was twenty-two, her baby son two years later, and shortly thereafter two of her sisters.

Yet for all she was a woman of the nineteenth century, she also swept beyond the limitations and restrictions which the society of that time placed upon half its members. Modern woman's liberation would have found in her a kindred spirit, a firm activist, a sound mind, a useful wit.

Deeply religious, an extensive reader of the Bible, a widely known and much-traveled speaker in the Society of Friends, she nevertheless held unorthodox views for the time. Her emphasis was not upon theology, but upon "practical righteousness," and she agreed with William Penn that "men are to be judged by their likeness to Christ rather than by their notions of Christ." If people are guided by a higher power, she said, whether

> it be called the Great Spirit of the Indian, the Quaker "Inward Light" of George Fox, the "Blessed Mary" Mother of Jesus of the Catholics, or Burmah the Hindoo's God— they will all be one, and there will come to be such faith and such liberty as shall redeem the world.

We are still seeking that broadmindedness.

A prime mover in the antislavery movement, involved in the temperance and peace movements as well, a defender of the young—parents "overlook the fact that a child, like all human beings, has inalienable rights"—she was a significant promoter of the rights of women. With Elizabeth Cady Stanton she was one of the chief organizers of the famed Women's Rights Convention held at Seneca Falls, New York in July 1848 and a principal speaker at subsequent public meetings to promote the cause. With skill and wit she dealt with the time-honored arguments that women should be confined to the home, that females were innately inferior to males. To those who resorted to the authority of St. Paul, who had placed upon women the obligation to obey their husbands, she wittily replied: "Many of the opposers of Woman's Rights who bid us to obey the bachelor St. Paul, themselves reject his counsel—he advised them not to marry." And to the argument that inferiority of intellect required that women be protected from involvement in public life, she responded: "Does one man have fewer rights than another because his intellect is inferior? If not, why should a woman?" In a surprisingly modern tone, she suggested that the development of woman's intellect may well have been stunted by long ages of repression, but such conditions of injustice did not in themselves indicate that woman was innately inferior to man; nor, she argued, should a condition brought about by injustice be urged as a reason for continuing the original injustice. But recognition of this condition, she well realized, made the task more difficult, and she warned Mrs. Stanton that

> Thou wilt have hard work to prove the equality of women with men, facts are so against such an assumption, in the present stage of woman's development. We need not however <u>admit</u> inferiority even tho' we may not be able to prove equality.

Full of common sense, she rejected the flattering but condescending support of males whose sympathy to the cause led them to eulogize women and to declare that by nature woman was "the better half of creation and man a tyrant." To that Mrs. Mott shrewdly replied that men had become so accustomed to handing out compliments to women that they made such statements without realizing that "man was not a tyrant by nature but had been made tyrannical by the power which had by general consent been conferred upon him."

What she wanted was not a false recognition of the superiority of women, but recognition that as human beings women should possess, as one of the resolutions at Seneca Falls proposed, "an equal participation with men in the various trades, professions and commerce." The issue, for Lucretia Mott, was the establishment of the principle of "coequality of woman with man, her right to practice those acts of life for which she is fitted by nature." The twentieth century has not said it better.

Only two years before her death she attended and spoke at the thirtieth anniversary of the famous convention at Seneca Falls, where at the age of eighty-five she proclaimed the right of women to hold property, receive wages equal to the task performed, enjoy higher education, and exercise the franchise.

At her death, Alfred Love said of her, "None but thyself can be thy parallel." Lucretia Mott would probably have wanted that applied to every woman.

Chapter 9
CULTURE IN THE NEW REPUBLIC

The Spirit of the Times
THE NEW EDUCATION

Established by law in 1848, the University of Wisconsin—the eleventh state university in the nation—saw its first college class begin in 1850. Its student enrollment up to the Civil War rarely rose over 300. Students came principally from Wisconsin but in 1856, a typical year, 36 out of 169 entered from other states and Canada. Most students were in their late teens or early twenties, but occasionally there was one of thirty or forty and in 1860 a man of fifty registered, apparently creating no more stir then than now.

Modern students attracted by the virtues of the simple life might find much appealing about student life at the University in the middle of the nineteenth century. Their parents might find even greater appeal in its cost. Although there were two residence halls, many out-of-town students roomed and boarded with Madison families or prepared their own meals. A room in one of the dormitories initially cost five dollars a term; tuition was ten dollars. By 1855, tuition and room rent was reduced to only twenty-five dollars for a year of three terms. Meals at the first mess hall were about eighty cents a week. When the South Hall dormitory was built, it became a residence hall with dining room where faculty and their families could eat with students, who were charged two dollars a week for their food. The Board of Regents provided for this arrangement, which also included resident faculty families, on the grounds that "the social and domestic influence of daily intercourse in the hall and elsewhere" would "tend to elevate the standard of good manners and good order in the institution."

Students in the dormitories were required to supply their own furniture. Isaac N. Stewart reported to his father that his purchases cost him eight dollars "new from the store"—including bed, table, chairs, bookstand, an oil lamp for light, and a spirit lamp for a cookstove. Mattresses were straw- or husk-filled, and students periodically visited neighboring farms to get mattress filler.

Many students did not care for dormitory meals—a complaint familiar to modern ears—or found the cost prohibitive, and so bought and cooked their own food. Samuel Fallows of the class of '59 walked twenty miles each weekend to the family

The campus of Wisconsin State University

farm for his week's supply. Many subsisted on meager fare. The naturalist John Muir recalled years later that when he arrived at the University a student assured him that "The baker and milkman come every day. You can live on bread and milk." Muir did a little better than that, spending fifty cents a week for his diet of "bread and molasses, graham mush, and baked potatoes." Other students supplemented their diet with fish caught in Lake Mendota or freshwater clams gathered in nearby streams.

As was typical in American colleges, attendance at chapel was daily and compulsory. But many students also began and ended each day with a prayer in their rooms, attended Sunday morning services at a local church, afternoon Sabbath services on the campus, and Sunday evening services at a local church.

Entertainment and recreation were limited and simple, but seemed to satisfy student needs. There were no organized sports, but students on their own played wicket, quoits, and baseball. They organized a military drill team in 1858, conspicuous for its ineptitude according to contemporary accounts, and founded a chess club the same year despite murmurs of disapproval that it was "morally wrong" to spend too much time on the game. Students also sought out other diversions, none approved by the faculty or the administration, including visits to saloons, gaming houses, and the theater. And they clashed with town youth, got into fights, and disturbed the peace. But such conduct was regarded by the faculty as less serious than failing to meet academic standards and more students were dismissed for academic than social misconduct.

In the 1850s student opinion frequently favored the admission of women. But when women students were first admitted in 1863 through a backdoor arrangement which created a normal or teacher-training department to which both sexes were admitted, male reaction was often hostile. James High fourteen years later still seethed with indignation: "We believed then and still believe that the problem of coeducation is not susceptible of perfect solution, and is incompatible with the highest culture of either sex." Perhaps this was because male students felt that the presence of women would divert them from preparing for the serious tasks ahead. These were solemn indeed, as one of the editors of the short-lived student literary magazine made clear:

> Man has no right to ignore the duties which devolve upon him, as a social being. He is so constituted that the path of happiness and the path of usefulness are one. He who would reap the fruits of his vast acquisitions and varied powers must employ them in the service of mankind. Let him acquire knowledge in the school of experience; learn wisdom in solving the all-important problems of his own daily duties; and cultivate the finer feelings of his nature by carrying joy and gladness to the abodes of want and suffering, and by sowing the seeds of virtue and intelligence in the moral wastes of the earth.

There was some public doubt that the University was successful in so preparing students. When the first two students graduated in 1854—Charles T. Wakeley and Levi M. Booth—the editor of the Madison Argus and Democrat was not exactly sympathetic with what the University had wrought: "The former entered the University with thorough practical habits and strong native good sense as the basis of an education and has not been much injured by his scholastic . . . associations. The latter has much good sense yet to acquire to make his college learning of any avail to himself."

But the students seemed to think it all worthwhile. Many looked back on their life at the University as one of the most exciting periods in their lives. And John Muir later recalled sentimentally that when he left the University he had climbed to a high hill overlooking the campus "where I had spent so many hungry and happy and hopeful days. There with streaming eyes I bade my blessed Alma Mater farewell."

Education and Knowledge

The Americans have always talked a great case on the value of education, arguing that most of the world's social and economic ills would be solved if people were educated, and proclaiming that the fate of the American republic hung on the capacity of its citizens to absorb knowledge. "There can be no fear of our institutions as long as education is cherished," wrote Schoolcraft. At the same time the Americans have frequently been reluctant to put their money where their mouths were, whether the fate of the nation was at stake or not. This was often the case even after the battle for free tax-supported public schools had been fought and won in most of the legislatures of the country.

The Growth of Schools   Especially in the West there was a reluctance to spare the money for adequate school systems. Many families were reluctant, in an era when struggling to get ahead materially was a major concern, to divert a portion of their limited funds to the support of schools. To many farmers there and in the rest of the nation, there were more important things for the young to do than fritter away their time behind a book. One observer commented that the smart farmer kept his sturdy sons at home to walk behind the plow, while those less endowed by nature he "sent to Dartmouth." But hostility to the support of education extended to more than the colleges.

The result was what might be expected. Schools frequently operated on meager resources, buildings were cheaply constructed and ill-furnished, had inadequate sanitation and ventilation, and were badly equipped. Teachers were by and large poorly trained and underpaid. One reason why women came to dominate in elementary teaching was that they would accept low wages, generally less than half those paid to men, who were themselves underpaid. As late as 1861, men teachers averaged $6.30 a week and women $4.05 in rural areas, while in urban districts men were getting $18.07 and women $6.91.

Stern discipline and rote memory were the methods of the average schoolroom, perhaps not surprisingly in view of the lack of training for teachers and the ungraded schools in which pupils of all ages sat in the same room. Men teachers were frequently hired not on the basis of their mental prowess, but for their ability to subdue physically the older boys in the school. One even resorted to a brace of pistols to back up his authority.

The effects of these conditions on the general populace were noticeable. John Mason Peck, a Baptist missionary in Illinois, wrote that "Many adults, especially females, are unable to read or write, and many more, who are able to read a little, cannot readily understand what they attempt to read, and therefore take no pleasure in books and study." But that was in the West. In New England, with a long educational tradition, this was less generally true. As one loyal resident noted: "I have lived more than forty years in New England, and have not . . . met with ten individuals . . . who could not read and write."

But in spite of all obstacles, significant changes began. Education gradually shifted emphasis, and schools grew and expanded.

The traditional aims of education, character and moral development, mental discipline, literacy, and citizenship, dominated the first half of the nineteenth century—which meant that learning and knowledge were secondary. But even within this framework changes did occur. Thus even though reading, spelling, writing, and arithmetic were the main offerings in most of the one-room elementary schools in the country, by mid-century states such as Massachusetts had added English grammar and geography, and some towns had introduced history and even music. On the secondary level, the old Latin grammar school, designed to prepare boys for college, had concentrated on Latin, Greek, and arithmetic. By 1860 geography, English grammar, algebra, geometry, and ancient history had been added.

The private academies that sprang up in profusion all over the country were secondary schools which tended by 1860 to offer parallel courses: the traditional classical program and what was called the English course, which substituted English grammar and literature for Latin and Greek. Within the

English program courses in the natural sciences, astronomy, chemistry, botany, American history, algebra and geometry, even in some instances manual training, became part of the curriculum. In many such programs in the academies an attempt was made to relate these courses to "practical" matters: navigation, surveying, business writing and procedures. In the colleges and universities a similar expansion of the curriculum took place, and the sciences, history, and modern languages made their appearance. Moreover, the interest in science resulted in the creation of special scientific institutions such as Rensselaer Polytechnic Institute, and special scientific schools at Harvard, Yale, and Dartmouth. Overall, it must be remembered that from common school to college, variation in offering was great, ranging from few courses to many, and the quality of instruction was equally varied, from very poor to excellent.

Perhaps the most obvious characteristic of American education in these years was growth. By 1860 there were thousands of elementary schools in the country, most of which had come into being by requirement of law, although there were many private and church schools also. By 1860 the desire to make additional education available to those who were not intending to enter college had resulted in the beginning of a significant expansion in secondary education. The full extension to the secondary level of the principle of free tax-supported schools still lay in the future. Nevertheless by 1860 there were some three hundred public high schools in the country and approximately six thousand private secondary schools and academies, many of these partly supported by public funds.

Growth also occurred in higher education. In 1780 there were 9 colleges in the new nation. By 1861, there were some 182 colleges which had managed to survive, and numerous others which failed to do so. Despite the fact that the vast majority of college students no longer intended to become ministers, most of the new colleges were founded by religious denominations whose intent was apparently to make sure that the nation's future leaders would be morally and theologically sound. Since the supply of colleges far exceeded the demand, most barely survived, and enrollments were generally below 200 students.

Although the state universities still lay ahead, they had been conceived. Early in the century there were a handful of state colleges, including those in North Carolina, Vermont, and Virginia, but they received little or no public support. The University of Michigan, the first successful state university with free tuition for residents of the state, was assured of survival after Henry Tappan became its president in 1851. The federal government established a precedent for support with federal land grants. All states admitted to the Union before the Civil War, except Vermont, Kentucky, Maine, and Texas, received educational land grants from the public domain. Such grants were ill-used, however, with the exception of those to the University of Michigan.

Significant in these years was the opening of educational opportunities to women. Not only was elementary education made available to girls by the expansion of schools, but they began to be admitted to the secondary schools

Massachusetts	Harvard	1636	Michigan	University of Michigan	1817
Virginia	William and Mary	1693	Missouri	St. Louis University	1818
Connecticut	Yale	1701			
New Jersey	Princeton	1746	Alabama	Athens College	1822
Pennsylvania	University of Pennsylvania	1751	Louisiana	Centenary College	1825
New York	Columbia	1754	Mississippi	Mississippi College	1826
Rhode Island	Brown	1764			
New Hampshire	Dartmouth	1769	Delaware	University of Delaware	1833
South Carolina	College of Charleston	1770	Arkansas	College of the Ozarks	1834
North Carolina	Salem College	1772			
Kentucky	Transylvania University	1780	Illinois	McKendree College	1837
			Iowa	Loras College	1839
Maryland	Washington College	1782	Texas	Southwestern University	1840
Georgia	University of Georgia	1785	Wisconsin	Carroll College	1840
Vermont	University of Vermont	1791	California	American Baptist Seminary	1841
Tennessee	Tusculum College	1794	Oregon	Willamette University	1842
Maine	Bowdoin	1794			
Ohio	Ohio University	1804	Minnesota	University of Minnesota	1851
Indiana	Vincennes University	1804	Florida	University of Florida	1853

Present names are used.

THE FIRST COLLEGE FOUNDED IN EACH STATE, 1636–1860

and to attend academies founded especially for them. The admission of women to colleges began at Oberlin, although everywhere they were segregated from men in classes.

With the expansion of the nation, training in the professions became of obvious importance, and this fact was reflected in the founding of a number of medical and law schools before the Civil War. But even in the best the standards were often low and instruction was given on a part-time basis by practicing doctors and lawyers. The majority of doctors and lawyers were still trained by the old apprentice system.

By 1860 formal education was much improved. A basic school system had been established. Though the commitment to public education was largely confined to the elementary level, its application to higher levels had begun. At the same time, large numbers of children were denied an adequate education, or any at all. Tens of thousands, even where public education existed, were kept out of the schools by their parents or attended only a few terms. The existence in some states of an additional tax on parents with children in school often contributed to this. In many places, moreover, instruction was minimal and children were lucky if they learned to read and write. Higher up the educational ladder student enrollments were shockingly small. In a society still predominantly rural, schooling seemed to offer to many people little help in their everyday life, and therefore was a luxury few could afford.

But education is more than formal training, as we keep telling ourselves even today, and there were other developments that helped to make the Americans a more learned and informed people than they would otherwise have been. As one writer of the time noted: "As a nation, we are educated more by contact with each other, by business, by newspapers, magazines, and circulating libraries, by public meetings and conventions, by lyceums, by speeches in congress, in the state legislatures, and at political gatherings, and in various other ways than by direct instructions imparted in the school room."

Newspapers, Magazines, Books and Libraries   The expansion of the publishing business both reflected and nourished the demand for self-education. In 1828 there were some 852 newspapers in the country, and their annual circulation was about six issues per person. By 1850 it was almost four times that amount. The appearance in 1833 of the *New York Sun*, the first of the many penny newspapers, and the adoption by Congress in 1851 of cheap and uniform postal rates helped circulation greatly. Publishers also found a wide market in the middle class for such items as gift books, which helped both to create and to meet the demand for "better literature and art." Harper's brought out a series of Boys' Libraries, Girls' Libraries, a Family Library which ran to 187 volumes, and a Library of Select Novels which eventually reached 615 titles. Other publishers were quick to imitate. Publishers also issued translations of major works by European philosophers and men of letters, while cheap books of useful information, history, religion, travel, and biography began to appear. By 1825 there were almost 100 periodicals in the country, although their circulation was not large. By 1860 dozens of other magazines had appeared, many with a wide audience. These included *Harper's Weekly*, the *Magazine of Useful and Entertaining Knowledge, Graham's, Godey's Lady's Book*, and others. The agricultural press also expanded, and though their publications contained perhaps too many articles on the sins of the city and the virtues of the farm, they also had informational pieces on soil care, federal and state aid to agriculture, household hints, and other items useful to the farming family.

The growing public interest in knowledge was also reflected by the rise of libraries. Skilled workers had available the resources of the libraries established by the mechanics' and apprentices' institutes. The first of these was the Apprentices' Library in Boston in 1820, and soon practically every city possessed such a library. By 1857 the New York Apprentices' Library was reporting three-quarters of a million book checkouts, mostly by working people. And the mercantile libraries founded by clerks and young merchants made their appearance in the 1820s. Both types sponsored lectures, debates, discussions, and some evening classes.

Such libraries were, of course, semi-private institutions supported not by public funds but by fees and donations. The first libraries supported by public funds were the school district libraries in the state of New York in 1838. Confined principally to New York and New England and restricted in purpose, they may have been small and inadequate, but they helped pave the way for the idea of public responsibility for libraries.

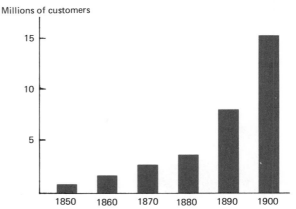

THE GROWTH OF NEWSPAPERS

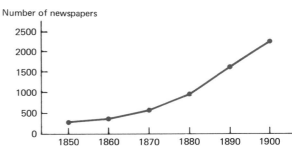

Libraries for general public use that were backed by public monies had a tentative start in the late 1820s and 1830, but it was not until 1848 that the first genuine public library as we know it today came into being. In that year the Massachusetts legislature allowed public funds in Boston to be used to support the projected Boston Public Library. Various other states began to pass laws permitting towns to establish tax-supported libraries and the movement was underway.

To the older proprietary or subscription libraries existing by the end of the eighteenty century there were added some 250 new libraries in the first quarter of the nineteenty century, and 550 libraries of all kinds (not counting school libraries) between 1825 and 1850.

The Lyceum   Broader in impact on the spread of knowledge among the common people was the lyceum movement, a voluntary association of citizens seeking to improve their knowledge. The first lyceum appeared in 1826 in Millbury, Massachusetts, organized by Josiah Holbrook, who wanted to bring knowledge of science to the people. By 1835, there were some three hundred lyceums in fifteen states, most of them east of the Alleghenies. In the next fifteen years, the movement quickly spread throughout the West.

While the lyceum became important in promoting the common-school movement and the establishment of libraries, it also did much to stimulate

Lecturer and His Audience, *at Clinton Hall, 1838. An etiquette was developing for attending the lyceum, among which were dictums against rowdiness, standing in one's place, and wearing hats that were too high. Apparently some members of this audience were unaware of their responsibilities.*

an interest in science and in popular topics of interest. While there was a natural reliance on home-town talent in the lectures, discussions, and demonstrations that characterized lyceum activities, their great popularity rested on the lectures of visiting scholars and men of letters who delighted in the opportunity to ride the lyceum circuit, popularizing ideas and causes and making money from their fees as they did so. Professor Benjamin Silliman of Yale and Professor Louis Agassiz of Harvard dazzled the populace with the wonders of science, while in Cincinnati Ormsby Mitchel lectured so successfully on astronomy that the citizens bought him a telescope surpassed only by that in Greenwich, England. The reformed drunkard, John B. Gough, extolled the virtues of temperance, and Horace Mann those of public education. William Lloyd Garrison denounced slavery on the lyceum platform, and Susan B. Anthony spoke for women's rights. Famous English authors such as Charles Dickens and William Makepeace Thackeray placed the literary world before the public. A favorite of lyceum audiences was Elihu Burritt, "the learned blacksmith," whose extraordinary achievement in learning over thirty languages showed ordinary people the potential in themselves. And so it went.

The public enthusiasm for knowledge was widespread, although obviously less able of expression in rural districts than in towns and cities. On some occasions, enthusiasm got out of hand. A Boston crowd filling the street to hear the Silliman lecture on chemistry was so great that it crushed in the windows of the Old Corner Book Store where the tickets were being distributed.

Observers from abroad were amazed at this American eagerness for knowledge. A British Member of Parliament, Thomas Wyse, wrote in Great

Britain that because of the lyceum "thousands of children of not more than 8 or 10 years old, know more geology, mineralogy, botany, statistical facts, etc., of what concerns their daily and national interests and occupations, than was probably known 30 years ago by any five individuals in the United States." While that observation was an exaggeration of the wildest sort it does serve to indicate the belief commonly held in Europe that the Americans as a whole were more generally knowledgeable than were the masses of the people in any other country, as indeed they were.

The Advance of Knowledge   If the Americans led the Western World in possessing a superficial knowledge of many matters, they did not lead in the advancement of knowledge. And the work which Americans did was often heavily dependent upon European fundamental research, study, and method.

Particularly in the first few decades of the republic the advance of knowledge rested in the hands of members of well-to-do families whose resources were such that they had time and money for study, research, and publication. Plantation wealth, for example, enabled John Izard Middleton to study archeology abroad and to publish a pioneer work in 1817. By assuming the printing cost of $12,000, Nathaniel Bowditch was able to translate and publish for serious American students Laplace's classical *Mécanique Céleste.* The wealthy Scotch-American, William Maclure, published in 1817 his geological survey on the eastern United States, *Observations on the Geology of the United States,* the first such study of any large area. And Chancellor James Kent paid for the publication of the first of the eight volumes of his monumental *Commentaries on American Law.*

But new trends were underway. The expansion of colleges and universities provided security for scholars to do their work. Harvard, Yale, Columbia, the College of New Jersey, even small institutions such as Bowdoin and Amherst and the new state university in Michigan, saw pioneer work in various fields. The appearance of museums, institutes, and societies also provided a stimulus to the advancement of knowledge. The New York Historical Society was founded in 1804, the American Antiquarian Society in 1812, and the Lyceum of Natural History was founded in New York in 1817. Learning was also furthered by the founding of the American Association for the Advancement of Science, and of professional journals such as the *American Journal of Science* and others devoted to special disciplines.

A crucial step in the advancement of knowledge was the gradual emergence of government, especially federal government, as an agency supporting and promoting investigative projects. Key governmental institutions were established in this period: the Naval Observatory, and the famed Smithsonian Institution, which was to become a major research center in physics, archeology, and ethnology. Of equal importance were projects supported by the government in spite of much public opposition.

Before the Civil War almost every state sponsored geological surveys, a process initiated by North Carolina in 1824. Later, surveys of the flora and

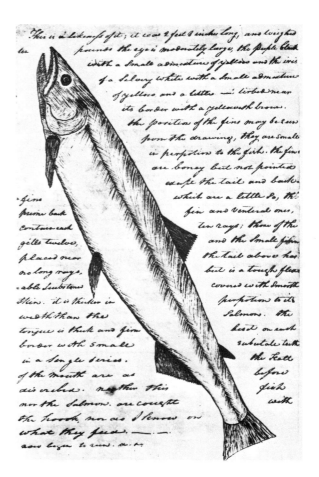

Drawing and account of a salmon from the Journal *of William Clark. The entry is typical of the care and precision of the observations made on the expedition. Those observations included records of temperature and weather, maps, accounts of Indian culture, and collections of geological and botanical specimens, all of which not only furthered the scientific knowledge of the wilderness, but spurred interest in its possibilities for trade and settlement.*

fauna of states were also undertaken. After the Lewis and Clark expedition sent out by President Jefferson, which yielded valuable knowledge of the geography, geology, and natural history of the West, the federal government found itself involved in more and more such enterprises. The most important among the early government expeditions to the West was that of Stephen Long in 1820 which led to extensive knowledge about the Rocky Mountain region and the discovery of new animals, insects, and plants.

The later United States Coastal Survey, which occupied decades, was a major achievement, as was the great study by Matthew Maury whose work as director of the National Observatory and Hydrographic Office resulted in the publication in 1855 of *The Physical Geography of the Sea* and led to the establishment of new sea routes saving time and diminishing the risk from storms. Maury's study indeed laid the foundation for a new science, oceanography, and was of great value to all maritime countries.

The great achievement in government-sponsored research was the United States Exploring Expedition of 1838–1842, commanded by Lieutenant Charles Wilkes. The Expedition surveyed 800 miles of coast and streams in

Passenger Pigeon, *an 1829 aquatint by R. Howell, after Audubon.*

North and South America and some 280 islands in the South Atlantic and South Pacific, and proved as well the existence of Antarctica. It also assembled vast data on navigation, geology, meteorology, terrestrial magnetism, and hydrography. The civilian scientists with the Expedition ultimately produced some twenty volumes on mineralogy, geology, biology, and ethnology, including Dr. Charles Pickering's *Chronological History of Plants* as well as studies of Polynesian dialects, the geographical distribution of races, and the physical history of humanity. Furthermore, the Expedition brought back specimens that formed the basis for the collections of the United States National Museum and the United States Botanical Garden. Subsequent expeditions surveyed areas in Latin America, the Dead Sea, the Arctic, and the China Seas. Commodore Perry's famous visit to Japan resulted in a three-volume work on that hitherto isolated land.

Much research and study was promoted by the curiosity of inquiring minds. Thomas Say's volumes on *American Entomology* are an example, as are James Audubon's magnificent *Birds of America.* So are the studies of the brilliant, eccentric Constantine Rafinesque, an immigrant whose scientific inquiries brought him in 1833 to anticipate Darwin by declaring that plants and animals had developed over a long period through deviations and mutations that exemplified "the great universal law of perpetual mutability in everything." So is Caleb Atwater's studies of prehistoric mounds in the West, which led eventually to the publication of his *Description of the Antiquities Discovered in the State of Ohio and other Western States*. In 1847 Maria Mitchell, who studied astronomy with her father, discovered a telescopic comet, which gained her international recognition.

At the same time much study and research was stimulated by utilitarian needs and motives. Commercial interests were greatly aided by the work of the Coast Survey and of Maury. The development of the West as a new and growing region was promoted by the expanding knowledge of that area gained from the various governmental expeditions and studies. The rising industrial system was served not only by the colleges that began to offer courses useful to young men embarking upon such careers, but also by work done by professors of science. At Yale, Silliman's analysis of oil specimens from Pennsylvania sent to him by George Bissell suggested that a worthwhile illuminant could be made from petroleum at low cost, and thus underwrote Bissell's promotion of a new industry.

Medical research also had important utilitarian interests. The major American contribution was probably the discovery of anesthesia, first experimented with by Dr. Crawford Long and Dr. Horace Wells, but not proved conclusively to the profession until Dr. W. T. G. Morton, a Boston dentist, successfully administered ether to a surgical patient in the Massachusetts General Hospital in 1846.

Although the expansion of knowledge in America in the decades before the Civil War was, by comparison to later developments, a modest achievement, nevertheless the foundations for an American commitment to knowledge were established and the factors involved in that commitment became visible during these years, including a skepticism about devoting time, money, and resources to studies which seemingly have no relation to social need. There is a familiar ring in the complaint of one Congressman on government support for the United States Exploring Expedition. He declared the money would better be spent on practical needs at home rather than in remote regions, and suggested that an expedition to the moon made about as much sense.

American Literature and the Arts

American writers and artists in the first half of the nineteenth century were inevitably affected by the Romantic movement, which had already begun in Western Europe. The Romantic view of life and art differed from that of the Age of Reason in the eighteenth century by stressing freedom and feeling rather than order, restraint, and reason. Romanticism glorified the individual and worshiped wild, untrammeled nature, was less interested in an ordered society and more in the unrestrained freedom of the individual. The romantic admired the tempestuous Byronic hero and at the same time idealized the "noble savage" and the common people. It gave free play to the imagination, and saw society as a living, growing organism rather than a structure determined by intellect, reason, and immutable law.

To a greater or lesser degree, all early nineteenth-century American writers and artists were influenced by Romanticism, though the influence was so varied that the connection often seems slight. But the Romantic spirit chimed with the larger democratic and nationalistic mood of a country devoted to the ideal of the common people, which believed that America and Americans were capable of any accomplishment, was suspicious of formal learning, and was convinced that the instincts of the ordinary citizen were in the last analysis the best touchstone of what was right.

Popular Literature Most of the popular novels as well as the stories, essays, poems, and journalistic observations that filled the magazines and newspapers, were banal and sentimental rather than genuinely romantic. Magazine verse tended to exploit such themes as sorrow at the death of a young maiden or an infant. Popular novels weren't much better, as evidenced by the following from *Guy Rivers,* by the prolific South Carolina writer William Gilmore Simms, in which the villain threatens the heroine with a typical set of horrors:

> "Hark ye, if ye fear not death, there is something worse than death to so romantic a damsel, which shall teach ye fear. Obey me, girl—report the route taken by this fugitive, or by all that is black in hell or bright in heaven, I—" And with a whisper, he hissed the concluding and cruel threat in the ears of the shuddering and shrinking girl. With a husky horror in her voice, she cried out:—"You dare not! monster as you are, you dare not!" then shrieking, at the full height of her voice—"Save me, uncle! save me! save me!"

Women novelists such as Susan Warner, Marie Cummins, Mary Jane Holmes, and Catherine Sedgwick, as well as male writers such as Simms and John Pendleton Kennedy, enjoyed exceptional sales. Over a million copies of Mary Jane Holmes's books were sold, and Simms at his peak earned $6,000 a year from his writing, an astonishing sum for the time. Among more serious writers, Washington Irving glorified the American West in *Astoria,* wrote a humorous *History of New York,* and with gentle affection described the rich culture of the Dutch patroon in upstate New York in such stories as "Rip Van Winkle" and "The Legend of Sleepy Hollow." James Fenimore Cooper romantically portrayed the American frontier in five novels called the Leatherstocking Saga, stirring accounts of pursuit and escape involving Indians, hunters, and charming young ladies wandering in the woods. And the poet William Cullen Bryant wrote graceful lyrics on nature that gave him not only a reputation at home, but even among some critics abroad.

In the second quarter of the nineteenth century other competent writers appeared. Henry Wadsworth Longfellow became a professor of literature at

The Crockett Almanac. Violence as well as sentimentality had its place in the hearts of the reading public.

Harvard and one of the most respected figures of the time. He had great technical competence, and his musical verses sang of "The Village Blacksmith" or hailed "The Ride of Paul Revere." His long narrative poems on the American past *(Evangeline)* and the American Indian *(The Song of Hiawatha)* were great romantic successes. Almost as popular was John Greenleaf Whittier, whose "Snowbound" and "A Barefoot Boy" captivated a basically rural society to whom the simple life had great appeal. Also widely appreciated were the light verses and witty essays of Boston physician Oliver Wendell Holmes. His patriotic plea for the preservation of the U.S.S. *Constitution,* "Old Ironsides," and his romantic restructuring of "The Chambered Nautilus," stirred many readers; and his series of essays for the *Atlantic Monthly,* "The Autocrat of the Breakfast Table," helped put that new magazine on a solid footing. James Russell Lowell's major work was as editor of the *Atlantic.* His own essays, criticism, and poetry lacked depth and originality. His chief contribution to literature lay in the *Bigelow Papers,* a series of humorous stories satirizing the Mexican War that he had written in a New England dialect.

American Literature Comes of Age   In the 1840s and 1850s a new generation of serious writers clearly indicated that American literature had come of age. These giants were Emerson, Thoreau, Hawthorne, Poe, Whitman, and Melville.

Ralph Waldo Emerson was the leading thinker among these, not only because of the power of his perceptions and his skill with the language, but because of his influence as the major spokesman for transcendentalism. This highest expression of romanticism in America held that individuals could grasp moral and religious truths intuitively and had no need for outside authority. The transcendentalists took the position that humanity, as a part of nature, contained within itself the divine essence. Emerson believed that all individuals had the truth within them and could safely rely upon themselves. "I have taught one doctrine," he declared, "namely the infinitude of the private man." In his popular essay, "Self-Reliance," he told his readers: "Trust thyself: every heart vibrates to that iron string." In his small book *Nature,* he asked: "Who can set bounds to the possibilities of man? Once inhale the upper air, being admitted to behold the absolute natures of justice and truth, and we learn that man has access to the entire mind of the Creator, is himself the creator in the finite." "Let man stand erect, go alone, and possess the universe," he wrote. With this kind of potential, restrictions upon freedom were not needed. Indeed, "the appearance of character makes the state unnecessary."

Emerson provided, in his immensely popular lectures, his essays, and his poetry, an influence that helped to liberalize people's thinking, to stimulate them to rely upon themselves, to change and reform, to abandon ideas which no longer had purpose. Emerson took a benevolent view of things. To him the universe was an expression of God, and events would always turn for the best. This was optimism in tune with the times. Emerson was disturbed by the drive and direction of a growing industrial America, but never came to terms with the fact that the doctrine of self-reliance he preached might have grim as well as happy consequences. His ideas also fed the nationalistic spirit of the country when, in his famous address "The American Scholar," he called upon Americans to reject the European influence and to rely upon themselves, their own surroundings and experiences, their own ideas.

Henry David Thoreau was a follower and a close friend of Emerson, but also a complete individualist, carrying Emerson's ideas on self-reliance beyond the spiritual to the material and the political. As much disturbed as Emerson by the materialistic bent of American society, Thoreau was willing to prove that you could get along on your own if necessary with very little and gain freedom in the process, and he ran his two-year experiment at Walden to prove the point. "Most men," he wrote, "are so occupied with the factitious cares and superfluously hard labors of life, that its finer fruits cannot be plucked by them." Too busy making a living to savor life, they lived "lives of quiet desperation." He, on the other hand, "went to the woods because I wished to live deliberately, to confront only the essential facts of life, and see if I could not learn what it had to teach, and not, when I came to

Henry David Thoreau

die, to discover that I had not lived." The self-reliance he accepted not only made him object to all restrictions on the freedom of the individual—"That government is best which governs not at all"—but to argue that each man knows what is best for himself—"If a man does not keep pace with his companion, perhaps it is because he hears a different drummer." Thoreau never argued that his was the only way, making the point that each individual should "find out and pursue *his own way,* and not his father's or his mother's or his neighbor's instead." Thoreau's conviction that *his* way was right for him was dramatized by his refusal to pay his Massachusetts poll tax because he believed the war with Mexico was immoral. He ended in jail, but only for one night when his aunt paid the tax, an act he could hardly object to since in doing so she was presumably marching to her own drummer. But out of this experience came his most famous essay, "Civil Disobedience," in which he argued the case for defying the law if the law went contrary to one's conscience. "Under a government which imprisons any unjustly," he wrote, "the true place for a just man is also a prison." That essay may have been responsible for putting a lot of just men in jail, but it also influenced the destiny of nations, reaching out in the twentieth century to influence Mahatma Gandhi in South Africa and India, and through him coming full circle and affecting Martin Luther King and the civil rights movement in the United States in the 1950s and 1960s.

Also influenced by Emerson was the exuberant poet of American democracy and nationalism, Walt Whitman, whose poems reflect Emerson's self-reliance, since Whitman believed he wrote best by rejecting the traditional rules of meter and rhyme and relying on his own instincts. His main work was *Leaves of Grass,* published first in 1855 and continually revised and expanded through nine editions. Whitman saw himself as the poet of democracy, and indeed believed that writers and artists must provide the emotional power underlying democracy:

> Of all races and eras, These States, with veins full of poetical stuff, most need
>   poets, and are to have the greatest, and use them the greatest,
> Their Presidents shall not be their common referee so much as their poets
>   shall.

He identified himself with the mass of ordinary Americans, and was thus not merely being boastful in his "Song of Myself:"

> I celebrate myself, and sing myself
> And what I shall assume you shall assume,
> For every atom belonging to me as good belongs to you.

Whitman's example encouraged others to write experimentally, and to search out topics wherever their inclinations and instincts led them. But no other writer of the time so consciously spoke for democracy or so represented the best of its ideas.

Edgar Allan Poe is sometimes called a minor figure—even Emerson dismissed him as insignificant—but as a romantic writer his influence was great, not only at home but abroad, and his talent was clearly superior. His personal life reads like a romantic novel by a fashionable "authoress" of the day. Unstable of character, he became an alcoholic, could not hold a steady job, was frequently ill mentally as well as physically, married a girl of thirteen, was obsessively dependent upon his mother-in-law, lost his young wife, and died at forty. But he was a brilliant literary critic, as his editorship of several magazines demonstrated, was a shrewd political observer, and had a remarkable talent for expression in both prose and poetry. Mood dominated his writing, and in short stories such as *The Cask of Amontillado, The Fall of the House of Usher, The Pit and the Pendulum,* and poems such as "The Raven," "Annabel Lee," "To Helen," and "Ulalume," he created an unforgettable atmosphere and played upon and explored the emotions of fear, terror, loneliness, horror, the sense of loss, and love. He practically invented the detective story, as shown in his tales of *The Murders in the Rue Morgue* and *The Purloined Letter.* Poe was a supreme and self-conscious stylist, and would have been gratified and surprised to learn that he was to become an inspiration of the symbolist movement in France at the end of the nineteenth century.

Nathaniel Hawthorne, an introspective New Englander brought up in virtual isolation until he was thirty, was fascinated with the American past, and with the emblematic meanings he found in the ironies of nature and human events. He thus shared Poe's romantic love of the strange, but added to it an ethical sense Poe seldom showed. Though associated for a time with the transcendentalists, Hawthorne rejected their optimistic view of life. His main concern was not with society, but with the struggles of individuals with sin and guilt and with the curse of loneliness and isolation that is the fate of the sinner, for the worst thing that can happen to a human being is to be cut off from the common stream of humanity. In his major work, *The Scarlet*

Letter, the sin is adultery, yet the society that condemned it is as guilty as those who sinned against its laws. Hawthorne's other novels, The *House of the Seven Gables, The Blithedale Romance,* and *The Marble Faun,* deal less successfully with the same themes of sin, guilt, and retribution. Hawthorne's great talent lay in his skillful use of symbols, in his capacity to evoke mood, and in his psychological probing into the lives of his characters.

Herman Melville, from one point of view, is a classic example of how America has tended to treat her literary talent. When you write things of popular interest, the public cheers; when you are then encouraged to write what really moves you, the public ignores you. As a young man Melville served on a whaler, jumping ship in the South Seas where the mighty whale "rolls its island bulk," living in the Marquesas among cannibals, and beachcombing in Tahiti for a year. *Typee,* published in 1846, was his account of life among the islanders, and his glorification of primitive innocence in a setting few people had ever seen appealed enormously to the romantic tastes of the American public. Some were offended by his disparaging view of missionaries, but then how can you glorify primitive innocence without criticizing those who would interfere with it? *Omoo,* a sequel, appeared a year later, and then came other books based loosely on his experiences as a sailor on a merchant ship and in the navy. But Melville was not content with facile and shallow romanticizing. He thought deeply about human destiny, good and evil, and man's place in the universe. After an unsuccessful attempt to develop these ideas in an allegory, *Mardi,* he turned to what became his greatest achievement, *Moby Dick,* perhaps the finest novel ever written by an American and of the first rank in the literature of the world. But the public got lost in his symbolism, and his deeper concerns did not interest them. Subsequent books were ignored or dismissed, and so even though he lived until the 1890s he practically ceased writing until, near the end of his life, he completed the short novel *Billy Budd,* which was not published until 1924.

Moby Dick is a superb account of whaling, some say the best ever written, but it is much more than that. The great white whale, Moby Dick, was "the gliding great demon of the seas of life;" he was "that intangible malignity which has been from the beginning; to whose dominion even the modern Christians ascribe one-half of the world. . . . All that most maddens and torments; all that stirs up the lees of things; all truth with malice in it; all that cracks the sinews and cakes the brain; all the subtle demonisms of life and thought; all evil . . ." And as for Captain Ahab, his obsession with killing the whale symbolized the belief that evil could be met and conquered by courage and iron will. But he does not succeed, and he and his ship the *Pequod* are destroyed by Moby Dick. In part Melville seems to be saying that evil exists in the very nature of the universe, that it is part of God's design for humanity, and that to seek to destroy it is to defy God and invite the supreme punishment. Melville also seems to admire and praise those who have the courage and the iron will to defy a hostile universe even if they inevitably go down to defeat. If on another level Moby Dick also represented nature and its forces, then Melville seems here to be saying that individuals cannot conquer nature any more than they can evil, and indeed will be destroyed in their attempt—an observation given further meaning in our own time when technological encroachments on nature threaten to backfire. Melville pondered humanity's fate, as the greatest writers have always done, but he did not resolve it. Even if he was defeated in this attempt, perhaps it was the attempt that mattered.

Music and the Arts   If the United States produced men of extraordinary talent and originality in literature, it was not quite so fortunate in the other arts. Yet music and the fine arts became vital to American life, even though there were no American Beethovens or Rembrandts.

Aspiring and serious composers tried their hands at symphonies, oratorios, and even operas. Americans enthusiastically welcomed touring European artists such as the great Norwegian violinist, Ole Bull, and "the Swedish Nightingale," Jenny Lind. Indeed the enthusiasm for Jenny Lind, whose success paved the way for other touring artists, was probably unequaled until the first tour of the Beatles, and perhaps not even then. Thousands of people swarmed the wharf to see her arrival, the crowds were so dense that her carriage could barely make its way to her hotel, which was surrounded by thirty thousand people. One enterprising operator, who possessed what he said was one of her gloves, charged twenty-five cents to kiss the outside of it, fifty cents to kiss the inside. Hats, coats, oysters, cigars, and other items were named after her. Said one paper: "New York is conquered, a hostile army or fleet could not effect a conquest so complete."

Americans also began to support the introduction of music into the public schools, and they purchased song books by the thousands—so many, in fact, that one gets the impression a majority of Americans spent their time around pianos harmonizing. The New England composer of hymns, Lowell Mason—still known for such compositions as "Nearer, My God, to Thee"—was enormously successful as a publisher of hymn books. His *Carmina Sacra* of 1841 brought him over $100,000, an incredible sum for the time. Other hymn books and popular songbooks were equally successful.

The tradition of folk music was strengthened and extended as humble people preserved the old songs and composed new ones to celebrate or ease their labors in the field, at sea, on the canals and steamboats, and in the forests. And spirituals and work songs provided sounds of inner and community strength for slaves. Popular songs or ballads dominated the American musical scene with their romantic sentimental tunes and lyrics on such themes as love lost and found, death, hope and sorrow, home, family, nostalgia—songs which, as the touring English baritone, Henry Russell, said, "made music the vehicle of grand thoughts and noble sentiments." It was the vehicle for a large bank account as well, for Russell himself made a fortune from singing such songs. Many of these are still widely known, among them "Woodman, Spare that Tree," "Rocked in the Cradle of the Deep," "Bury Me Not on the Lone Prairie," "Listen to the Mocking Bird," and "My Darling Nelly Gray."

Christy's Minstrels. This ornate poster advertised the varied talents of the Minstrels' blackface entertainers.

Starting in the 1830s or earlier, the minstrel show became one of the most popular forms of musical and theatrical entertainment. A variety show and a forerunner of vaudeville, the minstrel show consisted of a group of white singers and dancers in blackface performing "darky" songs, jokes, and dances, and it did a great deal to crystallize the nineteenth-century stereotype of black character and humor. It drew from a wide variety of sources for songs, many of which became immensely popular. It helped to promote Dan Emmett's ballads and walkarounds, such as "Blue Tail Fly," and "Dixie." But the greatest of the song writers was Stephen Foster whose famous minstrel songs, "My Old Kentucky Home," "Old Black Joe," "Old Folks at Home" (or "Swanee River"), and others, made minstrel leaders and song publishers rich, but brought little financial reward to Foster. The widespread popularity of such songs is suggested by a newspaper report of the effect of "Old Folks at Home" a year after it first appeared:

> Pianos and guitars groan with it, night and day; sentimental young ladies sing it; sentimental young men warble it in midnight serenades . . . all the bands play it; amateur flute players agonize over it . . . the street organs grind it out at every hour.

Most of Foster's songs were sentimental ballads as popular as his minstrel tunes, songs such as "Jeanie with the Light Brown Hair," "Gentle Annie," and "Beautiful Dreamer." His themes and melodies had great appeal to the romantic sentiments of the age.

The Arcade, Providence, Rhode Island. An example of Greek Revival architecture designed by Russell Warren.

In architecture, the great achievements of the colonial and early Federal periods were replaced by a spreading mediocrity and increasingly feeble imitation, and by mid-century American buildings, public as well as private, were greatly influenced by the so-called Greek Revival and the Gothic style, neither of which really reflected the American environment, physical or social. A bustling, expanding America, however, seeking to proclaim its own progress, delighted in throwing up buildings loosely inspired by Greek temples but often with no recollection of their balance and proportion. Capitol buildings, courthouses, customs houses, banks, college buildings, churches, and private homes all felt the impact of an ill-remembered classical influence or the heavy-handed weight of the gothic. Early Federal architects such as Charles Bulfinch, Richard Upjohn, James Renwick, and others had created buildings under these influences that often had charm and appeal. But sometimes they failed, and the worst products of their successors sometimes achieved a grotesque abandon that could be comic, and have at last acquired a certain dignity simply by the passage of time.

Although the goal of aspiring painters and sculptors was to study in Europe, the home of the Old Masters, competent professional training became a reality in America with the founding of such institutions as the Pennsylvania Academy of Fine Arts. A limited public found it possible at least to become acquainted with the arts, if not tastefully informed about them, through the establishment of art museums and galleries, such as Peale's in Philadelphia, although the early museums offered a hodgepodge of attractions besides painting. Touring exhibitions from Europe also helped broaden public acquaintance with the arts, although many of the presumed Old Masters on exhibit were not the originals but copies. Private American collectors, moreover, such as Lumen Reed and Thomas Jefferson Bryan of New York, began to open their collections occasionally for public viewing.

An important development in the promotion of American art, as well as in the stimulation of public appreciation and taste, was the founding of the American Art-Union in New York in 1839. By using what was essentially a lottery technique the Art-Union raised funds for the purchase of paintings by Americans, got their works distributed, and made available to members thousands of engravings and prints. The Cosmopolitan Art-Union of Ohio, founded after the New York operation violated the antilottery laws of that state, had some thirty-eight thousand members, distributed an art magazine, and made grants for study abroad by young American artists. Government, too, became involved in the arts. State and local governments commissioned portraits, busts, statues, and paintings to adorn their public buildings, and although the federal government also granted some commissions for works of art, efforts to establish a national policy and program of government patronage and sponsorship were not realized. American artists profited, of course, from such commissions, although many foreigners did also.

The work of American artists varied greatly in accordance with their interests, their conception of what the public wanted, and the larger influences of nationalism and romanticism. Early in the life of the republic, Gilbert Stuart, who had had a successful career in England, returned to the United States to paint several portraits of Washington and other prominent Americans. Samuel F. B. Morse painted a portrait of Lafayette to celebrate the French general's return to America in 1824. Grand themes were treated on a huge scale by such painters as John Trumbull, Rembrandt Peale, and Washington Allston. George Catlin devoted his skill to hundreds of pictures of Indian life, highly detailed and of great historical value. Painters such as William Mount and George Caleb Bingham painted pictures of everyday life—Mount of the lives of his Long Island neighbors, and Bingham of life in Missouri, particularly on the great rivers.

Dozens of artists were commissioned by Currier and Ives to record scenes familiar to Americans: horse racing, barns in winter, trains, hunting and fishing, almost every conceivable moment in American life. Their lithographs sold by the thousands. Romanticism found strong expression also in landscape painting by American artists. Painting the natural beauties of the Hudson River area and the Catskills occupied a number of artists known as the "Hudson River school." Later, other painters caught on canvas the natural wonders of the Rockies.

Sculptors found a good market for classical figures and portrait statues for the homes and gardens of the wealthy, as well as for public buildings, such as Greenough's statue of Washington. Hiram Powers created the sensation of

Raftsmen Playing Cards *by George Caleb Bingham.*

the times with his nude *Greek Slave,* small miniatures of which graced tables in thousands of homes.

American art was vigorous in the first decades of the republic, though it hardly offered serious competition to the European tradition.

Recreation and Entertainment

One of the most popular forms of entertainment was the theater. Although some condemned it and popular opinion generally took a dim view of actors—a view not altogether without justification—the theater soon became an established feature of American life. By 1850 there were theaters and resident companies in all the larger towns and cities as far west as Iowa, and touring companies both American and English traveled extensively through the country. Famed English actors such as Edmund Kean and William Charles Macready, and well-known actresses such as Fanny Kemble made frequent appearances in the United States and acquired loyal fans. Such loyalty, which was granted to American actors and actresses as well, was sometimes carried to extremes. In 1849 a mob of New York supporters of the

American actor Edwin Forrest charged the theater where the English actor Macready was playing, and in the ensuing riot twenty-two persons were killed and a large number injured.

The quality of performances was greatly affected by the variety of offerings a company felt compelled to present. In a single week it might present a melodrama, a Shakespearean tragedy, an opera, an eighteenth-century comedy, and a fairy-tale play. All theatrical evenings ended with an afterpiece, a farcical takeoff on any subject. Nothing was immune from its barbs: Shakespeare, opera, politicians, contemporary events, historical incidents.

Shakespeare was the most performed playwright in America in these years, although his works were almost always altered drastically. Scenes were dropped, new ones were added, lines were changed, and emphases shifted, all to make sure that morality triumphed and to achieve the happy ending so pleasing to audiences of the day. *King Lear* was altered so that both Lear and Cordelia survived, which destroyed the tragedy. Since audiences loved special effects, irrelevant pageantry and song were often added to Shakespearean plays. Other English dramatists were frequently performed, and Sheridan's *School for Scandal* was particularly popular. Many plays by continental dramatists were translated for the American stage.

But it was the melodrama which was most popular and which set the tone for the American theater. The melodrama had no limits on character, time, place, or subject matter. Its tone could be equally varied: serious, comic, happy, tragic. Its purpose, however, never varied—to promote virtue. The early American playwright and theater manager, William Dunlap, wrote: "The stage paints Virtue in her holiday garments, and though storms sometimes gather around her radiant head, the countenance of the heavenly maid, resigned, serene and meek, beams forth, after a season of patient suffering, with ineffable refulgence." And virtue was embodied in "that height of human good, enchanting woman." The conflict and excitement of the melodrama came from the danger posed to the heroine's goodness and virtue. That danger was always presented in physical, sexual terms, and it came in the person of the villain who was completely despicable and unprincipled, a man who rejected all morality: "Away with conscience—justice—all the checks that lie upon my path!" Villains were often foreign, and if not were characterized by foreign manners. The villain, of course, was always defeated. The hero, though his goodness could be occasionally marred (though always repaired), was generally perfect, his characteristics described by one play's villain in this manner:

> He is filled to the very brim with the old fashioned principles of virtue, chastity, sobriety, and all that sort of stuff. . . . This pious, chaste, virtuous, timid young man has lived all his days in the country. His body has been fed with milk and his mind with sermons.

Practically every melodrama also had an old father, whose constant advice defined the moral points of the play in case the audience failed to get them through the action. Though farmers or workmen were seldom heroes, they were treated with great veneration, being regarded as the repository of all sound wisdom. It was the friend from the countryside who always came up with the crucial wisdom that saved the day, as in this bit of advice to a city businessman whose family was falling victim to fashionable and foreign ways:

> You must sell your house and all these gee-gaws, and bundle your wife and daughter off to the country. There let them learn economy, true independence and home virtues, instead of foreign follies.

The melodrama, despite or perhaps because of its false conventions, stilted language, stereotyped characters, and simplified morality, was immensely popular; for it emphasized American superiority, the greatness of the United States, the virtues of the soil and simple labor, and the triumph of good.

In the city Americans seeking diversion could also be entertained by the exhibits of P. T. Barnum, who developed the best-known amusement center in the United States, with its collection of curiosities both genuine and "humbug" drawn from all parts of the world. These included the famous midget, General Tom Thumb, giants over seven feet tall, fat men, bearded ladies, trained fleas, mermaids, and other wonders. The traveling animal shows and acrobatic troupes of earlier days had by the 1840s been brought together with the rings and riding shows of the city amphitheaters, and the American circus was born—a form of mass entertainment that was to delight generations to come.

In the West where life was hard, men in the early days sought relief from their labors in boisterous competition, testing their strength and skills in a variety of sports. Pitching quoits (pushing a twenty- to sixty-pound stone from the shoulder somewhat like the modern shotput), lifting weights, running, jumping, pole-vaulting (for distance, not height), tug-of-war, and wrestling were always popular. A game that many today would regard as cruel was gander pulling, in which men rode bareback toward a gander hanging by its feet from a tree and tried to pull off its neck. The gander's greased neck and constant fluttering made this a difficult task at best. Horse racing was also popular, and organized racing appeared with advancing settlement and the rise of the county fair by 1840. The inevitable betting brought frequent charges against these "unlawful assemblages of idle and dissolute persons who had congregated for the purpose of *running horses*," but such opposition met with no success.

In frontier areas contests to prove who was the better man were common. Friendly "rasslin" ended when one man was thrown and usually produced no injuries, but with rowdies and whiskey present fights took place in which the rules allowed for striking, biting, hair-pulling, scratching, kicking, eye-gouging, and stomping on a downed man.

Shooting matches were another way of proving who was the better man, and a common sport, with perhaps a half barrel of whiskey or a beef or a turkey as prize. Targets were from seventy-five to a hundred yards away, usually consisting of an inch square of white paper with a diamond hole in the center set in a blackened circle on a board.

Women did not participate in such activities, or even watch them. But they were involved in the "sociables" which brought people together, often for a combination of work and play such as house-raising, logrolling, and corn-husking. In corn-husking, for example, neighbors young and old, male and female, would gather at the appointed barn, leaders would be picked, sides chosen, the corn divided into equal piles, and the battle was on to see which side finished first. Whooping, shouting, and much merriment marked the contest, enlivened when some young fellow found a red ear of corn and exercised the right this granted to kiss the girl of his choice. Afterward the company enjoyed food, liquid refreshments, and a barn dance. Quilting parties, spinning parties, apple-parings, rag-cuttings, carpet-tackings, wool-pickings, and chicken- and goose-pickings were all turned into sociable occasions in the West and rural America.

Among young men and women, a gathering known as a frolic, a hoedown, or a bussing bee was popular. Among Quakers, Disciples of Christ, Methodists, Baptists, and Presbyterians who frowned on dancing such a gathering was known as a play party. It was really the same thing, but the participants did not have to feel they were engaged in sinful activity. Frolics involved many variations of singing, marching, choosing partners, skipping, shuffling, and kissing:

Green grow the rushes, O!
Kiss her quick and let her go!
But don't you muss her ruffle, O!

Weddings were important occasions in the West for socializing and entertainment. Everybody in the neighboring area was invited and the celebrating usually lasted several days. Spelling bees and singing schools were also made into social activities. Spelling contests were not confined to the one-room schoolhouse and involved not just girls and boys, but young and old, families, and even communities. In the villages and towns, debating clubs, moot courts, and literary societies also let people get together and were as much social as intellectual in purpose and character.

Though the Americans were a hard-working people, they also clearly found time to play and to enjoy themselves. For most of rural America, such activities were simple and unsophisticated, but they lightened the burdens of everyday life and bound families and communities together in ways which the developing mass entertainments of the rising cities did not.

Profile: HORACE MANN

Without question the most important and influential educator in America in the decades before the Civil War, Horace Mann was a classic example of the power of self-improvement through education. Born in 1796 into an old but poor Massachusetts family, Mann had a miserable childhood marked by poverty, ill health, repression, and fear. Learning little by day in a totally inadequate school run with a cruel discipline, he suffered the torments of the damned at night brought on by the grim and terrifying visions preached by the local minister.

At the age of twenty he studied for six months under a tutor and gained admittance to Brown University, from which he graduated with high honors. Unusually talented, he studied law and was admitted to the Massachusetts bar in 1823. He became a highly successful lawyer and politician, serving in the state legislature for ten years from 1827 to 1837. Interested in various reform causes, he was particularly and not unnaturally concerned about education.

With the establishment of a state board of education in 1837, Mann to everyone's surprise gave up his law practice and political career to become secretary to the board, seeing in the position the opportunity to bring about fundamental reforms in education. Education had been the instrument for his own success in conquering a disabling background, and he wanted to see this opportunity extended to all.

In the twelve years he held the office of secretary to the state board he managed to transform completely the Massachusetts school system from one characterized by short terms, dilapidated buildings, untrained and underpaid teachers, and unproductive teaching methods to one identified by minimum required terms, public support, higher salaries, professionally trained teachers, an enriched curriculum, and new and effective teaching methods. To bring this about he organized teachers' conventions and institutes, established teacher-training schools, founded and edited the <u>Common School Journal</u>, visited and studied school systems in England, Ireland, Scotland, Holland, Belgium, France, Switzerland, and Germany, and carried his message on change to the public in numerous speeches and lectures and to private and influential citizens in letters and conversations. But most importantly, he issued a series of twelve annual reports which contained not only extensive statistical data on the state of education, but discussions of educational problems and needs and their proposed solutions. These reports circulated widely abroad and in the other states of the Union. The New York legislature, for example, printed and distributed eighteen thousand copies of his Fifth Report. Mann's influence abroad was considerable. He greatly influenced, for instance, the South American educational reformer and political figure, Domingo Sarmiento who became President of Argentina. Sarmiento became a close friend of Mann and his wife, and used Mann's ideas and American teachers and teaching methods to promote educational development in Chile and Argentina.

Mann attached special importance to education not only as a practical tool for getting ahead in the world, but as essential to developing good citizens. Seeing education as the key to the success of the republic led him to insist that the process and direction of education must also be democratic, a reflection of the society it nourished.

His own assessment of his task appeared in a letter to his wife: "If I can be the means of ascertaining what is the best construction of schoolhouses; what are the best books, what is the best mode of instruction; if I can discover by what application of means a non-thinking, non-reflecting, non-speaking child can most surely be trained into a noble citizen, ready to contend for the right and to die for the right; if I can only obtain and diffuse throughout the state a few good ideas on these and similar subjects, may I not flatter myself that my ministry has not wholly been in vain?"

Mann closed out his life with two terms in Congress, an unsuccessful campaign for the governorship of Massachusetts, and then the presidency of Antioch College in Yellow Springs, Ohio in 1852. Badly in debt and shaken by internal dissension and poor management, the college was sold for debt in 1859 and then reorganized. His health shattered by these and other troubles, Mann died within a few weeks of this disaster. But he lived long enough to give the Commencement Address that year, which concluded with words often used to characterize the principal motivation of his life. He told the graduates of that year: "Be ashamed to die until you have won some victory for humanity." He must have died in some pride himself.

Chapter 10
THE CIVIL WAR

The Spirit of the Times
IN THE EYES OF EUROPE

Whenever the Americans abandon the plow and take up the sword, from the Revolution to Vietnam, others seem irresistibly drawn to the spectacle. This has held true not only when the Americans have taken up arms against other peoples, but even when they have turned upon one another. Certainly this was the case in the Civil War, which much of the Western world watched in horrified fascination.

For many, the spectacle of the United States engaged in bloody internal conflict confirmed their suspicions of the fraudulent character of democracy itself and hopefully promised the removal from the international scene of a powerful united democratic nation that might well pose a threat to older established institutions and traditions. When news of the conflict reached England, it was the reactionary Sir John Ramsden who proclaimed in Parliament, "The republican bubble has burst," and Sir Edward Bulwer-Lytton explained in a public speech why this would benefit Europe:

> If it could have been possible that, as population and wealth increased, all the vast continent of America ... could have remained under one form of government ... why, then, America would have hung over Europe like a gathering and destructive thunder-cloud. No single kingdom in Europe could have been strong enough to maintain itself against a nation that had once consolidated the gigantic resources of a quarter of the globe.

In Spain, editorial opinion used the occasion of the war to denounce the horrors of democracy and republicanism:

> The history of the model republic can be summed up in a few words. It came into being by rebellion. It was founded on atheism. It was populated by the dregs of all the nations in the world. It has lived without the law of God or man. Within a hundred years, greed has ruined it. Now it is fighting like a cannibal, and it will die in a flood of blood and mire.

Yet there were those who took a very different view. In England the great liberal Member of Parliament, John Bright, who had long argued for reform at home on

285

THE EAGLE'S NEST.
"THE UNION: IT MUST AND SHALL BE PRESERVED"

*Anti-Confederate propaganda. Northern bitterness towards Southern
disruption of the Union is reflected in this cartoon with vipers and rats
hatching from the eggs representing the Southern states.*

the American example, wrote reassuringly to his American friend, John Greenleaf
Whittier, that

> we are witnessing a great change of opinion, or opinions hitherto silent are being
> expressed. In every town a great meeting is being held to discuss "the American
> question" and the vote is almost everywhere unanimously in favor of the North. The
> rich and the titled may hate the republic, but the people do not.

Not only in England, but on the Continent as well, workers whose jobs were
wiped out as a consequence of the cotton shortage stemming from the Northern
blockade of Southern ports held firm for the North in the midst of their own
economic distress. The unemployed cotton mill workers of Manchester, for example, sent a letter of support to Lincoln and praised the Emancipation Proclamation. Workers in many other towns as well did much the same. In France, the
journalist Eugène Forcade summed up the opinion of equally distressed factory
workers in Normandy:

> While our government shows definite partiality for the Southern cause, in the hope of
> obtaining the raw material for our cotton workers, these same workers take a very

different view of the matter. If they were asked the following question: "Which do you prefer—victory for the South, with the reappearance of cotton on our markets and the continuance of slavery, or the emancipation of the whole of the Negro race with unemployment and hunger persisting among you as a result?"—we are quite certain that their answer would be: "Without a moment's hesitation, we would rather go on suffering poverty and hunger than see four million human beings continue to live in bondage."

There is no doubt that many ordinary people everywhere felt that the cause of democracy—not only in terms of black freedom but a free society itself—was tied up with the successful defense of the Union by the North. When the war ended, common people everywhere gathered to praise the North for its victory. In England, the official labor paper, the Beehive, summed up the meaning of the great conflict as part of the larger struggle of peoples everywhere to improve their lot in the world:

> But in the presence of the glorious triumph of our principles on the other side of the Atlantic let us take heart. Our opponents told us that Republicanism was on its trial. They insisted on our watching what they called its breakdown. They told us plainly that it was forever discredited in England. Well, we accepted the challenge. We staked our hopes boldly on the result. We forced them to keep their hands off when they wanted to break into the ring. We cheered on our Republican friends to their work, bidding them remember that the eyes of Europe were upon them. They have not disappointed us. Under a strain such as no aristocracy, no monarchy, no empire could have supported, Republican institutions have stood firm. It is we, now, who call upon the privileged classes to mark the result. They may rely upon it that a vast impetus has been given to Republican sentiments in England, and that they will have to reckon with it before long.

The Beehive was right. The day of reckoning came two years later when the workingmen of England at last gained the franchise from a conservative government. In Holland a conservative regime was overthrown and a new liberal government came into being that carried a bill abolishing slavery in the Dutch colonies. And in Sweden constitutional reforms partly modeled on the American experience were achieved, prompting the American minister in Stockholm to write: "Who shall not say that the great example of our own beneficent institutions has not had much to do with this, and other liberal efforts in various directions?"

The Growing Gap Between

It is not easy to understand the coming of the Civil War without some sense of the widening gap that had developed between the South and the rest of the country in the decades before the conflict began. For despite things held in common, the historic ties that bound North and South together, the fact is that the South increasingly found itself outside the mainstream of American development.

Even the most casual knowledge indicates that the South was not deeply involved or participating significantly in the major experiences that were shaping and influencing so much of American society in the first half of the nineteenth century. By 1860 industry and manufacturing had become a significant element in the life of the rest of the nation. Yet the South possessed only fifteen percent of the manufacturing establishments of the country, and these were almost entirely small-scale operations. Of the almost $2 billion worth of manufactured goods produced in the United States in 1860, less than ten percent came from the South. Moreover, the South had not developed the necessary technical resources to support an expanding industrial system. Its textile enterprises relied upon the North for machinery, skilled workers, and technicians. The South was little affected by the growth and life of cities, which were important influences in the North and West. In 1860 there were only 5 Southern towns with populations between 20,000 and 50,000: Charleston, Richmond, Mobile, Memphis, and Savannah, and only one city with over 50,000, New Orleans with 168,000. Yet New York City had over 1,000,000, Philadelphia 500,000, and Boston 177,000. By 1860, in fact, approximately thirty-five percent of the population of the Northeast lived in cities, and the large city was becoming familiar in the West, as witness Chicago and Cincinnati. Along with industrial and urban growth the North had a wealthy urban business class and an industrial urban working class, both minor elements in Southern life. All this meant that attitudes of mind, values, points of view, interests, experiences were developing elsewhere in the nation that were beyond the ken of most Southerners.

But this was not the full story of an increasing Southern isolation from major American experiences. The South had nothing like the influx of immigrants of the rest of the country. Approximately six million immigrants entered the country in the decades between the founding of the republic and the Civil War, and less than fifteen percent of them settled in the South, which was one reason why the South in 1860 had less than one-third of the population of the country.

Furthermore, the South was not swept up in the great democratic reform impulse that affected the North. Of the dozens of communitarian experiments, only two were tested on Southern soil. The peace movement had little or no appeal. The free public school movement was largely ignored. The abolition movement was actively repressed. The women's rights movement found the South totally unresponsive, and Southern feminists such as the Grimke sisters had to go North to satisfy their urge to agitate. Union organization was sporadic, limited, and aroused little interest. The movement for penal reform did find support in the South, but many states refused to vote the taxes necessary to support state penitentiaries. The temperance movement also had support in the South, but was destined to failure here as elsewhere in the country. The only significant Southern expression of humanitarian reform came in the founding of schools and institutions for the physically and mentally handicapped.

In terms of the major experience of westward migration and settlement, once the move into the Old Southwest had been completed, the "boundaries" of the South had been drawn. Southerners, it is true, had migrated into lower Ohio, Indiana, and Illinois, but this had been before 1830 for the most part, and furthermore they could not take slavery with them. The net result was that the South remained unaffected by the influence of the free farming class which formed the basis of Western society. Moreover, by 1860 the South had lost its political and economic ties with the West, which in the past had seen Western produce flow through Southern ports and had made it possible for a Southerner, Andrew Jackson, to be looked upon as much the spokesman of the West as he was of the South. By 1860 the West was linked by rail to the Northeast, not to the South, and the flow of economic, social, and political traffic was between those regions.

Finally, the South increasingly found itself outside the main arena of American nationalism, and indeed after 1830 began to develop conceptions and points of view that defined the Southern experience in national terms of its own. Certainly by 1830 the South was proposing a political definition of the nation quite different from that held by the rest of the country. More and more Southerners were accepting Calhoun's argument that the Constitution came from a compact of separate sovereign states rather than from the authority of the people as a whole, and that therefore a state could pass on the constitutionality of an act of Congress and decide its own terms of association with the Union. Moreover, the South had consistently challenged key aspects of economic development as defined by Northern spokesmen of nationalism, seeing, for example, the rise of a protected manufacturing interest as weakening the Southern economy within the nation. Furthermore, the South increasingly regarded national expansion westward not as contributing to its own security but as weakening it, unless slavery were allowed access to the West. Significantly, Southern talk of expansion began to direct attention toward Mexico, Central America, and the islands of the Caribbean. In terms of cultural development as well, the South was little involved in the call for a literature and art distinctly American in tone and geared to an expression of American national interests, themes, and experiences. The South tended to rely on an imported culture, such as it was, seeing more in Sir Walter Scott than it did in Emerson. Its own writers starved, left, or like William Gilmore Simms were painfully conscious of never being accepted as an integral part of Southern society. Pro-South to the core, William Lowndes Yancey declared that the South did not need literature: "our poetry is in our lives; our fiction will come when truth has ceased to satisfy us; and as for our history, we have made about all that has glorified the United States."

In all these ways, then, the South steadily became isolated from the main lines of American development. Many Southerners were left with the uneasy feeling that the North was a foreign country where things were done differently and with whom the South had less and less in common. Looked at from the broad perspective of time, no one today would say that this gap implied that the South was inferior to the rest of the country. But that differences existed was undeniable, and those differences increasingly made it difficult for the sections to *understand* one another. The gap that had opened up between the South and the rest of the country made difficult the kind of communication that was essential to any reasonable solution of disputes— North and South were simply operating on different wavelengths and the messages were garbled or not getting through at all. As so often happens, the state of cultural communication lagged behind that of technical communication. These differences in themselves were not the cause of war, though men have gone to war for less cause. But they did create a situation in which war became possible if disagreement should arise so serious that either side felt threatened by the other.

The Root of Conflict

Serious disagreement did indeed arise, and that disagreement centered on slavery. Lincoln observed in the Second Inaugural what few doubted at the time, that "the slaves constituted a peculiar and powerful interest. All knew that this interest was somehow the cause of the war."

Somehow the cause of the war—that may be as close as we are ever likely to get in seeking the precise source of the conflict. But it is hard to escape the conviction that it was slavery that lay at the root of the Civil War. For behind every conflict of interest between the South and the rest of the country, behind every distinction that tended to set the South off from the rest of the nation, behind every disputed value, behind every disagreement in policy lay the influence of slavery. Thus, though slavery was confined to the South, the effects of the institution stretched throughout the country, entangling the lives of Americans even where there were no slaves, even among those who cared no more for slaves as human beings than did those who owned them.

Ironically, the South that enslaved the black became itself enslaved, a prisoner of the very institution it sought to protect and preserve. Even its political victories could not have been won without the persons it held in bondage. It is worth remembering that at the center of every major Southern political victory on the national scene lay the extra votes the Southern states had in the House of Representatives as a consequence of the rule in the Constitution that allowed a slave to be counted as three-fifths of a person in the determination of the population figures upon which the assignment of congressional representation was made. This was the case, for example, in the Kansas-Nebraska Act of 1854, which repealed that part of the Missouri Compromise of 1820 forbidding slavery in all lands north of 36° 30', and which declared that the people of the territories were free to determine the nature of their own institutions, thus reopening the whole issue of slavery in the West.

But the irony was even greater. For after 1830 the South, home of Jefferson, developed a defense of slavery that involved a rejection of the democratic heritage to which Jefferson had contributed so much. It was Calhoun, in his elaborate intellectual defense of the South, who laid the philosophical base for the justification of slavery. Men were not born free and equal, he argued. Nor could civilization progress on such an assumption. Those who are less blessed in competence support by their labor the superior and wiser who can then devote their higher abilities to the advance of the public good and the progress of civilization and culture, including the successful achievement of self-government. So it had been in ancient Greece. So indeed, ran the argument, it was in the industrial North where the industrial wage slave supported the progress of Northern society. But the black slavery of the South was a superior system, for it provided benevolent care and treatment of the inferior slave labor absent in the brutal exploitation of the wage slave of the North. Because of its superiority, therefore, black slavery should not only be protected and preserved in the South, but it should be given sanction throughout all America. If the South could not be guaranteed the means to preserve its institutions from assault within the Union, then it should be permitted to withdraw and go its own way.

These ideas were developed and embroidered by many others in the South. George Fitzhugh argued that extending liberty to those unfit for it, as was done in the North, led to the disorder and insecurity characteristic of Northern society. William Grayson, in *The Hireling and the Slave,* took to heroic couplets to make the point that slaves enjoyed a more pleasant and secure existence than factory workers. Dr. Josiah Nott and George Gliddon explained the presumed inferiority of the black by marshaling evidence that they claimed proved the separate origin of the races. This argument caused some confusion since it contradicted the Scriptures, which were heavily relied upon in *The Pro-Slavery Argument,* a collection of essays published in 1852 to prove that slavery was an institution sanctioned by God. Such views not only conflicted with the more liberal turn in religious thought developing in the rest of the country with its emphasis upon the Christian ethic of the New Testament, but also clashed with the democratic conception of basic human dignity and with the clearly held belief that all men were equal in their right to rise in accordance with their abilities. Those in the North who had not yet risen as far as they wished, or who had ambitions for their children, were not to be persuaded that the answer to present inequalities or injustices lay in permanent servitude. At any rate, in sermons, newspaper editorials, public speeches, and novels, the argument defending slavery was spread throughout the South and widely accepted from 1830 on.

At the same time, the South closed off all discussion that challenged its views and instituted a censorship which would have shocked Jefferson who had strongly believed in the necessity of free speech, a free press, and the virtues of an open mind. Abolitionist literature was seized by Southern postmasters and destroyed. Outspoken, even mild, opponents of slavery were harassed out of the region. College professors were dismissed from their posts for views uncongenial to Southern defenders of slavery. The press was literally closed to any opposition views, as was the church and the public forum. The net result was that the heralded democratic process of resolving problems by free and open discussion was effectively muzzled.

Yet the challenge went beyond the borders of the South itself. For the slave states worked to suppress antislavery activity in the rest of the Union. They sought to get the nonslave states to suppress antislavery societies, activities, and publications, and succeeded in getting the House of Representatives to pass a resolution forbidding the discussion of slavery in that branch of Congress for eight years. Moreover, the passage of the Fugitive Slave Act in 1850 permitted any slaveholder to enter a nonslave state, take a fugitive before any judge, and on the sole basis of the slaveholder's testimony receive legal permission to return the fugitive to servitude. Thus in states whose citizens took pride in their moral commitment to due process of

*The idyllic and the real. The Currier and Ives image of slaves as joyous
and carefree, their lives full of singing and dancing thanks to the generosity
of their owner helped to sustain the Southern defense of slavery as a
benevolent system.*

law, such rights as those to legal counsel, habeas corpus, trial by jury, and
questioning of witnesses were violated in their very midst. It was in part this
situation that brought a favorable response to Lincoln's observation that "if
free negroes should be made *things,* how long, think you, before they will
begin to make *things* out of poor white men?"

But the threat of the proslavery argument pushed into Northern society in
other ways as well, notably in the dispute over slavery in the western territories. Here the slave states won a menacing victory in 1854 with the passage
of the Kansas-Nebraska Act, which reversed the exclusion of slavery from
the Louisiana Purchase north of 36° 30' except for Missouri. Different views
of what constituted the nation were at stake here, since the slave states
argued that the territories were the property of the states and so any individual could take slaves into the territories, while the nonslave states argued
that the territories were the property of the people of the nation, and so the
national government, which possessed the power to grant statehold, could
set the conditions for admission including that of the exclusion of slavery.
But the heart of this issue was the presence of slaves in the West.

It is idle now to speculate on how serious was the possibility of slavery
becoming a successful institution in the West, but we do know the reaction

In sharp contrast to the comfortable existence depicted on the left is this
stereograph of slaves in a Georgia cottonfield.

of Western farmers and others to the idea. The free farming class of the West
had no desire to see the full paraphernalia of a slave society—elitist, restric-
tive, unprogressive, as they perceived it—move in on their established communities where they pretty much ran their own show. The very contempt
that Western farmers had for blacks, whom they did not regard as their
equals, made them suspicious of and hostile to any attempt to introduce
slavery in the West. Lincoln understood this fear and played upon it with
great success. In Illinois he declared:

> The whole nation is interested that the best use shall be made of these
> Territories. We want them for homes of free white people. This they cannot
> be, to any considerable extent, if slavery shall be planted within them. Slave
> States are places for poor white people to remove from, not remove to. New
> free States are the places for poor people to go to, and better their condition.
> For this use the nation needs these Territories.

Immigrants and eastern workers alike were also swayed by the argument
that slavery must be confined to the South and not allowed to expand in the
West.

And so on all matters of vital interest there arose grave differences between the South and the rest of the nation, and at the heart of those differences was the institution of slavery.

Southerners had become committed to a system, a way of life, strongly influenced by the institution of slavery. The vast majority of Southerners did not own slaves and in all likelihood never would, but they lived in a society where slaves were all about them and always had been, where ownership of black human beings seemed natural, where such ownership was a sign of social and economic status. Like many others in American society, less wealthy Southerners looked forward to rising in the world and acquiring the visible signs of success and advancement—that is, to owning slaves. Moreover, in a society in which blacks were deliberately kept down and prevented from expressing their natural abilities, there was little to suggest to the ordinary Southerner that blacks were not inferior beings. It occurred only to a few that the forms of inferiority had been imposed by man, not nature.

Few Southerners, moreover, were willing or able to see the degree to which their entire society was shaped and conditioned by slavery. While they certainly defended slavery as an institution, they also thought in broader terms that they were defending a way of life distinctly their own, and came to believe that only by secession could they preserve it.

But even here the South ran headlong into dispute with the North. To most people in the rest of the country the commitment to the nation as a whole, to the concept of the Union and to the democratic principles upon which it had been founded, was very strong. To them secession was the final Southern threat to *their* way of life, since the South was now proposing simply to junk the whole experiment. It was too much. If secession were accepted, where was the rule of law, of order, of stability in society? If withdrawal and fragmentation were acceptable for one minority, why not for any other? If such a process was legalized by success, what community would be safe? The newspapers raised the point bluntly: "If [the] doctrine of secession as illustrated and enforced by [its] practice is true, then there is no such thing as governmental authority or social obligation."

In sum, then, the South was making proposals and operating along lines that seemed not only contrary to but a distinct threat to the rest of the country. It turned its back upon the Northern concept of democracy, suppressed free and open discussion, tried to cut off the right to petition, kept three and a half million people in bondage, suggested that black slaves were better off than many free white laborers, argued that black slavery should be carried everywhere within the Union, demanded that the national government sanction and support all this, and when thwarted in its endeavors sought refuge in the ultimate challenge to law: secession, a doctrine which, it should be noted, was carefully left out of the constitution of the Confederacy itself. And so the war came.

The Course of the War

The election of Lincoln on a Republican party platform that, among other matters, pledged that "The normal condition of all the territory of the United States is that of freedom," was followed by the secession of the seven states

Fort Sumter. After thirty-four hours of bombardment, the flag of the Confederacy replaces the Union flag. The presence of the federal fort within the newly formed Confederacy and the crisis which developed over its exhausted supplies became the final, polarizing issue between North and South. The Southern need to assert its independent status and the Northern desire to sustain the Union clashed on the morning of April 12.

of the Deep South from December 1860 to February 1861. The Confederacy then began to take shape. After Lincoln took office on March 4, 1861, he reached the decision to resupply with food the beseiged Fort Sumter in Charleston harbor. Having already seized all other federal property in the

South except Sumter and Fort Pickens at Pensacola, Florida, the Confederacy saw no point in allowing Sumter's reinforcement. They began a bombardment on April 12, and 34 hours later Fort Sumter's commander surrendered. Reluctant to take the first shot, Lincoln's responsibility for such an action was removed by the attack. He promptly called for seventy-five thousand volunteers, the remaining Southern states of Arkansas, North Carolina, Tennessee, and Virginia then seceded, and the war was on.

The Americans have always begun their wars playing a kind of improvised, catch-up brand of conflict. They are never ready. Armies have to be created and troops trained, factories have to be converted to war production, strategy has to be conceived, and generals, who have a tendency to fight according to the experience of the last war, have to become educated to the exigencies of the one confronting them. The Civil War was no exception. Both sides were unprepared and inexperienced, as the first battle between them at Bull Run in July 1861 demonstrated. Inexperienced Northern troops broke and ran, and inexperienced Southern troops were too disorganized to pursue. After that, both sides settled down to the serious business of developing military machines appropriate to the tasks at hand.

The political goals that each side set for the war determined the military strategy of each. The South sought independence as a nation to preserve its "way of life." It had no wish to conquer and impose its will on the rest of the country. Southern strategy, therefore, was defensive: fight off the enemy, keep Union forces out of the South, and wear down the North's will to continue. The North on the other hand sought the preservation of the Union under the Constitution, and this required invasion and conquest of the seceding states.

Comparative Resources   Strategy was also influenced but not dictated by recognition of available resources. Southern leaders were well aware that they lacked the capacity to carry the war into the North, and Northern leaders were confident that they possessed the material and human resources to carry on a sustained invasion of the South. In the last analysis, resources were crucial because, other things being equal, they determined who was to win. And the South was at a clear disadvantage in basic resources.

The eleven Confederate states had a population of only nine million (three and a half million of whom were slaves), a third that of the North. Less than one million white males were of military age and over eighty percent of them ended up in uniform, which is pushing use of manpower to the limit. The South lacked an extensive industry and transportation system adequate to the speedy movement of supplies and troops from one sector to another. The South did develop an efficient munitions industry and imported much from abroad, especially in the early years of the war. It lost no battle for lack of arms and munitions, but it did become sadly deficient in other supplies both

The Gun Foundry *by John F. Weir. The industrial capacity of the North was one of its strongest assets.*

military and civilian. Finally, the concentration of Southern wealth in agriculture severely limited the Confederacy's ability to tax and to borrow, and thus finance the war.

The North on the other hand had extensive resources in manpower, industry, and money. Heavy Northern losses in battle could quickly be replaced. From May to June 1864, for example, Grant took in succession devastating losses at the Battles of the Wilderness, Spotsylvania Court House, and Cold Harbor in a major attempt to crush Lee, and still ended with his Army of the Potomac larger than when the campaign began, which was not the case with Lee. The wealth of the North enabled the government to borrow over $2.2 billion, raise $667 million in taxes, and issue additional hundreds of millions in greenbacks without the disastrous inflation and incredible shortages that had struck the South by 1864.

The North, therefore, had the capacity to carry on the kind of offensive war its political goals required. The South did not have the resources to pursue an offensive strategy, and events proved that it lacked the resources to carry out the sustained defensive strategy dictated by its political goals.

Napoleon III rejecting Confederate overtures. Jefferson Davis had failed to gain the support of Great Britain, which had signed a proclamation of neutrality, and his efforts with France proved equally unsuccessful.

Political Miscalculations   Southern leaders, however, assumed that their weakness in resources would be offset by aid from abroad and by a collapse of will in the North. Aid from abroad would come in the form of supplies, diplomatic recognition, and, they hoped, even war between Great Britain and the United States. The South relied on the need for Southern cotton to feed the mills of Britain and Western Europe, upon which depended both the livelihood of mill workers and the profits of mill owners. The South also expected to win the sympathy that usually goes to an invaded people defending their soil, their homes, and their families. Many Southerners felt that in the eyes of the world there would be an irresistible logic to their claim of the right of a people to determine their own destiny. After all, this claim had justified the American Revolution. As for the collapse of the Northern will to fight, the South was convinced that aid from abroad, internal dissension in the North, heavy casualties, and the absence of a quick victory would create sufficient public revulsion to force Lincoln to abandon the struggle.

But none of these things came to pass. The South underestimated the repugnance slavery aroused abroad. It failed to understand the identification that working-class and liberal elements abroad had with the North as a model of democracy. It failed to consider the availability of Egyptian and

Indian cotton as an alternate source of supply for European mills. It miscalculated British leadership, which was not willing to offer support until it was clear that the South was winning. It mistakenly assessed Northern public opinion, which did become discouraged and weary on occasion, but which also became angrier and more determined. And it misjudged Lincoln's political skill in keeping Northern opinion united and in fending off European involvement in the conflict.

Leadership Given Southern weakness and miscalculation, the war should have ended earlier. The fact that it did not suggests that Northern leadership was not so shrewd as it later appeared to be, after the war was over and victory was secured. In retrospect, as with nearly all wars, it is easy to impose upon the course of war a pattern of military strategy and tactics that demonstrates why the losers lost and the winners won. And this suggests that the high command of the winning side had a keener conception of the military situation than their opponents. But in many wars, the winning side simply slides sideways into victory and the losing side the same way into defeat. Successful war, like successful politics, is often a matter of trial and error until someone discovers the winning combination. Partly because many of the best officers were Southerners and chose the Confederacy, the North was plagued with a succession of overcautious and incompetent commanders, and it was not until Grant's successes in Tennessee and along the Mississippi proved his talents to Lincoln that the Union armies had a determined leader. It is astonishing, particularly early in the war, how many times Northern generals failed to follow up their opportunities. In September 1862 General George B. McClellan declined to pursue the advantage he had over Lee after the battle of Antietam when Lee's troops were exhausted and had their backs to the Potomac. Instead he allowed Lee to retreat across the river and return to Richmond. Even Grant at Shiloh earlier in that year had failed to follow and destroy an exhausted Confederate army, allowing it to escape, and thus lost the chance to end the war in the West. In short, there were blunders, missed opportunities, and tactical blindness.

Overall Strategy In looking back over the war, however, a pattern emerged that provided victory, though it was less planned from the beginning than that it simply happened to work out that way. Broadly put, this pattern included: a blockade of Southern ports which reduced successful blockade runners from nine out of ten in 1861 to one out of two in 1864; a western campaign down the Mississippi, which by 1863 with the capture of Vicksburg had cut off Texas and Arkansas and split the Confederacy; and the destruction of Southern troops, material, and supplies in a series of devastating campaigns until the Confederacy no longer had the capacity to continue, a process that began with Grant's victories in Tennessee, continued with Sherman's march through Georgia and then north through South and North Carolina in 1864–1865, and concluded with Grant's ravaging of Lee's

The battle for Vicksburg. Grant had assessed Vicksburg as the key to the Mississippi and began his attack with the assistance of Admiral David Porter, whose gunboats were used to run Grant's army past the batteries defending the city to a point on the same side of the river from which they could launch their attack. The struggle for the city was not an easy one, and Vicksburg withstood siege for eight months until it finally surrendered.

forces in Virginia during the same period and the capture of Richmond on April 3, 1865.

The major Southern effort to counteract all this climaxed in July 1863 when Lee, recognizing that defense was no longer adequate as a successful strategy, struck north into Pennsylvania, hoping for the psychological advantage of a victory on Northern soil. But in what was probably the crucial battle of the war at Gettysburg in July 1863, his forces were broken by the Union army under General George C. Meade. Although Meade did not press his advantages after the battle and Lee retreated to safety, the main question now became how long the war would last. Northern manpower and resources were beginning to take their toll. It would be almost two more years, but inexorable pressures were at work. The blockade increasingly deprived the Confederacy of access to major overseas supplies. The Mississippi River campaign severed its nation East from West. Sherman's devastation of the Southeast reduced home supplies and divided the Confederate armies in the East. The succession of bloody battles so depleted Southern manpower that by 1864 over half of its 800,000 men had been killed, wounded, or captured. Finally, Grant's relentless encirclement of Richmond pinned Lee's dwindling

The Charleston blockade. Bales of unshipped cotton choke the piers at Charleston. As the strength of the Union blockade increased it devastated the Southern economy, despite the efforts of the sizable force of blockade runners.

army to a single spot. At the end, on April 9, 1865, Lee and Grant met at Appomatox Court House west of Richmond, and the long and bitter struggle was over.

The Impact of the War

The Effect on the South The immediate ravages of war most deeply affected the South, since most of the fighting took place there with the usual consequences. Crops were destroyed, homes and farm buildings went up in flames, cities and towns were occupied. Even before he took Atlanta and began his march through Georgia to the sea, Sherman wrote to his wife that "We have devoured the land. . . . All the people retire before us and desolation is behind. To realize what war is one should follow our tracks." But this was only the most dramatic example of the misery wrought by the war.

The relentless pressure of the Federal naval blockade of Southern ports, the presence on Southern soil of Union armies, the cutting-off of Texas and Arkansas by Grant's campaign along the Mississippi River, the steady shrinking of Southern resources chewed up by military demands—all these combined to ruin the Southern economy and make miserable the lives of the people. The transportation system broke down, shortages of many goods

Richmond in ruins.

developed, coffee disappeared, salt became scarce, and inflation by 1864 led
to butter selling at $25 a pound and flour at $275 a barrel. Impoverishment
was the fate of many, and disease the byproduct of poverty. Women and
children tried to carry on the work of the farms and the shops, but by 1864
the task had become too great for many, the penalties in suffering too high.
One North Carolina woman wrote to Governor Vance pleading that her
husband be allowed to come home so that her children might be fed: "i
would like to know what he is fighting for he has nothing to fight for i don't
think that he is fighting for anything only for his family to starve." One man
wrote to his brother advising him to desert: "I would advise you to . . . go to
the other side whear you can get plenty and not stay in this one horse
barefooted naked and famine striken Southern Confederacy."

Intellectual and cultural life in the South suffered devastating blows under
the impact of the war. Many private plantation libraries were destroyed; the
importation of books was severely limited by the blockade; book publishing
was greatly restricted by lack of paper, some of the books published came
out on coarse brown paper or even wallpaper, and in all cases the number of
copies was far below the demand. Newspapers and periodicals were equally
hard hit, some being forced to suspend publication, others coming out on
half-sheets, mere slips of paper, or wallpaper. Except for a few isolated
instances, the public school system broke down, private academies closed or
survived on a day-to-day basis, colleges closed for lack of private or public

funds. The war was clearly an economic, social, and cultural disaster for the South. Scarcely a single aspect of life remained unaffected.

It is ironic that in spite of the magnitude of its defeat the South refused to accept psychologically what had happened on the battlefield. Americans have always hated to admit that they may have been wrong, and in this instance the South was completely American. Out of its postwar literature and oral reminiscences there emerged the myth of the Old South: gentle, humane, gracious, chivalric, devoted to the land, blessed with the virtues of the countryside, and sensitive to the finer things of life. Indeed this notion was what many Southerners came to believe they had been defending against the crude and vulgar materialism of Northern business and urbanism. To them the defense of that mythical Old South had been a worthy cause and still was. Few who have read *Gone With the Wind* can doubt that the South finally won in fiction what it had lost in life. It may well be that some such romanticizing had a kind of necessary therapeutic value in reassuring people that they had done no wrong, that the cause had been good; but it was later used to justify Southern treatment of blacks as inferior and also led to many absurdities. Such was the case of the South Carolina teacher who forty years after the war made his pupils hold up their right hands and swear they would never read *Uncle Tom's Cabin.* The South was to be a long time recovering from the economic, social, cultural, and psychological consequences of the war.

The Effect on the North   In the North the picture was different. Here there was no devastation of the kind that shattered the South. Economically the North did not suffer during the war. Industrial productivity, under the impetus of government contracts, held firm, though its rate of growth was slowed. The mass-production industries, such as clothing, shoes, weapons, iron and steel, did well. Opportunities for making money abounded, and new millionaires were plentiful. The business class acquired new status and influence, and out of the war came legislation reflecting business interests: higher tariffs, a national banking system, a national currency, support for transcontinental railroads. The West continued to receive Americans on the move as well as immigrants from abroad, and although farmers or their sons were often drawn from the plow to fill the ranks of Western regiments, agriculture expanded.

Culturally and intellectually the North seemed unaffected in any adverse way by the war. Public education suffered little, for while male teachers volunteered in large numbers, the gap was filled by women. Two states in the West established elementary school systems; six new normal schools for training teachers were established in as many states; and teachers' associations continued to meet regularly. Although enrollments declined on almost every campus, higher education remained by and large unaltered. Only an occasional faculty member went to war. New colleges, in fact, were founded during the war, including the Massachusetts Institute of Technology and

Vassar; and there was a marked increase in private funds for higher education from philanthropic capitalists making money from the war. It was during the war that the Morrill Act was passed, granting every state thirty
thousand acres of public land for each senator and representative in its
congressional delegation, the endowment to be used to establish colleges
primarily devoted to agriculture and the mechanical arts.

Although some periodicals may have suffered from the loss of Southern
subscribers, magazines by and large increased their circulation during the
war. Newspapers, given the great interest of the public in following the war,
boomed and expanded. Sunday issues, in fact, came into being during the
war. The number of books on loan from libraries increased, and book publishing flourished from the effort to get reading material to the soldiers in the
field.

Scientists and scholars devoted energy to the war effort, especially in such
areas as medicine, hygiene, ballistics, weights and measures, and explosives.
Some scientific studies were postponed, the meetings of some scientific
organizations suspended. But generally scientific and other scholarly work
continued unhampered. During the war James Dwight Dana published his
monumental *Manual of Geology,* Charles Francis Hall continued his arctic
explorations and researches, George Ticknor published the revised edition
of his great *History of Spanish Literature,* Dr. Thomas Parsons pursued his
translation of Dante, John Draper brought out his *History of the Intellectual
Development of Europe,* and there was a new edition of Webster's *American
Dictionary.* Scholarly organizations increased in number. The National Academy of Sciences was founded during the war, and new historical societies as
well.

With victory the North exhibited insufferable pride and self-righteousness. Ignoring its own past acceptance of slavery, forgetting its own prejudice against the blacks, conveniently putting aside memories of the break-
down of the democratic process that civil war represented, many in the
North now saw the war as a triumphant crusade, proof that they had been
right and that their institutions were not just valid but better. After all the
Union had been saved, the evil of slavery abolished from the land. The cause
was right and it had been victorious. Victory reaffirmed, although in a dis-
torted fashion, the old conviction of American superiority. This was as great
a case of myth making as the South indulged in after the war, and as
unattractive.

This myth was to be one of the painful heritages of the war. It not only
contributed to the air of sanctity assumed by the Republican Party, it helped
underwrite the power of the business interests which had contributed so
much to the victory. It prompted many to believe that Americans could do
no wrong in their relations with other peoples, an assumption of arrogance
that was to plague us as much as a hundred years later.

The End of Slavery   The war brought an end to slavery, an achievement
of enormous magnitude. Yet the damage done by the institution of slavery

PRINCIPAL CAMPAIGNS OF THE CIVIL WAR

was to be long-lasting. Racial prejudice remained; equality was not granted along with freedom. Blacks were still inferior in the eyes of most white Americans, and that view was to create a whole new series of problems with which the nation is still contending. But no move to improve the condition and status of the black American, to open up new roles for blacks in America, to broaden choices available to these new citizens, was possible until slavery as an institution had been wiped out. If most white Americans had no urge to respond to this challenge for a long time to come, blacks could now do so, and they began a long struggle that has not yet ended.

The War and National Unity   The Civil War at last made the United States a nation. The old fears for its survival were wiped out, the ghost of states' rights and secession had been exorcised in the fires of war. A new sense of national unity, of national *being,* came into the American consciousness. People no longer talked about the Union with the suggestion that its fate was in doubt. Daniel Webster in the old days was always rising to toast "the Union, now and forever, one and inseparable," as though by speaking he could make it so. After the war that use of the word Union largely disappeared from the American language, so that today anyone toasting the Union may be assumed to mean the United Steelworkers, not the United States. New problems, new issues, were to face the American people, but they were now to be dealt with within the context of a genuine nation whose fate was no longer in doubt.

The Great American Drama

The Civil War has stimulated more research, speculation, and analysis than any other event in the American experience. It grips our attention because it casts up in bold relief the extremes of the human condition. It contains both the lightest and the heaviest of the human elements; it gives us humanity in its worst moments and in its noblest.

Torn Loyalties   All war is tragic, but civil conflict is particularly so. Family against family, brother against brother, father against son, kin fighting kin. This was no simple contest with sides drawn sharply by geography, language, culture, and national boundaries. There were staunch partisans of the Union in nearly every Southern state, and defenders of the Confederacy throughout the North. Justice Wayne of Georgia remained on the bench of the Supreme Court whose Chief Justice had no sympathy with the Union cause. Thousands of Northerners served in the Confederate forces, and thousands of Southerners fought for the Union. The split in loyalties was most acute in the border states. In Louisville, Kentucky, recruits for the Union marched up one side of a street as Confederate volunteers passed down the other. Later, men from the same village would meet in battle, their opposing regiments often bearing the same name. One young Massachusetts soldier who with his fellows broke a Confederate charge, and then in pursuit of the fleeing enemy stopped to turn over the body of a fallen foe, found it to be that of his own brother.

Robert E. Lee was offered the command of the military forces on both sides, and chose the Confederacy, of which he disapproved, because of his loyalty to his native state of Virginia. Mrs. Lincoln's brothers donned the Confederate gray, and two Crittenden brothers ended as generals in opposing armies. The commander of the Confederate navy saw his son serving in the Union Navy. There is no way of knowing how many confronted the ultimate civil war on the secret battlefields of their own minds.

The Best and the Worst The war had its moments of unforgettable gallantry. Recall General Pickett heading his division on the road to Gettysburg. Passing a little girl waving the Federal flag, he took off his hat and bowed to her. When asked why he saluted the flag of the enemy, Pickett replied: "I did not salute the enemy's flag. I saluted the heroic womanhood in the heart of that brave little girl and the glorious old banner under which I won my first laurels." Or one of Grant's veterans in Virginia in 1864 at a time when it was hard to get new recruits: "Well, if new men won't finish the job, old men must, and as long as Uncle Sam wants a man, here is Ben Falls." But not for long. Two months later he fell in the battle at Spotsylvania Court House. Or sixteen-year-old Theodore Upson, explaining to his father why he was enlisting: "Father, we must have more soldiers. . . . I can go better than some others. I don't feel right to stay home any longer." And thrice-wounded Oliver Wendell Holmes, looking back upon the great fraternal struggle and recording: "You could not stand up day after day in those indecisive contests, where overwhelming victory was impossible because neither side would run when they ought when beaten, without getting at least something of the same brotherhood for the enemy that the north pole of a magnet has for the south."

Near the opposite end of the scale were incidents that border on the ridiculous. Consider the fashionable crowd which swarmed out of Washington to watch the first Battle of Bull Run as though it were a play—taking lunches, whiskey, wine, and spyglasses to observe the action. One Congressman noted that the carriages of the visitors gave the area "the appearance of a monster military picnic," and William Russell of the London *Times* wrote sarcastically that "The French cooks and hotel-keepers . . . have arrived at the conclusion that they must treble the prices of their wines and of the hampers of provisions which the Washington people are ordering to comfort themselves at their bloody Derby." Or consider the young son of Governor and then General Wise of Virginia, who fought as a cadet at New Market and rode as messenger for his father. When the Confederacy collapsed he was sent North to the home of his uncle where at dinner he was not allowed to eat with the adults because he was too young, and so ate in the nursery with the other children!

There was also a darker side to the spectacle of Americans fighting Americans, revealing the ignoble in man's nature and the less admirable but no less human side of men caught in terrible conflict with one another.

There were, in the midst of calls to duty, those who found they could not answer. Some men purchased their way out of service, paying "bounty men" to fight for them. Others fled the field of battle. The Federal rout at the first Battle of Bull Run saw men abandoning their arms and equipment and fleeing to the sanctuary of Washington—"a most woebegone rabble," Frederick Law Olmstead called them. The correspondent for the London *Times* was even less sympathetic: "I saw the beaten foot-sore, spongy-looking soldiers, officers and all the *débris* of the army filing through the mud and rain, and forming crowds in front of the spirit stores." And a captain who had witnessed the Confederate rout at Winchester wrote: "The Ladies of

Andersonville Prison. The business of supplying a prison camp became lost in the priorities of financing and managing a war for which both sides were ill-prepared. Incomplete when prisoners began arriving in enormous waves, the prison was never adequate for human survival. Even in death Andersonville failed its prisoners, unable to provide the tools with which to dig their graves.

Winchester came into the streets and begged them crying bitterly to make a stand for their sakes if not for their own honor, but to no avail. The cowards did not have the shame to make a pretense of halting." But one can easily sympathize with those for whom the strain and terror of battle became too great. Sometimes duty demands too much and offers too little.

The true ugliness in men that war releases could be seen in the side-effects of the conflict: the murder, pillage, and rape that marched with some soldiers on both sides who saw license for conduct not sanctioned in peace. Particularly horrifying was the collapse of human decency in some prisoner-of-war camps, the most notorious of which was Andersonville in Georgia where 13,000 of some 32,000 Federal prisoners died of neglect, misery, cruelty, and the unwillingness of the Federal government to exchange prisoners. Descriptions of life at Andersonville, where men died of dysentery, scurvy, gangrene, typhoid, and other ailments of neglect, still make the mind tremble as though on the rim of hell. An inspecting medical officer "observed men urinating and evacuating their bowels at the very tent doors and around the little vessels in which they were cooking their food. . . . Masses of corn-bread, bones, old rags, and filth of every description were scattered around or accumulated in large piles." And the secretary to visiting surgeon Joseph

Jones wrote to his wife: "In my travels in China, and various sections of the globe, I have witnessed many an awful sight, and beheld the dead and dying in various stages. I even now recall to mind most vividly some fearful scenes of death within the prison at Shanghai, and also cases of Cholera in the North of China, but all is nothing to what I am now beholding." Many of the prisoners lost all sense of human decency and turned upon one another, fighting, killing, stealing. One new prisoner wrote in horror: "there was a fellow next to our Tent died & some of the old prisoners went through him like a dose of salts before he had bin dead 5 minits miserable wretches hope to god I may never see sutch a case again."

The Ultimate Cost

In terms of the forces involved and the population on both sides, the Civil War was the deadliest in American history. North and South, more than 600,000 lost their lives, vast numbers of them not in glory on the field of battle but in hospitals and first-aid shelters at the hands of inept surgeons and ignorant attendants, from the absence of proper medical supplies, and a multitude of illnesses. The magnitude of the loss was equal to that in all other American wars combined, from the Revolution to Vietnam. Given the size of the population at the time, Civil War losses were enormous. The number of American dead in World War II would have had to be six times greater than it actually was to have equaled Union Army losses alone, and ten times to have equaled Confederate losses. And this does not include the tens upon tens of thousands of wounded, many of them permanently disabled.

Few Americans really expected or wanted the war. Secretary of State Seward may have talked of an "irrepressible conflict," but few believed that the crisis could be so serious as to lead to war. In this each side misjudged the other. The South, swathed in its chivalric legend of superiority, could not conceive of the commercial North fighting for something that did not fill its pocket. Yet as Grant wrote to his Southern father-in-law at the beginning of the crisis: "It is all a mistake about the Northern pocket being so sensitive." What was important was the Union, and most people in the North agreed with the sentiment expressed by then Captain Philip Sheridan that "This government is too great and good to be destroyed."

Yet the North also misjudged. There had been talk of secession before in states both north and south of the Mason-Dixon line: at the Hartford Convention over the War of 1812, in the South Carolina Nullification Crisis over the tariff, in Massachusetts at the time of the Mexican War. But nothing had ever happened, and it seemed impossible that it could happen now.

Part of this tragedy of the unexpected happening lay in the shock Americans experienced at the failure of their great experiment in democracy. For the instruments of democracy—the ballot, the rule of law, minority rights, the art of compromise—hailed as man's best hope, failed in time of crisis, and force, the instrument of kings and autocrats, became the last resort. Where in

COMPARISON OF U.S. WAR
CASUALTIES

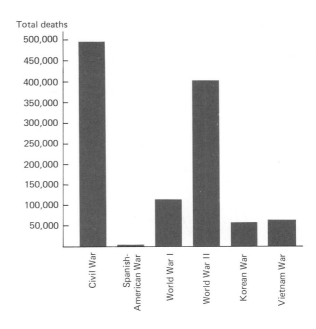

this was the vaunted superiority of democracy? For Americans who had long
seen themselves playing the role of model for mankind, it was a shock to be
regarded as the fallen idol. So the war was a blow to the American ego, to
American pride. Perhaps this is why both North and South almost frantically
proclaimed themselves still to be democratic, the true defenders of the faith.
Both sides insisted they had acted under the Constitution, and each made its
legal brief. Jefferson Davis went to his grave claiming that Lincoln had
violated the Constitution.

Lincoln, on the other hand, tried to rise above this aspect of the tragedy in
his Second Inaugural Address. "Let us judge not that we be not judged," he
said, and turned for an explanation to God, whose motives are beyond
understanding:

> The Almighty had His own purposes. . . . If we shall suppose that American
> slavery is one of those offences which, in the providence of God, must needs
> come, but which, having continued through His appointed time, He now wills
> to remove, and that He now gives to both North and South this terrible war as
> the woe due to those by whom the offence came, shall we discern therein any
> departure from those divine attributes which the believers in a living God
> always ascribe to Him? Fondly do we hope, fervently do we pray, that this
> mighty scourge of war may speedily pass away. Yet, if God wills that it
> continue until all the wealth piled up by the bondsman's two hundred and
> fifty years of unrequited toil shall be sunk, and until every drop of blood
> drawn with the lash shall be paid by another drawn with the sword, as was
> said three thousand years ago, so still it must be said, "The judgments of the
> Lord are true and righteous altogether."

If slavery were the one offence, he was probably right. Not only Southern hands were stained. So too were those of Americans outside the South who had profited from the slave trade and tolerated the "peculiar institution" when the Republic was founded. However compassionate in the assigning of blame, Lincoln's view was an even more tragic vision of the conflict than that which saw each side seeking to place the burden of guilt upon the other. For this was a burden not eased by sharing.

Profile: ABRAHAM LINCOLN

No other American has quite the same hold on the American imagination as Abraham Lincoln. Indeed, no other American, with the possible exception of Franklin D. Roosevelt in modern times, has been held in such high esteem by ordinary people throughout the world. Lincoln statues, busts, and portraits abound in countries as different in culture as England and Japan. Statesmen everywhere have acquired status in quoting The Great Emancipator. Not even Washington, either at home or abroad, has drawn the revered attention that Lincoln has. Books about him have averaged one a week since his death, and there is a steady stream of newspaper and magazine articles, pamphlets, novels, plays, and poetry.

Although any man who held the Presidency during the Civil War would have drawn considerable historical attention, Lincoln was much more than just the President. John Hay, who knew him as well as it was possible for any man to know Lincoln, called him "the greatest character since Christ"—a comparison in tune with the popular vision of Lincoln as a man who assumed the burdens of his people, rose by virtue of his character above the vindictiveness of the struggle, and was martyred by a bullet on Good Friday, the anniversary of the Crucifixion. No other political figure in history has been placed in such exalted company.

Lincoln was at once a simple and a highly complex man, a man of genuinely simple virtues sincerely held, who knew the value of simplicity. On the public platform he said: "I presume you all know who I am—I am humble Abraham Lincoln. . . . If elected I shall be thankful; if not it will be all the same." He was naturally honest and candid, and when he referred to "my poor, lean, lank face," or "my old, withered, dry eyes," it was not for political effect but because he saw himself that way. When a campaign document in 1860 declared that he was a reader of Plutarch, he immediately made the report accurate by reading Plutarch's Lives; and though candidates for public office have always been willing to stretch a point in referring to their military careers if they had any, Lincoln simply joked that in the Black Hawk War in which he briefly served he only fought "a good many bloody struggles with the mosquitoes."

Though humble—"I was born and have ever remained in the most humble walks of life"—he was ambitious. His law partner Herndon later said of him that "His ambition was a little engine that knew no rest;" and when from 1849 to 1854 it seemed as though a major political career was beyond his grasp, he became deeply discouraged. He was, in the face of immense difficulties, a decisive and clear-headed leader, uniting his party, the North, and so the nation; yet he was to say in 1864 that "I claim not to have controlled events but confess plainly that events have controlled me." And though he desperately wanted the Presidency, once he had it there was, as he noted, no glory, only "ashes and blood."

More than anyone else, Lincoln saw the Civil War as the great challenge to the American nation and American democracy, and he realized clearly that a successful rebellion would not only destroy the nation but cast into doubt the great experiment of democracy. He believed that democracy was unlikely to survive the collapse of the Union. It was this concern for the Union that caused him to delay on the issue of emancipation, to the great despair of the abolitionists in the North and the nation's democratic friends abroad. "I would save the Union," he told Horace Greeley," . . . if I could save the Union without freeing any slave, I would do it; and if I could do it by freeing all the slaves, I would do it." When freeing the slaves became necessary, as he saw it, to save the Union, he issued the Emancipation Proclamation. Its value, of course, was primarily psychological, since genuine emancipation came only with the Thirteenth Amendment, which Lincoln did not live to see ratified. But his influence was crucial in getting the amendment through the House of Representatives. He moved slowly and surely, and in the end the country got both emancipation and the Union.

Yet the point of saving the Union was to preserve the great experiment of democracy, "the last best hope on earth." This was the heart of the matter. As he told John Hay: "For my part, I consider the central idea pervading this struggle is the necessity that is upon us of proving that popular government is not an absurdity. We must settle this question now, whether in a free government the minority have the right to break up the government whenever they choose. If we fail it will go far to prove the incapability of the people to govern themselves." Accepting the idea that America was the proving-ground of democracy, he told the Congress on July 4, 1861, that:

> This is essentially a People's contest. On the side of the Union it is a struggle for maintaining in the world that form and substance of government whose leading object is to elevate the condition of men. . . . Our popular government has often been called an experiment. Two points in it our people have already settled—the successful <u>establishing</u> and the successful <u>administering</u> of it. One still remains—its successful <u>maintenance</u> against a formidable attempt to overthrow it. It is now for them to demonstrate to the world that those who can fairly carry an election can also suppress a rebellion—that ballots are the rightful and peaceful successors of bullets; and that when ballots have fairly and constitutionally decided, there can be no successful appeal except to ballots themselves at succeeding elections.

In the last analysis, Lincoln's extraordinary hold on the imaginations of people everywhere comes from the fact that he was simply a great human being. He had, as Jane Addams later said, "the largest share of the common human qualities and experiences." His humaneness, his decency, his kindness to all, his tolerance and understanding, his compassion—these are the finest of human qualities, and in Lincoln none of them was smothered and lost by the pressures of war and power, but instead they flourished. No other American leader has ever put so well the case for goodness and decency as Lincoln did in the closing remarks of his Second Inaugural Address:

> With malice toward none; with charity for all; with firmness in the right, as God gives us to see the right, let us strive on to finish the work we are in; to bind up the nation's wounds; to care for him who shall have borne the battle, and for his widow, and his orphan—to do all which may achieve and cherish a just, and a lasting peace, among ourselves and with all nations.

We could find no better guide for the troubles of our own time.

Chapter 11
THE CRISIS OF
RECONSTRUCTION

The Spirit of the Times
MYTH VERSUS REALITY

The era of Reconstruction after the Civil War has long loomed in the public mind, North as well as South, as a tragedy of horrors. Certainly no one would look upon this period as a pleasant romp of jovial reconciliation between victors and vanquished. And the experience did indeed leave lasting scars in American society. But it is also true that in the long record of rebellions fought and lost, the treatment of the losers has often been marked by a ferocity of oppression and punishment not found in the aftermath of the American Civil War.

Punishment for those Confederates involved in the war, the rank-and-file as well as the leadership, was mild or nonexistent. Ordinary soldiers and supporters of the Confederacy achieved full pardon by simply taking an oath of allegiance. Furthermore, no military officers were ever arrested or brought to trial for treason. A few public officials were arrested—including Jefferson Davis, the Confederate President—but none were brought to trial and all except Davis, who remained in prison for almost two years, were shortly released. By the 1870s, in fact, Congress had issued a blanket pardon for all but a few, and former Confederate leaders were shortly holding local, state, and national offices again—not exactly a scene of stern retribution.

Brutal punishment of the losers was not an element in Reconstruction. Nor was destructive exploitation of a defeated and helpless people. It used to be argued that the South, placed under military occupation, was turned over to Northern carpetbaggers, Southern scalawags, and freed blacks now possessed of political rights under the Fourteenth and Fifteenth Amendments who all embarked upon an orgy of corruption and greed for their own enrichment. No one would deny that mistakes were made in the administrations of the Reconstruction governments, that corruption was present, that self-serving operators took advantage of the economic confusion of the times.

But corruption was a fact of national political life in the years after the Civil War, and total corruption in the South was minor compared to the large-scale corruption going on elsewhere in the country. The Tweed Ring drained more from

Reconstruction. *The Christian ideal as envisioned by Horatio Bateman was never realized.*

the public till in New York City than filled the pockets of all malefactors in the South. Moreover, although blacks held office, their influence was never dominant except for a brief period in two Southern states. And of those blacks who served, the majority were able men who displayed no evidence of vindictiveness toward whites. Far from ruining social and political life, the Reconstruction governments initiated important reforms and began many projects of improvement. Social services were expanded and public education was greatly extended. Although economic development was slow, especially in comparison to national growth, the Southern economy began to recover. Agriculture began its march back toward prewar levels of productivity. Railroad construction totaled seven thousand miles of track, and manufacturing and mining gains in tobacco, textiles, coal, and iron were made. By the official end of Reconstruction rule in 1877, conditions had greatly improved rather than deteriorated. The South, of course, remained behind the rest of the nation in economic growth, but this had been true in the prewar era as well.

Finally, it should be noted that military occupation itself was relatively mild and certainly did not result in violent suppression of the white population. In fact, the violence that occurred under Reconstruction came primarily from those whites who most resented the political role thrust upon blacks. Secret societies arose, the best-known of which was the Ku Klux Klan, which sought by terrorist tactics to drive blacks out of politics. Blacks were threatened and terrified by mysterious hooded nightriders, they were beaten and whipped, and hundreds were brutally murdered. Federal troops were used to help the federal government break up the Klan. But this force was of a completely different nature than that used by the Klan to force blacks from political life in the South.

Reconstruction can indeed be called a tragedy. No myth here. But the tragedy lay not in any presumed repression of the South or punishment for those who fought in the war or supported the Confederacy. Nor did it lie in the brutal exploitation of the vanquished by the victors. Its tragedy lay in the failure to achieve some kind of social, economic, and political integration of blacks into the life of the South—and indeed the nation—on terms acceptable to both blacks and whites, North and South alike. This failure was the tragic reality of the Reconstruction era, and responsibility for it lay with all Americans. If the majority of Americans by the 1870s had given up on the implementation of those rights granted blacks by the Fourteenth and Fifteenth Amendments, at least these protections were now in the law of the land for subsequent generations to draw upon.

The Reconstruction Period

The Confederate vision of an Athenian democracy, Southern-style, resting on white citizenship and black slavery, vanished at Appomattox Courthouse on April 9, 1865. Although slavery died, for American blacks the century to come was to be a long winter of disappointment, frustration, and despair. Yet at its beginning was a period of hope, the dozen turbulent years known as the Reconstruction. This era briefly held out the possibility that a genuine political and social revolution might be imposed upon the South, one that would alter the terms and conditions of livelihood and therefore the status of the black population. But Reconstruction proved to be a revolution that failed to ignite. After a generation, the status of the blacks was gradually reaffirmed at a level only somewhat short of actual legal slavery. White attitudes toward the blacks did not change. The national view of the place of the black in society became indistinguishable from the Southern view; and there was a successful counter-revolution in race relations.

The plight of the South after Appomattox was grievous for both its white and its black populations. Everywhere roads, wharves, machinery, buildings, and even land were destroyed or run down through neglect. Specie and loans were almost impossible to secure. Organized authority vanished in many areas and banditry was rife. Hundreds of thousands of blacks quit their rooted existence on farms and plantations and in cities and towns. Confederate veterans straggled home from the remnants of their armies and from Northern prisons, and picked up as best they could their former lives. Demoralization of the white ruling class accompanied its loss of political power. Southern society had apparently gone with the wind. What forces would move into the political and economic vacuum of the South?

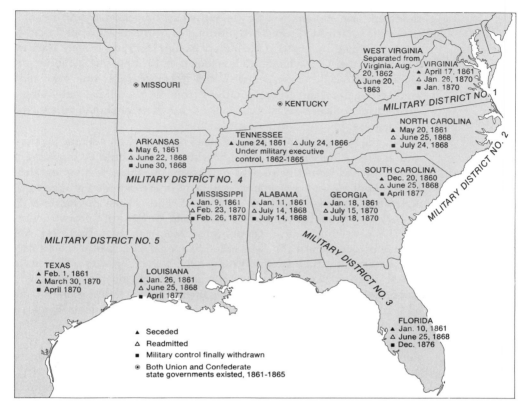

RECONSTRUCTION, 1865–1877

Lincoln's plans for the South unfolded after his Emancipation Proclamation of January 1, 1863. He later won Congressional approval for the Thirteenth Amendment and universal emancipation, but he did not ask that blacks be given citizenship and equal rights. Rather, in December 1863 he put forth his Ten-Percent Plan, issued as an executive proclamation of amnesty and Reconstruction. This plan required that if a minimum of ten percent of the qualified voters of 1860 would take an oath of allegiance to the Union, their state might set up a state government, the President would recognize it, and readmission of the state to the Union would follow. Lincoln's announced policy was one of rapid reconciliation with the Southern states. But he had no opportunity to put it into effect. His assassination immediately after the war has left only speculation about how Lincoln would have adjusted the renewed Union with the subsequent demands for black equality.

Johnson versus the Radical Republicans   After Lincoln's assassination, President Andrew Johnson took over the Ten-Percent Plan in slightly modified form and enacted it by executive proclamation. By the end of 1865, new state governments had been formed in every state except Texas. Johnson proclaimed amnesty for the bulk of ex-Confederates in May 1865, and as a result, former Confederate leaders took over the new state governments. In December 1865 Johnson declared that Reconstruction was over and that elected Senators and Representatives from the Southern states—many of them former officers and officials in the Confederacy—should take their seats in Congress.

But the Radical Republicans—a hard-line anti-Confederate persuasion—had entirely different ideas about how the South should be treated. During 1865 they had fumed helplessly as Johnson put through his program; now they simply refused to seat any Southern Congressmen on grounds that the states had not been legally reconstructed. Thus began the battle of Presidential Reconstruction versus Congressional or Radical Reconstruction.

Who were the Radical Republicans? Many of them had been foes of slavery before the war. They included Salmon P. Chase in Lincoln's cabinet, Charles Sumner and Benjamin Wade in the Senate, Thaddeus Stevens in the House of Representatives. Generally favorable to business interests, they had nonetheless diverse views among themselves on tariffs, money, banking, and internal improvements. They were united on advancing black rights, ultimately to the point of granting complete political and legal equality; and they favored excluding ex-Confederates and the former ruling class from political influence in the postwar South. The popular sentiment of the North after the war was understandably vindictive, and the Radicals sought to exploit this sentiment to advance black rights, an issue in which most Northern citizens had little or no interest. In the main, it would be accurate to say that what distinguished the Radical Republicans was their insistence on advancing the blacks to equality and their effort to create a political and social structure in the South that would guarantee that equality. The Radicals were the dynamic political and moral element in Reconstruction. During the war, they had dominated the Joint Committee on the Conduct of the War, a powerful agency in their hands. By the end of the war they had moved into open opposition to Lincoln's program for Reconstruction.

President Johnson revered Lincoln and followed the general lines of Lincoln's program, though without flexibility or tact. A man with definite views, he was fully determined to use his office to enforce them. His personal limitations were real enough; he unquestionably treated political opponents rudely and dealt unfairly with his critics, even those trying to help him. But the leniency of his program is sufficient explanation for his devastating collision with the Radical Republicans.

Johnson believed that the planter class, by promoting secession, had irresponsibly brought on the war and manipulated the Southern small farmer into supporting it. He reasoned that with peace the small farmers would come to recognize the full depth of their betrayal by the planters, would refuse to follow their leadership, and would ally themselves with their free-farmer counterparts in the North and West. Johnson's political ideal was to unite moderate and conservative Republicans with Union Democrats in a new national coalition, one in which the preponderant white farmer class would feel secure. With the classes roughly in balance, social harmony would prevail throughout the nation. America would return to the principles of the early republic.

Johnson maintained that the blacks, like everyone else, could work out their destiny without special favors and within an economic system governed by the laws regulating capital and labor. He strongly supported the Thirteenth Amendment and universal emancipation: free labor would not only undermine the power of the planter class but would establish a more efficient set of labor relations. The Southern economic situation would improve as white inventive and productive talents were released; and black economic fortunes would rise with those of the region. Politically, socially, and legally, the blacks would remain under white tutelage. Class and racial relationships would remain fixed. Johnson said nothing about changing the lot of the blacks in any special or positive sense. They would remain an unskilled, uneducated, and propertyless laboring class, and the South itself a white man's country.

The moderate and conservative Republicans, apostles of the waxing capitalist interests, were willing to work with Johnson, finding his propositions about the economic order acceptable enough as a place to start. But they envisaged a far larger role for their interest in the new order than Johnson would have found tolerable. And he would have been staggered, for example, by the vision of Secretary of State William H. Seward of a future mighty industrial America and of an American empire. But Johnson's program shattered on the conscience and power of the Radicals.

In the tangled history of Reconstruction, it is still possible to assert that the subservient place President Johnson assigned to the blacks in the Southern social order was the central issue that made any compromise with the Radicals impossible. More than anyone else, he turned Reconstruction into an issue of moral principle. Already in 1865, while Johnson proceeded confidently with Reconstruction by executive proclamation, the Freedmen's Bureau and the Black Codes illustrated the opposing forces that were to divide Presidential and Congressional Reconstruction.

The Freedmen's Bureau Congress set up the Freedman's Bureau within the War Department just before the end of the war. Under General Oliver O. Howard, a high-minded philanthropist, the Bureau cut a wide humanitarian swath throughout the South. It also aroused white Southern anxieties. The Bureau was given "control of all subjects relating to refugees and freedmen," an elastic mandate in itself, which Howard and his fellow commissioners interpreted liberally. The situation indeed called for quick measures and considerable initiative and ability to improvise. As the war came to an end, hundreds of thousands of blacks took to the road. Many simply wanted to indulge their sense of adventure, muted so long on the plantation. Others set off to look for kin and friends separated from them during slavery. Footloose blacks roamed the countryside, picking up rations from the Union army or

A freedmen's camp on the outskirts of the city of Richmond.

living by theft. Eventually, most of them fell into dire need, as did a great many Southern whites as well. The Freedmen's Bureau gave help zealously and effectively. Thanks to its issue of food, clothing, and medicine, it saved untold numbers of lives and tempered much misery. The Bureau lent legal and moral support to blacks by acting as a court of law, assuring blacks the right to choose their own employers, and arranging fair labor contracts for them. Its widespread intervention in labor relationships struck a particularly delicate Southern nerve, and Southern whites resented the publicity the Bureau gave to many instances of mistreatment of blacks.

The initial successes of the Bureau in protecting blacks turned it into a lever that pried open the South to idealistic Northerners. Thousands of schoolteachers, ministers, and enthusiastic young people followed in the wake of the Bureau, working with it and augmenting its projects. Free public schools were set up on a wide scale, open to blacks and whites alike. Countless charities were established, supported by donations from benevolent societies in the North. Many white Southerners came to hate and fear the Bureau for such educational and charitable activities and were anxious lest they be perpetuated. The activities of the Bureau exposed the blacks to ideas and influences that stimulated black self-respect and that were in every way at odds with the picture of the world and of themselves that Southern paternalistic ideology had impressed upon the blacks in the past.

The Black Codes   The Black Codes were the immediate Southern answer to the emancipation of the slaves and particularly to the difficulties of securing the services of the black labor force. The Codes were enacted by the Johnson state legislatures in 1865. They remained until struck down in April 1866 by the Civil Rights Act—passed by Congress over Johnson's veto—

which guaranteed equal civil rights to blacks. The Codes varied throughout the Southern states. Although most Codes recognized certain legal rights for blacks, they also restricted their freedom. Generally they forced labor contracts upon the blacks in one form or other; for example, by arresting them for vagrancy and then as punishment putting them to work. The Codes were in fact not enforced unless agents of the Freedmen's bureau acquiesced. The Bureau, its own resources frequently stretched thin, often found in the Codes a convenient device to hold down black migrancy. But the Codes did enforce conditions on blacks so closely resembling those of slavery that many thoughtful Southern leaders became alarmed, particularly since they could perceive the Radical Republican reaction building up in the Congress.

Debate over Reconstruction The Radicals in Congress were willing to believe the worst about the South in any event. Reports by the end of 1865 seemed to them conclusive evidence that Johnson's Reconstruction really meant the restoration of the antebellum South in all important essentials. In early 1866, the Joint Committee on Reconstruction held hearings. Witnesses attested to the degrading treatment of blacks under the Black Codes, and letters from Southern Unionists added to the complaints. The highly respected Carl Schurz toured the South and made a straightforward and particularly impressive report to the Joint Committee. Schurz stressed that the South was resigned to its military defeat, but that the blacks in general were being badly treated and required federal protection. And a former large slaveholder, R. W. Flournoy of Mississippi, told Thaddeus Stevens: "To leave the negro to be dealt with by those whose prejudices are of the most bitter character against him, will be barbarous."

Such evidence enabled the Radicals to criticize more effectively the return of ex-Confederates to leadership in the new state governments in the South. And Johnson's expectation that the Southern farmers would disavow their former leadership proved utterly mistaken. This fact added enormously to Johnson's political difficulties and was of persistent importance during Reconstruction and beyond.

The Radicals Reign Radical Reconstruction was forced through by a determined minority. Its leader in the House of Representatives was Thaddeus Stevens, representative from Pennsylvania and Chairman of the important House Committee on Reconstruction. Charles Sumner of Massachusetts led the Radicals in the Senate. Outside the Congress, men like Wendell Phillips, Boston patrician and former abolitionist, and E. L. Godkin, editor of the New York *Nation,* channeled powerful moral sentiments from the larger community into the Congress. These sentiments were well received by the Radicals.

The Radicals were united above all on the question of human equality. Many got their primary convictions from the Declaration of Independence with its principle of universal human equality; others rooted their views in

Charles Sumner. The powerfully outspoken Republican leader steadfastly pursued his consuming goal, that of "absolute human equality, secured, assured, and invulnerable." It was through Sumner's tenacious effort that seceded states had to provide equal suffrage in order to be readmitted to the Union. But in his pursuit of his goal of equality for all Sumner's vision became increasingly limited and his intolerance of those who disagreed with him grew out of proportion to the disagreement. His last years in the Senate were spent in vehement denunciation of those he considered his enemies.

Christianity. In many Radicals, of course, these views fell into easy combination. Such articles of faith protected the Radicals against the prevalent folklore that was spread rather evenly amongst Northern and Southern whites concerning the natural inferiority of blacks.

Thaddeus Stevens was the clearest head amongst the Radicals in Congress. He had a tough-minded estimate of social forces, a program, a realistic awareness of the strength of the obstacles blocking its attainment, and a practical vision of what the reunited and democratized American Republic might be like. No dreamer, and equipped with balanced qualities of moral fervor, political adroitness and tenacity, he possessed also the decisiveness and audacity to act.

Radical Reconstruction was really an attempt to achieve a political and social revolution from the top, to be carried through by the Congress. It aimed at nothing less than modernizing the American republic which, after all, still largely conformed to the pattern of a simpler age of agrarianism and commercial capitalism. The Republican party was to supply the propelling force. The national government would be strengthened at the expense of the states; Northern farmers, workers, commercial, financial, and industrial interests would find allies among the freed blacks and, following destruction of the planter interest, ultimately with Southern white farmers as well. Native Southern capital and resources, no longer sidetracked into human chattels and plantation mortgages, would join in a swelling mainstream of capitalist industry and finance, to expand with them in a truly national market. Although the Radicals were not marked by unanimity of opinion on economic matters, nevertheless they shared the general view that the new society would be economically dynamic and prosperous, politically stable and free.

Those moderate and conservative Republicans who were representative of the new capitalist forces accepted the Radical economic suppositions, which in principle were much the same as President Johnson's in stressing an unregulated capitalism. All Republicans knew clearly that the "party of the Union" had come into being as a sectional party and still had not put down deep national roots. Under Radical urging, there was Republican concurrence that the party must be moved into the South; that therefore the blacks must be made voting citizens with such help as was needed to make their votes effective—that is, Republican. For the Radicals, to see a return of the Southern Democrats to the Congress in strength, to have to compromise again with them continually, was an intolerable thought. The Congressional elections of 1866, it was recognized, would be decisive. The Radicals flung all their resources into the campaign.

The campaign was marked by bitterness and invective. President Johnson attacked Radical leaders individually, and added name-calling for good measure. The Radicals replied in kind, reminding Northerners that in the late war Southern bullets had been fired mostly by Democrats, that the white South was unrepentant, and that matters of conscience could not be put aside regarding treatment of the blacks in the South. Economic issues got little attention in the campaign; all guns were turned on Johnsonian Reconstruction. The campaign showed that Johnson's program commanded at best a wide indifference. The Radicals were rewarded with a large Congressional majority that would enable them to override Johnson's vetoes with ease.

Radical Policies   Radical Reconstruction called for breaking the power of the planter class. Radicals were agreed that the blacks must be enfranchised and their civil rights guaranteed. The Congress put through the First Reconstruction Act (1867) over Johnson's veto, and this was subsequently reinforced by three other acts. The South was placed under military rule backed by the full force of the national government. Ten states were divided into five military districts. The Supreme Court, aware of the force behind the Radicals, chose not to sit on cases involving the Reconstruction Acts. Constitutional conventions set up new state governments in the South, replacing those established by Johnson. Blacks could vote in all these proceedings, but former Confederate leaders could not.

On constitutional guarantees of black rights, three famous amendments were enacted in the early Reconstruction years. The Thirteenth Amendment (1865) freed the slaves. No land was given to the freedmen, nor compensation paid to their former owners. The Americans thus confiscated private property on a scale unknown in the West in modern times until the Russian Revolution of 1917. The former slaveholders, still politically disorganized, and accepting emancipation as the likely limit of change, did not protest strongly. The Fourteenth Amendment (1868), opposed by Johnson, made the blacks citizens. The Fifteenth Amendment (1870) gave black males the vote.

The importance of these amendments cannot be overrated. Even though for practical purposes they were ignored in the decades to come, they remained the law of the land. In the changed circumstances of our time their existence came to represent a realizable ideal, putting on the defensive those who resisted their fulfillment. In the Reconstruction era itself, their importance was enormously magnified by the failure to give the blacks a stake in society through land ownership.

Land Reform   To the Radicals, land reform as a matter of course meant confiscation of the plantations. A division of land among the blacks, and including the poorer whites as well, would undermine the economic base for the political leadership of the planter class. Guaranteed the possession of a freehold farm, the blacks would be freed from the necessity of letting their labor on unfavorable terms to the landowner through sharecropping and tenantry, a system already fastening itself on the Southern landscape in the 1860s.

In spite of the considerable obstacles the more militant Radicals, with Stevens as usual at their head, were willing to make a try and to employ such precedents as were near at hand.

During the war, the Union armies had liberated thousands of slaves in their advance into the Southern states. In South Carolina the Sea Islands had been occupied in 1861 by Union forces. The plantations there were divided among black families, the blacks managed their local affairs successfully, and the community prospered. At Davis Bend, Mississippi, in 1864–1865 following their liberation by the Union army, blacks with government help undertook a cooperative agricultural venture that turned a handy profit. The Sea Islands experiment outlasted Reconstruction, but after the war President Johnson returned the land of the Davis Bend plantations to its former white owners. Though limited in the numbers of freedmen involved, both these experiments suggested success for more widespread application. Stevens did not fail to point to the liberation of the serfs, and the assignment of land to them, carried out in the Russian Empire from 1861 to 1866. The analogy with the American experience was weak, but Stevens affirmed that the Russian tsar had correctly recognized that freedom was severely limited unless economic security accompanied it.

Land reform had been discussed periodically by Northerners since the last years of the war. It was Stevens again who made the greatest issue of it, since he attempted to get it included in the First Reconstruction Act of 1867. Stevens used government statistics to work out the elements of a plan that would at first confiscate about 400 million acres of land held by five percent of Southern white families, the "chief rebels," as Stevens put it; some seventy thousand planters each holding more than two hundred acres would lose their land. The confiscated land would be distributed to freedmen's families in forty-acre parcels; the remainder would be sold to help pay the public debt and provide veterans' pensions as well as compensation to Southern Unionists who had lost property during the war. The blacks thus established as small freehold farmers would get long-term guidance from the Republicans in Congress till they could master the responsibilities of managing their farms. Land and the vote would guarantee their freedom while they made the difficult transition into self-respecting citizenship; and the "party of the Union" would acquire a firm base in the South.

Stevens and the Congressional hardcore Radicals tried to get the forty-acre plan written into the First Reconstruction Act of 1867. It received only slight support in the House, and the debate fizzled out by the end of the sixties. Land reform was the most revolutionary change asked by the Radicals, and its failure left Southern blacks helpless to control their economic destinies. Public opinion was unable to accept such a proposal.

E. L. Godkin's *Nation,* normally a Radical supporter, warned that "A division of rich men's land amongst the landless . . . would give a shock to our whole social and political system from which it would hardly recover without the loss of liberty." Northerners who had bought up Southern plantations after the war resisted the idea of confiscation as a matter of course. Even Northern workmen took a dim view of confiscation, since it seemed to be setting blacks up in business. Those in the factories, themselves with little or no property, could not understand why blacks should be given a special advantage. Individual skill, initiative, and the notion of making it on one's own were the virtues esteemed by the Americans. Most of the support Stevens got for his forty-acre plan came from those who saw in confiscation and land sales a way of reducing the public debt and hence taxes. But the general verdict was that with emancipation the blacks would be free to sell their labor wherever they could, at what price they could get, just like anyone else. Beyond that the nation would not go.

The Impeachment of Johnson   The progress of Reconstruction as designed by the Congress was marked by a series of confrontations between the Radicals and President Johnson—of bills vetoed and vetoes overridden, of Johnson's lack of restraint in dealing with those with whom he disagreed, and of an emotionally intense Congressional reaction to Johnson's behavior. Radical fury against his opposition to the Congressional program of Reconstruction climaxed in the attempt to remove him from office. The Republican argument was that Johnson had failed to fulfill his constitutional duty to enforce the laws of the land, but this was an unfounded argument. His real "crime" was political disagreement with the Radicals over Reconstruction. The issue on which the case hinged was the Tenure of Office Act of 1867, which forbade the President to remove any official appointed with the consent of the Senate without first securing the approval of the Senate.

Johnson in February 1868 dismissed his Secretary of War, Edwin M. Stanton, an avowed supporter of the Radicals. This precipitated Johnson's impeachment and trial, which the Radicals were convinced they had the votes to win. But the dubious nature of the charges, the malice apparent in the prosecutor's handling of the case contrasted with the dignity of the defense conducted by Johnson's lawyers, the dislike some senators had of

The Sergeant-at-Arms of the Senate
serves the summons of impeachment
on President Johnson.

Benjamin Wade, the president of the Senate who would assume the Presidency if Johnson were removed, and the realization that Johnson's effectiveness was nil and he would shortly be out of office anyway, all combined to convince seven Republican senators to vote against conviction. Johnson won acquittal by one vote.

The Grant Administration—Incompetence and Corruption With Johnson unacceptable to anyone, Republican or Democrat, the Republicans happily turned in 1868 to war hero General Ulysses S. Grant. Grant's presidential victory in 1868 over Horatio Seymour was overwhelming in the Electoral College, but his narrow popular majority was clearly attributable to black voters enfranchised in Republican-dominated Southern states under Reconstruction rule. Ironically, Grant's majority would have been much larger had not various Northern states rejected constitutional moves to permit blacks to vote in those states.

Grant was willing to permit Congress to assume control of Reconstruction. Brilliant on the battlefield, he was completely ineffective in the White House and his political naiveté was exploited not only by the Congress, which was also increasingly disturbed by his ineptitude, but by his friends and associates as well. His administration was marked by one of the worst periods of corruption in American political history, even though Grant personally was not involved. The Whiskey Ring scandal, which involved cheating the government of millions in tax revenue, involved Grant's private secretary. His Secretary of War took bribes in connection with the management of Indian affairs. Other scandals involved officials in the Navy and Treasury departments. To compound the problem, Grant out of a misguided sense of loyalty

This cartoon mocked Grant's failure to recognize corruption in his friends or take any action against it once discovered. General William W. Belknap, Grant's Secretary of War, received a kickback of nearly $25,000 as a result of an appointment he made to Fort Sills.

protected those who had betrayed him. Although the infamous Credit Mobilier scandal occurred before Grant became President, it broke during his second administration and he was forced to assume part of the blame. The scandal involved the bribing of key members of Congress with Credit Mobilier stock in order to cover up the granting of fraudulent contracts by the Credit Mobilier, a construction company involved in the building of the Union Pacific. A congressional investigation of the matter after Grant took office revealed that a number of prominent officials had been involved, including the man who had become Grant's Vice President.

Grant's inability to govern effectively allowed Congress considerable opportunity to increase its power and consequently institute significant change with the development of its Reconstruction programs.

The Impact of Reconstruction

The South remained under military rule until 1877. A variety of Northerners moved South. Some wanted to settle there in the fashion of "going West," others went to work with the Freedmen's Bureau to help blacks and poor whites, swelling the migration of such idealists begun earlier. The Union League, an arm of the Republican Party, penetrated into the South to organize the black vote. Most of the Northern immigrants supported the Republicans; Southerners labelled them all "carpetbaggers," attributing somewhat indiscriminately a get-rich-quick-and-leave motive to all the newcomers.

The Republicans also found allies among white Southerners themselves: former Southern Unionists, some Southern businessmen, some Southern humanitarians, and various Southern opportunists.

Southern resentment of Reconstruction governments is reflected in this cartoon of the "Solid South" shackled and burdened with "carpetbag and bayonet rule." An army of occupation was stationed in each of the military districts to enforce what at times was a flagrant disregard of civil rights. In some Southern states any commemoration of the Confederacy was outlawed, government officials were removed, and courts were replaced by military tribunals when they failed to punish violence against blacks.

The Radicals and their Southern adherents wrought considerable transformation in the South. Democratic state constitutions were set up, and a free public school system was established that drew in uneducated whites as well as blacks. Women's rights were expanded, taxes were made more equitable, and there were better facilities for the care of the physically and mentally handicapped and of the poor. Penal codes were reformed, punishments for minor crimes were made less harsh, and the number of crimes punishable by death was reduced. The blacks participated in making these changes. Black legislators sat in all the Southern state legislatures, but in only two, Mississippi and South Carolina, did they become the majority. No blacks became governors. On the whole, except for staunchly maintaining political and legal guarantees, the blacks were remarkably conservative, not even using their influence in the state governments to urge land reform strongly.

It was in personal human terms that Reconstruction had the greatest impact on the South. The coercion of black labor was relieved by the Radical influence. Blacks rushed eagerly into the free schools. They were able to develop a family life more nearly approximating that of the country at large. The simple fact of emancipation did away with the worst aspect of slavery, the fear of arbitrary separation from relatives and friends. Beatings, threats of beatings, and worse punishments were outlawed. Blacks continued to work very hard, but they could keep something of what they earned; consequently they ate better as well. Reconstruction generally made a genuine break with the black past and launched a serious program to incorporate blacks as equals into American life.

The Failure of Reconstruction   What failed to change during the Reconstruction years were white thoughts and attitudes towards the blacks. Changes in attitudes towards people as a class or race require changes in status within wider social relationships. Reconstruction supplied the political conditions for a change of status by making the black a voting citizen. Resistant Southern whites accepted Reconstruction at the time only because it was less painful to do so than not. But when the authority of the national government no longer enforced it, the white South fell back upon its conventional attitudes.

Why did Reconstruction finally fail? Purely political considerations within Republican ranks explain much. The Republican Party had risen as a sectional political force in the 1850s, dedicated to preserving the Union and the national market and augmenting federal power to these ends. The "party of the Union" had achieved astonishing success. Nationalist and patriotic feeling, greatly intensified by the war experience, and the increasing market for their goods in the East and in Europe, bound the Western farmers to Republicanism. As the Republicans won the West, the Southern blacks became politically expendable. Under these circumstances, the Republicans felt far less urge to push for the establishment of a party base in the South. The idealism of the Radicals, expressed originally in human terms of helping the blacks to citizenship, shaded off into the less dramatic goals of civil service and other reform as age overtook the Radicals and their energies declined.

A series of growing economic problems related to the stock market, the tariff, industrial expansion, and the shortage of money that climaxed in the Panic of 1873 increasingly commanded the attention of the voters throughout the country and correspondingly reduced their interest in the fate of the blacks of the South and the problems of Reconstruction.

With waning support from their own party, the Radicals gradually lost their zeal. Pressing changes upon an unwilling people is not inherently pleasant work. The South quickly developed techniques of resistance, first subtly, then more openly. White Southerners, as during the war itself, were fighting on their own ground and within a society that they knew well. The carpetbaggers, the Northern idealists, and others working in the South were far from home, living in a society that they did not fully understand and that did not want them. Northerners who provoked Southern resentment, whether with justification or not, came to feel isolated in the region.

In the South, opposition to Reconstruction was accompanied as time went on by a good deal of terror in the fashion of the counter-revolution following the radical phase of the French Revolution. A host of vigilante and secret societies blossomed in the late 1860s, of which the Ku Klux Klan was merely the earliest and best known. In the early 1870s, the military governors, aided by Congressional enactments, dealt with these successfully by force; but the appearance of these lawless elements sent a shudder throughout the black communities in the South.

Disappointment with President Grant as well as confirmation of a waning Republican interest in Reconstruction were clearly evident when the Democrats won control of the House of Representatives in the election of 1874. In

The Regulators. *White extremists turned to terrorism and violence in their reactions to Reconstruction.*

the following year Grant, who had earlier been willing to use federal troops to protect black voters from intimidation in the South, refused to send troops to Mississippi in response to an appeal from its Republican carpetbag governor, declaring that "The whole public are tired out with these annual autumnal outbreaks in the South, and the great majority are now ready to condemn any interference on the part of the government."

Thus Grant, who had originally represented the hope of the Radical Republicans in the reconstruction of the South, ended up presiding over its final failure.

The presidential election of 1876 confirmed the end of Reconstruction. The Republicans nominated Governor Rutherford B. Hayes of Ohio, the Democrats chose Governor Samuel J. Tilden of New York. Tilden apparently won the election, possessing a popular majority. But his claim to victory rested upon the votes of the last three Southern states—Florida, South Carolina, and Louisiana—which still remained in Republican hands. In the long and complicated dispute over who was to be awarded the electoral votes from these three states, it seems clear that both sides were guilty of fraud and corruption. Less than a month before inauguration day in 1877, the Electoral Commission created by Congress awarded the disputed votes to Hayes, thus insuring him election by one electoral vote. While Northern Democrats were furious and even talked of a military march on Washington to put their man in the White House, Southern Democrats had other things on their mind. Many Southern Democrats believed they were more likely to get federal economic aid for their section from a Republican administration interested in economic growth. More importantly, many Southern Democrats wanted to be left alone to run the South as they saw fit, and if Republicans could assure them that Hayes would go along with this point of view, they were willing to accept his victory.

Whether deals were actually made in this regard is still in doubt. What is clear is that Reconstruction had run its course, the entire country wanted to put the issue behind it, interest in providing special protections and privileges to blacks had long since disappeared in the minds of most Americans, and sectional harmony was eagerly sought by most. At any rate, after he became President, Hayes removed the last of federal troops stationed in the South, and the era of Reconstruction formally ended. A new era began, an era of national neglect of the black in American society that was not to be reversed until the second half of the twentieth century.

Profile: THADDEUS STEVENS

Few men of influence in American history have ever been so reviled as Thaddeus Stevens. And some would say few deserved it more. After his death on August 11, 1868, he was referred to by the New York <u>Times</u> as "the Evil Genius of the Republican Party." James Gordon Bennett of the New York <u>Herald</u> called him "malevolent, even malignant," and the New York <u>World</u> declared that Stevens was "the author of more evil and mischief than any other inhabitant of the globe since the end of the civil war." In the South, where for years he had been detested by whites, his death prompted one paper to exalt that "The prayers of the righteous have at last removed the Congressional curse."

Yet his achievements were of great significance. He served in the Pennsylvania House of Representatives from 1833 to 1842, and then in Congress from 1849 to 1852 and from 1858 until his death. He was uncompromisingly opposed to slavery before the war—he denounced any extension of slavery into the territories, prophetically declared the Compromise of 1850 would be "the fruitful mother of future rebellion," defended fugitive slaves without fee, and was opposed to the Supreme Court's decision in the Dred Scott case. His profound concern for the fate of blacks led him to play a key role in securing the Thirteenth and Fourteenth Amendments and in laying the groundwork for the Fifteenth, which he did not live to see enacted. He helped greatly to make American nationalism a political reality by his work to consolidate federal power both during and after the war. He was also a life-long supporter of free public education. In a powerful and eloquent speech in the Pennsylvania legislature in 1835 he carried the day for a free school law about which, over thirty years later as he lay on his deathbed, he said: "That was the proudest effort of my life."

The source of controversy over Stevens as a powerful political leader in Congress and the nation arose in essence out of his own character. He was a man of considerable wit, but seemed impelled to use it to the discomfiture of others. On one occasion he asked a legislator who had voted against a bill Stevens supported if his opponent was a married man with children. When his opponent replied yes, Stevens said, "I am sorry to hear that. I was in hopes, sir, that you were the last of your race." But there were larger flaws than this. He had a streak of vindictiveness that drove him to seek punishment for those he considered guilty of wrongdoing. And he possessed a fanatical commitment to principle that made him turn against all who did not see the truth as he did. Early in his political career he had proudly declared that "I would sooner lose every friend on earth than violate the glorious dictates of my own conscience." If this was his ambition, he came very close to attaining it. He would not admit of the possibility of his being badly advised by his conscience—the truth was his and his alone. This vindictiveness and his fanaticism about principle gave him a pathological conviction that if things did not go the way he thought they should the country was doomed to ruin and destruction. As he lay dying, he remarked, "My life has been a failure. . . . I see little hope for the Republic."

His unforgiving nature was apparent in his hatred of the "bloated aristocrats" of the South whose property, he believed, should be confiscated by the government. And opposing speedy and conciliatory reunion of the states, he believed rebellion justified the view that the Southern states should be treated as conquered territories not as errant sons to be welcomed home with open arms. But his vindictive streak was most apparent in his insistence on the impeachment and trial of President Andrew Johnson. It was Stevens who forced this matter to its sorry pass, even though he knew that the real issue was the political clash between Johnson and the Radical Republicans, not the indictable offenses under the Constitution of treason, bribery, or other high crimes and misdemeanors. So great was his hatred of Johnson that when the President was acquitted on May 16, 1868 by one vote, Stevens (though a dying man) doggedly but futilely tried to keep the issue alive by concocting new articles of impeachment.

Thaddeus Stevens was an enormously complex man, his life full of inner conflicts and personal contradictions, and as such he was not only hard to understand but difficult to appreciate. He took an essentially Calvinist view of human nature, believing humanity inherently evil, but at the same time he held the utopian belief that it was possible to legislate total equality overnight. He could be unsparing in his attacks on those who he believed stood in the way of progress, and yet he had a profound commitment to human rights. The social and economic revolution he wished to impose on the South was unacceptable to his contemporaries, but his work for the Fourteenth and Fifteenth Amendments was of crucial political importance for the advancement of civil rights in twentieth century America. His fear that his life had been wasted and useless was born of his innate pessimism, but was unwarranted by the long-range impact of his achievements. In the last analysis, his virtues outweighed his flaws.

Selected Reading

General Works

The following general works survey different aspects of American development and should be referred to for their pertinent references throughout chapters one to eleven.

The most comprehensive study of American cultural and intellectual life and institutions is Merle Curti, *The Growth of American Thought* (Harper & Row, New York, 1964) which also contains a superb bibliography current to the last revised edition. Stow Persons, *American Minds* (Holt, Rinehart, & Winston, New York, 1958) concentrates on certain intellectual themes with great illumination. Harvey Wish, *Society and Thought in America* (2 vols., David McKay, New York, 1962) looks at social and intellectual life in great detail. Daniel Boorstin's three volumes on *The Americans* (Vintage, New York, 1959, 1965, 1973) are exciting and original works. Extremely thoughtful essays by important scholars compose *Paths of American Thought* (Houghton Mifflin, Boston, 1963) edited by Morton White and Arthur M. Schlesinger, Jr. Stephen B. Oates, *Portrait of America* (2 vols., Houghton Mifflin, Boston, 1973) is an excellent anthology of historical essays. Carl Degler, *Out of Our Past* (Harper & Row, New York, 1959), is a superior general interpretation.

The best general sources for brief biographies of Americans are the multivolume older *Dictionary of American Biography* (Scribner's, New York, 1936), the *Encyclopaedia Britannica* 15th edition (Encyclopaedia Britannica, Inc., Chicago, 1974), and the one-volume *Encyclopedia of American Biography* (Harper & Row, New York, 1974) edited by John Garraty. Roderick Nash has written a biographical history of the United States, *From These Beginnings* (Harper & Row, New York, 1973), in which he shows what can be done with this approach in the study of a limited number of key Americans.

The Comparative Approach to American History (Basic Books, New York, 1968), edited by C. Vann Woodward, demonstrates the importance of viewing American experience in relation to that of other peoples. The two-volume *The Underside of American History* (Harcourt Brace Jovanovich, New York, 1971), edited by Thomas R. Frazier, reminds us of the unhappy side of America's past. G. D. Lillibridge's essay, "The American Impact Abroad: Past and Present," in *The American Scholar*, Winter 1965–1966, outlines the theme of American influence abroad. Also see Lillibridge, ed., *The American Image* (Heath, Lexington, Mass., 1968) and Michael Kraus, ed., *The North Atlantic Civilization* (Van Nostrand, Princeton, N.J., 1957). Gerald Stearn has edited *Broken Image* (Random House, New York, 1972) which establishes a grimmer side to this theme.

Other books on particular subjects include Ronald W. Hogeland, ed., *Women and Womanhood in America* (Heath, Lexington, Mass., 1973) and Edith

H. Altbach, *Women in America* (Heath, Lexington, Mass., 1974) on the neglected sex. Carl Wittke, *We Who Built America* (Prentice-Hall, Englewood Cliffs, N.J., 1964) and Maldwyn Jones, *American Immigration* (University of Chicago Press, Chicago, 1960) survey the immigrant experience. Norman F. Cantor and Michael S. Werthman, eds., *The History of Popular Culture Since 1815* (Macmillan, New York, 1968), which leaps back and forth across the Atlantic, and Russel B. Nye, *The Unembarrassed Muse: The Popular Arts in America* (Dial, New York, 1970) explore this subject. Hans Kohn studies *American Nationalism* (Macmillan, New York, 1957) and Ross M. Robertson surveys the *History of the American Economy* (Harcourt Brace Jovanovich, New York, 1960). Richard Chase surveys *The American Novel and its Tradition* (Doubleday, Garden City, N.Y., 1957) and Robert E. Spiller exhaustively examines *The Literary History of the United States* (Macmillan, New York, 1964) in three volumes. William T. Hagan sums up the story of the *American Indians* (University of Chicago Press, Chicago, 1961), Oliver W. Larkin looks at *Art and Life in America* (Holt, Rinehart, & Winston, New York, 1962), and R. Freeman Butts and Lawrence A. Cremin examine the *History of Education in American Culture* (Holt, Rinehart & Winston, New York, 1953). John Hope Franklin gives a general history of blacks in *From Slavery to Freedom* (Knopf, New York, 1956).

The great majority of these books and those subsequently listed are in paperback.

Chapter 1

The best biography of Columbus is Samuel Eliot Morison, *Admiral of the Ocean Sea* (Little, Brown, Boston, 1942). See also Cecil Jane, Jr., *The Journal of Christopher Columbus* (Crown, New York, 1960). For background on the European world see J. H. Parry, *The Age of Reconnaissance* (New American Library, New York, 1963), Charles E. Nowell, *The Great Discoveries* (Cornell University Press, Ithaca, New York, 1954), J. H. Elliott, *The Old World and the New, 1492–1650* (Cambridge University Press, New York, 1972), Wallace Notestein, *The English People on the Eve of Colonization* (Harper & Row, New York, 1954). For the mood of Europe, the early part of Howard Mumford Jones, *O Strange New World* (Viking, New York, 1964). For the American impact on Europe, Michael Kraus, *The Atlantic Civilization: Eighteenth-Century Origins* (Cornell University Press, Ithaca, 1949), A. L. Rowse, pertinent chapters in *The Elizabethans and America* (Harper & Row, New York, 1959), E. J. Hamilton, *American Treasure and the Price Revolution in Spain* (Octagon Books, New York, 1934).

Chapter 2

Edmund S. Morgan tells the story of John Winthrop in *The Puritan Dilemma* (Little, Brown, Boston, 1958). On immigration see the pertinent chapters in Jones and Wittke as well as Marcus Hansen, *The Atlantic Migration* (Harper &

Row, New York, 1940). Also see Darrett B. Rutman, *The Morning of America 1603–1789* (Houghton Mifflin, Boston, 1971), a brief and thoughtful colonial survey, and Thomas J. Wertenbaker's *The Founding of American Civilization* (3 vols., Scribner's, New York, 1938, 1942, 1947). For more specific examples, George F. Willison, *Saints and Strangers* (Reynal & Hitchcock, New York, 1945), Ian Charles Graham, *Colonists from Scotland* (Cornell University Press, Ithaca, N.Y., 1956), and W. F. Dunaway, *The Scotch-Irish in Colonial Pennsylvania* (University of North Carolina Press, Chapel Hill, 1944). Philip Curtin studies the *Atlantic Slave Trade* (University of Wisconsin Press, Madison, 1970). Curti sums up European influences as does Louis B. Wright, *The Cultural Life of the American Colonies* (Harper & Row, New York, 1957). Curtis P. Nettels, *The Roots of American Civilization* (Crofts, New York, 1963) contains an analysis of the impact of the American environment.

Chapter 3

Edmund S. Morgan examines family life in *The Puritan Family* (Peter Smith, Gloucester, Mass., 1966) and *Virginians at Home* (Holt, Rinehart & Winston, New York, 1963). Kenneth A. Lockridge, *A New England Town: The First Hundred Years* (Norton, New York, 1970) and John Demos, *A Little Commonwealth* (Oxford University Press, New York, 1970) study social change and family structure in two small communities. Julia C. Spruill covers *Woman's Life and Work in the Southern Colonies* (Norton, New York, 1952). See also pertinent material in Hogeland and Altbach. On religion, Alan Simpson, *Puritanism in Old and New England* (University of Chicago Press, Chicago, 1955), Perry Miller, *The New England Mind: From Colony to Province* (Harvard University Press, Cambridge, 1953), Darrett B. Rutman, *American Puritanism* (Lippincott, Philadelphia, 1969), Edmund S. Morgan, *Visible Saints* (Cornell University Press, Ithaca, N.Y., 1963), E. S. Gaustad, *The Great Awakening in New England* (Harper & Row, New York, 1957), Alan Heimert, *Religion and the American Mind* (Harvard University Press, Cambridge, 1966). See also the pertinent material in Curti and in Daniel Boorstin, *The Americans: The Colonial Experience* (Random House, New York, 1958). On class structure see pertinent material in Nettels, Marcus Jernegan, *Laboring and Dependent Classes in Colonial America* (University of Chicago Press, Chicago, 1931), A. E. Smith, *Colonists in Bondage* (University of North Carolina Press, Chapel Hill, 1947), Bernard Bailyn, *The New England Merchants in the Seventeenth Century* (Harvard University Press, Cambridge, 1955), Louis B. Wright, *The First Gentlemen of Virginia* (Huntington Library, Pasadena, Cal., 1940), and Jackson T. Main, *The Social Structure in Revolutionary America* (Princeton University Press, Princeton, N.J., 1965). On slaves, see Franklin, and for the rise of prejudice, Winthrop D. Jordan, *White over Black: American Attitudes Toward the Negro* (University of North Carolina Press, Chapel Hill, 1968). On the economy see pertinent material in Fred A. Shannon, *America's Economic Growth* (Macmillan, New York, 1951) and the Wertenbacker volumes on *The Founding of American Civilization*. Also Carl Bridenbaugh, *The Colonial Craftsman* (New York University Press, New York, 1940).

Chapter 4

Carl Van Doren has the best biography of *Benjamin Franklin* (Viking, New York, 1938). William L. Sachse discusses colonial contacts abroad in *The Colonial American in Britain* (University of Wisconsin Press, Madison, 1956). Urban life is covered thoroughly by Carl Bridenbaugh, *Cities in the Wilderness* (Ronald, New York, 1938) and *Cities in Revolt* (Knopf, New York, 1955). A comprehensive view of colonial culture is found in Louis B. Wright, *The Cultural Life of the American Colonies* (Harper & Row, New York, 1957). See also the chapter in Curti on the arts and sciences. Persons has illuminating material on American and the European enlightenment. See also Brooke Hindle, *The Pursuit of Science in Revolutionary America* (University of North Carolina Press, Chapel Hill, 1956).

Chapter 5

The multivolume biography *Jefferson and His Time* (Little, Brown, Boston, 1948–1974) by Dumas Malone has five volumes to date. Adrienne Koch analyzes *The Philosophy of Thomas Jefferson* (Columbia University Press, New York, 1943). A brief selection of *Thomas Jefferson on Democracy* (Greenwood, New York, 1939) has been edited by Saul K. Padover. See also Edwin T. Martin, *Thomas Jefferson: Scientist* (Macmillan, New York, 1961) and Merrill D. Peterson, *The Jeffersonian Image in the American Mind* (Oxford University Press, New York, 1960). General and good accounts of the Revolution include John R. Alden, *History of the American Revolution* (Knopf, New York, 1969), E. S. Morgan, *The Birth of the Republic* (University of Chicago Press, Chicago, 1956), and Gordon Wood, *The Creation of the American Republic* (University of North Carolina Press, Chapel Hill, 1969). Dan Lacy analyzes *The Meaning of the American Revolution* (New American Library, New York, 1964) and Bernard Bailyn examines *The Ideological Origins of the American Revolution* (Harvard University Press, Cambridge, 1967). R. R. Palmer sets the Revolution in the larger context of the European world in *The Age of the Democratic Revolution* (Princeton University Press, Princeton, N.J., 1959), while Durand Echeverria notes its impact on the French in *Mirage in the West* (Princeton University Press, Princeton, N.J., 1957). See also Richard B. Morris, *The American Revolution Reconsidered* (Harper & Row, New York, 1967) and Elisha P. Douglas, *Rebels and Democrats* (University of North Carolina Press, Chapel Hill, 1955).

Chapter 6

J. C. Miller provides a good account of *Alexander Hamilton: A Portrait in Paradox* (Harper & Row, New York, 1959). On nationalism see pertinent chapters in Kohn and Curti. Also Reginald Horsman, *The Causes of the War of 1812* (A. S. Barnes, New York, 1962), A. K. Weinberg, *Manifest Destiny* (Johns Hopkins Press, Baltimore, 1935), Frederick Merk, *Manifest Destiny and Mission in American History* (Knopf, New York, 1963), and George Dangerfield, *The Awakening of American Nationalism* (Harper & Row, New York,

1965). On economic developments see Douglas C. North, *The Economic Growth of the United States* (Norton, New York, 1966), John Shover, *American Railroads* (University of Chicago Press, Chicago, 1961), George R. Taylor, *The Transportation Revolution 1815–1860* (Harper & Row, New York, 1968), and Carter Goodrich, ed., *Canals and American Economic Development* (Kennikat Press, Port Washington, New York, 1961). For the European reaction to American technology and industry, Marvin Fisher, *Workshops in the Wilderness: the European Response to American Industrialization 1830–1860* (Oxford University Press, New York, 1967). On the Marshall Court, see J. C. Garraty, ed., *Quarrels That Have Shaped the Constitution* (Harper & Row, New York, 1964).

Chapter 7

On Jackson see J. C. Ward, *Andrew Jackson: Symbol for an Age* (Oxford University Press, New York, 1955) and Robert V. Remini, *Andrew Jackson* (Harper & Row, New York, 1969). On reform and change, see Chilton Williamson, *American Suffrage: From Property to Democracy* (Princeton University Press, Princeton, N.J., 1960), Alice Felt Tyler, *Freedom's Ferment* (Harper & Row, New York, 1944), Saul K. Padover, *The Meaning of Democracy* (Praeger, New York, 1963), Arthur E. Bester, *Backwoods Utopias* (University of Pennsylvania Press, Philadelphia, 1950), Merle Curti, *The American Peace Crusade 1815–1861* (Duke University Press, Durham, 1929), Louis Filler, *The Crusade Against Slavery* (Harper & Row, New York, 1960), Eleanor Flexner, *Century of Struggle* (Harvard University Press, Cambridge, 1970). International reform ties may be seen in Frank Thistlethwaite, *The Anglo-American Connection in the Early Nineteenth Century* (Russell and Russell, New York, 1959) and G. D. Lillibridge, *Beacon of Freedom: The Impact of American Democracy on Great Britain 1830–1870* (University of Pennsylvania Press, Philadelphia, 1955). On labor see Foster R. Dulles, *Labor in America* (Thomas Y. Crowell, New York, 1960) and Norman Ware, *The Industrial Worker 1840–1860* (Peter Smith, Gloucester, Mass., 1924), and for the rise of poverty, R. H. Bremner, *From the Depths* (New York University Press, New York, 1956).

Chapter 8

For biography, see Lloyd C. M. Hare, *The Greatest American Woman, Lucretia Mott* (Greenwood, New York, 1937) and Othelia Cromwell, *Lucretia Mott* (Russell & Russell, New York, 1958). On women see pertinent chapters in Robert E. Riegel, *American Women: A Story of Social Change* (Fairleigh Dickinson University Press, Rutherford, N.J., 1970), Hogeland, *Women and Womanhood in America,* and Jean E. Friedman and William G. Shade, *Our American Sisters* (Allyn and Bacon, Boston, 1973), and some useful material in the dated Arthur Calhoun, *A Social History of the American Family* (AMS Press, New York, 1918). Family life is also found in Robert Riegel, *Young America* (Greenwood, New York, 1949), and in the descriptions of farm life in R. C. Buley, *The Old Northwest Pioneer Period, 1815–1840,* 2 vols., (Indiana Historical

Society, Indianapolis, 1950). On children, see Bernard Wishy, *The Child and the Republic* (University of Pennsylvania Press, Philadelphia, 1968). On religion, see pertinent chapters in Curti, also in W. W. Sweet, *The Story of Religion in America* (Harper & Row, New York, 1939), and W. L. Sperry, *Religion in America* (Macmillan, New York, 1946). Also Bernard A. Weisberger, *They Gathered at the River* (Quadrangle, Chicago, 1958) for revivalism. For social life, see Wishy and also Edward Pessen, *Riches, Class, and Power Before the Civil War* (Heath, Lexington, Mass., 1973). For slavery, see Kenneth Stampp, *The Peculiar Institution: Slavery in the Ante-bellum South* (Knopf, New York, 1956), Norman R. Yetman, *Life Under the "Peculiar Institution"* (Holt, Rinehart & Winston, New York, 1970), John Blassingame, *The Slave Community* (Oxford University Press, New York, 1972), Stanley Feldstein, *Once a Slave* (Morrow, New York, 1971), and *Time on the Cross* (Little, Brown, Boston, 1974), a controversial examination by Robert W. Fogel and Stanley L. Engerman.

Chapter 9

For biography see Jonathan Messerli, *Horace Mann: A Biography* (Knopf, New York, 1972) and the chapter in Merle Curti, *The Social Ideas of American Educators* (Scribner's, New York, 1935). For cultural life, Curti, *The Growth of American Thought* is indispensable. Also Russel B. Nye, *The Cultural Life of the New Nation* (Harper & Row, New York, 1960). For education, see Butts and Cremin. Check pertinent material in Larkin for art. For literature, see Spiller. On recreation and entertainment, see Carl Bode, *The Anatomy of American Popular Culture 1850–1861* (Southern Illinois University Press, Carbondale, 1970) and also pertinent material in Cantor and Werthman as well as Nye, *The Unembarrassed Muse.*

Chapter 10

The best one-volume biography is Benjamin P. Thomas, *Abraham Lincoln* (Knopf, New York, 1952). See also Herbert Mitgang, ed., *Lincoln as They Saw Him* (Collier, New York, 1962). Foreign views of the war are found in Belle Baker Sideman and Lillian Friedman, eds., *Europe Looks at the Civil War* (Orion Press, New York, 1960). Allan Nevins, *Ordeal of the Union* (Scribner's, New York, 1947–1971) is the most thorough coverage of the war. Bruce Catton's three-volume *The Centennial History of the Civil War* (Doubleday, New York, 1961, 1963, 1965) covers the military aspects. An excellent one-volume account is J. G. Randall and David Donald, *The Civil War and Reconstruction* (Heath, Lexington, Mass., 1961). E. M. Coulter, *The Confederate States of America* (Louisiana State University Press, Baton Rouge, 1950) covers the impact of the war on the South. Robert Cruden, *The War that Never Ended* (Prentice-Hall, Englewood Cliffs, N.J., 1973) describes the impact on common people. Bell I. Wiley describes both *The Life of Johnny Reb* (Bobbs-Merrill, Indianapolis, 1943) and *The Life of Billy Yank* (Doubleday, New York, 1952) for the impact on those who fought. Benjamin Quarles discusses *The*

Negro in the Civil War (Little, Brown, Boston, 1953), and Edmund Wilson calls it *Patriotic Gore: Studies in the Literature of the Civil War* (Oxford University Press, New York, 1966). Curti discusses the impact of the war on intellectual life, and Robert Penn Warren looks thoughtfully at *The Legacy of the Civil War* (Random House, New York, 1960).

Chapter 11

For biography, see Fawn M. Brodie, *Thaddeus Stevens: Scourge of the South* (Norton, New York, 1959). For a general treatment of Reconstruction see Randall and Donald, *The Civil War and Reconstruction*. Also Kenneth Stampp, *The Era of Reconstruction* (Knopf, New York, 1965) and John Hope Franklin, *Reconstruction After the Civil War* (University of Chicago Press, Chicago, 1961).

The Declaration of Independence

When in the Course of human events, it becomes necessary for one people to dissolve the political bands which have connected them with another, and to assume among the Powers of the earth, the separate and equal station to which the Laws of Nature and of Nature's God entitle them, a decent respect to the opinions of mankind requires that they should declare the causes which impel them to the separation.

We hold these truths to be self-evident, that all men are created equal, that they are endowed by their Creator with certain unalienable Rights, that among these are Life, Liberty and the pursuit of Happiness. That to secure these rights, Governments are instituted among Men, deriving their just powers from the consent of the governed, That whenever any Form of Government becomes destructive of these ends, it is the Right of the People to alter or to abolish it, and to institute new Government, laying its foundation on such principles and organizing its powers in such form, as to them shall seem most likely to effect their Safety and Happiness. Prudence, indeed, will dictate that Governments long established should not be changed for light and transient causes; and accordingly all experience hath shown, that mankind are more disposed to suffer, while evils are sufferable, than to right themselves by abolishing the forms to which they are accustomed. But when a long train of abuses and usurpations, pursuing invariably the same Object evinces a design to reduce them under absolute Despotism, it is their right, it is their duty, to throw off such Government, and to provide new Guards for their future security.—Such has been the patient sufferance of these Colonies; and such is now the necessity which constrains them to alter their former Systems of Government. The history of the present King of Great Britain is a history of repeated injuries and usurpations, all having in direct object the establishment of an absolute Tyranny over these States. To prove this, let Facts be submitted to a candid world.

He has refused his Assent to Laws, the most wholesome and necessary for the public good.

He has forbidden his Governors to pass Laws of immediate and pressing importance, unless suspended in their operation till his Assent should be obtained; and when so suspended, he has utterly neglected to attend to them.

He has refused to pass other Laws for the accommodation of large districts of people, unless those people would relinquish the right of Representation in the Legislature, a right inestimable to them and formidable to tyrants only.

He has called together legislative bodies at places unusual, uncomfortable, and distant from the despository of their Public Records, for the sole purpose of fatiguing them into compliance with his measures.

He has dissolved Representative Houses repeatedly, for opposing with manly firmness his invasions on the rights of the people.

He has refused for a long time, after such dissolutions, to cause others to be elected; whereby the Legislative Powers, incapable of Annihilation, have returned to the People at large for their exercise; the State remaining in the mean time exposed to all the dangers of invasion from without, and convulsions within.

He has endeavoured to prevent the population of these States; for that purpose obstructing the Laws of Naturalization of Foreigners; refusing to pass others to encourage their migration hither, and raising the conditions of new Appropriations of Lands.

He has obstructed the Administration of Justice, by refusing his Assent to Laws for establishing Judiciary Powers.

He has made Judges dependent on his Will alone, for the tenure of their offices, and the amount and payment of their salaries.

He has erected a multitide of New Offices, and sent hither swarms of Officers to harass our People, and eat out their substance.

He has kept among us, in times of peace, Standing Armies without the Consent of our legislature.

He has affected to render the Military independent of and superior to the Civil Power.

He has combined with others to subject us to a jurisdiction foreign to our constitution, and unacknowledged by our laws; giving his Assent to their acts of pretended legislation:

For quartering large bodies of armed troops among us:

For protecting them, by a mock Trial, from Punishment for any Murders which they should commit on the Inhabitants of these States:

For cutting off our Trade with all parts of the world:

For imposing taxes on us without our Consent:

For depriving us in many cases, of the benefits of Trial by Jury:

For transporting us beyond Seas to be tried for pretended offences:

For abolishing the free System of English Laws in a neighbouring Province, establishing therein an Arbitrary government, and enlarging its Boundaries so as to render it at once an example and fit instrument for introducing the same absolute rule into these Colonies:

For taking away our Charters, abolishing our most valuable Laws, and altering fundamentally the Forms of our Governments:

For suspending our own Legislature, and declaring themselves invested with Power to legislate for us in all cases whatsoever.

He has abdicated Government here, by declaring us out of his Protection and waging War against us.

He has plundered our seas, ravaged our Coasts, burnt our towns, and destroyed the lives of our people.

He is at this time transporting large armies of foreign mercenaries to compleat the works of death, desolation and tyranny, already begun with circumstances of Cruelty & perfidy scarcely paralleled in the most barbarous ages, and totally unworthy the Head of a civilized nation.

He has constrained our fellow Citizens taken Captive on the high Seas to bear Arms against their Country, to become the executioners of their friends and Brethren, or to fall themselves by their Hands.

He has excited domestic insurrections amongst us, and has endeavoured to bring on the inhabitants of our frontiers, the merciless Indian Savages, whose known rule of warfare, is an undistinguished destruction of all ages, sexes and conditions.

In every stage of these Oppressions We have Petitioned for Redress in the most humble terms: Our repeated Petitions have been answered only by repeated injury. A Prince, whose character is thus marked by every act which may define a Tyrant, is unfit to be the ruler of a free People.

Nor have We been wanting in attention to our British brethren. We have warned them from time to time of attempts by their legislature to extend an unwarrantable jurisdiction over us. We have reminded them of the circumstances of our emigration and settlement here. We have appealed to their native justice and magnanimity, and we have conjured them by the ties of our common kindred to disavow these usurpations, which, would inevitably interrupt our connections and correspondence. They too have been deaf to the voice of justice and of consanguinity. We must, therefore, acquiesce in the necessity, which denounces our Separation, and hold them, as we hold the rest of mankind, Enemies in War, in Peace Friends.

We, therefore, the Representatives of the united States of America, in General Congress, Assembled, appealing to the Supreme Judge of the world for the rectitude of our intentions, do, in the Name, and by Authority of the good People of these Colonies, solemnly publish and declare, That these United Colonies are, and of Right ought to be Free and Independent States; that they are Absolved from all Allegiance to the British Crown, and that all political connection between them and the State of Great Britain, is and ought to be totally dissolved; and that as Free and Independent States, they have full Power to levy War, conclude Peace, contract Alliances, establish Commerce, and to do all other Acts and Things which Independent States may of right do. And for the support of this Declaration, with a firm reliance on the Protection of Divine Providence, we mutually pledge to each other our Lives, our Fortunes and our sacred Honor.

The Constitution of the United States

We the people of the United States, in Order to form a more perfect Union, establish Justice, insure domestic Tranquility, provide for the common defence, promote the general Welfare, and secure the Blessings of Liberty to ourselves and our Posterity, do ordain and establish this CONSTITUTION for the United States of America.

ARTICLE I

Section 1. All legislative Powers herein granted shall be vested in a Congress of the United States, which shall consist of a Senate and House of Representatives.

Section 2. The House of Representatives shall be composed of Members chosen every second Year by the People of the several States, and the Electors in each State shall have the Qualifications requisite for Electors of the most numerous Branch of the State Legislature.

No Person shall be a Representative who shall not have attained to the Age of twenty-five Years, and been seven Years a Citizen of the United States, and who shall not, when elected, be an Inhabitant of that State in which he shall be chosen.

Representatives and direct Taxes shall be apportioned among the several States which may be included within this Union, according to their respective Numbers, which shall be determined by adding to the whole Number of free Persons, including those bound to Service for a Term of Years, and excluding Indians not taxed, three fifths of all other Persons. The actual Enumeration shall be made within three Years after the first Meeting of the Congress of the United States, and within every subsequent Term of ten Years, in such Manner as they shall by Law direct. The Number of Representatives shall not exceed one for every thirty Thousand, but each State shall have at Least one Representative; and until such enumeration shall be made, the State of New Hampshire shall be entitled to chuse three, Massachusetts eight, Rhode-Island and Providence Plantations one, Connecticut five, New-York six, New Jersey four, Pennsylvania eight, Delaware one, Maryland six, Virginia ten, North Carolina five, South Carolina five, and Georgia three.

When vacancies happen in the Representation from any State, the Executive Authority thereof shall issue Writs of Election to fill such Vacancies.

The House of Representatives shall chuse their Speaker and other Officers; and shall have the sole Power of Impeachment.

Section 3. The Senate of the United States shall be composed of two Senators from each State, chosen by the Legislature thereof, for six Years; and each Senator shall have one Vote.

Immediately after they shall be assembled in Consequence of the first Election, they shall be divided as equally as may be into three Classes. The Seats of the Senators of the first Class shall be vacated at the Expiration of the second Year, of the second Class at the Expiration of the fourth Year, and of the third Class at the Expiration of the sixth Year, so that one-third may be chosen every second Year; and if Vacancies happen by Resignation, or otherwise, during the Recess of the Legislature of any State, the Executive thereof may make temporary Appointments until the next Meeting of the Legislature, which shall then fill such Vacancies.

No Person shall be a Senator who shall not have attained to the Age of thirty Years, and been nine Years a Citizen of the United States, and who shall not, when elected, be an Inhabitant of that State in which he shall be chosen.

The Vice President of the United States shall be President of the Senate, but shall have no vote, unless they be equally divided.

The Senate shall chuse their other Officers, and also a President pro tempore, in the absence of the Vice President, or when he shall exercise the Office of the President of the United States.

The Senate shall have the sole Power to try all Impeachments. When sitting for that purpose, they shall be on Oath or Affirmation. When the President of the United States is tried, the Chief Justice shall preside: And no person shall be convicted without the Concurrence of two thirds of the Members present.

Judgment in Cases of Impeachment shall not extend further than to removal from Office, and disqualification to hold and enjoy any Office of honor, Trust, or Profit under the United States: but the Party convicted shall nevertheless be liable and subject to Indictment, Trial, Judgment, and Punishment, according to Law.

Section 4. The Times, Places and Manner of holding Elections for Senators and Representatives, shall be prescribed in each state by the Legislature thereof; but the Congress may at any time by Law make or alter such Regulations, except as to the Places of Chusing Senators.

The Congress shall assemble at least once in every Year, and such Meeting shall be on the first Monday in December, unless they shall by Law appoint a different Day.

Section 5. Each House shall be the Judge of the Elections, Returns and Qualifications of its own Members, and a Majority of each shall constitute a Quorum to do Business; but a smaller number may adjourn from day to day, and may be authorized to compel the Attendance of absent Members, in such Manner, and under such Penalties, as each House may provide.

Each House may determine the Rules of its Proceedings, punish its Members for disorderly Behavior, and, with the Concurrence of two thirds, expel a Member.

Each House shall keep a Journal of its Proceedings, and from time to time publish the same, excepting such Parts as may in their Judgment require Secrecy; and the Yeas and Nays of the Members of either House on any question shall, at the Desire of one fifth of those Present, be entered on the Journal.

Neither House, during the Session of Congress, shall, without the Consent of the other, adjourn for more than three days, nor to any other Place than that in which the two Houses shall be sitting.

Section 6. The Senators and Representatives shall receive a Compensation for their Services, to be ascertained by Law, and paid out of the Treasury of the United States. They shall in all Cases, except Treason, Felony, and Breach of the Peace, be privileged from Arrest during their Attendance at the Session of their respective Houses, and in going to and returning from the same; and for any Speech or Debate in either House, they shall not be questioned in any other Place.

No Senator or Representative shall, during the Time for which he was elected, be appointed to any civil Office under the Authority of the United States, which shall have been created, or the Emoluments whereof shall have been increased, during such time; and no Person holding any Office under the United States shall be a Member of either House during his continuance in Office.

Section 7. All Bills for raising Revenue shall originate in the House of Representatives; but the Senate may propose or concur with Amendments as on other bills.

Every Bill which shall have passed the House of Representatives and the Senate, shall, before it become a Law, be presented to the President of the United States; If he approve he shall sign it, but if not he shall return it, with his Objections, to that House in which it shall have originated, who shall enter the Objections at large on their Journal, and proceed to reconsider it. If after such Consideration two thirds of that House shall agree to pass the bill, it shall be sent, together with the objections, to the other House, by which it shall likewise be reconsidered, and if approved by two thirds of that House, it shall become a Law. But in all such Cases the Votes of both Houses shall be determined by Yeas and Nays, and the Names of the Persons voting for and against the Bill shall be entered on the Journal of each House respectively. If any Bill shall not be returned by the President within ten Days (Sundays excepted) after it shall have been presented to him, the Same shall be a Law, in like Manner as if he had signed it, unless the Congress by their Adjournment prevent its Return, in which Case it shall not be a Law.

Every Order, Resolution, or vote to which the Concurrence of the Senate and House of Representatives may be necessary (except on a question of Adjournment) shall be presented to the President of the United States; and before the Same shall take Effect, shall be approved by him, or being disapproved by him, shall be repassed by two thirds of the Senate and House of Representatives, according to the Rules and Limitations prescribed in the Case of a Bill.

Section 8.   The Congress shall have Power To lay and collect Taxes, Duties, Imposts and Excises, to pay the Debts and provide for the common Defence and general Welfare of the United States; but all Duties, Imposts and Excises shall be uniform throughout the United States.

To borrow money on the credit of the United States;

To regulate Commerce with foreign Nations, and among the several States, and with the Indian Tribes;

To establish an uniform Rule of Naturalization, and uniform Laws on the subject of Bankruptcies throughout the United States;

To coin Money, regulate the Value thereof, and of foreign Coin, and fix the Standard of Weights and Measures;

To provide for the Punishment of counterfeiting the Securities and current Coin of the United States;

To establish Post Offices and post Roads;

To promote the Progress of Science and useful Arts, by securing for limited Times to Authors and Inventors the exclusive Right to their respective Writings and Discoveries;

To constitute Tribunals inferior to the Supreme Court;

To define and punish Piracies and Felonies committed on the high Seas, and Offences against the Law of Nations;

To declare War, grant Letters of Marque and Reprisal, and make Rules concerning Captures on Land and Water;

To raise and support Armies, but no Appropriation of Money to that Use shall be for a longer Term than two Years;

To provide and maintain a Navy;

To make Rules for the Government and Regulation of the land and naval forces;

To provide for calling forth the Militia to execute the Laws of the Union, suppress Insurrections and repel Invasions;

To provide for organizing, arming, and disciplining the Militia, and for governing such Part of them as may be employed in the Service of the United States, reserving to the States respectively, the Appointment of the Officers, and the Authority of training the Militia according to the discipline prescribed by Congress;

To exercise exclusive Legislation in all Cases whatsoever, over such District (not exceeding ten Miles square) as may, by Cession of particular States, and the acceptance of Congress, become the Seat of Government of the United States, and to exercise like Authority over all Places purchased by the Consent of the Legislature of the State in which the Same shall be, for the Erection of Forts, Magazines, Arsenals, dock-Yards, and other needful Buildings;—And

To make all Laws which shall be necessary and proper for carrying into Execution the foregoing Powers, and all other Powers vested by this Constitution in the Government of the United States, or in any Department or Officer thereof.

Section 9.   The Migration or Importation of such Persons as any of the States now existing shall think proper to admit, shall not be prohibited by the Congress prior to the Year one thousand eight hundred and eight, but a tax or duty may be imposed on such Importation, not exceeding ten dollars for each Person.

The privilege of the Writ of Habeas Corpus shall not be suspended, unless when in Cases of Rebellion or Invasion the public Safety may require it.

No Bill of Attainder or ex post facto Law shall be passed.

No capitation, or other direct, Tax shall be laid unless in Proportion to the Census or Enumeration herein before directed to be taken.

No Tax or Duty shall be laid on Articles exported from any State.

No Preference shall be given by any Regulation of Revenue to the Ports of one State over those of another: nor shall Vessels bound to, or from, one State, be obliged to enter, clear, or pay Duties in another.

No Money shall be drawn from the Treasury, but in Consequence of Appropriations made by Law; and a regular Statement and Account of the Receipts and Expenditures of all public Money shall be published from time to time.

No Title of Nobility shall be granted by the United States: And no Person holding any Office of Profit or Trust under them, shall, without the Consent of the Congress, accept of any present, Emolument, Office, or Title, of any kind whatever, from any King, Prince, or foreign State.

Section 10. No state shall enter into any Treaty, Alliance, or Confederation; grant Letters of Marque and Reprisal; coin Money; emit Bills of Credit; make any Thing but gold and silver Coin a Tender in Payment of Debts; pass any Bill of Attainder, ex post facto Law, or Law impairing the Obligation of Contracts, or grant any Title of Nobility.

No State shall, without the Consent of the Congress, lay any Imposts or Duties on Imports or Exports, except what may be absolutely necessary for executing its inspection Laws: and the net Produce of all Duties and Imposts, laid by any State on Imports or Exports, shall be for the Use of the Treasury of the United States; and all such Laws shall be subject to the Revision and Control of the Congress.

No State shall, without the Consent of Congress, lay any duty of Tonnage, keep Troops, or Ships of War in time of Peace, enter into any Agreement or Compact with another State, or with a foreign Power, or engage in War, unless actually invaded, or in such imminent Danger as will not admit of delay.

ARTICLE II

Section 1. The executive Power shall be vested in a President of the United States of America. He shall hold his Office during the Term of four years, and, together with the Vice-President, chosen for the same Term, be elected, as follows:

Each State shall appoint, in such Manner as the Legislature thereof may direct, a Number of Electors, equal to the whole Number of Senators and Representatives to which the State may be entitled in the Congress; but no Senator or Representative, or Person holding an Office of Trust or Profit under the United States, shall be appointed an Elector.

The Electors shall meet in their respective States, and vote by Ballot for two persons, of whom one at least shall not be an Inhabitant of the same State with themselves. And they shall make a List of all the Persons voted for, and of the Number of Votes for each; which List they shall sign and certify, and transmit sealed to the Seat of the Government of the United States, directed to the President of the Senate. The President of the Senate shall, in the Presence of the Senate and House of Representatives, open all the Certificates, and the Votes shall then be counted. The Person having the greatest Number of Votes shall be the President, if such Number be a Majority of the whole Number of Electors appointed; and if there be more than one who have such Majority, and have an equal Number of Votes, then the House of Representatives shall immediately chuse by Ballot one of them for President; and if no Person have a Majority, then from the five highest on the List the said House shall in like Manner chuse the President. But in chusing the President, the Votes shall be taken by States, the Representation from each State having one Vote; a quorum for this Purpose shall consist of a Member or Members from two-thirds of the States, and a Majority of all the States shall be necessary to a Choice. In every Case, after the Choice of the President, the Person having the greatest Number of Votes of the Electors shall be the Vice President. But if there should remain two or more who have equal votes, the Senate shall chuse from them by Ballot the Vice-President.

The Congress may determine the Time of chusing the Electors, and the Day on which they shall give their Votes; which Day shall be the same throughout the United States.

No person except a natural-born Citizen, or a Citizen of the United States, at the time of the Adoption of this Constitution, shall be eligible to the Office of President; neither shall any Person be eligible to that Office who shall not have attained to the Age of thirty-five years, and been fourteen Years a Resident within the United States.

In Case of the Removal of the President from Office, or of his Death, Resignation, or Inability to discharge the Powers and Duties of the said Office, the same shall devolve on the Vice President, and the Congress may by Law provide for the Case of Removal, Death, Resignation, or Inability, both of the President and Vice President, declaring what Officer shall then act as President, and such Officer shall act accordingly, until the disability be removed, or a President shall be elected.

The President shall, at stated Times, receive for his Services a Compensation, which shall neither be increased nor diminished during the Period for which he shall have been elected, and he shall not receive within that Period any other Emolument from the United States, or any of them.

Before he enter on the execution of his Office, he shall take the following Oath or Affirmation:—"I do solemnly swear (or affirm) that I will faithfully execute the Office of President of the United States, and will, to the best of my Ability, preserve, protect, and defend the Constitution of the United States."

Section 2. The President shall be Commander in Chief of the Army and Navy of the United States, and of the Militia of the several States, when called into the actual Service of the United States; he may require the Opinion, in writing, of the principal Officer in each of the executive Departments, upon any subject relating to the Duties of their respective Offices, and he shall have Power to Grant Reprieves and Pardons for Offences against the United States, except in Cases of Impeachment.

He shall have Power, by and with the Advice and Consent of the Senate, to make Treaties, provided two thirds of the Senators present concur; and he shall nominate, and by and with the Advice and Consent of the Senate, shall appoint Ambassadors, other public Ministers and Consuls, Judges of the supreme Court, and all other Officers of the United States, whose Appointments are not herein otherwise provided for, and which shall be established by Law: but the Congress may by Law vest the Appointment of such inferior Officers, as they think proper, in the President alone, in the Courts of Law, or in the Heads of Departments.

The President shall have Power to fill up all Vacancies that may happen during the Recess of the Senate, by granting Commissions which shall expire at the End of their next Session.

Section 3. He shall from time to time give to the Congress Information of the State of the Union, and recommend to their Consideration such Measures as he shall judge necessary and expedient; he may, on extraordinary occasions, convene both Houses, or either of them, and in Case of Disagreement between them, with respect to the Time of Adjournment, he may adjourn them to such Time as he shall think proper; he shall receive Ambassadors and other public Ministers; he shall take Care that the Laws be faithfully executed, and shall Commission all the Officers of the United States.

Section 4. The President, Vice President and all civil Officers of the United States, shall be removed from Office on Impeachment for, and Conviction of, Treason, Bribery, or other high crimes and Misdemeanors.

ARTICLE III

Section 1.   The judicial Power of the United States, shall be vested in one supreme Court, and in such inferior Courts as the Congress may from time to time ordain and establish. The Judges, both of the supreme and inferior Courts, shall hold their Offices during good Behaviour, and shall, at stated Times, receive for their Services, a Compensation, which shall not be diminished during their Continuance in Office.

Section 2.   The judicial Power shall extend to all Cases, in Law and Equity, arising under this Constitution, the Laws of the United States, and treaties made, or which shall be made, under their Authority;—to all Cases affecting ambassadors, other public ministers and consuls;—to all cases of admiralty and maritime Jurisdiction;—to Controversies to which the United States shall be a Party;—to Controversies between two or more States;—between a State and Citizens of another State;—between Citizens of different States,—between Citizens of the same State claiming Lands under Grants of different States, and between a State, or the Citizens thereof, and foreign States, Citizens or Subjects.

In all Cases affecting Ambassadors, other public Ministers and Consuls, and those in which a State shall be Party, the supreme Court shall have original Jurisdiction. In all the other Cases before mentioned, the supreme Court shall have appellate Jurisdiction, both as to Law and Fact, with such Exceptions, and under such Regulations as the Congress shall make.

The trial of all Crimes, except in Cases of Impeachment, shall be by Jury; and such Trial shall be held in the State where the said Crimes shall have been committed; but when not committed within any State, the Trial shall be at such Place or Places as the Congress may by Law have directed.

Section 3.   Treason against the United States, shall consist only in levying War against them, or in adhering to their Enemies, giving them Aid and Comfort. No Person shall be convicted of Treason unless on the Testimony of two Witnesses to the same overt Act, or on Confession in open Court.

The Congress shall have power to declare the Punishment of Treason, but no Attainder of Treason shall work Corruption of Blood, or Forfeiture except during the Life of the Person attainted.

ARTICLE IV

Section 1.   Full Faith and Credit shall be given in each State to the public Acts, Records, and judicial Proceedings of every other State. And the Congress may by general Laws prescribe the Manner in which such Acts, Records, and Proceedings shall be proved, and the Effect thereof.

Section 2.   The Citizens of each State shall be entitled to all Privileges and Immunities of Citizens in the several States.

A Person charged in any State with Treason, Felony, or other Crime, who shall flee from Justice, and be found in another State, shall on demand of the executive Authority of the State from which he fled, be delivered up, to be removed to the State having Jurisdiction of the crime.

No Person held to Service or Labour in one State, under the Laws thereof, escaping into another, shall, in Consequence of any Law or Regulation therein, be discharged from such Service or Labour, but shall be delivered up on Claim of the Party to whom such Service or Labour may be due.

Section 3.   New States may be admitted by the Congress into this Union; but no new State shall be formed or erected within the Jurisdiction of any other State; nor any State be formed by the Junction of two or more States, or parts of States, without the Consent of the Legislatures of the States concerned as well as of the Congress.

The Congress shall have Power to dispose of and make all needful Rules and Regulations respecting the Territory or other Property belonging to the United States; and nothing in this

Constitution shall be so construed as to Prejudice any Claims of the United States, or of any particular State.

Section 4.   The United States shall guarantee to every State in this Union a Republican Form of Government, and shall protect each of them against Invasion; and on Application of the Legislature, or the Executive (when the Legislature cannot be convened) against domestic Violence.

ARTICLE V

The Congress, whenever two-thirds of both Houses shall deem it necessary, shall propose Amendments to this Constitution, or, on the Application of the Legislatures of two-thirds of the several States, shall call a Convention for proposing Amendments, which, in either Case, shall be valid to all Intents and Purposes, as part of this Constitution, when ratified by the Legislatures of three-fourths of the several States, or by Conventions in three-fourths thereof, as the one or the other Mode of Ratification may be proposed by the Congress; Provided that no Amendment which may be made prior to the Year One thousand eight hundred and eight shall in any Manner affect the first and fourth Clauses in the Ninth Section of the first Article; and that no State, without its Consent, shall be deprived of its equal Suffrage in the Senate.

ARTICLE VI

All Debts contracted and Engagements entered into, before the Adoption of this Constitution, shall be as valid against the United States under this Constitution, as under the Confederation.

This Constitution, and the Laws of the United States which shall be made in Pursuance thereof; and all Treaties made, or which shall be made, under the Authority of the United States, shall be the supreme Law of the Land; and the Judges in every State shall be bound thereby, any Thing in the Constitution or Laws of any State to the Contrary notwithstanding.

The Senators and Representatives before mentioned, and the Members of the several State Legislatures, and all executive and judicial Officers, both of the United States and of the several States, shall be bound by Oath or Affirmation to support this Constitution; but no religious Test shall ever be required as a qualification to any Office or public Trust under the United States.

ARTICLE VII

The Ratification of the Conventions of nine States shall be sufficient for the Establishment of this Constitution between the States so ratifying the same.

Done in Convention by the Unanimous Consent of the States present the Seventeenth Day of September in the Year of our Lord one thousand seven hundred and Eighty seven, and of the Independence of the United States of America the Twelfth. In Witness whereof We have hereunto subscribed our Names.

Articles in Addition to, and Amendment of, the Constitution of the United States of America, Proposed by Congress, and Ratified by the Legislatures of the Several States, Pursuant to the Fifth Article of the Original Constitution.

AMENDMENT I [1791]

Congress shall make no law respecting an establishment of religion, or prohibiting the free exercise thereof; or abridging the freedom of speech, or of the press; or the right of the people peaceably to assemble, and to petition the Government for a redress of grievances.

AMENDMENT II [1791]

A well regulated Militia, being necessary to the security of a free State, the right of the people to keep and bear Arms shall not be infringed.

AMENDMENT III [1791]

No Soldier shall, in time of peace, be quartered in any house, without the consent of the Owner, nor in time of war, but in a manner to be prescribed by law.

AMENDMENT IV [1791]

The right of the people to be secure in their persons, houses, papers, and effects, against unreasonable searches and seizures, shall not be violated, and no Warrants shall issue, but upon probable cause, supported by Oath or affirmation, and particularly describing the place to be searched, and the persons or things to be seized.

AMENDMENT V [1791]

No person shall be held to answer for a capital or otherwise infamous crime, unless on a presentment or indictment of a Grand Jury, except in cases arising in the land or naval forces, or in the Militia, when in actual service in time of War or public danger; nor shall any person be subject for the same offence to be twice put in jeopardy of life or limb; nor shall be compelled in any criminal case to be a witness against himself, nor be deprived of life, liberty, or property, without due process of law; nor shall private property be taken for public use, without just compensation.

AMENDMENT VI [1791]

In all criminal prosecutions, the accused shall enjoy the right to a speedy and public trial, by an impartial jury of the State and district wherein the crime shall have been committed, which district shall have been previously ascertained by law, and to be informed of the nature and cause of the accusation; to be confronted with the witnesses against him; to have compulsory process for obtaining witnesses in his favor, and to have the Assistance of Counsel for his defence.

AMENDMENT VII [1791]

In suits at common law, where the value in controversy shall exceed twenty dollars, the right of trial by jury shall be preserved, and no fact tried by a jury, shall be otherwise reexamined in any Court of the United States, than according to the rules of the common law.

AMENDMENT VIII [1791]

Excessive bail shall not be required, nor excessive fines imposed, nor cruel and unusual punishments inflicted.

AMENDMENT IX [1791]

The enumeration in the Constitution, of certain rights, shall not be construed to deny or disparage others retained by the people.

AMENDMENT X [1791]

The powers not delegated to the United States by the Constitution, nor prohibited by it to the States, are reserved to the States respectively, or to the people.

AMENDMENT XI [1798]

The Judicial power of the United States shall not be construed to extend to any suit in law or equity, commenced or prosecuted against one of the United States by Citizens of another State, or by Citizens or Subjects of any Foreign State.

AMENDMENT XII [1804]

The Electors shall meet in their respective States and vote by ballot for President and

Vice-President, one of whom, at least, shall not be an inhabitant of the same State with themselves; they shall name in their ballots the person voted for as President, and in distinct ballots the person voted for as Vice-President, and they shall make distinct lists of all persons voted for as President, and of all persons voted for as Vice-President, and of the number of votes for each, which list they shall sign and certify, and transmit sealed to the seat of the government of the United States, directed to the President of the Senate;—The President of the Senate shall, in the presence of the Senate and House of Representatives, open all the certificates and the votes shall then be counted;—The person having the greatest number of votes for President, shall be the President, if such number be a majority of the whole number of Electors appointed; and if no person have such majority, then from the persons having the highest numbers not exceeding three on the list of those voted for as President, the House of Representatives shall choose immediately, by ballot, the President. But in choosing the President, the votes shall be taken by states, the representation from each state having one vote; a quorum for this purpose shall consist of a member or members from two-thirds of the states, and a majority of all the states shall be necessary to a choice. And if the House of Representatives shall not choose a President whenever the right of choice shall devolve upon them, before the fourth day of March next following, then the Vice-President shall act as President, as in the case of the death or other constitutional disability of the President.—The person having the greatest number of votes as Vice-President, shall be the Vice-President, if such number be a majority of the whole number of Electors appointed, and if no person have a majority, then from the two highest numbers on the list, the Senate shall choose the Vice-President; a quorum for the purpose shall consist of two-thirds of the whole number of Senators, and a majority of the whole number shall be necessary to a choice. But no person constitutionally ineligible to the office of President shall be eligible to that of Vice-President of the United States.

AMENDMENT XIII [1865]

Section 1. Neither slavery nor involuntary servitude, except as a punishment for crime whereof the party shall have been duly convicted, shall exist within the United States, or any place subject to their jurisdiction.

Section 2. Congress shall have power to enforce this article by appropriate legislation.

AMENDMENT XIV [1868]

Section 1. All persons born or naturalized in the United States, and subject to the jurisdiction thereof, are citizens of the United States and of the State wherein they reside. No State shall make or enforce any law which shall abridge the privileges or immunities of citizens of the United States; nor shall any State deprive any person of life, liberty, or property, without due process of law; nor deny to any person within its jurisdiction the equal protection of the laws.

Section 2. Representatives shall be apportioned among the several States according to their respective numbers, counting the whole number of persons in each State, excluding Indians not taxed. But when the right to vote at any election for the choice of electors for President and Vice-President of the United States, Representatives in Congress, the Executive and Judicial officers of a State, or the members of the Legislature thereof, is denied to any of the male inhabitants of such State, being twenty-one years of age, and citizens of the United States, or in any way abridged, except for participation in rebellion, or other crime, the basis of representation therein shall be reduced in the proportion which the number of such male citizens shall bear to the whole number of male citizens twenty-one years of age in such State.

Section 3. No person shall be a Senator or Representative in Congress, or elector of President and Vice-President, or hold any office, civil or military, under the United States, or under any State, who, having previously taken an oath, as a member of Congress, or as an officer of the United States, or as a member of any State legislature, or as an executive or judicial officer of any State, to support the Constitution of the United States, shall have engaged in insurrection or rebellion against the same, or given aid or comfort to the enemies thereof. But Congress may by a vote of two-thirds of each House, remove such disability.

Section 4. The validity of the public debt of the United States, authorized by law, including debts incurred for payment of pensions and bounties for services in suppressing insurrection or rebellion, shall not be questioned. But neither the United States nor any State shall assume or pay any debt or obligation incurred in aid of insurrection or rebellion against the United States, or any claim for the loss or emancipation of any slave; but all such debts, obligations, and claims shall be held illegal and void.

Section 5. The Congress shall have the power to enforce, by appropriate legislation, the provisions of this article.

AMENDMENT XV [1870]

Section 1. The right of citizens of the United States to vote shall not be denied or abridged by the United States or by any State on account of race, color, or previous condition of servitude.

Section 2. The Congress shall have power to enforce this article by appropriate legislation.

AMENDMENT XVI [1913]

The Congress shall have power to lay and collect taxes on incomes, from whatever source derived, without apportionment among the several States, and without regard to any census or enumeration.

AMENDMENT XVII [1913]

The Senate of the United States shall be composed of two Senators from each State, elected by the people thereof, for six years; and each Senator shall have one vote. The electors in each State shall have the qualifications requisite for electors of the most numerous branch of the State legislatures.

When vacancies happen in the representation of any State in the Senate, the executive authority of such State shall issue writs of election to fill such vacancies: *Provided,* That the legislature of any State may empower the executive thereof to make temporary appointments until the people fill the vacancies by election as the legislature may direct.

This amendment shall not be so construed as to affect the election or term of any Senator chosen before it becomes valid as part of the Constitution.

AMENDMENT XVIII [1919]

Section 1. After one year from the ratification of this article the manufacture, sale, or transportation of intoxicating liquors within, the importation thereof into, or the exportation thereof from the United States and all territory subject to the jurisdiction thereof for beverage purposes is hereby prohibited.

Section 2. The Congress and the several States shall have concurrent power to enforce this article by appropriate legislation.

Section 3. This article shall be inoperative unless it shall have been ratified as an amendment to the Constitution by the legislatures of the several States, as provided in the Constitution, within seven years from the date of the submission hereof to the States by the Congress.

AMENDMENT XIX [1920]

The right of citizens of the United States to vote shall not be denied or abridged by the United States or by any State on account of sex.

Congress shall have power to enforce this article by appropriate legislation.

Section 1.   The terms of the President and Vice-President shall end at noon on the 20th day of January, and the terms of Senators and Representatives at noon on the 3d day of January, of the years in which such terms would have ended if this article had not been ratified; and the terms of their successors shall then begin.

Section 2.   The Congress shall assemble at least once in every year, and such meeting shall begin at noon on the 3d day of January, unless they shall by law appoint a different day.

Section 3.   If, at the time fixed for the beginning of the term of the President, the President elect shall have died, the Vice-President elect shall become President. If a President shall not have been chosen before the time fixed for the beginning of his term, or if the President elect shall have failed to qualify, then the Vice-President elect shall act as President until a President shall have qualified; and the Congress may by law provide for the case wherein neither a President elect nor a Vice-President elect shall have qualified, declaring who shall then act as President, or the manner in which one who is to act shall be selected, and such person shall act accordingly until a President or Vice-President shall have qualified.

Section 4.   The Congress may by law provide for the case of the death of any of the persons from whom the House of Representatives may choose a President whenever the right of choice shall have devolved upon them, and for the case of the death of any of the persons from whom the Senate may choose a Vice-President whenever the right of choice shall have devolved upon them.

Section 5.   Sections 1 and 2 shall take effect on the 15th day of October following the ratification of this article.

Section 6.   This article shall be inoperative unless it shall have been ratified as an amendment to the Constitution by the legislatures of three-fourths of the several States within seven years from the date of its submission.

Section 1.   The eighteenth article of amendment to the Constitution of the United States is hereby repealed.

Section 2.   The transportation or importation into any State, Territory, or possession of the United States for delivery or use therein of intoxicating liquors, in violation of the laws thereof, is hereby prohibited.

Section 3.   This article shall be inoperative unless it shall have been ratified as an amendment to the Constitution by conventions in the several States, as provided in the Constitution, within seven years from the date of the submission hereof to the States by the Congress.

No person shall be elected to the office of the President more than twice, and no person who has held the office of President, or acted as President, for more than two years of a term to which some other person was elected President shall be elected to the office of the President more than once.

But this Article shall not apply to any person holding the office of President when this Article was proposed by the Congress, and shall not prevent any person who may be holding the office of President, or acting as President, during the term within which this Article becomes operative from holding the office of President or acting as President during the remainder of such term.

Section 1.   The District constituting the seat of Government of the United States shall appoint in such manner as the Congress may direct:

A number of electors of President and Vice President equal to the whole number of Senators and Representatives in Congress to which the District would be entitled if it were a State, but in no event more than the least populous State; they shall be in addition to those appointed by the States, but they shall be considered, for the purposes of the election of President and Vice President, to be electors appointed by a State; and they shall meet in the District and perform such duties as provided by the twelfth article of amendment.

Section 2. The Congress shall have the power to enforce this article by appropriate legislation.

AMENDMENT XXIV [1964]

Section 1. The right of citizens of the United States to vote in any primary or other election for President or Vice President, for electors for President or Vice President, or for Senator or Representative in Congress, shall not be denied or abridged by the United States or any State by reason of failure to pay any poll tax or other tax.

Section 2. The Congress shall have the power to enforce this article by appropriate legislation.

AMENDMENT XXV [1967]

Section 1. In case of the removal of the President from office or his death or resignation, the Vice President shall become President.

Section 2. Whenever there is a vacancy in the office of the Vice President, the President shall nominate a Vice President who shall take the office upon confirmation by a majority vote of both houses of Congress.

Section 3. Whenever the President transmits to the President pro tempore of the Senate and the Speaker of the House of Representatives his written declaration that he is unable to discharge the powers and duties of his office, and until he transmits to them a written declaration to the contrary, such powers and duties shall be discharged by the Vice President as Acting President.

Section 4. Whenever the Vice President and a majority of either the principal officers of the executive departments, or of such other body as Congress may by law provide, transmit to the President pro tempore of the Senate and the Speaker of the House of Representatives their written declaration that the President is unable to discharge the powers and duties of his office, the Vice President shall immediately assume the powers and duties of the office as Acting President.

Thereafter, when the President transmits to the President pro tempore of the Senate and the Speaker of the House of Representatives his written declaration that no inability exists, he shall resume the powers and duties of his office unless the Vice President and a majority of either the principal officers of the executive departments, or of such other body as Congress may by law provide, transmit within four days to the President pro tempore of the Senate and the Speaker of the House of Representatives their written declaration that the President is unable to discharge the powers and duties of his office. Thereupon Congress shall decide the issue, assembling within 48 hours for that purpose if not in session. If the Congress, within 21 days after receipt of the latter written declaration, or, if Congress is not in session, within 21 days after Congress is required to assemble, determines by two-thirds vote of both houses that the President is unable to discharge the powers and duties of his office, the Vice President shall continue to discharge the same as Acting President; otherwise, the President shall resume the powers and duties of his office.

AMENDMENT XXVI [1971]

Section 1. The right of citizens of the United States, who are eighteen years of age or older, to vote shall not be denied or abridged by the United States or by any State on account of age.

Section 2. The Congress shall have power to enforce this article by appropriate legislation.

Presidential Elections, 1789–1972

Year	Candidates	Party	Popular vote	Electoral vote	Percentage of popular vote
1789	**George Washington**	No party designations		69	
	John Adams			34	
	Minor Candidates			35	
1792	**George Washington**	No party designations		132	
	John Adams			77	
	George Clinton			50	
	Minor Candidates			5	
1796	**John Adams**	**Federalist**		71	
	Thomas Jefferson	Democratic-Republican		68	
	Thomas Pinckney	Federalist		59	
	Aaron Burr	Democratic-Republican		30	
	Minor Candidates			48	
1800	**Thomas Jefferson**	**Democratic-Republican**		73	
	Aaron Burr	Democratic-Republican		73	
	John Adams	Federalist		65	
	Charles C. Pinckney	Federalist		64	
	John Jay	Federalist		1	
1804	**Thomas Jefferson**	**Democratic-Republican**		162	
	Charles C. Pinckney	Federalist		14	
1808	**James Madison**	**Democratic-Republican**		122	
	Charles C. Pinckney	Federalist		47	
	George Clinton	Democratic-Republican		6	
1812	**James Madison**	**Democratic-Republican**		128	
	DeWitt Clinton	Federalist		89	
1816	**James Monroe**	**Democratic-Republican**		183	
	Rufus King	Federalist		34	
1820	**James Monroe**	**Democratic-Republican**		231	
	John Quincy Adams	Independent Republican		1	
1824	**John Quincy Adams**	**Democratic-Republican**	108,740	84	30.5
	Andrew Jackson	Democratic-Republican	153,544	99	43.1
	William H. Crawford	Democratic-Republican	46,618	41	13.1
	Henry Clay	Democratic-Republican	47,136	37	13.2
1828	**Andrew Jackson**	**Democratic**	**647,286**	**178**	**56.0**
	John Quincy Adams	National Republican	508,064	83	44.0
1832	**Andrew Jackson**	**Democratic**	**687,502**	**219**	**55.0**
	Henry Clay	National Republican	530,189	49	42.4
	William Wirt	Anti-Masonic	33,108	7	2.6
	John Floyd	National Republican		11	

The percentage of the popular vote for any given year may not total 100 percent since candidates who received less than 1 percent of the popular vote have been omitted.

Data from *Historical Statistics of the United States, Colonial Times to 1957* (1961), pp. 682–683, and *The Official Associated Press Almanac 1975.*

Year	Candidates	Party	Popular vote	Electoral vote	Percentage of popular vote
1836	**Martin Van Buren**	**Democratic**	**765,483**	**170**	**50.9**
	William H. Harrison	Whig		73	
	Hugh L. White	Whig	739,795	26	49.1
	Daniel Webster	Whig		14	
	W. P. Mangum	Whig		11	
1840	**William H. Harrison**	**Whig**	**1,274,624**	**234**	**53.1**
	Martin Van Buren	Democratic	1,127,781	60	46.9
1844	**James K. Polk**	**Democratic**	**1,338,464**	**170**	**49.6**
	Henry Clay	Whig	1,300,097	105	48.1
	James G. Birney	Liberty	62,300		2.3
1848	**Zachary Taylor**	**Whig**	**1,360,967**	**163**	**47.4**
	Lewis Cass	Democratic	1,222,342	127	42.5
	Martin Van Buren	Free Soil	291,263		10.1
1852	**Franklin Pierce**	**Democratic**	**1,601,117**	**254**	**50.9**
	Winfield Scott	Whig	1,385,453	42	44.1
	John P. Hale	Free Soil	155,825		5.0
1856	**James Buchanan**	**Democratic**	**1,832,955**	**174**	**45.3**
	John C. Frémont	Republican	1,339,932	114	33.1
	Millard Fillmore	American	871,731	8	21.6
1860	**Abraham Lincoln**	**Republican**	**1,865,593**	**180**	**39.8**
	Stephen A. Douglas	Democratic	1,382,713	12	29.5
	John C. Breckinridge	Democratic	848,356	72	18.1
	John Bell	Constitutional Union	592,906	39	12.6
1864	**Abraham Lincoln**	**Republican**	**2,206,938**	**212**	**55.0**
	George B. McClellan	Democratic	1,803,787	21	45.0
1868	**Ulysses S. Grant**	**Republican**	**3,013,421**	**214**	**52.7**
	Horatio Seymour	Democratic	2,706,829	80	47.3
1872	**Ulysses S. Grant**	**Republican**	**3,596,745**	**286**	**55.6**
	Horace Greeley	Democratic	2,843,446	66	43.9
1876	**Rutherford B. Hayes**	**Republican**	**4,036,572**	**185**	**48.0**
	Samuel J. Tilden	Democratic	4,284,020	184	51.0
1880	**James A. Garfield**	**Republican**	**4,453,295**	**214**	**48.5**
	Winfield S. Hancock	Democratic	4,414,082	155	48.1
	James B. Weaver	Greenback-Labor	308,578		3.4
1884	**Grover Cleveland**	**Democratic**	**4,879,507**	**219**	**48.5**
	James G. Blaine	Republican	4,850,293	182	48.2
	Benjamin F. Butler	Greenback–Labor	175,370		1.8
	John P. St. John	Prohibition	150,369		1.5
1888	**Benjamin Harrison**	**Republican**	**5,447,129**	**233**	**47.9**
	Grover Cleveland	Democratic	5,537,857	168	48.6
	Clinton B. Fish	Prohibition	249,506		2.2
	Anson J. Streeter	Union Labor	146,935		1.3
1892	**Grover Cleveland**	**Democratic**	**5,555,426**	**277**	**46.1**
	Benjamin Harrison	Republican	5,182,690	145	43.0
	James B. Weaver	People's	1,029,846	22	8.5
	John Bidwell	Prohibition	246,133		2.2

The percentage of the popular vote for any given year may not total 100 percent since candidates who received less than 1 percent of the popular vote have been omitted.

Year	Candidates	Party	Popular vote	Electoral vote	Percentage of popular vote
1896	**William McKinley**	**Republican**	**7,102,246**	**271**	**51.1**
	William J. Bryan	Democratic	6,492,559	176	47.7
1900	**William McKinley**	**Republican**	**7,218,491**	**292**	**51.7**
	William J. Bryan	**Democratic; Populist**	**6,356,734**	**155**	**45.5**
	John C. Wooley	**Prohibition**	**208,914**		**1.5**
1904	**Theodore Roosevelt**	**Republican**	**7,628,461**	**336**	**57.4**
	Alton B. Parker	Democratic	5,084,223	140	37.6
	Eugene V. Debs	Socialist	402,283		3.0
	Silas C. Swallow	Prohibition	258,536		1.9
1908	**William H. Taft**	**Republican**	**7,675,320**	**321**	**51.6**
	William J. Bryan	Democratic	6,412,294	162	43.1
	Eugene V. Debs	Socialist	420,793		2.8
	Eugene W. Chafin	Prohibition	253,840		1.7
1912	**Woodrow Wilson**	**Democratic**	**6,296,547**	**435**	**41.9**
	Theodore Roosevelt	Progressive	4,118,571	88	27.4
	William H. Taft	Republican	3,486,720	8	23.2
	Eugene V. Debs	Socialist	900,672		6.0
	Eugene W. Chafin	Prohibition	206,275		1.4
1916	**Woodrow Wilson**	**Democratic**	**9,127,695**	**277**	**49.4**
	Charles E. Hughes	Republican	8,533,507	254	46.2
	A. L. Benson	Socialist	585,113		3.2
	J. Frank Hanly	Prohibition	220,506		1.2
1920	**Warren G. Harding**	**Republican**	**16,143,407**	**404**	**60.4**
	James M. Cox	Democratic	9,130,328	127	34.2
	Eugene V. Debs	Socialist	919,799		3.4
	P. P. Christensen	Farmer-Labor	265,411		1.0
1924	**Calvin Coolidge**	**Republican**	**15,718,211**	**382**	**54.0**
	John W. Davis	Democratic	8,385,283	136	28.8
	Robert M. La Follette	Progressive	4,831,289	13	16.6
1928	**Herbert C. Hoover**	**Republican**	**21,391,993**	**444**	**58.2**
	Alfred E. Smith	Democratic	15,016,169	87	40.9
1932	**Franklin D. Roosevelt**	**Democratic**	**22,809,638**	**472**	**57.4**
	Herbert C. Hoover	Republican	15,758,901	59	39.7
	Norman Thomas	Socialist	881,951		2.2
1936	**Franklin D. Roosevelt**	**Democratic**	**27,752,869**	**523**	**60.8**
	Alfred M. Landon	Republican	16,674,665	8	36.5
	William Lemke	Union	882,479		1.9
1940	**Franklin D. Roosevelt**	**Democratic**	**27,307,819**	**449**	**54.8**
	Wendell L. Willkie	Republican	22,321,018	82	44.8
1944	**Franklin D. Roosevelt**	**Democratic**	**25,606,585**	**432**	**53.5**
	Thomas E. Dewey	Republican	22,014,745	99	46.0
1948	**Harry S. Truman**	**Democratic**	**24,105,812**	**303**	**49.5**
	Thomas E. Dewey	Republican	21,970,065	189	45.1
	J. Strom Thurmond	States' Rights	1,169,063	39	2.4
	Henry A. Wallace	Progressive	1,157,172		2.4
1952	**Dwight D. Eisenhower**	**Republican**	**33,936,234**	**442**	**55.1**
	Adlai E. Stevenson	Democratic	27,314,992	89	44.4

The percentage of the popular vote for any given year may not total 100 percent since candidates who received less than 1 percent of the popular vote have been omitted.

Year	Candidates	Party	Popular vote	Electoral vote	Percentage of popular vote
1956	**Dwight D. Eisenhower**	**Republican**	**35,590,472**	**457**	**57.6**
	Adlai E. Stevenson	Democratic	26,022,752	73	42.1
1960	**John F. Kennedy**	**Democratic**	**34,227,096**	**303**	**49.9**
	Richard M. Nixon	Republican	34,108,546	219	49.6
1964	**Lyndon B. Johnson**	**Democratic**	**43,126,506**	**486**	**61.1**
	Barry M. Goldwater	Republican	27,176,799	52	38.5
1968	**Richard M. Nixon**	**Republican**	**31,785,480**	**301**	**43.4**
	Hubert H. Humphrey	Democratic	31,275,165	191	42.7
	George C. Wallace	American Independent	9,906,473	46	13.5
1972	**Richard M. Nixon**	**Republican**	**47,167,319**	**521**	**60.7**
	George S. McGovern	Democratic	29,168,509	17	37.5
1974	**Gerald R. Ford**	**Republican**	Appointed as Vice President after Spiro T. Agnew resigned in 1973. Sworn in as President on August 9, 1974, after Richard M. Nixon resigned.		

The percentage of the popular vote for any given year may not total 100 percent since candidates who received less than 1 percent of the popular vote have been omitted.

ART CREDITS

page ii courtesy Plimouth Plantation, Plymouth, Mass.

pages 2–3 Photo Researchers

Chapter 1
page 5 Rare Book Division, The New York Public Library, Astor, Lenox and Tilden Foundations   page 8 American Museum of Natural History   page 10 Brown Brothers   page 13 Rare Book Division, The New York Public Library, Astor, Lenox and Tilden Foundations   page 14 Hispanic Society of America   page 16 The Metropolitan Museum of Art, gift of J. Pierpont Morgan, 1900

Chapter 2
page 20 courtesy of Pioneer Village, Salem, Mass.   pages 23, 27, 29 Rare Book Division, The New York Public Library, Astor, Lenox and Tilden Foundations   page 32 The National Maritime Museum, London   page 35 courtesy Secretary of the Commonwealth of Massachusetts   page 39 American Antiquarian Society

Chapter 3
page 44 Philadelphia Museum of Art, photograph by A. J. Wyatt, Staff Photographer   page 48 The New York Historical Society, New York City   page 53 Massachusetts Historical Society   page 56 The Thomas Gilcrease Institute of American History & Art, Tulsa, Okla.   page 58 The Henry Francis Dupont Winterthur Museum   page 61 National Gallery of Art, gift of Edgar William and Bernice Chrysler Garbisch   page 62 Prints Division, The New York Public Library, Astor, Lenox and Tilden Foundations   page 67 Redrawn by permission from THE AMERICAN HERITAGE PICTORIAL ATLAS OF UNITED STATES HISTORY, © 1966.   page 69 Boston Public Library   page 71 Arents Collection, The New York Public Library, Astor, Lenox and Tilden Foundations   page 72 National Archives   page 75 Charleston Library Society, Charleston, S.C.

Chapter 4
page 80 I. N. Phelps Stokes Collection, The New York Public Library, Astor, Lenox and Tilden Foundations   page 82 Rare Book Department, Free Library of Philadelphia   page 85 reproduced from collections of the Library of Congress   page 88 American Antiquarian Society   page 91 Historical Society of Pennsylvania   page 97 right: Massachusetts Historical Society; left: Historical Pictures Service, Chicago   page 99 Worcester Art Museum   page 100 Ewing Galloway   page 103 Colonial Williamsburg Foundation photograph   page 106 The Bettmann Archive   page 108 The Library Company of Philadelphia

Chapter 5
page 111 Virginia Chamber of Commerce, photo by Flournoy   page 114 The Public Archives of Canada   page 117 I. N. Phelps Stokes Collection, Prints Division, The New York Public Library, Astor, Lenox and Tilden Foundations   page 118 Colonial Williamsburg Foundation photograph   page 121 Prints Division, The New York Public Library, Astor, Lenox and Tilden Foundations   page 127 Yale University Art Gallery, The Mabel Brady Garvan Collection   page 131 The Architect of the Capitol, Washington, D.C.   page 133 The Henry Francis DuPont Winterthur Museum   page 136 National Archives   page 143 National Museums, France   page 147 The New York Historical Society, New York City

pages 150–151 The Public Library of Cincinnati and Hamilton County

Chapter 6
page 153 courtesy of Davenport West, Jr., photo from American Heritage   page 161 I. N. Phelps Stokes Collection, Prints Division, The New York Public Library, Astor, Lenox and Tilden Foundations   page 165 Redrawn by permission from THE AMERICAN HERITAGE PICTORIAL ATLAS OF UNITED STATES HISTORY, © 1966.   page 170 Worcester Art Museum   page 172 Connecticut State Library, photo by Gus Johnson   page 174 Brown Brothers   page 177 Historical Society of Pennsylvania   page 180 Museum of the City of New York   page 183 The New York Historical Society, New York City

Chapter 7
page 187 Historical Society of Pennsylvania   page 192 Boatmen's National Bank of St. Louis   page 194 The Bettmann Archive   page 199 Brown Brothers   page 201 Historical Society of Pennsylvania   page 205 Schomburg Center for Research in Black Culture, The New York Public Library, Astor, Lenox and Tilden Foundations   page 206 reproduced from collections in the Library of Congress   page 210 Museum of Science and Industry, Chicago   page 214 The Bettmann Archive   page 221 International Museum of Photography at George Eastman House, Rochester

Chapter 8
page 225 collection of The Newark Museum   page 228 The Bettmann Archive   page 231 collection of Matthew Isenberg, Hadlyme, Conn.   page 233 Massillon Museum, Ohio   page 237 courtesy of the Union Pacific Railroad Company   page 239 The Whaling Museum, New Bedford, Mass.   page 243 Museum of Fine Arts, Boston   page 248 The New York Historical Society, New York City   page 252 Historical Pictures Service, Chicago

Chapter 9
page 257 University of Wisconsin   page 264 Museum of the City of New York   page 266 Missouri Historical Society   page 267 reproduced from collections of the Library of Congress   page 270 Princeton University Library, Sinclair Hamilton Collection of Illustrated Books   page 272 Brown Brothers   page 276 J. Clarence Davies Collection, Museum of the City of New York   page 277 Rhode Island Historical Society   page 279 St. Louis Art Museum, Ezra H. Linley Fund   page 283 Historical Pictures Service, Chicago

Chapter 10
page 286 Connecticut Historical Society   page 292 reproduced from collections of the Library of Congress   page 293 The New York Historical Society, New York City   page 295 National Archives   page 297 Putnam County Historical Society, Cold Springs, New York   page 298 reproduced from collections of the Library of Congress   page 300 courtesy Kenneth M. Newman, Old Print Shop, New York City   page 301 South Carolina Historical Society   page 302 reproduced from collections of the Library of Congress   page 308 The Bettmann Archive   page 311 reproduced from collections of the Library of Congress

Chapter 11
page 315 The New York Historical Society, New York City   page 320 Historical Pictures Service, Chicago   page 322 The Bettmann Archive   page 326 New York Public Library   page 327 The Bettmann Archive page 328 Culver Pictures pages 330, 331 The Bettmann Archive

Maps drawn by Dick Sanderson

Index